THE GILDED DINOSAUR

Also by Mark Jaffe

And No Birds Sing

THE GILDED DINOSAUR

The Fossil War Between
E. D. Cope and O. C. Marsh and
the Rise of American Science

by Mark Jaffe

Crown Publishers   New York

For My Mother

Published by Crown Publishers, 201 East 50th Street, New York, New York 10022. Member of the Crown Publishing Group.

Random House, Inc. New York, Toronto, London, Sydney, Auckland
www.randomhouse.com

CROWN is a trademark and the Crown colophon is a registered trademark of Random House, Inc.

Printed in the United States of America

Design by Sue Maksuta
Triceratops drawing by Joseph Daly

Library of Congress Cataloging-in-Publication Data
Jaffe, Mark.
The gilded dinosaur : the fossil war between E.D. Cope and O.C. Marsh and the rise of American science / by Mark Jaffe. — 1st ed.
1. Cope, E. D. (Edward Drinker), 1840–1897.   2. Marsh, Othniel Charles, 1831–1899.   3. Paleontologists—United States Biography.
4. Fossils—West (U.S.)—Collection and preservation—History—19th century.   I. Title.
QE707.C63J34   1999
560′.978′09034—dc21   99-38510

ISBN 0-517-70760-8

10 9 8 7 6 5 4 3 2 1

First Edition

Acknowledgments

Writing this book has been a journey both across the American West and through American history. But whether on the road or locked deep in some archive, I was fortunate to have some savvy and patient guides.

In Philadelphia, Carol Spawn at the Academy of Natural Sciences and Roy Goodman and Scott DeHaven at the American Philosophical Society were invaluable. In New York City, Barbara Mathe at the American Museum of Natural History was a great help. Barbara Narenda assisted me in perusing the archives at Yale's Peabody Museum of Natural History, and Bruce Kirby guided me through the Smithsonian Institution Archives.

Some wonderful archivists and librarians also opened the West for me including Chelle Somsen at the South Dakota Historical Society, Daniel Davis at the University of Wyoming American Heritage Center, William Grace at the Kansas Historical Society, Barbara Day at the Colorado Historical Society, and Brian Shovers at the Montana Historical Society.

I also offer my special thanks to Thelma Jennings, who opened the Fort Wallace Museum just for me on a blustery and snowy day, and Cecil Sanderson, assistant superintendent at the Fort Bridger Historical Site.

I also had the advice of four prominent paleontologists—Peter Dodson, John Ostrom, David S. Berman, and Edward Deaschler—who tried to prevent me from making any mistakes in the science.

Robert Eveleth of the New Mexico Bureau of Mines and Mineral Resources was a tremendous help in reconstructing the history of western mining, and Michael F. Kohl, head of special collections at Clemson University, clued me in to some excellent Smithsonian sources.

A good part of the work on this book was done while I was Nieman Fellow at Harvard University, and I offer my deepest thanks to Bill Kovach, the Nieman curator, for his support. Harvard historian Evertt Mendelsohn was kind and patient in tutoring me in how a historian looks at science, and Anne Bernays and Justin Kaplan pushed, probed, and guided me in my word-smithing.

When I finally started pounding out pages, three of my *Philadelphia Inquirer* colleagues—Paul Nussbaum, John Fried, and Charles Layton—were good-hearted enough to read them and to give me sharp, but compassionate feedback.

David Black, my agent, was supportive from the first casual pitch of the Cope and Marsh story to the finished manuscript. My thanks also to Crown Publishing, especially to Karen Rinaldi, the first editor to support this project, and to Robert Mecoy and Peter Fornatale for bringing the book to fruition.

Finally, my deepest thanks and love to my first, best editor always, my wife, Sandy. Her careful reading of the manuscript made my work better—as it always does.

The evolution of geological time

Charles Lyell—1833	James Dwight Dana—1874			
Recent				
New Pliocene				Pliocene
Older Pliocene	Age of Mammals …Tertiary			Miocene
Miocene				Eocene
Eocene				
		Cretaceous		Upper
				Middle
				Lower
Cretaceous Group				
Wealden Group	Age of Reptiles			Wealdon Epoch
Oolite or Jura Group		Jurassic		Oolytic Epoch
Lias Group				Liassic Epoch
		Triassic		
			Permian	
Carboniferous	Carboniferous Age		Carboniferous	
			Subcarboniferous	
			Catskill	
	Devonian Age (*Age of Fishes*)		Chemong	
			Hamilton	
			Corniferous	
		Upper Silurian		Oriskany
				Lower Helderberg
				Salina
	Silurian Age (*Age of Invertebrates*)			Niagara
		Lower Silurian		Trenton
				Canadian
				Cambrian

Cenozoic	Quaternary	Pleistocene	*Modern humans*	
	Tertiary	Pliocene	*Homo erectus*	1.6 mya
		Miocene		5 mya
		Oligocene	*Large mammals*	24 mya
		Eocene		37 mya
		Paleocene	*Diverse mammals*	58 mya
	Cretaceous		*Dinosaurs Extinct*	65 mya
Mesozoic	Jurassic		*Age of Dinosaurs*	144 mya
	Triassic		*Early Dinosaurs*	208 mya
Paleozoic	Permian		*90% extinction*	245 mya
	Carboniferous	Pennsylvanian	*First Reptiles*	286 mya
		Mississippian	*Early forrests*	323 mya
	Devonian		*First Amphibians*	360 mya
	Silurian		*First land plants*	408 mya
	Ordovician		*Primitive Fish*	438 mya
	Cambrian		*Shelled Invertebrates*	505 mya
Precambrian	*The first single-celled organisms appeared about 3.4 mya*			570 mya
				Origin of Earth 4.6 bya

The Modern Geological Timeline

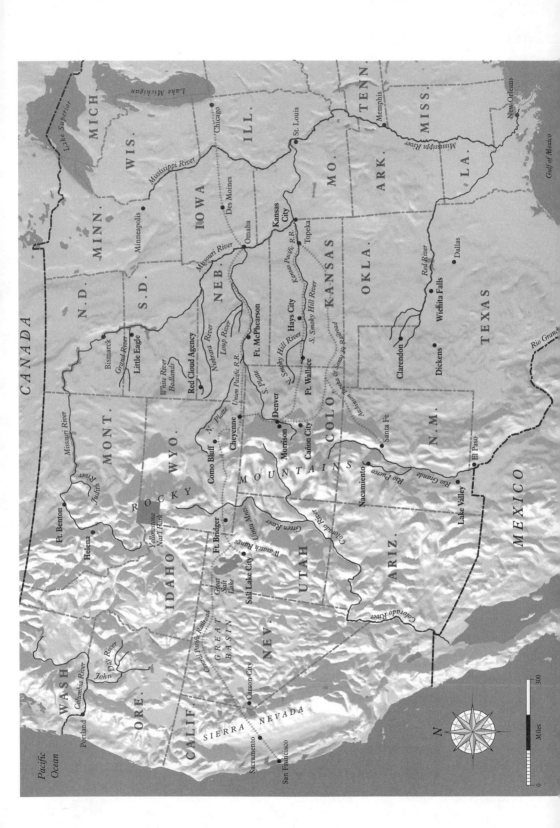

Chapter One

OTHNIEL CHARLES MARSH hurried from the Syracuse train station and made his way through the late autumn twilight toward the pavilion of the great giant. He joined the crowd shuffling slowly toward the entrance, paid his fifty cents, and went inside. Thousands had already passed this way. Oliver Wendell Holmes had come. The great transcendental poet Ralph Waldo Emerson had peered at the giant in awe and announced, "It is beyond me."

Marsh had only a twenty-minute layover, so his pilgrimage would have to be brief. Accompanied by a member of the staff, who proudly pointed out the giant's finer aspects, the Yale professor made a swift, but close survey. He did not need much time. He looked, and he must have smiled with glee. He raced back to the station and got on his train. O. C. Marsh knew the truth about the Cardiff Giant.

It had all begun on Saturday morning, October 16, 1869, in the rural village of Cardiff, New York. Two workmen digging a well on William Newell's farm struck something about three feet below the surface. Further spade work revealed a massive, gray, weathered statue—ten feet long with a three-foot shoulder span and an inscrutable visage.

Newell set up a tent and started charging a dime a look. The crowds came. The price of admission went up to fifty cents, and still they came. Was it a petrified man? Was it the statue of some ancient Indian tribe? A carving left by the first Jesuit missionaries sent to America? Yale theologian Timothy McWhorter opined that this was proof positive that the Phoenicians had reached North America centuries before Leif Ericson and his Vikings.

A syndicate of prominent Syracuse businessmen bought the giant for thirty thousand dollars and moved it the thirteen miles from Cardiff to Syracuse. Special trains carried the curious north, where four thousand tickets were sold in a single day. Word was that Spencer Baird, of the Smithsonian Institution, was considering bringing the giant to the nation's capital.

The great showman, P. T. Barnum, sent a man up to Syracuse offering sixty thousand dollars for a three-month lease on the giant. Rebuffed, Barnum hired a local sculptor to create a plaster copy.

1

What cheek. It was almost sacrilegious. The Cardiff Giant had been pronounced an important discovery by men of science and learning. Dr. John Boynton, a respected geologist living in Syracuse, estimated that the statue was at least three hundred years old and noted that it bore an odd resemblance to former New York governor DeWitt Clinton. "This is one of the greatest curiosities of the early history of Onondaga County," Dr. Boynton concluded.

A few days later, James Hall, director of the New York State Geological Survey and a true pillar of American science, pronounced the giant "the most remarkable object yet brought to light in this country, and although, perhaps not dating back to the stone age, is, nevertheless deserving of the attention of archaeologists."[1] Henry Ward, professor of natural sciences at Rochester University, took a look at the statue and agreed with Hall.

Yet here was Barnum ready to perpetrate a fraud. How could he do it? Perhaps it was because Barnum, the showman, like Marsh, the Yale paleontologist, knew the truth that had somehow escaped Boynton, Hall, and Ward.

Besides, who better than Barnum to dance the dance between science and scam. When Barnum was charged with putting a fake whale in his museum, hadn't he asked Harvard's Louis Agassiz, the most famous scientist in the country, to vouch for it? And when there were charges that his Burmese elephant Toung Taloung wasn't white, but rather whitewashed, Barnum would ask Joseph Leidy, professor of anatomy at the University of Pennsylvania and a leader of the Philadelphia Academy of Natural Sciences, to verify the beast's natural opalescence. (The truth was that Toung Taloung *was* a sacred white elephant smuggled out of Burma at a cost to Barnum of six thousand dollars. Unfortunately, it wasn't actually white. It was pinkish. So Barnum had resorted to a touch of whitewash just for effect.)

Unfailingly the scientists seemed to oblige the hucksters, for truth be told, this thing called "science" was still a raw and unsettled discipline in a raw and unsettled land. Indeed, the ideas that this thing called science was churning out made stone giants and white elephants seem tame. Just imagine saying Earth was created not by God in seven days, as Genesis assured, but by geological forces working over millions of years, that huge creatures, bigger than the biggest elephants, roamed the land and then mysteriously disappeared. And most astounding of all, insisting that man came forth not from God, but from monkeys. Why, Phoenicians in upstate New York seemed completely plausible.

This vision of the wild, impractical, and bumbling professor, closely allied with the flimflam man, pained America's little scientific community, and little it truly was, composed of no more than one thousand or, depending on how one counted, perhaps as few as three hundred men. (The number of women could be tallied on the fingers of a single hand.)

Most people weren't even sure what a "scientist" was, the term having only come into fashion in the 1840s, about the same time the word *dinosaur* was coined for the prehistoric behemoths. Both were surely odd creatures. Before that, there had been savants, naturalists, natural philosophers, and alchemists.

Many of America's scientific men were medical doctors. It wasn't the kind of training the Europeans gave their scientists, but in utilitarian America, as the author Henry James observed, medicine managed to unite the "realm of the practical" with "the light of science—a merit appreciated in a community in which the love of knowledge has not always been accompanied by leisure and opportunity."[2]

But it really didn't require any particular training to be a "scientist," and many of the American men of science had no particular training at all. John Wesley Powell had no diploma, no degree, no published scientific papers, and not much schooling, yet he was well on his way to becoming a vital force in American science.[3]

Just six weeks before the Cardiff Giant was discovered, Powell had completed the first descent of the Colorado River, through the Grand Canyon, and was now back at Illinois State Normal University, where he was professor of geology.

Nevertheless, even though they were homemade, self-made, part-time scientists, there was a growing air of seriousness and professionalism. The American scientific community craved respectability. After a tour of European universities and laboratories, Joseph Henry, the nation's most distinguished scientist, wrote, "I am now more than ever of [the] opinion, that the real working men in the way of science in this country should make common cause . . . to raise their scientific character. To make science more respected at home."

How? America had no great universities like the Germans, no academies like the French, no royal societies like the English. That was one reason Henry left his Princeton University laboratory in 1847 and became the head of the newly created Smithsonian Institution, the first federal establishment committed solely to the advancement of knowledge.

The real problem, however, was that Americans saw science as impractical at best, humbug at worst. It was, as Henry James said, an exercise of "leisure and opportunity." Consider Joseph Henry's own work in physics.

True, it was cutting-edge research on electricity and magnetism, and it went stride for stride with the work of England's Michael Faraday. But it was Samuel B. Morse who took the magnet toys from the laboratory and turned them into the moneymaking telegraph. Now, that was American.

As a young man, J. P. Morgan was offered a junior post in the mathematics department at Germany's University of Göttingen. He turned it down and instead of becoming a professor he returned to the United States to rule Wall Street.

These sentiments were especially strong now. Released from the woe and weight of civil war, Americans were ready to build their fortunes and their nation. Industry was booming, the West with its abundant minerals, timber, and land was opening, and immigration, offering cheap labor and new consumers, was surging. Riches were waiting to be won. Why play with magnets and microscopes?

Two weeks before the Cardiff Giant had been exhumed, the nation had held its breath while the financier Jay Gould sent the investment world reeling as he tried to corner the gold market. The bubble burst on Black Friday when President Ulysses S. Grant ordered federal gold into the market, even though Gould had tried to prevent that by giving stock in his venture to the president's sister and wife.

"There's no doubt but money is to the fore now," said Bromfield Corey, the Boston patrician in the 1885 novel *The Rise of Silas Lapham*. "It is the romance, the poetry of our age. It is the thing that chiefly strikes the imagination." The celebration was in Morgan's manipulating bonds and Gould's savvy with gold, not Professor Joseph Henry's knowledge of magnetism.

"I am tired of all this thing called science here," Pennsylvania senator Simon Cameron told Henry during an 1861 Smithsonian appropriations hearing. "What do we care about stuffed snakes, alligators, and all such things?"

But while American scientists might be able to endure the label of dreamers, the specters of fraud and flummery were serious threats as far as Henry was concerned. "Our newspapers are filled with puffs of quackery," he lamented, "and every man who can burn phosphorous in oxygen and exhibits a few experiments to a class of young ladies is called a man of science."

And yet it seemed scientists could not help but get embroiled in shenanigans with white elephants and giants. It was hard to separate fact from fakery. Down in Philadelphia, Joseph Leidy would find himself chairing a University of Pennsylvania committee assessing the value of seances. There were also attempts to build a meter to measure the power of prayer. "Scientists were in agreement that all references to occult qualities should be excluded from science," historian David Hull observed, "but they were not clear as to what it was about a quality that made it occult."[4]

Henry even found himself rubbing elbows with Barnum as the showman generously donated the carcasses of his exotic animals to the Smithsonian. While America's fledgling museums and universities could never afford to purchase such specimens, Barnum could, and when they expired—which they invariably did because no one knew how to care for such animals—he'd pass them along to the grateful scientists.

Henry's assistant Spencer Baird, who was responsible for building up the Smithsonian collections, was most appreciative, even asking Barnum for his bust so that it could be put in a place of honor. Barnum would boast that Henry himself was a "good friend" and that the great physicist had even called the impresario's American Museum—with its bogus mermaids and real monkeys—"a scientific establishment."

What a muddle. Science needed standards. Science needed rigor. Science had to steer clear of buffoonery. Henry despaired. If science didn't put an end to quackery, he warned, then quackery would put an end to science.

Barnum, confident that nothing—not even science—could put an end to quackery, was preparing to unveil his faux giant in New York City when O. C. (he hated to be called Othniel) Marsh stopped in Syracuse to see the real Cardiff Giant. In many ways, the thirty-eight-year-old Marsh was the epitome of what Henry was striving for in American science. Unlike James Hall, who had gained his expertise in geology doing surveys for the Erie Canal; Henry, who was largely self-taught; or Boynton, who had come to science by way of medicine, Marsh was university trained.

He had graduated from Yale and received a master's degree from Yale's Sheffield Scientific School, the best science program the nation had to offer. Then he had studied at the venerable German universities in Berlin, Heidelberg, and Breslau. Marsh returned to Yale to become the first professor of paleontology in America. So it was an educated eye he cast upon the giant.

Stocky and of middling height, with a receding hairline and small, close-set blue eyes over a full beard, Marsh circled the stone giant, bending down here and there to inspect details. Then he hurried back to his train. The following morning, he sat down to write a letter to the old college friend who had urged him to examine the giant, "I saw the 'Cardiff Giant' last evening and in accordance with your request I will tell you what I think of it. . . . A very few minutes sufficed to satisfy me that my first suspicions in regard to it were correct, viz; that it is of very recent origin, and a most decided humbug."

Marsh's examination revealed that the gypsum block had probably been water worn before the statue was carved and that tool marks were still visible in places where they had not been obliterated by polishing. He went on to point out that since gypsum is soluble in about four hundred parts of water, a "very short exposure of the statue in the locality at Cardiff would suffice to obliterate all traces of tool marks and also to roughen the polished surfaces, but these are both quite perfect, and hence the giant must have been very recently buried when discovered."

Marsh concluded, "The work is well calculated to impose upon the general public, but I am surprised that any scientific observers should not have at once detected the unmistakable evidence against its antiquity."

Barnum had known it without even seeing the giant. In truth, the Cardiff Giant was the concoction of farmer Newell's cousin, George Hull. The gypsum block had been purchased in Iowa, cut into the form of a giant in Chicago, "aged" with ink and sulfuric acid, and then buried in Cardiff a few days before it was "discovered."

Marsh's letter made its way into the *Buffalo Courier* on November 29, the *New York Herald* on December 1, and then across the wires to the nation. The Cardiff Giant hoax had been unmasked. In Marsh's wake, James Hall and John Boynton—or at least their apologists—said they knew all the time that it was a hoax.[5] They apparently had simply forgotten to mention it to anyone.

Showing up Hall was no casual exercise, for he was a formidable figure—powerful, egotistical, and quick tempered—with a shotgun on his office wall ready to serve as final arbiter in any dispute. Hall's own paleontological work on life in the Devonian period, four hundred million years ago, was considered a classic, and he was also able to badger and bully the New York state legislature into amply funding his geological survey, making it one of the most productive scientific agencies in the country.

Hall's influence extended well beyond the state borders, as he sent expeditions to the western territories and personally served, from time to time, as state geologist for Iowa and Wisconsin. But even a big reputation and a shotgun weren't going to scare Marsh.

Marsh simply could not resist. He took as much delight in the Cardiff Giant as Barnum. If it came at Hall's expense, so be it. In fact, it wasn't the first time the young professor had displayed a penchant for one-upmanship.

In 1860, Marsh had returned to Yale with an interesting fossil found on a summer expedition to Nova Scotia. At first, he thought it looked like "the backbone of a halibut." But at the suggestion of his geology professor, James Dwight Dana, he sent it to Louis Agassiz at Harvard for examination. Agassiz was the world's fossil-fish expert, having written the five-volume *Researches on Fossil Fishes,* and Marsh's find greatly excited him. In a letter published in the *American Journal of Science* in January of 1861, Agassiz said of the specimen, "We have here undoubtedly a nearer approximation to a synthesis between Fish and Reptile than has yet been seen."

If Marsh's fossil had real value, he was not about to let anyone, even the august Agassiz, steal his thunder. He immediately reclaimed the specimen and wrote a quick description, naming the fossil *Eosaurus acadianus.* For the next six months, Marsh conducted a detailed study and ultimately reported that Agassiz had got it wrong. The fossil was not some direct link between fish and reptile. It was really the remains of a twelve-foot-long, cold-blooded, air-breathing amphibian. The Yale graduate student had no compunctions about correcting the Harvard professor.

One scientist who clearly didn't want to be lumped with Hall, Boynton, or Barnum was the Smithsonian's Spencer Baird. "I *never* . . . thought of it as to purchasing the Cardiff Giant, which I have simply looked on as a humbug from the first. I wrote to one or two persons about it simply for information to prove my postulate," he assured Marsh.[6]

There were, of course, those with true faith. One man who simply wouldn't give up his belief in the giant was Reverend McWhorter, still sure that it was a Phoenician stone man. When Marsh returned to New Haven, McWhorter lit into the young professor.

"You are wrong, sir, absolutely wrong," McWhorter shouted as he waved his cane in Marsh's face. "You do not know what you are talking about, sir!"

"The whole thing's a fraud," Marsh coolly replied.

"I tell you, sir," McWhorter fumed, "that in three months it will be in the British Museum!"[7]

To Barnum, it made no difference, none at all. Science could never put an end to quackery. On December 12, his version of the Cardiff Giant—christened the "True Goliath"—went on display at Wood's Museum. Goliath lay in state amid black drapes, in a dimly lit room. The crowds came just as Barnum knew they would.

They even continued to flock to Syracuse. As one satisfied customer explained, "I paid my half dollar to see the thing because my neighbor Jones told me it was a genuine petrified man, but if it's a humbug as a Yale professor says, I would pay a dollar because the fraud's such a good one."[8]

Within a few weeks of Goliath's debut, the original Cardiff Giant arrived in New York City at Apollo Hall, just two blocks away from Wood's. But despite the big banner out front proclaiming GENUINE. CARDIFF GIANT. ORIGINAL. TALLER THAN GOLIATH, business was thin. Desperate, the Cardiff syndicate went to court to get an injunction against Barnum. The case was heard by Judge George Barnard, who had obligingly provided Cornelius Vanderbilt with injunctions and contempt orders against Jay Gould when the two tycoons had recently battled over control of the Erie Railroad. In this case, however, Barnard told the plaintiffs they would have to prove the "genuineness" of their giant and explained that "he had been doing some business in injunctions, but was going to shut down now."

"It is too bad that our men of science—paleontologists or ethnologists—should not only have the difficulties of nature and antiquity to strive against, but be also 'bothered' by rogueries of . . . their fellow man," the *New York Times* lamented.

Barnum was already looking past Goliath to his next venture. He was considering the circus business, and the prospects of a circus full of animals surely put his scientific friends into a state of expectation. Even Marsh was interested, and in years to come, he had a former Yale student, George Bird Grinnell, keep an eye on Barnum's doings. As a result, Marsh was able to pick up the skeletons of a Barnum kangaroo (seventeen dollars) and a shark (ten dollars). Grinnell cautioned, "Be careful of saying anything to Baird . . . for B. thinks he gets everything."[9]

"I am looking out for Barnum's cassowary. If it dies I shall have it . . . ," Grinnell reported to New Haven. "A two-horned rhinoceros died at Barnum's. . . . Barnum's Bactrian Camel departed this life yesterday and will of course, go to Baird."[10]

Why, some of these scientists were getting downright cheeky themselves. One day traveling home to Bridgeport, Connecticut, on the New Haven Railroad, Barnum was bemoaning to a fellow passenger the loss of some Mexican artifacts. Barnum had bought them and had them shipped to New York, where his agent, unaware of their value, put them up for sale.

"And were they sold?" Barnum's fellow passenger asked.

"Yes, some little cuss up in New Haven bought them," Barnum replied.

"I thought so," said the passenger, a stocky fellow with a receding hairline and close-set blue eyes over a full beard, as he handed Barnum his card. "I am the little cuss."[11]

Chapter Two

 IN THE SAME YEAR as the Cardiff Giant scandal, Marsh made a trip to see another set of specimens pulled from the bowels of Earth—specimens larger, more magnificent, and more bizarre than the Giant and, most astounding of all, absolutely genuine.

In many ways, this journey to Philadelphia was a true pilgrimage. For at that moment, the city was arguably the nation's science capital and undeniably its center for vertebrate paleontology. It was a splendid city, rich, growing, and willing to support a vibrant scientific community.

Walking its tree-shaded, cobblestone streets, lined with neat, brick townhouses trimmed in marble and brass, or sauntering along Broad Street, past the swiftly moving streetcars, the Union League's new beaux-arts brownstone palace, and the Academy of Music's great golden lanterns flickering with gaslight, Marsh found himself in a city palpably grander than his New Haven or even Boston. Was it any wonder that this the nation's second-largest city was a center of learning and intelligence?

And yet, there was also a self-satisfied provincialism, a primness, a close-mindedness about this place that called itself "America's Athens." Philadelphia, Henry James observed, was "A closed circle that would find itself happy enough if only it could remain closed enough." It was a sentiment that would one day taint and diminish the science practiced there and ultimately contribute to Philadelphia's eclipse as a science center.

Although the city was in the midst of its greatest surge in immigration—by 1870 slightly more than a quarter of its 675,000 residents would be from immigrant stock, mainly German and Irish—Philadelphia remained decidedly white, conservative, and Anglo-Saxon, with its 374 Protestant churches wildly outnumbering its 43 Catholic churches and 9 synagogues.[1]

Abolition Hall, a Negro orphanage called African Hall, and an Irish Catholic church had each in its turn been put to the torch by mobs, and the city was for a time a stronghold of the nativist American party, or "Know-Nothings," with their antiforeign, anti–Roman Catholic platform.

Even after the Civil War, when Octavius Catto, the black principal of the

Quaker-sponsored Philadelphia Institute for Colored Youth, was beaten to death as he tried to vote, no one was ever arrested for his murder.

So, political myopia and mean spirits suffused the "City of Brotherly Love" as much as civic pride and high-minded ideals. Still, when Marsh paid his visit in the first part of 1869, Philadelphia's science had no rival in America, save for Boston, and in his own chosen field—paleontology—there were only a few challengers in all the world.

The city's scientific reputation rested upon three key institutions. There were the American Philosophical Society—the nation's first scientific organization, founded by Benjamin Franklin in 1743; the University of Pennsylvania's medical school; and the Academy of Natural Sciences.

In 1869, there was no finer museum in the nation than the fifty-seven-year-old academy. Its collections were substantial, bigger than Louis Agassiz's at Harvard or Spencer Baird's at the Smithsonian. Its library was huge, more than twenty-five thousand volumes, and the scientific circle at its weekly Tuesday-evening meetings was stellar.

But most important for Marsh, it was the scientific home of Joseph Leidy and Edward Drinker Cope. Leidy, a professor of anatomy at the university medical school, had been studying American fossil life for more than twenty years and was the dean of American paleontology. He had identified the first dinosaur remains discovered in the United States, based on teeth brought back from an 1856 expedition to Montana. Two years later, he found the country's first dinosaur skeleton, the *Hadrosaurus.* Cope, a Leidy protégé, had discovered the second significant American dinosaur skeleton in 1866.

Cope's dinosaur, like Leidy's, was found in the muddy limestone marl of southern New Jersey. There was a hind leg, a portion of a jaw, and something that Cope said looked like "a cross between the talon of an eagle and the claw of a lion." The animal had been a two-legged meat eater, about twenty feet long.

Cope called it *Laelaps aquilunguis,* "eagle-clawed terrible leaper," and he envisioned an active predator jumping and attacking its prey with its great "birdlike" claw.[2] It was, Cope told his father, "altogether the finest discovery I have yet made." So exciting was the prospect of such discoveries that Cope moved his young wife and baby daughter to Haddonfield, New Jersey, to be closer to the marl pits.

⚜

The fact that the academy had the nation's only two dinosaur skeletons was in itself impressive. What drew Marsh to the city that year, however, was the fact that it now boasted the only reconstructed, fully mounted dinosaur skeleton in the entire world. Leidy's *Hadrosaurus* stood in the academy gallery—twenty-six feet long and fourteen feet tall. It was a monster far more imposing than the Cardiff Giant.

The *Hadrosaurus* mount was the handiwork of British sculptor Benjamin Waterhouse Hawkins. Hawkins was the world's first dinosaur artist, having already done several life-sized sculpts for the Crystal Palace Exposition Park, outside of London. Those models were a great success, drawing more than forty thousand people opening day.

Hawkins was in the United States to do a series of sculpts for a similar dinosaur garden in New York City's new Central Park. His commission stated, however, that this garden was to contain animals "representing ancient life on this continent."

Considering Philadelphia's preeminence in paleontology, it was natural that Hawkins would head there to do his research and that he would seek out Leidy and Cope.

When Hawkins saw the bones of Leidy's *Hadrosaurus,* he offered to mount them for the academy at no charge. The display was completed in late 1868. The academy officially thanked Hawkins, saying the model would "tend to benefit the community by expanding the minds of the masses . . . [and] advance science by increasing the number of those who can appreciate the labors of the men of science, sympathize in their labors, and secure for them objects of interest which would be thrown away or destroyed by the ignorant."[3]

There was a touch of prophecy in the academy's words, for Hawkins's New York City work would be destroyed and thrown away by the ignorant. When political control of the Central Park project shifted in 1871 to Tammany Hall, "Boss" William Tweed apparently felt the idea of dinosaurs was blasphemous. So he had a gang of toughs pay a visit to Hawkins's Central Park studio one night. They smashed a *Hadrosaurus* and several other models. The pieces were dumped in a nearby lake, and that was the end of dinosaurs in Central Park.

When Marsh visited Philadelphia, there was not only Hawkins's *Hadrosaurus* to see, but also Cope's newest project—the largest paleontological undertaking of his young career. Cope was trying to reconstruct a giant reptilian sea serpent that had lived in the waters that covered Kansas one hundred million years ago.

Cope and Marsh had first met in Berlin in the winter of 1863. Marsh, then thirty-two, was studying at the University of Berlin. The twenty-three-year-old Cope was making a grand tour of Europe, meeting men of science and visiting museums and collections.

The scion of a wealthy Philadelphia Quaker family, Cope had been dispatched to Europe to keep him out of harm's way—the harm being a Washington love affair that apparently budded while he was studying collections at the Smithsonian and the threat of being drafted into the Civil War.

A tall, handsome fellow with an interest in both natural history and the ladies (he wrote home with equal enthusiasm about visiting the Smithsonian and visiting Joseph Henry's daughters),[4] he was one of those self-made American scientists, his formal schooling having stopped with a Quaker boarding school at the age of sixteen.

Brilliant and precocious, Cope was already on his way to an outstanding career. When the young men met in Berlin, Marsh had two university degrees, but only two published scientific papers—both related to his Nova Scotia trip. While Cope had no degrees, he had already published thirty-seven scientific papers in five years.

It was rare for an American, so far from home, to find a colleague as well as a compatriot, so Cope and Marsh spent a few days together. When they returned to America, they pursued a scientific friendship.

They exchanged manuscripts, fossils, photographs, and correspondence. Their letters closed with "kind regards" and expressions of friendship.[5] In 1867, Cope honored Marsh by naming one of his amphibian fossil finds *Ptyonius marshii*. Marsh reciprocated the next year by naming "a new and gigantic serpent from the Tertiary of New Jersey" *Mosasaurus copeanus*.[6]

Cope, however, could not help fretting that Marsh had come to his very backyard and made off with an excellent fossil find, and so he referred to Marsh's *Mosasaurus* as "the one that got away." That same year, when Cope heard a rumor that Marsh was putting in a bid for a set of Irish elk skeletons, he wrote to Leidy saying, "How true the latter is I cannot say. Some one had better . . . stop the sale if possible."[7]

It was in this atmosphere of amiable, but growing competition that in the late spring or early summer of 1869, Marsh came to look at his friend's latest and most ambitious effort.

The specimen—a plesiosaur—had been sent to the academy in March of 1868 by an army surgeon at Fort Wallace, in western Kansas, and Cope made his initial report on the specimen at the academy's March 24 meeting. "Prof. Cope exhibited to the Academy several fragments of a large Enaliosaurian, discovered by the Academy's correspondent at Fort Wallace, Kansas, Dr. Theophilus H. Turner. . . . The general form is different from Plesiosaurus in the enormous length of the tail, the relatively short cervical region . . . the total length 34½ feet.

"He called it *Elasmosaurus platyrus* . . . [for] the great plate bones of the sternal and pelvic regions. It was a marine saurian whose progress was more largely accomplished by its tail than by its paddles."[8]

The exact nature of the animal, however, was still hidden in the jumble of fossil fragments. Turner had shipped more than one hundred bones—vertebrae, hip, shoulder, limbs, and most valuable of all, a skull. They had come to the academy wrapped in old newspaper, tied up in burlap sacks, and boxed in wooden crates.[9]

Cope unwrapped the fossils one by one and set about chipping away the clay encrusted on the bone surfaces. Then began the sorting and piecing together of the hotchpotch. To do that, Cope relied on the techniques of comparative anatomy developed by the great French anatomist, Baron Georges Cuvier.

Cuvier had reasoned that the form and function of skeletal structure was similar across species. For example, skulls are attached to backbones, legs are attached to hips. And so, by being able to identify a very few bones and taking account of their proportions, an entire animal could be reconstructed. Indeed, Cuvier boasted he could do it all with a single bone.

Cuvier's techniques were adopted by the foremost anatomists of the time, including Joseph Leidy. Having attended Leidy's anatomy classes at the medical school, in 1861, Cope set out using the same techniques to reassemble his Kansas sea serpent.

Finally, by the middle of 1869, Cope had made sense of the puzzle and reconstructed the animal. At thirty-five feet long, with large fins attached to platelike hip and chest bones, and a small angular head with sharp teeth, the *Elasmosaurus* easily surpassed *Laelaps* in size and magnificence. But what was most striking was its flexible neck. So odd was the neck that this animal needed a whole new taxonomic order for itself, which Cope proudly christened the Streptosauria, or "twisted reptiles." Cope had written a major paper, with lithographic plates, to be attached to the *Transactions of the American Philosophical Society* that summer, at his own expense.

Cope showed Marsh his craft, with some pride no doubt, and as the Yale professor cast his eye over the bones, he may have gotten the same rush as when he found tool marks on the Cardiff Giant. A monumental mistake had been made. And Marsh was going to notch friend Cope on his belt along with the likes of Agassiz and Hall.

"I noticed that the articulations of the vertebrae were reversed," Marsh recounted years later, "and suggested to him gently that he had the whole thing wrong end most." It was, Marsh said with some delight, "like Barnum's famous woolly horse, the head was where its tail should be." Cope had put the skull on the tail.

Marsh's criticism did not come across as gentle to Cope. When he retold the story to friends, Marsh had been "caustic," perhaps even gloating. Cope's first instinct was to defend his work. After all, he had spent the better part of a year studying and reconstructing the beast. He had followed Leidy's method, and Turner had said that when he found the bones, the skull and vertebrae had been arranged in this manner. Cope and Marsh picked over the bones. They wrangled and bickered. They called in Leidy to arbitrate. Leidy examined the skeleton.

Now, while Marsh might revel in controversy and showing up a colleague, Leidy surely did not. Leidy was a man of good cheer, striking good looks—one friend described him as "the Christ type"—and a hankering for black bread, Swiss cheese, and lager beer. He liked everyone, and everyone liked him.

Well, of course, he didn't like sick people, which was an occupational handicap for a doctor. Although he received a degree from the University of Pennsylvania Medical School in 1844, he gave up his practice after just two years, and at the age of twenty-three, devoted himself to research and teaching anatomy.

Leidy examined the *Elasmosaurus* and then quietly took the last vertebra from the tail and fitted it into the skull. Cope was mortified. He quickly set about buying up all the copies he could find of the transactions of the American Philosophical Society, although some remained rattling around town. (Both Leidy and Marsh had copies.) It was a humiliating blow for the twenty-nine-year-old scientist. Outside scientific circles, this would not carry the blemish or bite of Hall being duped by the Cardiff Giant. There would be no public scandal, but for Cope it was a small disaster. This was his biggest paleontological project ever, and he had muffed it. Not only had he muffed it, but it had been found out by his two most distinguished colleagues.

For Agassiz or Hall to make a mistake and be caught by Marsh was no more than stubbing a toe. They were both so well established, so preeminent in their fields. Cope, however, was young and without university credentials. His reputation rested entirely upon his work.

⚜

Although it was probably of little consolation to Cope, in truth, science was full of mistakes, particularly in this newest of sciences, paleontology. A bone was found, and it was thought to mean one thing. Then a second bone was found, and together the two bones indicated something entirely different. It was not surprising that a distinguished scientist like Agassiz could look at Marsh's Nova Scotia fossil and think it some new transitional form between fish and reptile, when it turned out to be an amphibian.

It was all uncharted territory. The map of this new prehistoric world—a world barely imagined just a few decades earlier—was still being fashioned. The first strokes were drawn in 1795 by Scottish physician James Hutton in his *Theory of the Earth,* a book that contended the world was neither created in seven days nor was only six thousand years old, as calculated by the generations of Genesis.

The Earth, Hutton said, had been built and sculpted through the processes of erosion and mountain building. It was the handiwork of sediments piling up and lava spewing out of volcanoes. All these forces were working in uniform ways, in vast cycles, over huge time periods. It was, Hutton said, a world with "no vestige of a beginning, no prospect of an end."

Hutton's ideas were still being debated in the first decade of the new century, when France's Cuvier, after analyzing fossil and living elephants, came to the conclusion in 1806 that some species from the world's distant and foggy past had completely disappeared from Earth. The animals had gone extinct.

The idea of extinction challenged another deeply held belief, one that stretched back to Aristotle, the notion of a fixed world. Central to this idea was the concept of the "plenum"—a place or space that is full and complete. God had filled the world with a cornucopia of life, life that could be linked from the smallest to the greatest, which of course, was man. Extinction would break the chain.

By comparing the corresponding anatomical features of living species and fossil species, Cuvier was able to show that the American mastodon and Siberian mammoth were distinct from the living elephant and apparently no longer alive. "Cuvier's detailed factual analysis in support of the mammoth's extinction finally shook man's faith in the plenum," said historian Adrian Desmond, "and removed the first link from the chain."[10]

Cuvier also noted that the further back one went into Earth's history, the less creatures resembled those of today. Soon the most remarkable animals were being exhumed from life's deep history, especially in England. First came the *Megalosaurus*—the "giant lizard"—discovered in 1815 by the Reverend William Buckland, professor of mineralogy at Oxford University. Then Gideon Mantell, a Sussex physician, found the *Iguanodon,* or "the iguana tooth," in 1822, and the *Hylaeosaurus,* the "woodland lizard" in 1832.

As their names indicated, these were the remains of reptiles, giant reptiles.

They were far bigger than their largest modern-day descendants, far bigger than the largest modern land animals. (Although Mantell's use of the modern lizard as a comparative guide led to vastly inflated size estimates. Just one more scientific mistake waiting to be rectified.)

The same year Mantell described the *Hylaeosaurus,* Charles Lyell, another Scotsman, completed the third volume of his *Principles of Geology,* a study that amplified Hutton's work. Lyell, by detailed observation and voluminous fact, attempted to show how the world was shaped by chemical, biological, and physical forces working incrementally over long time periods.

Lyell was trained as a lawyer, and his huge work was written like a skilled legal brief with articles of evidence. *Principles* drew a picture of an evolving Earth, a world shaped by the accumulation of small effects moving in no particular direction.

One of the aims of this new geology was to determine the sequence of Earth history and the age of the planet. Remarkably, the callow geologists were quickly able to develop a scheme for the former, although they remained uncertain about the latter.

The first tool they developed was a piece of logic called the law of superposition, which simply observed that rock layers on the bottom are older than rocks on the top. Another early technique was biological matching of rock layers. If the fossils of the same creatures or plants were found in two rock layers, no matter how far apart geographically or how different in physical constitution, it was a safe bet the rocks were the same age. It was this use of fossil dating that first made paleontology a valued exercise.

Using these techniques and paying close attention to the physical composition of the rocks, Lyell was able to identify roughly nine "ages," from the Carboniferous through the Cretaceous and Eocene to the present. It was the first rough sketch of the Earth's true history.[11]

Forty years after Lyell, America's foremost geologist, James Dwight Dana of Yale, had refined that sketch. Dana divided Earth history into seven ages, which were then again subdivided into about a dozen "periods," and those periods into more than forty "epochs."

This slow puzzle-piecing would continue decade after decade, until a century after Dana, the picture's resolution would be much sharper, with Earth history partitioned among twelve periods, thirty-five epochs, and seventy-two ages.

Precisely how far back did these epochs and ages go? No one was really sure. By using estimates based on observed rates of erosion and sedimentation, it was clear that it took millions of years to build rock strata. Dana noted that by one estimate, the Paleozoic period had lasted thirty-six mil-

lion years and the Mesozoic, nine million years. Another calculation estimated that the "minimum duration" for Earth was "200,000 million
years." It was, however, impossible to be more precise.

"Time is long—very long," Dana assured. But how long he couldn't
say.[12]

If the Earth's crust evolved, what of the life living upon it? Lyell did not
deal with that directly. He meticulously noted life's remarkable global distribution and variation and suggested there had been a gradual succession of
biological changes. But as more and more ancient extinct life forms were
discovered, and it became clear that species appeared and disappeared, the
unavoidable questions arose—how and why did that happen?

Some scientists believed that life, like the physical Earth, evolved, that it
"transmuted" from one form to another. Another heresy. Unlike geological
forces or extinction, there was far less proof to support this idea. Some,
including Cuvier and Agassiz, believed successive catastrophes, like Noah's
flood, had periodically wiped out a large number of species and then God
created a bunch of new ones.

In 1842, Richard Owen, a Cuvier disciple, completed the second part of
a detailed report for the British Association for the Advancement of Science
titled "Fossil Reptiles of Great Britain." In this study, Owen argued that the
huge prehistoric animals being discovered were completely separate and
particular from present-day reptiles and needed their own category, their
own taxonomic order. Owen proposed calling them Dinosauria—"fearfully great lizards."

Owen had anatomical reasons for placing the *Iguanodon, Megalosaurus,*
and *Hylaeosaurus* in a distinct order. For example, all of them had fused vertebrae in the lower back for additional support, and despite being reptiles,
their limb bones were similar to those of mammals. The model for these
"dinosaurs," Owen insisted, wasn't Mantell's lizard, but the huge land
mammals, elephants and rhinos. Owen was acclaimed as the "English
Cuvier."

Owen also had political and ideological motives for creating dinosaurs. It
was a gambit to best his rivals in developing an interpretation of the
expanding body of paleontological material, and it was a rebuff against the
growing speculation over the possibility of evolution. These fossil species,
Owen insisted, "never exhibit any indications that their forms graduated or
by any process passed into another species. They appear to have sprung
from one creative act."[13] It would not be the last time that fossils would be
used to tear down or build up the theory of evolution.

Owen, however, could not blunt the growing interest in evolution, and in

1859, a disciple of Lyell—a fellow who once said, "I often feel half my views come out of Lyell's brain"—published a detailed study on the subject. His name was Charles Darwin; his book was *On the Origin of Species by Means of Natural Selection.* Like Lyell's *Principles,* Darwin's *Origin of Species* was a thesis loaded with fact and observation. Still, Darwin freely conceded that since evolution was such a slow-moving process, it could not be documented in the modern world. Only by looking back through the millennia could proof be found. Darwin feared that such evidence would be hard to come by. But the message was clear: The key to the mystery of life lay in paleontology.

Without a doubt, the most valuable ammunition in this battle to understand the history of the Earth and its life was fossils. Geologists depended on them to help match and fix the ages of rock. Even more important, tracing the variation of life from strata to strata, starting at the deepest, most ancient horizon and working ever upward toward modern times, might show the lines of evolution, the ancestral forms and the transitions species made to adapt and survive.

Soon Darwin's own acolyte, Thomas Huxley (he was nicknamed "Darwin's Bulldog") was pushing the bounds of paleontology, challenging Owen, Cuvier, and anyone else who denied evolution.

From Hutton to Cuvier to Lyell to Owen to Darwin to Huxley, mankind's entire notion of creation and life had shifted in the space of a single human lifetime. "Geology, the youthful science," Marsh would scribble in his notes at the University of Breslau.[14]

Yes, geology and paleontology were young sciences and a young man's game. Lyell was thirty-three when he wrote the first volume of *Principles.* Cuvier was thirty-seven when he proved extinction. Owen was thirty-eight when he invented dinosaurs. And, although Darwin waited until he was fifty to publish *Origin of Species,* he had hit upon the book's central idea two decades earlier. If these sciences were studded with errors, they were the miscues of exuberance, impatience, imagination, and youth.

Sitting together in a Berlin cafe, just four years after *Origin of Species* had been published, Cope and Marsh must have felt they were on the verge of great things. They had arrived almost at the birth of their science and not long after the birth of their nation. Earth might be ancient, but their world was young, and they were ready to take their places in it.

❖

What to do about the wrong-headed *Elasmosaurus?* In the fall, Cope wrote a brief and very obtuse note—a correction of his restoration—without actually admitting there had been an error. It ran in the proceedings of the academy. This did not satisfy either Marsh or Leidy. And so, at the academy's Tuesday evening meeting on March 8, 1870, Leidy rose and delivered brief remarks on *Elasmosaurus,* noting for the record that "Prof. Cope has described the skeleton in a reverse position and in that view has represented it in a restored condition in figure 1, plate ii of his *Synopsis of the Extinct Batrachia and Reptilia . . .* August, 1869, published in advance of the fourteenth volume of the *Transactions of the American Philosophical Society."* Leidy went on to offer analysis of the animal's vertebrae.[15]

There is no record of whether Cope was among the twenty-five members in attendance that night, but Marsh was there. He read a paper on an extinct bird "allied to the turkey," from the green sands of Monmouth County, New Jersey. He also displayed the tooth from an extinct peccary from New Jersey's Shark River and some bones from a small *Hadrosaurus.*[16]

In a subtle way, Marsh's report was yet another cut, for by 1869, more and more of the Jersey marl fossils weren't going to Cope, Leidy, or the academy in Philadelphia. Instead, as Marsh's paper intimated, they seemed to be heading to New Haven. Marsh, it turned out, had engaged the services of the Reverend H. H. Beadle of Bridgeton, New Jersey, to hunt the marl and send fossils to Yale.

In September of 1869, *Frank Leslie's Illustrated Newspaper* had even reported on the excavation of "antediluvian" fossils at the Vincentown Marl Company near Burlington, New Jersey, at which time "Prof. Marsh took from the ground among other things the rib of a whale and the snout of a swordfish."

In March of 1870, the very same week Leidy corrected Cope's restoration of the *Elasmosaurus* before the academy, Cope turned up at two of the New Jersey sites Marsh men were prospecting. "Cope was at Felsinger's and to Stanley's about two weeks hence," Reverend Beadle reported to Marsh in a March 20 letter. "He told them you miss on payments—also that he has seen me and I had sent him out there to get what there was.

"But they did not trust the tale. So that his raid could not have paid him for the crossing . . . Cope left an envelope directed and stamped at Felsinger's. I had a mind to put a note in it and send it back. I leave that for you to do when you come down."[17]

Cope was surely stewing. When he found what he thought was an error in a Marsh paper, he could not help but write to him, "As we sometimes take the liberty of alluding to each others 'great mistakes,' I would like to make one criticism."[18]

Marsh dismissed Cope's caviling and claimed the fossil grounds he staked out as his and his alone. Relations between Cope and Marsh were definitely cooling. What neither man realized, however, was that the events of 1869 had done more than merely bring a chill to a professional friendship. They set a pattern that would to a great degree fix their life courses on paths that would be painfully intertwined.

They were in a competition for the treasure of old bones and also at odds over the story those old bones told. Cope would work quickly, gliding gracefully over his material, although he was prone to a mistake here and there. Marsh was methodical and calculating and ever patrolling for the miscues of his rivals. Both nurtured ambition and intellect. Neither man was prepared to yield.

With their science so young and the world so large, so untapped, one would have thought that there would be enough room for both Cope and Marsh. But their energy, ideas, and egos would prove to be great, so great that even the vast American West could barely contain them.

Yes, the West, that was where the future of paleontology truly lay. Everyone knew that the West was the most promising fossil field in the world—the greatest unknown—and Marsh was now determined to get there first.

Chapter Three

 IN ALL OF AMERICA, there was not a single Malayan tapir skeleton—not a one, and here was this fine specimen going on the market in London, for a mere ten pounds sterling. Why, Spencer Baird would have snapped it right up. He couldn't though, for he didn't have the money.

"It was my hope that the Smithsonian might purchase the specimen, but Prof. Henry thinks we cannot afford it," Baird lamented in an April 1870 letter to Marsh.[1] Baird could never get enough money out of Henry, the Smithsonian's parsimonious secretary.

In an effort to keep out of the congressional cross hairs and silence critics, like Pennsylvania senator Cameron, Henry ran a very frugal shop at the Smithsonian. The institution's role was to promote research and publication. Period.

Baird knew, however, that for zoology, geology, and archeology, collections were vital. Baird yearned for a great museum. It was, however, only a dream. He was left scrounging around for specimens, begging his fellow scientists, and Barnum, for their spare bits and pieces. What he gathered, he stored in hallways and basements, for Professor Henry thought spending money on a museum building imprudent.

There would be no new tapir skeleton for the Smithsonian. Perhaps Yale would like it for the new museum it was building, Baird suggested. As events would prove, Marsh didn't care much for the tapir one way or another, but he sent Baird a check for seventy dollars to purchase the specimen.

The tapir meant nothing. Alliance and political goodwill meant everything, and Marsh had already shown that he knew how to forge them using the dollar as a tool. It was a skill that must have been instinctive, for he had not grown up with money.

Born October 29, 1831, on a hardscrabble farm in Lockport, New York, to Caleb and Mary Marsh, Othniel spent his childhood going to rural schools and doing farm chores—or, rather, doing his best to avoid them.

Marsh was only three when his mother died from cholera. He and his five-year-old sister, Mary, were sent for a time to live with relatives. When they returned, Caleb had remarried. Soon there was a house full of half brothers and half sisters. But Othniel and Mary were their own family, and whatever affection and nurturing the boy received came from his one true sister. As his oldest son, Caleb expected a lot of work out of Othniel, and there was constant tension between the two.

One escape the boy discovered was the company of Colonel Ezekiel Jewett, a retired military man and gentleman geologist. Jewett had moved to the region because fossils were so plentiful, and he often took young Marsh on his collecting jaunts. Jewett's skill in the field impressed even James Hall in Albany. Marsh hunted game with Jewett as well and aspired to be as sharp with both the geological hammer and the rifle as the old soldier, who had ridden to Mexico with General Zachary Taylor.

Jewett opened Marsh's eyes to the world of science and in years to come would, in some small degree, be the father that Caleb Marsh had never been. When Caleb died in 1864, it was Jewett who would bring Marsh the news and console him. Years later, he would fuss over the dangers of the western expeditions. "I don't like the idea of your campaign to the west," he would write to Marsh. ". . . There is no great necessity to exposing one's hair when [the army] will quiet the rascals in a month or two."[2]

Still, at the age of twenty, Marsh was considering pursuing life as a carpenter or country schoolteacher. At that moment, he was rescued by his mother's brother, George Peabody, the mercantile banker and millionaire. Uncle George had started out as dry-goods clerk and was now a financier living in London. Self-made men tend to either revere or dismiss education. Uncle George was most definitely in the first camp. He staked young Marsh to an education at Phillips Exeter Academy and Yale College.

When he arrived in Andover, Massachusetts, in 1851, to start at Phillips Exeter, Marsh was already considerably older than his classmates and soon was nicknamed "Daddy." After the drudge work of the farm and the emotional warfare with his father, Marsh luxuriated in his freedom, spent a good deal of time hunting, and showed he was not much of a student.

Things changed that summer. Mary, who had married and moved to Lowell, Massachusetts, became seriously ill. Marsh rushed to her bedside. But at the age of twenty-three, almost the same age Marsh's mother had been, Mary died. Marsh mourned, and during a summer day spent on Dracut Heights, just outside of Lowell, he took stock of his life. Perhaps it was then he decided that the only person he could ever really depend on was himself. "I changed my mind during an afternoon spent on Dracut Heights," he told a biographer years later. "I resolved I would return to Andover and take hold, and really study."[3]

Marsh went on to Yale and graduated eighth in his class, with the Latin prize and a Phi Beta Kappa key. He also received the Berkeley Scholarship for the best examination in Greek. Marsh used the scholarship to help finance his studies at the Sheffield Scientific School and received a master's degree in 1862. All along the way, he courted his Uncle George by letter and reported to his Aunt Judith Peabody Russell in Danvers, Massachusetts.

With Uncle George living in London, Aunt Judith was Peabody's monitor and bursar. While applauding Marsh's scholarship, she was constantly scolding him for spending too much money and sending her the bills too late.

"I consider an irregular and careless way of keeping accounts dishonesty," she reprimanded Marsh in 1857. Three years later, she was still complaining about tardy bills and high living. She warned that Uncle George was displeased and that his open-ended agreement to finance Marsh's education was in jeopardy. "I gave no limits to Othniel's yearly expenses because I thought he would not be extravagant," Uncle George was reported to have said. "I observe that last year he spent $900. If he is likely to go over $1,000 this year, I withdraw what I did write."[4]

Money, it was a liberator, an enticement, a burden, a threat. But money had its uses. Marsh was studying in Berlin, still subsidized with Peabody money, when he heard that his uncle was going to make a large bequest to Harvard. (The Massachusetts Peabodys had a longstanding relationship with the university, and most of the Peabody boys went to Harvard. Marsh was the exception, heading for Yale because of its superior science studies.)

In November of 1863, Marsh wrote from Berlin to Benjamin Silliman Jr., then head of Yale's science faculty. "I had a long talk with Mr. P. in regard to his future donations. . . . I will tell you confidentially that Harvard will have her usual good fortune. . . . I can, assure you, however, I did [not] allow the claims of my Alma Mater to be forgotten."[5]

Marsh kept Silliman and James Dana, the eminent Yale geologist, posted on developments. Through the winter, the student and his professors exchanged letters on prospects and strategy. In the spring, Peabody, on his way to the spa at Wiesbaden to take the cure for his gout, met with Marsh in nearby Hamburg.

A few days later, Marsh was able to report to Silliman, "I take great pleasure in announcing to you that Mr. George Peabody has decided to extend his generosity to Yale College, and will leave a legacy of one hundred thousand dollars to promote the interest of Natural Science." The money was to be used to build the Peabody Museum of Natural History, and Marsh was pretty sure that Yale could get the money even before Peabody died. He had gotten Yale just as large a grant as Harvard and had managed to get himself named as one of the trustees for the new establishment. (In time, Marsh would wheedle another fifty thousand dollars out of Uncle George to help defray annual operating costs.)

In the same envelope with the triumphal message was another letter. This one was seeking advice on which studies to pursue to have the best chance of getting a position at Yale. Silliman wrote back saying that the faculty was "electrified" by the news of the grant. Regarding his career question, Silliman said, "The task of answering the important questions which you propound is much simplified by what has happened. It now seems clear that you have fit yourself by suitable studies for duty here in connection with the science of Geology and *Paleontology.*"

Silliman continued, "It is Prof. Dana's view that you should devote yourself with zeal and your well known perseverance to the study of Paleontology. . . . You have only to show your fitness . . . and you will receive the appointment."

Marsh had no illusions about what had transpired. "One result of your munificent donation to Yale," he told his uncle, "has been to more than realize my highest hopes of obtaining an honorable position." He explained that Dana and Silliman had proposed that he study paleontology because "there is no branch of science in America which offers so fine a field for a researcher."[6]

In 1866, Yale established a chair of paleontology, and Marsh immediately filled it. The university, however, didn't fund the post, the average professorial salary being about fifteen hundred dollars a year. Perhaps Yale was betting that Uncle George would provide a free professor, as well as a museum. If so, it was a good bet. As far as Marsh was concerned, that was just fine. He could live off a Peabody trust fund, and if Yale wasn't paying the piper, it couldn't call the tune. He would teach no courses, devoting himself to the Peabody Museum and research. It had all worked out admirably. Now, it wasn't that Marsh didn't merit the chair—paid or unpaid—but certainly bringing Yale a huge donation hadn't hurt his cause. Money definitely had its uses.

Seventy dollars for a tapir skeleton wasn't a great deal of money to Marsh—barely three weeks' salary for a Yale professor. It was more the thought, the show of support that counted. Even Baird realized that the London tapir would take a backseat to Marsh's planned expedition to the West. It was by all accounts going to be the biggest, most extensive fossil hunt ever conducted in the western states. "I hope you will have a good time in your excursion this summer," Baird wrote, "& will collect enough specimens for yourself and the Smithsonian. Do not forget to consider us first in the distribution of your duplicates. We, on our part, will not be backward in reciprocating."

Marsh had worked hard to put the expedition together, securing the backing of several businessmen to help finance the trip and recruiting a dozen Yale students, willing to hunt for fossils and pay their own way. He managed to get the railroads to provide passes and perhaps most important, had enlisted the backing of the War Department, receiving letters of support and introduction from General William Sherman, head of the army, General Phil Sheridan, who was in charge of the western forts, and the regional commander, General E. O. C. Ord.

Sheridan even saw some military value in providing Marsh with a military escort for such expeditions. "It will make it a little embarrassing to the Sioux," he explained to Ord, "by sending a force south of their reservation. The next objective is to gratify the professors of Yale College by letting Prof. Marsh gather the bones of dead elephants."[7]

Marsh's plan was to use the Union Pacific rail line as a base of operations and army posts across the frontier as staging grounds, provisioners, and protection for the Yale party.[8]

As June approached, all was in readiness. There had been a few forays into the West, most notably by Ferdinand Vandeveer Hayden in the 1850s and 1860s. He had collected some fossils in the Dakotas, Wyoming, and Montana, first for Hall and then for Leidy. The Indians thought Hayden, who never carried a gun and searched the ground and rocks frantically, was some sort of crazy, white mystic and named him "He Who Picks Up Stones Running." Still, the scientific value of the West had hardly been plumbed, and everyone knew that there were immense riches out there.

When Charles Lyell visited the United States in 1842, the value of the great weathered geological formations of the West was immediately clear to him. "We must turn to the New World if we wish to see in perfection the oldest monuments of earth's history," he said. "Certainly in no other country are these ancient strata developed on a grander scale or more plentifully charged with fossils."

In 1864, sitting in Ferdinand Roemer's paleontology class at the University of Breslau, Marsh wrote in his notebook, "The most inviting field for Paleontology in North America is in the unsettled regions of the west. It is not worthwhile to spend time on the thickly inhabited region." Roemer had visited Texas in 1842 and written a work on Cretaceous fossils, *Kreidebildung von Texas.*

Germany might have the great universities and France the academy, but America had the West. It was an immense, peerless laboratory. "Here the earth had a slow regular pulse," author and historian Wallace Stegner wrote. "It rose and fell for millions of years under Carboniferous, Permian, Triassic oceans, under Cretaceous seas, under the fresh-water lakes of the Eocene, before it was heaved up and exposed to rain and frost and running water and the sandblast of winds."[9]

What made the West so valuable was that this diverse patchwork of geological formations offered glimpses into so many epochs of life's primitive history. In Texas, there was a window into the Permian of 250 million years ago. A vision of life one hundred million years later in the Jurassic could be found in Colorado, and a peek at life one hundred million years ago in the Cretaceous was waiting in Kansas. Wyoming held some hint of the flora and fauna fifty million years ago during the Eocene, and embedded in Nebraska's chalk cliffs was a picture of life a mere five million years ago during the Pliocene.

It all became tangible for Marsh on his first visit to the West in 1868. In August, he had gone to Chicago for the annual meeting of the American Association for the Advancement of Sciences. One of the junkets arranged for the scientists was a ride to the terminus of the Union Pacific Railroad, whose tracks were then steadily creeping westward.

Marsh viewed the "new and strange" landscape from the rumbling coach. "The actual reality was far beyond my anticipations when I found myself in the middle of these plains, stretching in every direction as far as the eye could see," he wrote. As they approached the Rockies, the train passed over the bed of an ancient great freshwater lake. "I was eager to explore it," Marsh said, "for I felt sure that entombed in the sandy clays to the brim, there must be hidden the remains of many strange animals new to science, long waiting to be brought to light." Exploring the West, he felt "might require the labor of a life time."[10]

One stop Marsh particularly wanted to make was at Antelope Station, Nebraska. There had been press reports of the discovery of an ancient human skeleton, unearthed during the digging of a well. Marsh suspected that this "pre-Adamite man" was a humbug, and he wanted to investigate.

He persuaded the conductor to hold the train while he made a quick survey. Sure enough, there was the well and a mound of earth. Sifting through the dirt, Marsh found numerous bones and fragments. The mound was chock-full of bones. He lost track of the time, but the conductor didn't. The whistle blew, and the train began to leave. A bargain was quickly struck with the station agent to have all the bones picked from the pile, and Marsh caught the end of the last car as it left the station, heading west.

On the return trip, the agent had "a hat full of bones" for Marsh. "I left in his palm glittering coin of the realm, and we parted good friends,"

Marsh recounted. As the train lurched east, Marsh sorted through his catch, his fellow passengers watching with interest. No human bones, but the remnants of an ancient camel, pig, and turtle—evidence of no less than eleven extinct animals. Most interesting of all were the bones of a tiny horse. "The small horse was strongly in evidence, and interested all observers. He was then and there christened *Equus parvulus,*" Marsh wrote. "During his life he was scarcely a yard in height, and each of his slender legs was terminated by three toes."

Leidy had written the first paper on American fossil horses in 1847, noting the discovery of animal's remains, even though it had died out before the first Europeans arrived in the sixteenth century. There had, however, been a major change in the twelve years since then—Darwin's *Origin of Species.* From a Darwinian viewpoint, and Marsh was very much a Darwinian, *Equus parvulus* was a link in a chain of evolution that led from the diminutive, three-toed animal to the swift, hard-hoofed stallion. How had that happened? Could the answer be in the bottom of a Nebraska well or the rock faces of Wyoming buttes? Yes, the West was definitely America's laboratory, and Marsh could not wait to get started.

Unrest among the Sioux and Cheyenne scotched any plans for an expedition in 1869. Instead Marsh traveled in the East, visiting Philadelphia to see Cope's Kansas *Elasmosaurus,* one more good reason to follow the sun. At last, as the summer of 1870 approached, all was in readiness. Even the Indians appeared to be cooperating.

It was a spring filled with promise and good news. Baird wrote back informing Marsh that they had been successful in getting the London tapir. General Sheridan assured the Yale professor that the army would provide logistical support and protection. The letter he provided Marsh began, "To all officers of the Army."

The only annoying item came from Philadelphia. About three weeks before heading west, Marsh received a letter from Cope. The subject was some Ohio fossils that had been found by Dr. John Strong Newberry, a physician, Cleveland Medical School professor, geologist, and Hall protégé. The specimens were supposed to have been sent to Yale. Instead, they found their way to Philadelphia.

"I wish to mention briefly a matter which might be misunderstood in which I feel I am at great risk of appearing in a very unfavorable light," Cope said. Cope had written a paper describing the fossils, but it was only after publishing it that he learned from Newberry that the specimens were slated for Marsh's use. Cope vowed that Newberry's original letter, which came with the fossils, had stated, "You have the coal fossils to work up when you choose."

"Newberry," Cope wrote, "now tells me I did this *without any authority from him*. . . . I write to justify myself on this point and not to provoke disagreement between thyself & Prof. N. and I hope this will be considered strictly confidential. . . . If thee has felt aggrieved at my action . . . here is my explanation."[11]

Did Cope believe this would satisfy Marsh? Even as a Yale undergraduate, Marsh had shown himself to be compulsively possessive, keeping his large mineral and fossil collection under lock and key in an attic room at his boardinghouse. Sometimes he would carry his landlady's daughter piggyback up to his treasure room. "Libby, if you promise not to touch, I'll show you some wonderful things," Marsh told the little girl, and then displayed for her real gold and fool's gold, crystal and rock. Once Libby asked if one of the other student boarders, Arthur Hadley, who would become president of Yale, could come up. No, Marsh said he "couldn't trust him."[12]

But whatever irritation Cope's letter might have caused, Marsh did not have time to dwell on it for the West beckoned, and on June 30, the Yale expedition left New Haven.

✤

Fort McPhearson stood on the banks of the Platte River, at a place where the broad, shallow waterway split itself into a maze of channels, running between sandbars and little islands thick with willow and cottonwood trees. To the south stretched the endless rolling prairie of Kansas, to the north the rippling sand hills of Nebraska, more prairie, and finally the Dakotas.

The Union Pacific tracks now followed the riverbank, and in early July, the Yale men climbed down from rail coaches to begin their quest. They had spent a few days getting outfitted in Omaha and taking some target practice with their brand-new rifles. It looked like the guns might come in handy.

The day the Marsh company arrived, three antelope hunters straggled back to the fort, one man with an arrow still in him. The hunting party led by William Cody, who had recently won the nickname "Buffalo Bill," had been attacked by a band of about a dozen Sioux warriors. A young brave and one of the hunters, John Weister, exchanged fire at close range. The brave's arrow pierced Weister's arm. Weister's lead ball lodged in the Indian, who rode off a few hundred yards before tumbling from his horse dead. When they saw their chance, the hunters made a dash for the fort. "We stood the Indians off for a little while . . . ," Buffalo Bill said. "The Indians, however, outnumbered us, and at last we were forced to make a run for our lives."[13]

General Sheridan had written to Cody asking him to personally take care of Professor Marsh and the Yalies. Now the post commander, General Emory, wanted him to hunt the Sioux. Major Frank North, another experienced scout and Indian fighter, would guide the Marsh party. Cody and North had spent part of the past summer chasing the "Dog Soldiers," a particularly fierce and resourceful band of Cheyenne, who had two white women hostage.

After a five-hundred-mile chase, the Dog Soldiers had finally been caught that July at the Battle of Summit Springs. The tally had been fifty-seven Indians killed, seventeen women and children taken prisoner, and nearly four hundred mules and ponies captured.[14]

Cody, at Sheridan's request, selected saddle horses for the party from the herd of Cheyenne ponies. The general, Cody said, "always believed in my ability to select good horses."[15] On July 10, the Yale party rode out of the fort on their Indian ponies. Every Yale man was sporting a rifle, a bowie knife, a revolver or two, and a geological hammer.

Major North, who was, to hear Buffalo Bill tell it, the best pistol shot from the saddle in all the West, and his two Pawnee scouts led the way. Then came the Yalies and a company of the Fifth Cavalry commanded by Lieutenant Bernard Reilly Jr. and Lieutenant Earl Thomas. There were also six army wagons loaded with provisions, feed, tents, and ammunition. Buffalo Bill rode along with the fossil hunters for the first day. In all, there were seventy men in the fossil-hunting expedition.

The plan was to make a large circuit through Nebraska, first heading north over the Sand Hills, and across the Dismal River, until they reached the Loup Fork River. They would follow the river west for a while, then head north again to the Niobrara River. Finally, they would turn south, picking up the Platte and following it east back to the fort.

The prairies are often compared to the sea. The sea, however, has many faces. Southern Kansas is as flat as a sea becalmed, and the Dakotas are filled with the huge, gentle swells of buffalo grass. Nebraska's Sand Hills are sharp and pitched like an ocean whipped up by an oncoming storm.

The band moved slowly and with difficulty through the sand-dappled hills. The Pawnees led the way, creeping up over mounds, peering out from behind bunch grass for signs of the Sioux. Then came Major North trying to pick the smoothest path, for it was all too easy for a wagon wheel to crack the thin cover of green and rust-colored grass and stall in the sand beneath.

Marsh, however, was enthralled by the land and lectured from the saddle on how at one time all these hills were at the bottom of a great freshwater lake and how even before that, a vast inland sea covered most of the West and lapped at the foot of a young Rocky Mountains. At the end of the day, when they set up camp, Buffalo Bill remarked, "The Professor told the boys some pretty tall yarns today, but he tipped me a wink as much to say, 'you know how it is yourself, Bill.' " The next morning Bill left to go hunt Indians instead of fossils.

That night with the campfires crackling and casting shimmering light on the tents, with the soldiers "standing in picturesque groups," the horses picketed, and sentinels pacing the perimeter, Charles Wyllys Betts, one of the Yale students, could not help feel that the party was "in for something more than science."[16]

That was probably the hope of all twelve Yalies—a band of freshly graduated, mostly clean-shaven young men in their early twenties. For all but one, George Bird Grinnell, this was a summer's interlude before taking up the business of becoming lawyers, executives, and upstanding citizens. It was one last chance for an extraordinary adventure.

The next day, they marched for fourteen hours through the hot, treeless hills. The temperature edged up above one hundred degrees. There was neither shade nor water to be found. "What did God almighty make such a country as this for?" asked one of the troopers.

"God almighty made the country well enough," answered a comrade, "but it's this deuced geology the professor talks about that spoiled it all."

For five days, that would be their condition, broken only by a thunderstorm, from which the party filled its hats and drank. At last, they reached the Loup Fork River. The rippling hills came to an abrupt end in a series of white cliffs. Slithering away from the river were also small canyons of bare rock. "Our geological labors," Betts said, "now commenced."

There were signs that the Sioux were about. The Yalies thought they could hear Indian ponies in the night, and now as they began to work, they could see a tall column of smoke farther west along the river. Still, there had been no direct contact, no immediate threat. The Indians avoided confrontations with any large group of whites. They might boldly pick off a few antelope hunters—even if one of them was Buffalo Bill—but they would steer clear of seventy armed men, even if some of them were tenderfoot Yalies. The key was not to wander away, not to become a small group.

Every day the fossil hunters were protected by a strong guard, while the wagons and the rest of the column moved up the river. Soon the soldiers became active players in the game of finding fossils. The Pawnee scouts, however, would not touch the bones, believing them the remains of an ancient race of giants.

This moved Marsh to conduct a lesson in comparative anatomy for the Pawnees. Picking up the jaw of a fossil horse, he brought it close to the jaw of one of their ponies, showing how the two were similar. Cuvier in Indian County. It worked. "From that time," Betts said, the Pawnee scouts "rarely returned to camp without bringing fossils for the 'Bone Medicine Man.' "

Bone Medicine Man wasn't the only name Marsh earned from the Indians. An affectation of the professor's, a clearing of the throat, an exclaiming "What, what?" before speaking, was, the Pawnees thought, extremely curious. For this he was also known as the "Heap Whoa Man."

The fossil hunting was good. The clay surfaces offered up an array of Pliocene mammals—horses, camels, rhinos, and mastodons—and birds. Marsh was particularly interested in the horses. The Yalies were under orders to find as many horse fossils as possible. They responded by unearthing the remains of six different species.

In that baked and waterless plain, the river served as a magnet for game. Large herds of elk and antelope came to water, so fresh meat was plentiful. One day an antelope herd passed within two hundred yards of the fossil prospectors. To a man, they dropped their hammers and grabbed their rifles. The entire party opened fire at once, Betts said, "like a large package of firecrackers and with such effect that we had not only meat enough for a week, but brought the whole command sweeping down on us thinking that we were attacked by Indians."

The party also came across several Sioux funeral platforms. On one platform, they found a woman decked out in beads and bracelets. Next to her was a scalpless brave, with war paint still on his parchment cheeks. His crumbling hands held a rusty shotgun and a pack of playing cards. Such a vision of mortality left the young men silent and thoughtful. Marsh broke the mood. "Well, boys," he said, "perhaps they died of smallpox; but we can't study the origin of the Indian race unless we have those skulls."[17] The skulls were added to the Yale collection.

The live Sioux were also definitely out there. Smoke signals puffed up here and there in the valley. Still, no Indians came close. That didn't mean there wasn't any risk. One night, as the sun set amid thick, black thunderclouds, a line of orange light danced across the darkening plain. The Sioux had lit a prairie fire that was now advancing toward the fossil hunters on both sides of the Loup Fork. The party was camped in a bend along the river, and this purchased enough time to set a backfire, creating a cordon of charred ground between the camp and the burning prairie. They watched the spectacle of the fire moving along and beat out cinders drifting into the camp with blankets.

"Across the river wavy lines of fire crept up the rolling sand hills, and catching the clumps of cotton wood and pine trees wrapped them in cracking pyramids," Betts wrote, "while each gust of wind from the rising storm would sweep whole hillsides into a sheet of flames."[18] At last the thunderstorm broke, drenching the camp and quenching the fire.

The next day, the party marched across the charred prairie studded with roasted cactus and fried grasshoppers. Grass for the horses was difficult to find, and the river was narrowing with each mile, until it was nothing more than a stream and a few stagnant ponds. Water also became more scarce and more alkaline. They decided to turn south and head for the Platte. Another prairie march and then the wide shallow Platte. The Pawnees guided the party around the river's quicksand pools, and then they lead the Yale students on a mock raid on the town of North Platte. The "terrified inhabitants," Betts said, mistook the college boys for a party of Sioux and "rose up in arms to repel the invaders." The Yale boys were very amused, the good citizens of North Platte less so.

In North Platte, the Marsh party sat down to dinner at a table with china plates for the first time in more than two weeks. They also learned that the Franco-Prussian War had begun. Being a military man, Lieutenant Reilly was impressed. He ordered his men to fall in and announced with a flourish that war had been declared between France and Germany. One of the soldiers declared with "forcible profanity" how little he cared whether France and Germany were at war.[19] Perhaps if he realized that the fortunes of Prussian and French soldiers would ripple across the America West and affect the fate of the U.S. Cavalry and the Sioux nation, he would have been more concerned. But time and events would soon show how much smaller the world had become and how even America's western outposts, although they seemed remote from world events, really weren't.

Back at Fort McPhearson, General Emory congratulated the party on its safe return. The Yale men dined with the officers and crated their fossils for shipment back to New Haven. While the bones went east, the men went west to Wyoming, for the second leg of their expedition. Marsh now carried another letter of introduction, this one for General George Chamberlain in Denver.

"Permit me to introduce to you Prof. O.C. Marsh and a party from Yale College who are on a scientific expedition. They are not only distinguished people but very clever fellows and any attention that you can show them will go to the right place."[20]

They left the train at Cheyenne and made their way to Fort D. A. Russell. From the fort, they would set off to explore the region lying between the north and south forks of the Platte River. Again Marsh was given an escort, thirty men from Company I of the Fifth Cavalry. They headed south into Colorado, and there in the northeastern corner of the territory, Marsh discovered a previously unknown, unexplored badlands. The hard, white-rock washboard, whose western cliffs turned pink in the sunset, appeared to be of the same age and character as the Dakota badlands, some two hundred miles to the northeast.

The fossil hunters worked these badlands and found a variety of bones, including the remains of oreodons, which Betts described as "a remarkable animal combining characteristics of the modern sheep, pig, and deer." The lower deposits of the badlands yielded an even more interesting species, the *Titanotherium proutii,* a huge grazing beast with a four-foot-long jaw that looked a bit like rhino and stood as tall as an elephant.

So excited was Marsh by the discovery of these badlands that he immediately sent a letter back to Yale for publication in the next edition of the *American Journal of Science and Arts.*

PROFESSOR MARSH'S ROCKY MOUNTAIN EXPEDITION DISCOVERY OF THE MAUVISE TERRES FORMATION IN COLORADO

Prof. Marsh and party left New Haven on the 30th of June for Omaha and beyond. By a letter from him dated Cheyenne, August 4th, we learned he had already made a successful expedition to the Loup Fork and obtained a large collection of specimens, but they were prevented by Indians from going onto the Niobrara region. The following is the copy of a letter to J.D. Dana, dated Pine Bluffs, Wyoming Territory, August 12.

"The Scientific Expedition of the Yale College, while recently examining the geology of the Northern Colorado, discovered an extensive outcropping of the true Mauvise Terres of the White River formation. . . . The locality first detected, which contained all the characteristic fossils of the deposit, was on one of the branches of the Little Crow Creek about five miles south the Wyoming State Line. The strata there observed consisted of at least 150 feet of light colored clays, overlaid by sandstone and conglomerate about 200 feet in thickness. The lower portions of the clays are true Titanotherium beds. . . ."[21]

The party then moved into western Nebraska and stopped at Antelope Station, where they searched the old well. They also scoured the nearby cliffs and found three more species of fossil horse. Here rattlesnakes and not the Sioux were the main threat. Three draft animals were killed by snakes, and the constant rattling became "an old tune." One of the Yalies thought the snakes of at least some use and started collecting rattles to make a bracelet for his sweetheart.

They turned north and headed to Scotts Bluff on the banks of the Platte. Now they entered a bizarre prairie land, described by scientist and naturalist Loren Eisley as a "strange country of volcanic arches and cones, runnelled by rains, cut into purgatorial shapes."

The plain had been created some forty million years ago as silt and gravel washed down from the uplands. Then erosion began to lower this plateau, removing the sand and gravel, except where it was protected by hard rock caps and volcanic deposits. As the plain receded, the bluffs and cones rose. The tan walls of Scotts Bluff now tower five hundred feet over the mesa.

For decades, the bluff looming in the west was the sign that the first leg of the pioneer journey on the Oregon Trail was over. In those days, one could look east from the bluff and see line after line of wagon trains snaking across the prairie. But now as the Yale party rode toward the bluff over the Oregon Trail, grass was already growing thick in the deep wagon ruts.

Just sixteen months earlier, on May 10, 1869, the Union Pacific and Central Pacific had joined their tracks at Promontory Point, Utah. The iron rails now girdled the nation. Farther south, the Kansas Pacific had pushed all the way from the Mississippi River to the Rocky Mountains, and the Atchison, Topeka & Santa Fe had begun laying tracks toward the southwest. Pioneers no longer plodded along in Conestoga wagons. They road the rails. In 1850, there had been less than nine thousand miles of track in the country. By 1870, there were almost fifty-three thousand miles, and that figure was growing every year.

When the wagon train pioneers saw Scotts Bluff, it meant that they had covered six hundred miles of their two-thousand-mile journey. It had taken them two months. By train, they could easily make the same journey in a day.

Between the northern base of the bluff and the Platte was another wind- and rain-scarred patch of badlands, deep ravines choked with sagebrush. It was here that the Yale men once again searched for fossils, while soldiers stood guard scanning the river and the plains.

From the bluff, they made their way down Horse Creek, heading back toward Fort D. A. Russell. By this time, the Yale boys were beginning to feel at home in the Wild West, and two of them—George Bird Grinnell and John Reed Nicholson—decided to go off on their own for some duck hunting. They returned to camp unharmed, after getting lost for two days and setting the prairie on fire while smoking their pipes. (It was Grinnell who upon his return to New York would keep an eye on Barnum's menagerie for Marsh.)

The party reached the fort on August 23, about three weeks after setting out. Once again they climbed aboard the Union Pacific and headed west, this time setting down at Fort Bridger in western Wyoming.

Here Marsh met Judge William A. Carter, the post trader, justice of the peace, and generally one of the most influential men in the territory. He also met Carter's son-in-law, Dr. James Van Allen Carter, and the post commander, Major R. S. LaMotte. All three men would become valuable allies for the Yale professor.

Marsh was given a detachment from the Thirteenth Infantry as an escort, and a Mexican guide, Joe Talemans, accompanied the group. No horses were available at the post, so the expedition was mounted on mules.

Spurred by Indian tales of fabulous valleys strewn with huge petrified bones, Marsh's goal was to reach the junction of the Green and White Rivers in Utah. It was the end of August when the Yale party left the fort and headed south through the bottom of the Bridger Basin. They hurried past the green sands and gray clays of the basin, which would soon prove to be the most fruitful and most fought-over fossil grounds in the region. They kept moving south along the Green River, toward the legendary boneyard.

The going was rough, too rough. They tried to lighten the wagons by caching a load of grain. But the terrain was so rugged that the wagons were being shaken to pieces. They sent back to the fort to get packsaddles and ropes. The provisions were loaded on the mules, and off they went, down the Green River. This was the very same region—with its emerald waters bound by flaming red cliffs—that John Wesley Powell had navigated a year before, at the beginning of his descent of the Colorado River. This summer, Powell was in Washington trying to raise money from Congress. The Powell survey would take to the mountains again in the summer of 1871. For now, they belonged to Marsh.

They meandered south through mountain passes, already covered with snow, toward Fort Uinta in southern Utah. They never found those legendary bone valleys, but coming out of the mountains, they did come upon another fantastic scene, an expanse of stark Eocene rock, the Uinta badlands.

"We stood at the brink of a vast basin so desolate, wild and broken, so lifeless and silent that it seemed the ruins of the world," Betts wrote. It was a land "ragged, with ridges and bluffs of every conceivable form . . . rivulets that flowed from yawning canyons in mountain-sides stretched threads of green across the waste."

In traveling through this mountain region, the Yale party encountered a panorama of western life. There was "a company of old-time trappers clad in buckskin and living with their families in Buffalo skin lodges"[22] and a hunting party of Utes with horses pulling their lodge poles and papooses slung over saddle pommels. Nicholson, out duck hunting again, was chased by a grizzly bear. When rations ran low, the group feasted on a mule that had the misfortune of breaking its neck when it stepped in a badger hole. The mule was "tough, but pretty good."[23]

They met a posse tracking a gang called the Brown's Hole horse thieves and later met some members of the gang itself, who apparently had found the Yale grain cache. Marsh approached the men with the aim of getting his grain back, but when face to face with the bandits, who were "armed to the teeth," he tried engaging in amiable western banter.

"Well, where are your squaws?" Marsh asked.

"Sir," replied a dignified desperado, "this crowd is virtuous."

There is no indication that Marsh actually got the grain back. The party did manage to make Fort Bridger near the middle of September. Once again fossils were packed and sent east. The fossil hunters continued to move west, this time for some sightseeing in Salt Lake City, where the Yale boys "flirted with twenty-two daughters of Brigham Young in a box at the theater."[24] They went on to San Francisco and Yosemite, before heading back to Colorado.

Marsh's dispatches to New Haven weren't the only news of the Yale party filtering east. Ferdinand Hayden was also keeping Leidy posted in Philadelphia. A gaunt, complex, troubled figure, Hayden was a man with great ability and great flaws. He could be brash. He could be creative. He could be shifty. Perhaps it all went back to his broken home and a family in which the parents divorced, at a time when that simply wasn't done.

Hayden worked his way through Oberlin College and then studied medicine at the Cleveland Medical School, where he became an apprentice of John Newberry. Through Newberry, he met James Hall and abandoned medicine for science.

In 1858, Hayden wrote to Hall saying, "Nothing would give me greater pleasure than to be in your employ or in any way connected with you in exploration. There is no one whose good opinion I so earnestly desire."[25]

Hall arranged for Hayden to go on two western expeditions and introduced him to Leidy. Hayden switched allegiance once more. Leidy was able to help Hayden secure an associate professorship in geology at the University of Pennsylvania, and he also arranged for some expedition money.

By 1869, Hayden was turning the Geological Survey of Nebraska—he had recently been named its director—into the U.S. Geological and Geographic Survey. He was also practicing a shell game of promising western specimens to Baird at the Smithsonian, Leidy at the academy, and Dana and Marsh at Yale.

While science was his primary goal, he wasn't above taking five hundred dollars to write a five-page promotional booklet, "Colorado: Its Resources,

Parks and Prospects," for British land speculator and developer William Blackmere.[26]

On September 11, 1870, Hayden wrote to Leidy from Big Sandy Creek, Wyoming, saying that Marsh "has been ransacking the country and claims great success."[27] Indeed, Marsh had written to Hayden at Fort Bridger just a few days earlier saying that the Yale party had collected "some interesting fossils" and that Marsh would write up a notice for Hayden's survey report. "So please," Marsh asked, "if you should obtain any [fossils], let me describe them with mine, as that way we can get a better idea of the fauna of the ancient lake basin."[28]

Ten days later, Hayden sent what specimens he had to Leidy advising, "Do not let anyone have them who cannot commence their study at once. Marsh wrote me he mislayed a load of vertebrae remains. . . . I have written to him that all my vertebrae remains go to you. . . . I therefore send them to you. You can do with them as you please."

On October 10, Leidy received a Hayden letter from Fort Bridger.

"I advise you to publish your species as soon as described. Marsh is still down on the Green River. I may see him. I will send everything to you as soon as I get it.

"The recent fishes are in alcohol for Cope. Marsh, of course, wishes to make New Haven a scientific center. My interests are all in Philadelphia."

Finally, on November 12, Hayden sent Leidy a letter from Cheyenne marked "confidential." "Professor Marsh . . . feels very badly about my having provided [you with specimens]. . . . If you have not published the new species circled please do not delay. . . . He will be in Philadelphia in two weeks."

Leidy tried to calm the agitated Hayden. "I am sorry Prof. Marsh views things as he does. He has no reason to complain. You have been exploring western territories year after year and have at all times sent me the vertebrate remains . . . ," Leidy wrote. "When Prof. Marsh informed me he was going west, I had no right to complain nor did I even think so."[29]

Hayden, however, had felt the force of Marsh's determination and knew there was little chance of reaching an amiable understanding. "Marsh is more ambitious than Cope ever was . . . ," he warned Leidy. "He is raging ambitious."[30]

Meanwhile, the Yale party had retraced its steps to Denver and was now headed due east to Fort Wallace, Kansas, the very neighborhood of Cope's *Elasmosaurus platyrus.* This would be the expedition's final stop.

For three years, Fort Wallace had been on of the front lines of the battles and skirmishes with the Cheyenne and Arapaho. The fort consisted of about thirty low limestone buildings—bakery, blacksmith, armory, bar-racks—and a few corrals arranged around a large parade ground on the open prairie. There were no walls, just some rifle trenches around the perimeter, for if the Indians were not going to attack the Yale party, they certainly weren't going to attack an entire fort. The Butterfield Overland Stage was another story. The Cheyenne had repeatedly harassed and attacked the stage, which ran from Topeka to Denver, by way of Fort Wal-lace. The Indians had just about put the line out of business when the new Kansas-Pacific Railroad offered a speedier, safer alternative.

Marsh had come to Fort Wallace hoping to catch his own *Elasmosaurus,* but before hunting fossils, he was invited to go hunt buffalo. Everyone was hunting buffalo in those days. It was one of Kansas's biggest tourist attrac-tions. Would-be hunters could pay ten dollars and board a buffalo-hunt train. Each car had a rack with twenty-five breech-loading rifles and a box of cartridges. The hunters would shoot from open-air platforms, and the train would stop to harvest the tongues. Some travelers on regular passenger trains just shot their pistols from the coach windows, leaving dead buffalo along the train track. The whole region was swarming with so many buffalo that it was dangerous to run trains over the line at night.[31]

Just a few weeks before Marsh arrived, P. T. Barnum and a group of friends had been in the vicinity. General George Armstrong Custer, who was camped with the Seventh Calvary near Fort Hays, Kansas,[32] had outfit-ted Barnum with an escort of fifty cavalrymen, as well as horses, arms, and ammunition. "He received us like princes," Barnum said.[33]

"We were taken to an immense herd of buffaloes quietly browsing on an open plain," Barnum wrote. "We charged on them, and during an exciting chase of a couple of hours, we slew twenty immense bull buffaloes. Every man had killed his buffalo."

Although Barnum may have left Kansas with his buffalo, he failed, how-ever, to also bag Wild Bill Hickock, the sheriff in Hays City. Barnum wanted Wild Bill to join his circus, but in a card game, at Tommy Drum's Saloon, Wild Bill managed to win all the money Barnum had brought to lure him east.[34]

The officers at Fort Wallace were not quite as accommodating as Custer. The hunting party set out for the high tableland just south of the fort—an expanse of golden prairie, studded with tufts of green yucca, that stretched all the way to the Arkansas River. This great pasture was grazed by tens of thousands of buffalo, with the herds leaving each evening to water in the valleys that sliced the prairie.

The Yale men were assigned to an ambulance drawn by four mules. On the ride out, the captain, who was serving as master of the hunt, told stories about his previous buffalo hunts and treated his guests as if they were "all supposed to be tender-feet." This bothered Marsh. When they reached the tableland, he was even more irritated to learn that his group's role would be merely to "watch" the hunt. "Some of the Yale party used strong language," Marsh said, and then they set out on foot, hoping to get a shot in at a stray.[35]

Marsh remained in the ambulance and watched as the army officers dashed over the plain after individual buffalo. He thought it tame sport. The professor and the ambulance driver lit up a couple of good cigars and took in the day.

It was then that Marsh saw three buffalo crossing the tableland from a small herd to a larger one, a distance of perhaps three miles. An idea struck him.

"Driver, do you want a five-dollar bill?" Marsh asked.

"Mighty bad," came the reply.

"Then put me alongside of those three buffalo, where I can get a fair shot, and there is your money."

"I'll do it or bust these mules," the ambulance driver assured. With a crack of the whip, they were off.

The ambulance swayed from side to side as they careened over the prairie in pursuit of the ambling buffalo. As they drew closer, Marsh took out his field glasses and studied his quarry. The lead buffalo, he could tell by its darker coat and "more vigorous action," was a young bull. The other two were older bulls.

As they edged closer, Marsh singled out the last of the three animals as his target, and when they were even with the bull, he cradled his Winchester. Aiming low, just behind the foreleg where the heart should be, he squeezed off a shot. The last thing Marsh saw—before being pitched back in the wagon—was the bull going down. The sound of the rifle had spooked the mules, and they were now wildly straining, "each plunging for himself." The driver was fighting for control, as the ambulance barreled across the prairie rocking violently. "I thought every moment it would go over," Marsh said, "but I was willing to take the chance, and only lost my hat."

The other two buffalo were still ahead of the ambulance; Marsh's kill was out somewhere on the plain. Elated by his first shot, and with opportunity slipping away, he turned to the driver and asked, "Do you want another five?"

"You bet," he said.

"Then give me another shot at Number Two," Marsh ordered.

With some wrestling of the reins, the teamster swung the mules around, and they were off at a run. The buffalo had picked up their pace. Just as they drew near and Marsh was ready to fire, the mules broke again, and the driver had to fight to get them back on course. Marsh shot, the animal went down, and the mules again went careening over the prairie. Meanwhile the young bull continued toward the herd.

When the mules were under control once more, Marsh said to the driver, "I have one more five for you. Help me get that fine fellow, and we'll turn back."

It was a one-hundred-yard dash, and one more shot. The rifle report sent the mules wildly scrambling again, and it was some minutes before the driver could control them, and bring the ambulance back to the spot where the young bull lay. Marsh jumped down from the wagon.

"He was down but there was blood in his eye, as well as ground where he lay, Marsh recalled. "As I walked slowly toward him, with my rifle in my hand, the driver exclaimed. . . . Look out, he's going for you."

The bull sprang to his feet and charged. Marsh dodged and squeezed off one more shot. The bull went down for good. Marsh pulled out his hunting knife, rolled up his sleeves, and set to work. He cut off the head—which he thought would make a fine trophy. He was also hoping to rescue the hide and cut off the fore and hind feet, at the joint, as "evidence of what a fine animal I had slain." Having lost his hat, Marsh tied a handkerchief around his head.

It was in this sweaty, blood-splattered condition that the captain found him when he rode up. Marsh took all the blame for the episode. The driver, touching his vest pocket where the five-dollar bills were tucked, told the officer that the mules, frightened by the buffalo, had just run away on him—three times.

The cavalry officer helped Marsh load his trophies onto the wagon. (His two other kills were now several miles across the plain and would have to go unclaimed.) On the ride back, the captain was rather glum. It turned out that he had only managed two buffalo all day long. Trophies and meat were carted back to the fort.

The time had come now to do some serious work, and a few days later, Marsh and company set out with a guide, Ned Lane, and a military escort. It was already the middle of November, and the weather was turning cold. They moved east along the north fork of the Smoky Hill River. Soon the prairies gave way to buttes, canyons, and odd rock formations—chimneys, towers, pyramids, and spheres—with names like Castle Rock, Cobra Rock, and Old Chief Smoky. These chalky rock strata were once the floor of an ancient Cretaceous sea that stretched across North America from the Gulf of Mexico to the Arctic. This was a glimpse of Earth far older—150 to 65 million years ago—than anything the Marsh party had yet explored.[36]

Marsh's first destination was Twin Buttes, where Dr. Turner had discovered *Elasomsaurus platyrus*. Marsh wanted to "obtain additional remains of the same animal, if possible, and if not to find some comrades."

Meeting with only limited success, they moved down to the main branch of the Smoky Hill River. Here they struck pay dirt, finding a huge *Mosasaurus*—a marine lizard about fifteen feet in length—embedded in a yellow chalk bluff. It took several days to excavate the specimen and pack it in gunnysacks. The weather was becoming bitter, and sleeping on the bare ground became "less a pleasure than it had been throughout the summer."[37] To protect the tents from the piercing wind, they were pitched in the lee of a high bluff. For fear of Indians, the wagons were placed in a half circle at the foot of the cliff, and all the horses and mules were kept inside the cordon at night.

Buffalo came down to the Smoky Hill to drink every morning and evening, and there was always plenty of "choice cuts" for dinner. The smell of the meat brought coyotes sneaking around every night, but they were not bold enough to pierce the guarded circle.

Then one night, a shot cracked the dark, and the camp was thrown into chaos. Mules were braying. Horses were snorting. Tents were falling. Men were running and shouting. Everyone's first thought, first fear, was an Indian attack. Then all was still. No one was dead, no one wounded. Lanterns were lit. The camp was a mess, and all the animals were gone. A "council of war" was held, and the cause of the night's clamor was discovered. One bold coyote had jumped into camp from the bluff, lured by the smell of the fresh buffalo meat hanging outside the cook tent. That coyote had frightened and stampeded the mules and horses, provoking the sentry to fire his rifle.

There was nothing more to be done, and the men went back to bed. In the morning, only one old mule, Crazy Jane, could be found. A soldier was chosen to take Crazy Jane and follow the trail of the missing mules. The soldier tracking the animals soon realized that the mules were simply heading back to Fort Wallace, about fifteen miles to the west. So he prepared for a leisurely ride back to the fort.

In the meantime, the band of frightened mules with broken halters and dragging lariats arrived at the fort. It looked to the post commander, General Bankhead, as if the Marsh party had been ambushed. "Great God," Bankhead exclaimed, "the Indians have jumped the professor." And then perhaps seeing the newspaper headline "Yale Professor Scalped by Cheyenne," Bankhead quickly ordered a rescue mission. Lieutenant Braden was dispatched with a company. His orders: Rescue the fossil party, or bring back the remains.

The cavalry was already riding full speed to the Marsh camp when the soldier and Crazy Jane came moseying into the post. Before he could say anything, General Bankhead demanded, "Where's your gun?"

"I left it at camp," the private answered.

"Well," said the general, who clearly was having a hard day, "if you are damned fool enough to risk your own life in this Indian country, you shan't risk a government mule. Officer of the day, put that man in the guard-house."

The sun was setting when the Yale men heard the clamor of horses and wagons and saw Lieutenant Braden leading his men toward them in a cloud of dust. "He seemed greatly surprised at the quiet greeting we gave him and his men," Marsh said, "and inquired feelingly if we were all safe."

Once the tale was told and all was explained, the Yale men invited their rescuers to join them, as they were about to sit down to Thanksgiving dinner. There was no turkey, but there was buffalo tongue, steak, and roast rib, antelope meat in various forms, stewed jack rabbit, pork with beans, canned fruit and vegetables. It was all washed down with coffee and the "wine of Kentucky." College songs were sung by the Yalies, western stories were told the army officers. The coyotes, smelling the feast, howled.[38]

The time to leave was coming fast. On one of his last days in the field, Marsh worked into the late afternoon, with just a single soldier as a guard. The sun was setting, and the soldier was anxious to return to camp. They were riding along an old buffalo trail worn deep into the soft chalk of the riverbank when Marsh spied a small fossil bone about a dozen feet from the trail. He stopped and picked it up. It was hollow, about six inches long and one inch in diameter, with one end perfect and containing a peculiar joint Marsh had never seen before. He wanted to stay and search the area. Twilight was already covering the prairie, and his guard was growing more and more anxious. So the professor carefully wrapped the specimen and put it in one of his softest pockets. Then he cut a deep cross in the gray chalk rock beside the trail.[39]

It took another hour to make camp. By then a signal gun was being fired repeatedly to help them find their way. Even before supper, Marsh examined the bone again. It looked like the tibia of a gigantic bird. But it had a joint no bird possessed. The joint had a freedom of motion that no bird possessed. This was definitely something. But what?

It was packed with the rest of the specimens and sent on to Yale, the fourth big shipment since leaving New Haven more than five months before. Now the Yale band, tanned and grizzled, in army shirts and buckskin breeches, armed with their pistols and bowie knives and feeling like old western hands, climbed aboard a first-class "palace car" of the Kansas-Pacific, with its gleaming metal walls, polished spittoons, and plush seats. After a brief stop in Hays City, where Marsh also met General Custer, and the two talked of Indians and fossils, the band headed home, arriving in New Haven on December 18.

Marsh prepared to spend the winter unpacking, sorting, and most of all, figuring out what that strange little bone was that he found on the Kansas plains.

Chapter Four

MARSH'S LETTER IN THE SEPTEMBER *American Journal of Science,* announcing his Colorado badlands discovery, was the first published report of his explorations. The first, but certainly not the last. On December 24, 1870, just days after returning east, a lengthy account of the expedition, written by one of the students—Harry Zeigler—appeared in the *New York Weekly Herald*. Charles Betts was also at work on his own article for *Harper's Monthly*.

Sitting in Haddonfield, in the comfort of his home, with its marble fireplace and apple orchard, in the company of his wife and daughter, Cope may have felt a sharp tug from the stories of Marsh's adventures. Even more provoking than the popular press reports, however, had to be the string of scientific papers now coming out of New Haven.

The New Jersey marl pits had served Cope and Leidy well. Nevertheless, *Hadrosaurus* and *Laelaps* were the exceptions. It was rare that the marl would offer up a nearly complete skeleton. Most of the finds were individual, isolated bones. The West had so much more promise. Hadn't Theophilus Turner been able to send more than one hundred bones for a single specimen of the *Elasmosaurus?* Cope just had to go west.

There was, however, family and finances to consider. It might be easy enough for Marsh to leave Yale for six months, but Cope could not do the same to his wife, Annie, and four-year-old daughter, Julia. Besides he couldn't pay for such a journey. It was true that the family was wealthy. Cope Brothers Packet Ships was one of the largest merchant shipping companies in Philadelphia, and there were also warehouse and real estate interests. Alas, between Cope and the money stood his father, Alfred Cope.

The young Cope looked upon his father with a mixture of "awe and respect." No relationship would be so complex or so defining for Edward Cope as the one between father and son. That there was love between them, there is little doubt. It shines out in dozens of letters. That they looked at life very differently, and were both extraordinarily strong-willed men, is evident in those same pages.

Cope was born July 12, 1840, at his father's home, Fairfield, a great stone house on the outskirts of Philadelphia, surrounded by wide lawns and gardens. Like Marsh, Cope lost his mother, Hanna Edge Cope, when he was only three. But when his father remarried, his new wife, Rebecca Biddle, became very much a second mother, and Cope was as close to his little half brother James as he was to his two sisters. The family circle was drawn wide, and young Cope grew up among grandparents, uncles and aunts, and cousins. Yet, as wide as the circle was, it embraced an almost exclusively Quaker society.

He went to Quaker day and boarding schools, and it was at the Friends Select School in Westtown, Pennsylvania, that the struggle between father and son appears to have truly begun.

For the young Cope, Westtown was a mixture of Greek, mathematics, chemistry, and sledding, ice-skating, and "corner ball." The father was always chiding the son, an erratic student, to do better, and the son was always full of explanations. It was, you see, a sore finger that had been his downfall in penmanship.

As the years passed, the test of wills continued. At the end of 1855, a No. 4 in conduct, "not quite satisfactory," provoked a sharp rebuke. "A public disgrace what can he mean?" the fifteen-year-old Cope wrote to his sister Lille. "I'm sure I've done nothing to merit it *this* session at any rate. . . . I don't think I've been guilty of any more than one—if that—act of willful disorder."[1]

A few days later, son wrote to father, "Whatever may have been the reasons for my getting for getting No. 4 Conduct, I am sure there has been no ill will or feeling between any teacher and myself."

It was, however, farming, not schooling, that was their real battlefield. Starting at the age of fourteen, Cope spent the summers working on the farms of relatives and friends. It was his father's aim to make Cope a farmer. In part, this reflected Alfred Cope's desire to be sure that even though his son came from a wealthy family, he "be taught to work." Perhaps he had also seen in Edward the gathering storm clouds of a tempestuous spirit that was bound to get him in trouble in the world of men and affairs. Would not the rhythms of country life serve him better?

Edward did not think so. "Work, work, work, every day after day, I have no fancy for it," the fifteen-year-old Cope declared. The elder Cope persisted, and so did the younger. "The time spent cultivating in its present manner," Cope wrote to his father four years later, "almost seems wasted. . . . There must be more machinery about it and less poking."

But it was also on the farm that Cope's longstanding love of nature flourished, as he made studies of forest birds, swamp flowers, and field snakes. He read Charles Darwin's *Zoology of the Voyage of the Beagle* (the

American edition was titled *Voyage of the Naturalist)* and *Elements of Ento-mology.*

In 1860, Edward pled his case for going to Philadelphia to attend Joseph Leidy's anatomy classes as the University of Pennsylvania. It was an artful let-ter, displaying the guile, supplication, and single-mindedness that would mark the relationship between the father and the young man. In this letter, Cope gives a full report on the plowing and sowing of corn going on at his uncle's farm. He describes a book he has been reading on "the care and man-agement of horses." The author prefers brick flooring for barns, he notes.

The heart of the letter, however, is a proposal to attend the anatomy lec-tures and the suggestion that they would be "of immense service to one desiring a knowledge of the proper manner of treating stock."[2] Cope's father relented, and that winter marked a turning point. Cope was in the city and on the road to becoming a scientist.

The year before, he had undertaken the reorganization of the herpeto-logical collection at the Academy of Natural Sciences and had read his first paper—on the reclassification of salamanders—at one of the academy's Tuesday night meetings. In 1860, seven more papers would follow.

That same year, Alfred Cope bought his son a farm—McShag's Pinna-cle—in rural Chester County, Pennsylvania. Edward promptly rented it out and headed, in early 1861, for Washington, D.C., and the Smithsonian. He arrived in a town bracing for war. "Extensive accommodations for the mil-itary are being prepared, guards are doubled at the public buildings. . . . I am hurrying up matters as quickly as possible," he wrote home.[3]

Twelve weeks later, Confederate forces opened fire on Fort Sumter in Charleston harbor, and the Civil War had begun. A Quaker, and therefore in principle a pacifist, it was unlikely Cope would seek service in the mili-tary, although some young men from his set did. He was apparently ambiva-lent about serving, at one point expressing the thought of possibly becoming a hospital orderly or teaching emancipated slaves in the South. For the first years of the war, however, he simply followed his scientific interests, shuttling between Philadelphia and Washington.

(At the outbreak of the war, Marsh had been offered a major's commis-sion in a Connecticut regiment. He declined because of his poor eyesight. He remained in graduate school "drilling every day with the Graduate Guards." He told his father, "I shall go to war if necessary," but went to the University of Berlin instead.[4] He did, however, encourage his cousin to join up, and that drew serious fire from Aunt Judith.

"So you think it will be a great thing for James to 'go to the war' do you?" she wrote in the spring of 1862. "Why don't you go? I think it would be a great deal better for you to go, as you are older and stronger and in as much as you have no mother to suffer if you get shot.")[5]

In 1863, Cope was again at the Smithsonian, and Washington was now a city firmly in the grasp of the conflict. "I hear sundry stories of the war," Cope wrote home in January. "One Capt. Feilner told me that sometimes new men, unused to cavalry service, were sent to fight the enemy without drill. . . . Soldiers are occasionally knocked down and robbed on the streets of Washington now. Last night one was brought into the Smithsonian."[6] There was talk of moving the Smithsonian collections farther north, perhaps to the academy in Philadelphia.

In those days, the Smithsonian took on the ambience of a fraternity house, with visiting scientists actually boarding at the institution. Led by William Stimpson, a marine biologist and bon vivant, the scientists drank, caroused, and held footraces through the Smithsonian's Great Hall. Stimpson had dubbed this group the Megatherium Club, in honor of an extinct sloth. His fellows, Cope included, renamed the federal institution the Stimpsonian.[7]

As the war dragged on, the prospect of Cope being drafted grew, and the news from the front was ever grim. "I am afraid," Cope reported to sister Elizabeth, "Dick Chase was killed at the battle of Murfeesboro."

The war alone was enough for Alfred Cope to fret about, now added to this was a budding romantic liaison that had entangled his son in Washington. A number of the letters of this period were destroyed by Cope or never became part of his collected correspondence. In those that do remain, there are only veiled references to the affair. But something was up, and whoever the lady was, it was clear she was from outside the pure circle of Cope's life. So, with all this brewing, Alfred Cope dispatched his son to Europe in March of 1863.

What a turn of events. Cope had lobbied, struggled, and connived to get away from the farm. Now he was traveling Europe, with letters of introduction to some of the great scientists of the continent. Yet he made his pilgrimage in a deep depression. "I keep my resolution of occupying my mind constantly so as to crowd out painful thoughts. . . .' " he wrote to his father from shipboard. "It is perhaps a great advantage that I have had the outside of my sensibilities scorched into a crust."[8]

It was in such a condition that he arrived in Berlin. Years later, when much had passed, much that would color memories, Marsh recalled his first meeting with Cope this way. "I was a student at the University of Berlin. Professor Cope called upon me and with great frankness confided to me some of the many troubles that even then beset him. My sympathy was aroused, and although I had some doubts of his sanity, I gave him good advice and was willing to be his friend."[9]

Cope roamed through England, Belgium, Germany, Italy, Switzerland, and France. At one point, he was so despondent that he destroyed many of the notes, sketches, and letters he had compiled on the tour. Back in London in early 1864, his thoughts were finally turning to home, and the future, and that inevitably lead to questions of money.

It was clear that he did not want to return to McShag's Pinnacle. Although, getting a decent rent for the place—considering all the capital tied up in it—was a problem. "A man would have to own a considerable tract to derive an income in this way," Cope concluded in a letter to his father. "I feel considerably more interested in the matter of making money than I ever did before, from an apprehension that I might unhappily fall into the pit I was in a year or eighteen months ago (I don't mean the *very same*) and then have two persons instead of one to keep. Nothing but this could turn me five minutes from a life of study, for I am not constructed for getting along comfortably with the general run of people."[10]

Upon returning to Philadelphia in the spring of 1864, the Cope family made efforts to secure Edward a teaching post at Haverford College. It was a place where they had some influence. Edward's grandfather, Thomas Pim Cope, had been one of the college's founders, and a cousin, Charles Yarnall, was also founder and officer of the school. It did not take a Peabody-sized legacy to gain the post of professor of zoology. Then again, Haverford was a smaller, simpler, Quaker school. Yarnall wrote to Cope informing him of the appointment. Haverford simultaneously awarded him an honorary master's degree.[11]

Cope also became very active in the Society of Friends, passionate at times, displaying a fervor bordering on the fanatic, which embarrassed even his devout fellow Quakers. Then he announced to his father that he was thinking of marriage, a proper marriage, a marriage from within the circle. It was as if having won his independence from the farm, he wanted to assure Alfred Cope that the path he was taking was a solid one. At the end of 1864, he asked his father for counsel.

"I have often thought it would be an advantage to me to be married, in many ways, and have concluded to make a definite motion in that direction, provided no obstructions appear. Thy opinion is of course the first and most important to me—after that the way seems reasonably open. An amiable woman, not over sensitive, with considerable energy, and especially one inclined to be serious and not inclined to frivolity and display— the more christian of course the better—seems to me to be practically the most suitable for me, though intellect and accomplishments have more charms.

"As I have learned to rough it, and may sometimes be a little rough myself, a very sensitive woman would trouble herself and me—though I admire feminine sensitiveness. Be these things as they may, I have had a very strong inclination to open my mind to Mary Pim's daughter, Annie, that nothing but the recollection of my former experience as well as my desire for the advice of the more experienced has induced me to postpone it. Her amiability and domestic qualities generally, her capability of taking care of a house, etc., as well as her steady seriousness weigh far more with me than any of the traits which form the theme of poets!"[12]

No passion this time for young Cope. The match was certainly an acceptable one, Anne Pim, a distant cousin, having been raised and schooled within the society. On August 15, 1865, they were married at Mary Pim's farm in Chester County. The couple's only child, Julia, was born ten months later. Cope was obliged to keep McShag's Pinnacle, and Alfred Cope continued to try to persuade his son to take up farming.

The farm still held no appeal for Cope, and soon he began to chafe at college life as well. In 1867, he resigned his professorship, explaining to his father, "I despair for the place if the managers do not put it on a right bottom soon. . . . Flummery there is and will be at Haverford." As Cope himself had already observed, he simply was "not constructed for getting along comfortably with the general run of people." Alfred Cope must have known that all too well.

In Cope's defense, at that moment, the college was being "ambiguously run" with the administration split among the president, a superintendent, and a board of managers. This led to a fair amount of squabbling. So, after a total of five semesters, Cope left.[13]

The college wasn't the only institution with which the young Cope was losing patience. The entire polite, scientific establishment of Philadelphia seemed to be in the Quaker's gun sights. His brash and brusque demeanor was particularly unsettling at the academy and the Philosophical Society. These were gentlemen's clubs, as well as scientific organizations, and Cope's swagger rubbed many members the wrong way.

They were also largely gatherings of interested amateurs, and Cope had no patience or tact with mistakes or fuzzy thinking. He was witty with a sarcasm that cut, and he could be absolutely infuriating. Once, when academy member William Gabb was trying to make a point, Cope cut him short, saying "What, more gab, William?" At least Cope was amused.

And when words wouldn't do, Cope was ready to resort to more forceful argument. One evening, he and Persifor Frazer got into a fistfight in the elegant marble lobby of the Philosophical Society. When a friend saw Cope the next day, he said, "Good God, what happened to you?"

"If you think my eye is black," Cope replied, "you ought to see Frazer this morning."

It is worth noting that Frazer was a good friend. Years later, in a long tribute, Frazer would say that while Cope reveled in controversy and argument, he tended to brood over the words spoken—even in a friendly dispute.

"A temporary morbidity invested these words with a meaning entirely different from what was intended. . . . This weakness naturally increased with his years, and frequently precipitated acrimonious controversies," Frazer bemoaned.[14] "Meetings became more lively . . ." another Philosophical Society member said, "especially when the irascible Cope was involved."[15]

Leidy lamented that Cope continually "rendered himself obnoxious to members" of the academy. "He does things in an unnecessarily offensive manner," the gentle and gentlemanly Leidy complained.

A friend of both men observed that "whereas Leidy was essentially a man of peace, Cope was what might be called a militant paleontologist; whereas Leidy's motto was peace at any price, Cope's was war at whatever it cost."[16]

❖

After leaving Haverford, there was really only one place for Cope to go—New Jersey. Until the West began to open, New Jersey's southern coastal plain was considered the richest fossil field in the country.

The continent's first recorded dinosaur fossil—a large, black thighbone—was discovered at Woodbury Creek, New Jersey, in 1787, and was described at a meeting of the American Philosophical Society by Caspar Wistar, a Philadelphia physician.

Wistar knew that the bone came from some extraordinary animal "of enormous size." He calculated it had to be "nearly double the size of an elephant." But he did not know what to call it. It would be another sixty-five years before Richard Owen would coin the name dinosaur.

Sixty-nine years after Wistar's report, William Foulke was vacationing in rural Haddonfield when he heard about a fossil pit on a local farm. Foulke investigated, and the farmer showed him the hole in the soft marl. Foulke, a member of Philadelphia's Academy of Natural Sciences, suspected the pit might be valuable. He immediately contacted Leidy, who came to Haddonfield to supervise the site excavation.

Foulke's hunch was right, and the marl—which is actually a layer of ancient marine sediment laid down during the Cretaceous period—

yielded the most complete dinosaur skeleton that had ever been discovered. In December of 1858, Leidy and Foulke reported to the academy that the bones belonged to a "huge herbivorous saurian." Leidy named it *Hadrosaurus foulkii*—Foulke's bulky lizard.

With the aid of more bones than either Owen or Mantell had to work with, it was clear to Leidy that the *Hadrosaurus*'s front legs were much shorter than its back legs. In fact, they seemed more like arms. It appeared that the *Hadrosaurus* walked on two legs. Leidy's model wasn't Owen's rhino, but the kangaroo.

After his European trip, Cope, too, began searching the Jersey marl beds and in 1866, at the age of twenty-six, he discovered *Laelaps*. Again this was a bipedal dinosaur, which, Cope believed, moved with spring and speed. The work of Leidy and Cope was already challenging established ideas about dinosaurs. They were envisioning animals of a much different character, and they had the bones to prove it.

And so, in March of 1868, Cope moved his family—it took seven loads in a two-horse wagon—to Haddonfield. The Copes rented a spacious ten-room house, with its own grounds, on the town's tree-lined Kings Highway.[17] A few weeks later, Cope wrote to his father saying, "We are by this time pretty much at home. . . . We lost little in the moving, the most important was a dressing case glass. . . . Our stoves do well and our paint is dry."[18]

Just as Cope moved in, Marsh came for a visit. The two men spent a cold rainy week together exploring the marl beds. Cope hadn't wanted to go out while the weather was so bad. Marsh insisted.[19] Cope introduced Marsh to Albert Vorhees, owner of the West Jersey Marl Company. The phosphate-rich marl was used as a fertilizer, and the marl quarries were always a good source of fossils. Cope's *Laelaps* had come from Vorhees's quarry. (Marsh took the opportunity of meeting Vorhees to privately arrange for fossils to be sent to New Haven.)[20]

Now came Cope's money problems. He had given up a one-thousand-dollar-a-year salary when he abandoned his Haverford professorship, and he was now living on some rent from McShag's Pinnacle and periodic checks from his father. Ten dollars here, fifteen there. It was possible to live comfortably, if one lived simply. The McShag Pinnacle "milk business" alone was bringing in about three hundred dollars a month in sales.[21] But, how to finance research, publication, and exploration? "My occupation needs money for its successful prosecution; and there are few enough in this country whose circumstances allow them to follow it," he told his father.

"Whether it will be my place to remain here long I do not seek to know," Cope wrote in the same March letter. "It is best to be able to be a whole man at one thing at a time. I would I think it right rather to explore nature than spend the time farming."

But the money. "I could do more if I had my present capital," he told his father the following month.[22] Cope had a plan. If he sold McShag's Pinnacle and its livestock, he could buy the Haddonfield house for about twelve thousand dollars and invest the remainder. He would get a return equal to his present farm income, and have no rent to pay.

As it was, Cope was stretched thin. "The consequence is no money, account overdrawn a month at Cope Bros. and plenty of bills and notes due," Cope reported to his father. At last, Alfred Cope relented. McShag's Pinnacle would be sold. Edward Cope would never be a farmer.

In the months that followed, Cope patrolled the marl pits, finding four different species of mosasaurs, a mammoth, and an assortment of other fossils. He enjoyed Haddonfield's rural atmosphere. Unlike the city, it was not "infested with factory hands." He told his father, "Irish are few, but colored people abound." Haddonfield had a large Quaker community, and Cope was active in its meeting.

Then came Marsh's string of fresh, groundbreaking papers on the West, and that really put the spur into Cope. The first Marsh paper was on "new fossil Serpents from the Tertiary deposits of Wyoming." It was followed by a paper on "new fossil reptiles from the Cretaceous and Tertiary." It was, however, Marsh's third paper that truly created a buzz. This one dealt with the little hollow bone he had found on one of his last days on the Kansas plains.

Upon returning to Yale, Marsh had made a careful study of the small bone, which he said, "corresponded in many respects anatomically with the first joint of the little finger of the human hand." He compared it with the structure of other animals. "The only joint much like it that I could find, in any animal, living or extinct, was in the wing finger of the Pterodactyl, or flying dragon," he wrote in a memoir.[23]

Marsh, however, had some doubts. If it was one of these reptiles that flew through Mesozoic skies on leathery wings, it was the first discovered in America. That wasn't difficult to believe. The problem was its size. To that point, the pterodactyls found in Europe had been small, sparrow- to pigeon-sized specimens. But if Marsh's bone belonged to a pterodactyl it was, by Cuvierian calculation, twenty times larger and one hundred times bulkier than any pterodactyl known.

Although Marsh looked for some other explanation, he kept coming back to the pterodactyl. "Believing in my science, as taught by Cuvier," he wrote, "I determined to make a scientific announcement of what the fossil indicated and trust to future discoveries to prove whether I was right or wrong."

Marsh calculated that the wingspan of the animal was twenty feet. "Truly a gigantic dragon even in this country of big things," he said. Marsh decided to name the fossil *Pterodactylus owenii,* in honor of his English "friend," Professor Owen, who had already written extensively on these animals.

There was, no doubt, some flattery and currying of favor in the name. Marsh also gave Spencer Baird the opportunity to make the first announcement of the discovery and in the same letter raised the issue of getting first call on all the Smithsonian's fossil discoveries. By this time, Baird had made photographs and casts of the tapir skeleton and sent it on to Yale, with his enthusiastic thanks. Baird tried to reply diplomatically to Marsh's request.

"I am extremely obliged to you for giving me the privilege of making the first announcement in regard to the Pterodactyls, which I shall hasten to communicate to next week's paper . . . ," Baird wrote in late May. "We shall be glad to let you have any material that you can find at the Institution, although there is nothing here now but what you have already overhauled. With friendly relations to yourself, Leidy & Cope, it is a somewhat difficult matter for us to select the person to take charge of any new material, but probably there can be no harm in giving you a hint of what we have here, & if you come down & take possession of it, you have as much right to do so as anyone else."[24]

The June issue of the *American Journal of Science* carried a "Note on a New and Gigantic Species of Pterodactyl."[25] Now Marsh's career was barreling along. He would publish a series of five papers from the western expedition—on reptiles, mammals, and birds—and he was already making arrangements to take another band of Yale students into the field the coming summer of 1871. The plans for the Peabody Museum were moving slowly, although the money was in hand—collecting interest in a Yale account—and it was now only a matter of time, a year or two, before the project could begin.

But in a variation on the old saying "lucky in cards, unlucky in love," Marsh's personal life had not flourished quite as well as his professional one. He, like Cope, had left for Europe after an unsuccessful love affair and upon his return, again tried his hand at courtship, and again failed.

When turning toward affairs social, Marsh looked to the home of Elizabeth Cogswell Dixon, the wife of Connecticut senator James Dixon. It was through family connections that Marsh, the college student, found his way to the Dixons in 1858. (Mrs. Dixon's sister, Eliza, was married to Marsh's uncle Ezkiel.)

What an oasis the Dixon home was for twenty-seven-year-old Marsh. Coming from a threadbare farm and then spending years in the uniquely male domains of prep school and Yale, what a contrast it was. With Elizabeth Dixon and her two teenaged daughters, Clementine and Bessie, the Dixon home in Hartford was a more elegant and feminine place than Marsh had ever known, and he was a frequent visitor.

Elizabeth Dixon adopted Marsh as a nephew, something of a social project and a target for a bit of matchmaking. Hers was a world of Washington balls beneath Japanese lanterns and moonlight, of diplomatic teas, of strawberries and roses, and rides in a barouche through Central Park.[26] And always, it was a world of young ladies.

"Miss Ellen Collins was here also in a very becoming pink muslin couleur de rose," Mrs. Dixon wrote to Marsh. "Tonight there is a party to which we are all bidden & where you would see some very pretty persons."[27]

"Fanny Clark still lives & is as pretty as ever. I hope seeing her repaid you for coming up to Hartford," Elizabeth Dixon wrote later that same summer.[28]

While Elizabeth Dixon introduced Marsh to a number of "pretty persons," the one she seems to have tried to promote was her niece, Constance Kinney. Constance and daughter Bessie went down to Yale in the fall of 1859 to watch Marsh row in boat races, and both were very impressed, Elizabeth Dixon reported.

A few weeks later, Marsh received an invitation for a reception at the Kinney home in New York City. The Kinneys had "invited some young people for Miss Constance and requested that I send you an invitation," Mrs. Dixon explained.[29]

Marsh was duly attentive. "Constance wrote of your beautiful gift to her of an amethyst. She was much delighted. I ought to have said I wore mine to Mrs. Adams yesterday," Elizabeth Dixon wrote in early 1861.[30]

Unfortunately, it wasn't Constance who stirred Marsh's ardor, but Mrs. Dixon's eldest daughter, nineteen-year-old Clementine. Over the years, Marsh had invited Clemmie to art exhibitions and other events, and received the young lady's "kindest regrets."[31] Now more regrets were to be offered. Marsh's Aunt Eliza, who had first introduced him to the Dixons, tried to warned him that among the Dixon girls, he garnered more respect than affection.

His aunt saw his growing interest and cautioned him that perhaps he did not realize "how much you have staked in the thing." Aunt Eliza tried to soften the blow. "She is almost too much of a child yet to be seriously admired," she advised. A few months later, she counseled, "The process on your part must be slow rather than a direct attack. . . . I fear your plan for going ahead will be defeated." Still, Marsh pursued. Clemmie demurred. Nothing came of Marsh's efforts.[32]

At least, Aunt Eliza felt, Marsh could weather the disappointment. "I am glad you are one, whose preferences can be controlled in this line, and that you have other engrossing objects of pursuit and therefore your happiness is not at the mercy or caprice of any lady," she said.

When Marsh left for Europe, the correspondence with Mrs. Dixon continued. Now instead of balls and teas, Elizabeth Dixon wrote of war, of distributing flannels to Connecticut soldiers, and of working in the Army Square Hospital. (Bessie and Clemmie worked there, too.)[33]

Returning to the States and seeing Clementine again, Marsh resolved to try once more to win her hand. After all, things had changed. He was now on the verge of becoming a Yale professor. This time he sought Uncle George's counsel, blessing, and resources.

In a letter marked "confidential," Marsh laid the matter before his uncle. "You have several times given me advice in regard to matrimony, and I now find myself inclined to follow it somewhat sooner than I expected," he wrote. "I am happy to say, however, that the lady I hope to get possesses all the qualifications of high position and family which you deemed to important."[34]

"The lady in question is the daughter of Senator D of Ct. . . . ," Marsh announced, adding, "I think her far superior to any lady I ever knew. She is very highly educated, and especially accomplished in modern languages, painting, music, etc. I have admired her very much for a long time, and since my return from Europe my admiration has so increased that I am very anxious to secure her if possible."

Marsh already knew that it would not be easy. "I have faint hopes that the lady reciprocates in some degree my attachment that I do not feel perfectly sure that I should be at once accepted if I should propose."

There were, however, ways. Could he not win Clemmie's hand as he had won his Yale appointment? Perhaps a little monetary push was all that was needed? "I ought, of course, to offer the lady a home corresponding in some measure to the one she leaves," Marsh suggested to his uncle, "and this would be an expensive undertaking in a city like New Haven."

If Marsh could come as a suitor with a professorship and a fine house, maybe that would tip the balance in his favor. The Dixons paid a call on Peabody in his hotel suite during his visit to Washington. Uncle George found both Clemmie and Bessie charming. But it wasn't Uncle George's blessing or purse that would be wanting. Some things just couldn't be bought.

After that, Marsh tried courtship seriously only once more. This time it was the daughter of John W. Garrett, president of the Baltimore and Ohio Railroad. The young lady found Marsh "too demonstrative." Besides, the fact that Marsh would refer to a lady as "the prettiest little vertebrate" probably wasn't the sort of poetry that would win hearts.

The problem, one of Marsh's friends explained, was that the professor simply "lacked the light touch so helpful in social intercourse."[35] Years, later Marsh could joke that his mansion wasn't really a home because it hadn't been "properly Garrett-ed." While Miss Garrett had no interest, her father, at least, found Marsh useful as a mail drop.

"I have learned from my daughter that you are advised that Mr. and Mrs. Russell are on this side," Garrett wrote to Marsh. "Will you oblige me by forwarding the enclosed letter to Mr. Russell's present address."[36]

Enough of the parlor and the ladies. Aunt Eliza was right. It was time to turn to "other engrossing objects of pursuit." It was time to look westward. To get a group of good men and saddle up. There was, after all, that cross hacked into Niobrara chalk out in Kansas to be found. Would additional fossil bones prove that Marsh's pterodactyl really had a twenty-foot wingspan?

And while Marsh was getting his Yalies ready to head for the plains, down in Haddonfield, Cope was also preparing to go west. He would make a short journey—no more than a few weeks—and would go pretty much on his own. But he would go. If he could, he was going to bring home a prairie dog as a pet for Julia. At least he promised he'd try to bring one back. Yes, to the West. For it was the West that held the secrets of life's history and the future of the science of paleontology.

The first hunter to make it to the Kansas plains that summer was neither Marsh nor Cope, but Chief Red Cloud. The Sioux warrior had obtained permission from the Indian Bureau to lead a hunting party from his reservation on the edge of the Dakotas into Kansas buffalo country.

Army headquarters sent a letter to the commanding officer at Fort Wallace instructing that all troops "avoid any collision whatever with these Indians, unless such collision becomes actually unavoidable for self-defense of the settlers." A copy of the letter was forwarded to Marsh.[37] And so, while a year earlier he followed a buffalo-hunting P. T. Barnum into the

Kansas fields, this year Marsh waited for Chief Red Cloud to hunt the great beasts before venturing out.

Finally, on July 2, 1871, Marsh, ten Yale students, a military escort, and five army wagons left Fort Wallace in search of pterodactyls and anything else they could dig up. This time Marsh had no financial backing, and the entire cost of the trip—about fifteen hundred dollars, not counting the army's aid or personal expenses—was paid by the members of the expedition.

They headed back along the Smoky Hill River. The heat was ferocious, the mercury hovering between 95 and 120 degrees. For much of the trip, 110 degrees in the shade was the best that could be found.

When they had reached the general vicinity of the previous year's find, they made camp. As soon as the tents were pitched, Marsh and a few men rode out looking for the spot where he had found the bone.

Marsh rode the river bottom and found the buffalo trail. In his eagerness, he galloped ahead of his companions. His memory did not fail him, and he found the cross as distinct as when he had cut it. He could even see the impression left by his bone in the rock. He took out his hunting knife and cleared away the ground. There was another bone, one that fit into the fossil he already had in New Haven. He worked carefully, but anxiously. He uncovered another bone, and then another, until he had the whole series that supported the wing.

"These I measured as I took them up one by one, making a sketch of them as they were found," Marsh said. ". . . I was soon able to determine that my calculations based on the fragments were essentially correct, and that this first found American dragon was fully as large as my fancy painted him."

Marsh had the Yalies on their hands and knees scouring the hot ground and rocks for fossil fragments, especially for pterodactyls. He was rewarded with the remains of several specimens of the animal, including one that appeared to have an even larger wingspan—perhaps twenty-five feet.

This summer conditions on the Kansas plains were brutal. The river had shriveled to series of warm pools linked by the trickle of a stream. The buffalo grass was brown and withered. Rattlesnakes abounded and seemed to get more active the hotter it became. They were everywhere. During the course of a single day, more than twenty had to be killed. The tent camp was flattened by a thunderstorm one day and a hailstorm another. Provisions started to run low.

"Several of the party broke down entirely, unable to endure the fatigue, exposure, and hard-fare," according to a report in the Yale newspaper, the

College Courant, "and even the guide an Indian scout who had been on the plains for seventeen years, was stricken down by fever."[38]

After a month in the field, the Yale party broke camp and returned to Fort Wallace. They boarded the Kansas-Pacific for Denver, where they spent four days recuperating. Then it was on to Fort Bridger and after that Oregon. Now, the hot, dusty Kansas plains were wide open for Cope, and Cope was on his way.

Chapter Five

 IT WAS LATE AUGUST when Cope gazed out of the window of a Kansas-Pacific coach and saw the Great Plains for the first time. "They are wonderful and look more like the ocean than anything I have seen," he wrote Annie.[1] Where Marsh noted geological formations, Cope was struck by beauty. "The flowers . . . I did not suppose they were so tall; as high as a man's head or a steer's back. Sunflowers, Cornflowers and various composites of flax, sage, euphorgia, endless verbenas," he told his sister Lille.[2]

He watched as passengers fired their pistols at the massive herds of buffaloes, an exercise that left carcasses and bones lying on each side of the tracks for miles. He had, however, not come for the sight-seeing, but with the hope of "doing something in my favorite line of vertebrae paleontology." He wrote Annie that "Marsh has been doing a great deal I find, but has left more for me, and one of his guides is at Ft. Wallace, *left behind,* and in want of a job. . . . Marsh wouldn't let him go! I'll let him go!"

In September, Cope arrived at Fort Wallace and again heard "what Marsh and others have found is something wonderful." Cope's first foray was by rail to the town of Sheridan, east of the fort and near the Twin Buttes. This was an area Marsh had searched a year earlier. Still, Cope discovered a huge mosasaur sticking out of the bank of a narrow ravine. He also found beautiful, feather-shaped gypsum crystals. He sent one of these back east to Annie for her watch chain, with the hope in his letter that "may it please the mail not to break."

Back at the fort, Cope was outfitted with a wagon, six mules, and a five-man escort led by Lieutenant James Whitten. He was also offered a revolver and military hat. Cope refused the army paraphernalia, telling his wife, "I hate the sight of them."

He had arrived just before the garrison was about to be transferred, and Cope thought this was a bit of good luck. Many of the men and officers had worked with Marsh or Benjamin Mudge, a paleontologist at the state agricultural college, so they knew the things that interested fossil hunters and which areas had already been worked. "The new regiment will know nothing of this. The officers and men are by this time much interested in our studies and give us every aid," Cope wrote. To augment army rations for the trip, Cope bought cans of oysters, sardines, peaches, condensed milk, lime juice, and a couple of loaves of bread. These he shared with Lieutenant Whitten. The Cope party headed for some fresh territory south of Twin Buttes.

The plains of western Kansas are covered with a flat layer of sand and gravel sediments washed down from the Rocky Mountains, about ten to twenty-four million years ago during the Miocene. The Smoky Hill River cut deeply into this Miocene blanket, right down to the chalky rock of the Niobrara formation, which in Cretaceous times was the floor of the shallow sea that covered the middle of the continent and is sometimes called "the American Mediterranean." (Both the New Jersey marl and the Niobrara chalk are Cretaceous sea sediments, and that is the reason they share similar fossil faunas.) The Smoky Hill River and its creeks made their incisions, and then the wind and rain did the rest, breaking, carving, and sculpting the fissures into rocky badlands.

"Tracts of this kind are scattered over the country along the margins of the river and creek valleys and ravines," Cope wrote in 1875. "The upper stratum of the rock is yellow chalk, the lower bluish, and the brilliancy of the color increases the picturesque effect. From elevated points, the plains appear to be dotted with ruined villages and towns whose avenues are lined with painted walls of fortifications, churches and towers. . . . On level surfaces, denuded of soil, lie huge oyster-like shells, some opened and others with both valves together, like remnants of a half-finished meal of some titanic race."[3]

Now the life of that ancient world was being reconstructed by Cope and Marsh. Dinosaurs roamed the shores, strange birds and pterodactyls flew over the waters, which teemed with giant turtles, immense fish, and the seagoing reptiles—the plesiosaur and the mosasaur. The plesiosaurs, like Cope's *Elasmosaurus,* were snaky creatures, some fifty feet long, with large paddles to push themselves along. The mosasaurs, ancient kin to present-day monitor lizards, swam through the ocean with long, flexible tails and looked something like a cross between a lizard and a dolphin. They reached lengths of thirty feet.

When Cope traveled the plains and looked at the rock formations, it set his mind to work, taking him back through the millennia. "Far out in the expanse of this ancient sea might have been a huge, snake-like form, which rose above the surface, and stood erect, with tapering throat and arrow shaped head, or swayed about describing a circle of twenty feet radius above the water. . . . It probably swam many feet below the surface, raising the head to the distant air for breath, then withdrawing it, and exploring the depths forty feet below, without altering its body position."[4]

The collecting went well. The weather was good, except for a few gales that required the use of a handkerchief, with two small eyeholes, to protect against dust and bits of rock being blown into the face.

Cope described the discovery of his mosasaur as if he were battling that ancient creature. "A part of the face with teeth was observed projecting," he wrote, "and we attacked it with picks and knives. The lower jaws were recovered with glistening teeth. . . . The delight of the party was at its height when the bone of the pelvis and hind limb were laid bare for they had never been seen before in this species."[5]

In October, Cope made a third excursion into the field, this time with two wagons, fourteen mules, and seven soldiers. On this trip, Cope was also "collecting" for his daughter, Julia. "Thee must not be to sure about the prairie dog yet," he wrote her, "as I am not certain whether I can get one or not. But I will try. This little animal is not a kind of a dog really, but is a little like a big fat squirrel with a short tail."[6]

In words fashioned for a five-year-old, Cope described for Julia the "little canvass house" in which he slept, the prairie "as level as our parlor," and "the antelope, a very pretty animal as large as a little pony." At night, he told his daughter, "I take a roll of blankets and put them on the ground in the tent and unroll them, and when it is dark I get in between the blankets and go to sleep. In the night the coyotes bark. Does thee know what a coyote is? It is a kind of wild dog with a big tail about as large as Uncle George's Victor."

Cope also wrote of his experiences chasing buffalo—which were considerably different from those of Marsh. "When we were hunting one day, I rode up to a little place and came on two old buffaloes and ran at them with my mule. The old fellows ran away and I went after them for a while and they went another way." Cope apparently did not bring home a prairie dog. He did have a rattlesnake in a jar of alcohol to show Julia.

This was the first extended separation for Cope from his wife and daughter, and he carried a picture of them, which he showed to the soldiers. He signed his letters to Annie "take much love from thy Edward" and told her at one point, "I have been thinking of you all the time and were it not that I am in a situation to do a great deal for paleontology, I would return very soon."

In a letter to Julia, he wrote, "I am going to come home before very long to stay with thee and Mamma for a long time. Does thee remember the little songs thee used to sing . . . 'Tourtenay,' and 'Je suis un Prince.' I sing them often to remember thee by. Here is a big 'K' for Julia, she can give one to Mamma for me."

In roughly a month, Cope found fossils of mosasaurs, giant turtles, pterodactyls, and Cretaceous fishes. "I can now tell my own stories," Cope told Annie, "which for the time I have been here are not bad."

Indeed, he would announce the following March that his pterodactyl was bigger than Marsh's. "The largest Pterodactyl as yet . . . found on our continent," he would claim.[7] (In the end, this species turned out to be the same as the one Marsh had discovered.) In all, Cope would write four separate papers, all read before the American Philosophical Society the following winter.

Cope also stopped in Manhattan, at the Kansas State Agricultural College, where he examined the fossil collection of Benjamin Mudge, which included seven separate species of mosasaurs.

Mudge, born in Maine and trained as a lawyer, was another of those self-made scientists. In 1861, he was working as an oil-refinery chemist in Kentucky when his strong antislavery views made Kansas a more agreeable place to live.

He lobbied the Kansas legislature to fund a state geological survey and in 1864 became the survey's first director. A year later, he was elected professor of natural history at the agricultural college.

In 1870, Mudge undertook the first systematic search for fossils in the state, collecting from deposits along the Republican and Solomon Rivers. Mudge sent these to Cope. He also sent some specimens to Leidy.[8]

Mudge had met Marsh years before when he was practicing law near Andover, Massachusetts, and Marsh was a student at Phillips Exeter. Mudge offered to help Marsh on his second Kansas expedition; Marsh declined. But when he found out that Mudge had collaborated with Cope, Marsh was furious. Mudge apologized, assuring Marsh that Cope hadn't seen anything particularly new.

Cope left Fort Wallace for Denver in the middle of October and was back in Philadelphia by the end of the month. Evidently he didn't stay at home very long. On his travels through Kansas, he had met a young land surveyor, W. E. Webb, who was organizing an trip through the state later that year.

"My friend W. E. Webb the land agent here I find to be delightful young fellow, used to the plains, as a surveyor of land all over the state, very familiar with localities of fossils, which turn out to be very numerous and gigantic," Cope wrote to his sister.[9]

"I will . . . come out in the 11th month & spend a month on a special expedition with Webb . . . ," he told her. "Such an opportunity is very fine, with a man who knows the ground. Professor Marsh has been in that country for 3 weeks but has no such chance and it will cost nothing." He also advised Annie, "I am coming home soon, and will return the last of the 11th month . . . to make an exploration with Webb and a small party."[10]

In 1872, Webb published a book titled *Buffalo Land, an Authentic Narrative of the Adventures and Misadventures of a Late Scientific and Sporting Party upon the Great Plains of the West.*[11] The leader of this tongue-in-cheek narrative à clef is Professor Paleozoic, a man who could "tell cheese from chalk under the microscope."[12] The professor sounds remarkably like Cope. In fact, in the paleontology section of the book, Webb dispenses with Professor Paleozoic altogether and simply quotes Cope. The other members of the group were eastern sportsmen looking for some hunting and adventure.

The group arrived at Hays City by rail to begin their journey west through the Saline River Valley. As cities went, Hays was no Philadelphia. Why, unless saloons, card games, and gunfights were essential elements of the urban fabric, one could hardly call the whistle stop a town. On the other hand, if booze and whores made a city, Hays was a great metropolis.

A railroad town—the Kansas-Pacific tracks ran right down the middle of Main Street—Hays City was also the site of Fort Hays, and it was near the end of the Chisholm Trail, used by cowboys to drive Texas longhorn steers to the railhead at Abilene.

If the concoction of railroad men, soldiers, and cowboys wasn't volatile enough, all you had to do was add whiskey, and, lord knows, there was plenty of that in Hays City. "There is a row of saloons on the Kansas Pacific Railway called Hays City," a correspondent to the *Junction City Union* reported in July of 1871.

"Almost every other building is a liquor saloon or a house of ill fame," a reporter for the *Manhattan Standard* wrote. The reporter took a stroll through Hays "by moonlight" and found the Santa Fe Saloon "all ablaze with light, and soldiers staggering around in front . . . a good indication of what is going on within." The large, dilapidated building on Main Street with the sign GENERAL OUTFITTING turned out to be a bordello and not far away was the dance hall "kept by a Frenchman." A block farther on was a large "gambling hell," with billiard and faro tables, chuck-a-luck, and monte banks going "full blast."[13]

The soldiers would come riding down from Fort Hays, over the Big Creek, and along Fort Street until it intersected with Main. General Custer's brother, Tom, had earned a reputation, even in this rough place, by repeatedly riding his horse right into the saloons, which often seemed more like arsenals than taverns. At one establishment, the barkeep dispensed beer and whiskey while ringed by a "halo" of pistols and knives. The bar itself was as much a barricade for the bartenders' protection as a place for customers to put down their drinks.

Even with Wild Bill Hickok as sheriff, Hays could not be kept in line. Between 1869 and 1874, there were roughly thirty-five violent deaths—boys who died with their boots on—and at least three of those came at the hands of the sheriff.

Hays, however, turned out to be too wild even for Wild Bill. He was forced to flee town after a fight with Tom Custer and a couple of other soldiers in the summer of 1870. The reason for the fight is lost, although a good bet is that whiskey—or "Tarantula juice," as it was known—had something to do with it. Hickok was jumped by the soldiers. The sheriff pulled out his revolver and shot one of the men point-blank over his shoulder, killing him. Figuring that he couldn't fight an entire army post, Bill left town and ended up the city marshal in Abilene.[14]

Hays hadn't sobered up or calmed down in the year since Wild Bill's departure. "Hays City by lamplight was remarkably lively and not very moral," Webb wrote. "The streets blazed with the reflections from saloons, and a glance within showed the floors crowded with dancers. The gaily dressed women striving to hide with ribbons and paint the terrible lines that grim artist, Dissipation, loves to draw upon such faces."[15]

The group bought provisions, which included "something like fifty yards of bologna sausage," hired a wagon, a couple of Mexican teamsters, a guide, and then set out for the Saline River.

They were out less than two days when one member of the party, Shamus, went out ahead of the group to try to get a shot at a buffalo. He was, Webb said, "a poor rider" and "a miserable shot," so no one expected much, and they watched with amusement as Shamus came frantically galloping back, arms and legs flapping away, being chased, they supposed, by an angry buffalo.

It was only when their desperate friend came closer that they saw that his pursuers were not bison, but Indians. The Mexican teamsters grabbed their rifles, jumped in between the oxen, and started firing. The rifle shots spooked the horses and caused a general stampede, carrying the inexperienced easterners galloping across the plains.

The Indians stopped about a half mile from the group, for they were confronting nine armed, if somewhat befuddled, white men. The scout was able to quell the Mexicans' fire and shouted to his bounding clients to pull on their reins so that the horses would run in circles. Finally, when things calmed down, the scout and Cope rode out to talk to the Indians.

The Indians were a band of Cheyenne led by Chief White Wolf. They said they were hungry and asked for some food. The Webb party held its own council. "We dare not refuse them and go on," Cope advised. "They would be sure to dog our steps, and at the first convenient opportunity attack."

They decided to "invite" the Indians to return with them to Hays City. And so, they all went back to town. There a real powwow was held at the Land Office, which included the postmaster and several leading citizens, as well as the professor, Webb, and the guide. White Wolf produced a red clay pipe. As it was passed around, Webb said, the professor was faced with a dilemma. "He had never smoked. For an instant the professor hesitated, then reflecting that passing the pipe would be worse than choking over it, the excellent man put the stem to his mouth and gave a pull. . . . Gasping amid the stifling cloud, it poured from mouth and nose." After the council, Webb said, the Cheyenne ate three dinners within two hours.

The next day, the scientific, sporting party returned to the plains and headed for the Saline River. Just like Marsh, Cope could not help but lecture from the saddle. "The buffalo now feed over a surface strewn with the remains of those monsters which inhabited the waters of a primitive world," he told his companions.[16]

The valley of the Saline River is rolling land, broken by rock faces jutting here and there from the hills and strings of cottonwood trees that mark the whereabouts of the creeks that feed the river.

They camped in a grove near the river and not far from a tableland that would provide good shooting for the hunters. One of the marksmen had already bagged a wild turkey for dinner. Over the next few days, while the sportsmen combed the high plains for game, Cope searched for fossils. At the end of the day came the spectacle of sunset on the prairie, as the light of the sinking sun caught the clouds, turning those closest to the horizon deep lavender and those higher in the still, blue sky, rose and pale orange.

Sitting around the evening fire, Cope used a box as a desk, and Webb said he "looked more like the Arkansas traveler writing home, than a learned savant committing to paper the latest secrets wrung from nature."[17]

As they moved west, the band met the Sydney family, returning to their homestead on the Solomon River, a little to the north. They had been run off by a Cheyenne raiding party almost a year before. In that raid, Mr. Sydney had lost his wife, and his eldest daughter had lost her husband. They had run, but if they didn't return before the year was out, they would forfeit the homestead. So Sydney was taking his two daughters and grandchild back to what was left of their farm. They were, Webb said, a sad sight, a half-crazed father and his widowed daughter.

Cope's attention, however, was attracted by the younger daughter, Miss Flora. He began flirting, and apparently Flora responded. "The professor assured me confidentially that evening, and with much more than his wont enthusiasm on such a subject, that she preferred the language of rocks to that of fashion plates."[18]

Flora also proved to be crack shot, beating one of the party in a sharp-shooting contest. "Such a woman as that, the Professor said, was safe on the frontier, she could fight her own way and clear her vicinity of savages, whenever necessary, as well as any of us," Webb wrote. Flora was a mainstay for her beleaguered family. "No wonder," Webb said, "the Professor took early occasion to tell us that she was a noble woman, an honor to her sex."

Still, one of the party quipped that they appeared to have reached "the latitude of spooning." What was this? What about Annie's "loving Edward" and Julia's papa, who sang little French songs on the prairie to remember his daughter? It seems Cope wasn't insincere, but he couldn't help dallying. Be it a visit to Joseph Henry's daughters, a forbidden romantic liaison, or opening his mind to Annie Pim, the ladies always aroused Cope's ardor.

There would be other "Floras" over the years. Charles Knight, the artist of prehistoric life, who worked closely with Cope, said the gossip about the Philadelphia Quaker was that "in his heyday no woman was safe within five miles of him." Yet Cope would always return home and often recount his dancing and socializing in letters to Annie and Julia, a sign that at least he didn't believe he was doing anything improper.

The Sydney family moved off north, and the Webb band went west to Sheridan. Cope was once again in the "fossil belt." Riding along a canyon, they came upon something that looked "very much like a seventy-five foot serpent carved in stone," Webb said.

"This fossil, gentlemen," Cope explained, "is that of a *Mosasaur,* a huge reptile which existed in the Cretaceous Seas." At the Colorado line, the party turned back, and by the second week in December, Cope was at the academy's Tuesday-night meeting.

⚜

On his autumn trip, Cope had also hoped to reach Fort Bridger but couldn't manage to get a train pass to take him that far. Perhaps it was for the best, for when Cope was at Fort Wallace, Marsh's Yale party was at the Wyoming outpost.

When they arrived at Fort Bridger, the Marsh men found the garrison in a truculent mood. A cut in pay and inferior rations (soldiers survived mainly on hardtack, bacon, salt pork, and coffee) had prodded many enlistees to take the "Grand Bounce." Out of the 160 men in the fort's two companies, about 100 had already deserted. Some of the soldiers believed the poor pay and bad food were part of a plot by Congress to shrink the size of the army, without owning up to it.

Fort Bridger had been a strategic point for decades because it stood at the gateway to the low barren hills of the Red Desert—the easiest crossing of the Continental Divide. The route had been used by settlers, the Pony Express, and the Overland Stage Company.

It was the trader, trapper, and explorer Jim Bridger who had first exploited this advantage back in 1843, setting up a trading post. It became an army post fifteen years later. By the summer of 1872, however, the importance of the post had diminished considerably as a result of the coming of the Union Pacific (which used the same easy crossing to lay its tracks).[19]

The fort, which covered about forty acres on either side of a small stream called Black's Fork, sat in a pleasant valley. At the southern end of the compound were Judge Carter's big white house, his store, and saloon. Across the road was a string of log houses where the officers and their families were billeted.

Officers' Row was separated from the parade ground by Black's Fork and the aspen trees that lined its banks. On the northern end of the parade ground were the commissary, guardhouse, blacksmith, bakehouse, and laundry. The enlisted men's barracks were on the west side of the compound.

The Indian wars were long finished in this corner of the West, and with the railroad now running, the fort's role as a transportation hub had also faded. And so the officers and their ladies played croquet on the edge of the parade ground, and Judge Carter spent his time adjudicating civil complaints for alleged incidents of horse thievery.[20]

The scientific value of this region was, however, just beginning to emerge, as it proved to be a unique repository of Eocene fossils. The sediments of the Eocene had not collected anywhere else along the eastern front of the Rocky Mountains, having been either washed farther east or eroded over time.

But in this corner of the country, where Colorado, Wyoming, and Utah meet, the Eocene sediments were trapped between the Rockies and a series of smaller ranges to the east, including the Wind River, Uinta, and Wasatch Mountains.

There were three key areas near Fort Bridger where these Eocene sediments had collected. Just north of the Uinta Mountains was the Bridger Basin. To the east of the Uintas was the Wasahkie; to the south was the Uinta Basin. All were promising fossil lands.

Despite the dwindling manpower, Major LaMotte was able to find three wagons and a ten-man escort for Marsh. The going here was easier than it had been in Kansas. Although the Bridger Basin was pretty much a desert thickly grown with sagebrush, there were enough streams, with their cottonwood groves, to provide "agreeable relief from the gray expanse on either side."[21]

They camped on Henry's Fork, a stream between the Gizzly Buttes badlands and the Uinta Mountains. The many-fingered stream was thick with willow and cottonwood. The snow-capped Uintas provided a picturesque backdrop. The weather was good, and the fishing was excellent. During the two weeks on Henry's Fork, the Yale men caught more than a thousand trout. One day, Marsh himself landed 139 fish, weighing a total of more than one hundred pounds.

The pastoral nature of the place was marred by the vast fires the Indians repeatedly set in the mountain forests. Their aim was to burn down the woods and create more prairies in the hopes that the disappearing buffalo would return. "Day after day, we saw heavy clouds of smoke rising, and night after night the mountainsides were masses of flames," wrote one expedition member. "All argument with the Indians is in vain."[22]

The basin held more than trout and Indians. The Eocene beds had a remarkable array of early mammals—rhinos, elephants, tapirs, horses. The party even found two more horse species for Marsh, *Orohippus uintanus* and *O. pumilis.* Finding the bones was hard work. "We have literally had to crawl over the country on our hands and knees," one student said. "To see these minute bones the eye must be brought within three or four inches of the white clay on which they lie."

It was not, however, all work for the Yale boys. The soldiers drank a good deal, and the Yalies joined them. When the officers were not around, the Yalies and enlisted men held horse races with kegs of beer as prizes. One day after lunch, John Quigley, a Sheffield student, was so drunk that he had trouble staying on his horse and ended up with a black eye from banging his head on the pony's neck.[23]

By the summer of 1871, Marsh no longer had the Bridger Basin all to himself. John Wesley Powell had successfully shaken loose a government appropriation with the help of a junior congressman from Ohio named James Garfield. Powell and Garfield were kindred spirits, both midwesterners from humble beginnings, both Civil War veterans, both self-made men.

So, with his newfound federal dollars, Powell was working his way south down the Green River, surveying an area ten to twenty miles wide on either side.

Clarence King was also working his way east through the area with his U.S. Geological Survey of the Fortieth Parallel. The King Survey—financed by the War Department—was trying to document the natural resources along the western rail lines.

A classmate of Marsh's at Yale, King was conducting the most detailed, organized and scientific of all the western surveys. Fossils were not a high priority for King, but whatever he did find, he sent on to his old friend—Marsh.[24]

The fossils coming out of the Bridger Basin were extremely provocative. In the evolutionary maze, the Bridger Basin provided a look at that moment, about fifty-eight million years ago, when mammals were about to take over Earth. Clearly this was an immensely valuable resource, and as far as Marsh was concerned, it belonged to him. He had come first. He had laid claim.

This possessiveness was, even his admirers admitted, a flaw. The fact that he poached the Jersey marl beds or that Hayden had been in the Bridger Basin before him didn't seem to register with Marsh.

Even Dr. Carter could see the problem. "Out one day with Prof. Marsh and *under his vision* I found a few specimens which I wanted to send to you," Carter wrote to Leidy, "but felt under obligation to let him have [them]. . . . I noticed a very marked spirit of his shall I say jealousy . . . and confess a feeling of disappointment that I found it so."[25]

After leaving Wyoming, the Marsh party went west to the John Day River in Oregon, where they were met by Thomas Condon, who was both a pioneer minister and geologist. The Yale party had the benefit of both Reverend Condon's preaching in church and his guidance in searching the Miocene fossil beds of the John Day River basin.

Condon lent Marsh some of his specimens. At least, he thought he lent them to Marsh. Six years later, Condon wrote Marsh asking for them back. "The time . . . is more than up," Condon said. Nineteen years later, the minister—now a professor at the University of Oregon—was still pleading for the fossils. "I need them too," he said. Marsh, however, assumed that since he had paid Condon for his services that the specimens belonged to him.

It was while they were in Oregon that the Yalies heard of the great fire that started on the night of October 8 and destroyed most of Chicago. The crates containing the Kansas and Wyoming fossils had all been shipped through Chicago, so Marsh passed a few anxious days wondering whether his treasures had been burned up in the conflagration started when Patrick O'Leary's cow knocked over a lantern.

It turned out the Yale fossils had escape the Great Chicago Fire, and that was certainly a relief. But when Marsh learned Cope had been at Fort Wallace, he was furious. That, too, was his territory. And when he heard that Mudge had shown his fossils to Cope, Marsh fumed even more.

The West, however, was simply too big for Marsh to lock up in the attic like his mineral collection. The Bridger Basin was extremely valuable, and Marsh had already decided he would return again next summer, but Cope was heading that way, too. And so was Leidy. No one realized it yet, but a storm was brewing in the Bridger Basin.

Chapter Six

WHEN COPE ARRIVED AT Fort Bridger in late June of 1872, he came as the "chief paleontologist" of the U.S. Geological and Geographical Survey of the Territories. It sounded like an important position, but it wasn't. There was no pay and little financial aid. Still, Cope could claim to be on official government business and draw army supplies from post commissaries, and he was assured that his findings would be published in the survey's annual report.

Ferdinand Hayden apparently had misgivings about signing up Cope for his survey. Nevertheless, with the King Survey sending its fossils to Marsh, he felt he, too, needed a paleontologist. "I was anxious to secure the cooperation of such a worker, as an honor to my corps," Hayden explained to Leidy. "You will see therefore that while it is not a pleasant thing to work in competition with others it seems almost a necessity."

Hayden would have liked to continue to send his fossils to Leidy. But Leidy would never engage in competition or try to best another scientist. So, just as Hayden had abandoned his first mentor John Strong Newberry for James Hall and then jumped from Hall to Leidy, now he switched allegiances from Leidy to the more aggressive Cope.

At Fort Bridger, Cope learned the precise value of being Hayden's man—almost nothing. Just a few weeks earlier, Hayden had cleaned out the fort of wagons and horses and headed for Yellowstone, which the previous March had been designated America's first national park. Cope was left at Fort Bridger sleeping in the government hay yard and scrounging for supplies.

On June 22, Cope wrote for help to the regional commander, General Ord. "On reaching this post," Cope said, "Capt. Clift in command informs me that Dr. Hayden's first party have deprived him of all animals, bridles, saddles, etc. . . . The remaining teams are all employed in furnishing wood to Camp Douglas. The post has moreover no riding animals nor saddles. The men on duty tomorrow will number only fourteen (fourteen privates). Capt. Clift states that in ten days he can furnish one wagon and two men, but no saddles nor other animals."[1]

The big problem for a paleontology expedition, Cope explained to Ord, was getting to the fossil regions and carting back the specimens. "The wanting material," Cope wrote, "consists of mules, saddles, and men." Ord could do nothing. Two weeks later, Cope was still waiting.

"Prof. Cope has been here some time but has done nothing," Dr. James Van Allen Carter wrote to Marsh on July 6. "Hayden came some time ago and crippled Prof. Cope's prospects for transportation, etc."[2] Carter probably thought the news would cheer up Marsh, for since Cope's Kansas papers started coming out, the Yale professor had been complaining loudly, widely, and often.

Some of the things Cope was reporting on, Marsh had in his ample Kansas collection, but simply had not yet gotten around to studying. Marsh was methodical—and slow. While Cope might make mistakes, he was nimble.

Earlier that month, Carter had tried to soothe some ruffled feathers when a Cope paper apparently beat Marsh. "I am sincerely sorry to learn of another disappointment to you by the action of Prof. Cope. This is the first I knew of his having been over any of the fields explored by you. Knowing your great interest, and having seen how earnestly you labor personally to advance it and the cause, I am fully prepared to estimate how provoking it is—not to put it stronger—to be thus anticipated."[3]

In that same letter, Carter urged Marsh to come out to Fort Bridger to hunt fossils. Leidy had already accepted Carter's invitation. "I would be delighted to have you two together here, and my faith is that it will work beneficially to all in this way," Carter said. Leidy, Carter assumed, was "a genuine friend" of Marsh and that the two could reach an agreement on sharing fossils. What was Carter thinking?

But his duties at Yale and the pressure to publish brought on by Cope were tending to keep Marsh in New Haven. In fact, Marsh was lobbying the editors of the *American Journal of Science* to hold open the August issue until he could complete an article. Although not actually a Yale organ, the journal, founded in 1818 by Professor Benjamin Silliman Sr. and commonly called "Silliman's Journal," was closely allied with the university. But James Dwight Dana, who was now the editor, was reluctant to hold blank pages for Marsh. "I could not on any account leave with pages unfilled," he told Marsh. Couldn't his report go in the September edition? Marsh, Professor Dana felt, was becoming something of a nuisance.[4]

This year Marsh's foray into the West would be limited. Toward the end of the summer, he planned to take a small party—just four students—for a brief run into western Kansas and eastern Wyoming. He hoped that Dr. Carter and two hired fossil hunters would guard his interests in the Bridger Basin.

With Marsh in New Haven and Leidy not expected at Fort Bridger until late July, Wyoming was all Cope's, if he could only find a few mules and men. By this time, Annie and Julia had joined him at Fort Bridger. Cope planned to spend all summer exploring the basin, and he had moved from the hay yard into a rented house.

There was, however, only one way to get out of the fort. Cope had to buy what he needed with his own money. He purchased a wagon and four mules for $500 and hired another team and driver at $180 a month. He hired a teamster, a cook, and a guide and packer. He paid one dollar a day for each man and mule.

He was able to draw from the fort's commissary and quartermaster thirty days' rations of bacon, beans, rice, apples, onions, canned tomatoes, flour, hard bread, salt, pepper, and vinegar. For himself, he purchased some canned oysters, canned peaches, and a ham.[5]

Cope had also arranged for three young men from Chicago join him, young men who "wished to benefit by their chance for study," or so he thought. Just before leaving the fort, their leader, a fellow named Garman, demanded that they be paid for their time. Cope balked. The three threatened to leave. Cope told them to go. "I am glad to be rid of them at the outset," he told his brother, James. Garman had passed himself off as a Quaker, Cope wrote, but was probably a fraud. "I suspect . . . his whole scheme was to get up an expedition of his own."

On July 14, Cope wrote to Hayden apprising him of his difficulties in getting outfitted, adding that the prices he paid were "a little high." But he noted, "there have been some gigantic remains lately from here, which go to Prof. Marsh."[6] The very next day, Cope's five-man party left the fort and headed southeast, into the Bridger Basin. The fort's depleted ranks could provide no military escort. Cope didn't think they really needed one. They reach Smith's Fork, eight miles south of the post, and camped. From there, they pushed on to Cottonwood Creek. "It is a lovely creek and the birds sing all around," Cope wrote.

After a few of days in the field, Cope sent a teamster back to the fort with a letter for Annie. "I have had great success & in two days have found 25 or 30 species of which 10 are new. . . . Thee need not say anything about my success," Cope advised, "except that I am doing well & getting some things."[7]

At about the same time, Cope left Fort Bridger, Leidy and his wife, Anna, arrived. They had traveled all the way from Philadelphia to Carter Station—nine miles from the post—in the comfort of one of the new Pullman cars, with its polished wood interior, fresh towels, sitting rooms, and toilets. Folks had christened the new sleeper cars "yachts on wheels."

Dr. Carter and Dr. Joseph Corson, the post's army surgeon, had been sending Bridger Basin fossils to Leidy for more than two years. But this was the Philadelphian's very first visit to the West. "Dr. Leidy came about a week ago," Carter reported to Marsh in a July 23 letter, "& has had a four day trip among the 'badlands,' which he enjoyed very much."[8] Leidy was awed walking through the badland canyons. "It requires little stretch of the imagination to think oneself in the streets of some vast ruined deserted city," he wrote.

These small trips from the relative comfort of Fort Bridger would be Leidy's approach to fossil hunting. The forty-nine-year-old naturalist was not about to launch himself on one of the grueling fossil treks that Cope or Marsh might entertain. Indeed, for several years now, his prominence in paleontology had been slowly eroded by the vigor of Marsh and Cope.

When Leidy began applying his understanding of anatomy to American vertebrate fossils in 1847, he was pretty much alone in the field. For the next twenty years, his command of the subject was unchallenged, and specimens flowed to him from all over the country. Hall in Albany and Baird in Washington both deferred to Leidy when it came to fossils with backbones.

Then Cope and Marsh appeared, and things quickly changed. In 1867, Leidy published his *Cretaceous Reptiles of the United States*—the most detailed work to date on America fossils of that period. In England, it was savaged in a review.

"Altogether," the reviewer wrote, "we must, while expressing our thankfulness for the memoir, such as it is, say that it is the least able contribution to paleontology, that we can remember. Its best praise is that it contains no quackery, its worst condemnation is that it contains no science."

The review was signed "H." And everyone, including Leidy and Cope, thought that it was written by Thomas Huxley. It sounded like him. Stinging. As the leader of the young Turks of British science, the banner bearer for the Darwinian evolution, Huxley was famous for his stiletto prose. One of his favorite bêtes noires was Richard Owen, now a peer of the realm, with whom he was in a running battle over a variety of paleontology, evolutionary, and political issues. As for Sir Richard being "the English Cuvier," Huxley asserted, "he stands in exactly the same relation to the French as British brandy to cognac."

Leidy's transgression, as far as "H" was concerned, was his unwillingness to make any sense out of the huge reservoir of facts he was amassing. "I am too busy to make money or theorize," Leidy would say. Leidy just wanted to find the bones and describe them. However, for paleontologists, like Huxley, the value wasn't in the bones, but the story they told.

Then, throwing in an extra slap, "H" wrote, "We look forward with hope that the remains so precious will some day be elucidated and doubt not that the accomplished author . . . and discoverer of Laelaps [Cope] will make available to scientific students the descriptions of his Philadelphia brother Professor."

In a letter to his father, Cope said that while Huxley's review was "of the severest kind, not handsome, nor Christian . . . I cannot help feeling some gratification as it does not equal in unhandsomeness the manner in which both Leidy & Hawkins [the dinosaur sculptor] have treated me."[9]

However, John Strong Newberry, the physician and geologist, wrote to Leidy, saying that he had spoken to Huxley, who swore he had not written the review.[10]

Still, there was a change in scientific affairs afoot, and it continued that very summer in the Bridger Basin. Also working in the region was B. F. Meek, an expert on fossil shells. Meek and Hayden had worked together for Hall in Albany, and Meek, like Cope, was invited to work in the West under the auspices of Hayden's new survey.

Hayden was steadily building a cadre of scientists that would be affiliated with his survey, and he managed to attract some of the top names in geology, biology, and paleontology. As a result, his annual reports were filled with major scientific papers, and not coincidentally, Hayden became an important figure in the politics of American science.

Working near Black Buttes, about forty-five miles northeast of Fort Bridger, Meek and a coworker came upon some vertebrate remains. In years past, those bones would have gone to Leidy, but Meek now contacted Cope.

At Black Buttes, Cope found the fragments of an ancient animal lying in a bed of fossil leaves. He excavated sixteen vertebrae; the sacrum, ilia, and other pelvic bones; ribs; and some of the limbs.[11] Cope's examination showed that there was little doubt that this was America's third major dinosaur skeleton. He named it *Agathaumas sylvestris,* or "marvelous saurian of the forest."[12]

Though only a partial skeleton, the animal, at an estimated six tons, was huge. "If the reader will compare the measurements given for the species of the groups already known, he will observe that those of the present animal exceed those yet described for North America," Cope concluded.[13]

Despite being limited to brief forays into the field, Leidy was unearthing valuable fossils and making important discoveries. One of his most remarkable finds was the remains of a bizarre beast with a massive skull, approaching four feet in length. It had tusks and three sets of horns. Leidy named this extraordinary, rhinoceros-like mammal of the Eocene *Uintatherium robustum.*

While Leidy was making good progress and very much enjoying his visit to the West, Cope was having all sorts of problems. From Cottonwood Creek, the party had moved northeast to Bitter Creek, which unfortunately lived up to its name. The water was sharp and alkali, causing several members of the party to get sick. Then the spring gave out entirely.

Unlike picturesque Henry's Fork, Bitter Creek wasn't large enough to sustain cottonwood trees and had only a cordon of bushes along its banks, as it dribbled dun-colored water through a barren, white-rock valley. After three weeks, Cope was forced to break camp. "The stock began to look miserably and would have died had I not left when I did," he said.

The two teamsters "began to go wrong," as one of them used the grain set aside for the other team. The mules broke their tether one night, and one of the teamsters had to go off in search of them. He finally found them four days later and thirty-five miles away at Black Buttes. Then, instead of coming back directly, the man spent three days in a saloon.

"When he returned," Cope wrote, "he seems to have expected discharge, so he stole $20 or more worth of provisions etc. from our larder and 'cached' them. He drove on the return as far as the Buttes, and then tore up the collar, ran the wagon into a ditch and started out for another spree. I discharged him at once." In Green River City, Cope hired another wagon and teamster.

The hard rock faces made for exhausting work, requiring chisels, wedges, and stone hammers to free the fossils. It was also, Cope said, "a land of mosquitoes & midges and gnats." The party tried smoking out the bugs, with little effect. The only respite came with the cool of the evening, which drove off the insects. Still, as August moved along, Cope had collected more than fifty different species of fossil animals—mammals, fish, and reptiles—perhaps half of them new. One of the most curious discoveries was the remains of a huge, rhinolike mammal, with a massive skull sporting three sets of horns and tusks. Cope named it *Loxolophodon*.

In an attempt to ensure first claim to the discovery, Cope telegraphed his finding to the American Philosophical Society. But translating Greek words into Morse code was an exercise filled with risk, and the telegraph operator managed to bollix the name.

Back in Philadelphia, the officers at the society tried to make the best sense they could of the message and read a notice into their August 19 minutes stating, "The secretary announced that he had received a telegram from Professor Cope dated Black Buttes, Wyoming, August 17, 1872 reading (with conjectural corrections for specific words) as follows:

" 'I have discovered in southern Wyoming, the following species *Lefalaphon,* Cope.' "

✤

As the weeks, passed Marsh's summer plans were coming undone. The first hint of problems came in letter dated July 16, from John Chew, one of his hired fossil hunters. "I have been in your employ with Smith since the 12th of June, he is now with another party," Chew wrote. "I am continuing work until I hear from you."[14]

The Smith mention was the irascible B. D. "Sam" Smith. Where Smith had gone to Chew didn't say. Marsh was now down to one fossil prospector while Dr. Carter was busy entertaining Leidy. A few days later, however, Carter did write for he had some news, some very bad news.

"I regret *for human nature's sake as well* as your interests that Smith has proven false to his obligations to you," Carter wrote.[15] Smith was with Cope. Marsh immediately sent a telegram to Smith at Fort Bridger. The reply came not from Smith, but Judge Carter.

"Your telegram to Smith which came yesterday found him absent, in the employment of Prof. Cope. I had no idea he would prove so false to his engagement with you. . . . I learned that he had hired himself to Cope and was going out with him and that he had showed him some of the fossils gotten for you. Prof. Leidy and his wife have been with us for some time. The Doctor was out with Jeremy Carter and Dr. Corson on Wednesday last and has yet to return. Cope is also out with his party."[16]

What torture this must have been for Marsh, and a letter from Smith explaining himself certainly did nothing to assuage the professor's worries.

"Friend Marsh," Smith's letter began, "I thought I would write you a few lines and let you know how I am getting along. I was with Prof. Cope a few days, but have left him, my eyes were sore and I thought I would rest them a few days. . . . I got your letter and dispatch. . . . I am going to start for Pine Bluffs in the morning to collect for you. I think Cope has heard of the place and will be going there, but I don't intend he shall get ahead of me and if he does get there I don't think he will be much in the way for he don't understand collecting very well and he has fellout with his party and is all alone."[17]

Marsh must have suspected that Smith was painting an overly rosy picture—Cope was too smart and too resourceful to fail—and if there were any doubts, the coming weeks would dispel them. For Cope's papers on the Bridger Basin started to land even before he returned.

Cope was sending his papers back to the American Philosophical Society for quick publication. (Hayden's report was published only annually.) The society printed sporadically, but papers' being read into the record would help establish priority. Cope's first paper, "Descriptions of Some

New Vertebrae from the Bridger Group of the Eocene," named ten species and was dated July 29.[18] The following week came the "Second Account of the New Vertebrae from the Bridger Group," with five more species, including the first mention of an ancient reptile found at Black Buttes named *A. sylvestris.*[19]

While it is unlikely that any papers sent back during the dog days of summer received wide distribution, Marsh might have known about them. He was a member of the society, and his Philadelphia friends, such as Dr. Joseph LeConte, also a society member, tended to keep him posted on Cope's activities.

And so, in the middle of the summer, Marsh took his four Yale students and headed west. And even though he had told Dr. Carter he would not make it to western Wyoming this year, Fort Bridger was now on the itinerary. But he might never have gotten there at all if it hadn't been for a swift Indian pony named Pawnee.

Once more, Marsh's first stop was Fort Wallace. Outfitted with a military escort, led by Lieutenant James Pope, and with Ned Lane again serving as guide, the party headed east into the region of the Smoky Hill River badlands. Marsh was now almost as much at home on these prairies as his companions. They rode along together, Pope in his army cap and blue uniform; Lane in buckskin, Mexican spurs, and a wide sombrero; and Marsh in a slouch hat and old corduroy suit, the pockets bulging with specimens.

One day, as they came over a rise, stretching before them was the most massive buffalo herd any of them had ever seen. "The broad valley before us, perhaps, six or eight miles wide, was black with buffalo, the herd extending a dozen miles up and down the valley," Marsh recalled.[20] Lieutenant Pope calculated that there had to be at least one hundred thousand buffalo. "We must have one of those fellows for supper," Lane announced, and so the three men decided to hold an impromptu hunt.

Armed with a cavalry carbine and a pair of navy revolvers, Marsh rode down into the valley on his horse, Pawnee, and came close to the edge of the herd. He set his sights on a young cow and went off after the animal, which moved with surprising speed. As he was closing in, several shots snapped behind him. Marsh assumed that his comrades were at work. But he was fixed on his prey, and he said he brought down the buffalo "in the exact manner my first guide, Buffalo Bill, had taught me."

It was only then that he turned around and saw that the gunshots had stampeded this gigantic mass of buffaloes. At that moment Marsh also realized that the chase had carried him into the heart of the herd. "They began to lap around me," he said, "and I would soon be enclosed . . . liable at any moment to be trampled to death." His only chance was to ride with the stampeding mass and try to slide his way toward the edge. So he rode.

As he rode, he fired at the animals nearest to him, hoping to open a path of escape. "The whole mighty herd was now at full speed, the earth seemed fairly to shake under the moving mass, which with tongues out, and flaming eyes and nostrils, was hurrying onward, pressed by those behind," Marsh wrote. With each stride, the valley was narrowing, and even worse, they were heading into a large prairie-dog colony, filled with den holes. Buffalo began to stumble, pitch over, and trample one another. It was now that Marsh's Pawnee showed himself to be wise as well as fleet. "While running at full speed along with the herd, he kept his head down," Marsh said, "and whenever a dangerous dog hole was in his path, he either stepped short or leaped over it."

By now the herd had covered several miles, Marsh was nearly out of ammunition, and his horse was starting to tire. The valley had turned into a series of ravines, and buffalo were jumping and plunging into and out of the gullies. The buffalo were so packed around Marsh in the washes that he could have reached out and touched them. Coming out of a deep ravine, Marsh saw a glimmer of hope. Ahead was a low butte. The herd would have to divide to get around it. Marsh began firing at the buffalo on his left trying to clear a path to the butte. The closer they got, the more rapidly he fired. He swung his horse around to the back of the butte. From there, he watched as the herd streamed past on either side.

"Dismounting, I saw why my pony had seemed so foot-heavy during the last mile," Marsh said. "He was covered with dust, nearly exhausted, and with bleeding flanks, distended forelegs, and blazing nostrils, he stood quivering and breathing heavily, while the buffalo were passing within a few feet."

Soon all that was left were wispy eddies of the herd, and Marsh, still the hunter, downed a young heifer. With his hunting knife, he removed the tongue and hump steaks, an amount "sufficient for our small party."

Marsh unsaddled the horse and rubbed him down with the saddle blanket. His canteen was empty, but he offered the contents of his pocket flask. Pawnee declined. Marsh started to lead him back toward camp, but the horse, Marsh said, "soon made me understand that he was himself again." They rode back through the darkness, to the sound of a signal gun firing. Usually, one of the soldiers cared for the mounts, but that night Marsh rubbed down Pawnee himself.

Although the time spent in the Kansas plains was brief, one of Marsh's greatest discoveries came out of this journey. From the very first expedition, the Yale parties had collected the remains of fossil birds, and as early as 1870, Marsh had described three genera and five species of prehistoric aquatic birds, all related to modern birds. This summer, his small party was under orders to find more birds. They did, uncovering four individuals. Marsh himself found an almost complete skeleton of a huge, ancient bird, standing nearly six feet tall. All that was missing was its skull.

Fossil birds had become a very hot issue in paleontology circles, primarily due to the ever-controversial Huxley. In the war over evolution and fossil interpretation, Huxley had made old birds a major battleground. Gideon Mantell had originally thought of dinosaurs as giant lizards. Robert Owen had shaped them into reptilian elephants. Leidy had used kangaroos as the model for his dinosaur. But Huxley had promoted the idea of the similarity of dinosaurs and birds. One could even say, Huxley argued, birds had descended from dinosaurs. From an evolutionary viewpoint, this was an extremely beguiling position.

Opponents of Darwinian evolution argued that animals—certainly at the level of genera—were discrete creations. An eagle was clearly different than a snake. How could anyone dispute that? Still, if paleontologists could show similarities in form and function and carry development back to some common ancestor, if they could trace the branching and variation, it would go a long way toward bolstering Darwin.

Already evidence was beginning to pile up. In 1862, just three years after Darwin's *Origin of Species* was published, a striking discovery was made in the soft limestone of Solnhofen, Bavaria. There, in a quarry, was uncovered the complete fossil skeleton, save for the head, of a creature with a bony tail and the long claws of a reptile. But it also clearly had feathers. Here was the link between reptile and birds. The specimen was dubbed *Archaeopteryx,* or "ancient feather."

Then there was *Compsognathnus,* a small theropod dinosaur with a host of anatomical similarities to birds. Marsh had written a paper noting some of these. In 1867, Cope delivered remarks before the academy in which he "gave an account of extinct reptiles that approached birds." For years paleontologists had been puzzling over large three-toed tracks in the sandstone of the Connecticut River valley. It was thought that they must have been made by giant birds, but Cope argued that they had been made by dinosaurs. That same year Huxley published a study showing thirty-five similarities between *Archaeopteryx* and *Compsognathnus.* Huxley went so far as to suggest that dinosaurs might have been "hot blooded," and had bird-like hearts and lungs.[21]

Archaeopteryx was a Jurassic animal, Marsh was collecting in the Kansas Cretaceous, and his bird fossils were a one hundred million years closer to modern times. Still, there were still important bridging similarities. Marsh had some valuable specimens, but he was missing a crucial piece of the Cretaceous bird puzzle. It was a piece that Benjamin Mudge had discovered that very same summer and had put into a box he was preparing to send east—to Cope.

In August, Sam Smith wrote another letter to Marsh trying to defend his actions—having doubtless heard from the Carters of Marsh's anger and how everyone thought him a turncoat.

"My motive in going with Cope was to keep him off some places that I think is good bone country," Smith said. "I did not intend to quit you long. he got some things mostly turtle, very few things. Then I got your letter wishing me to go black buttes."[22]

Leaving Fort Wallace, Marsh stopped briefly at Fort D. A. Russell and then finally arrived in the Bridger Basin toward the middle of August. The Yale party immediately started fossil prospecting. One of the most impressive finds the party made was of the skull of a huge animal with three sets of horns and tusklike teeth. Marsh named the animal *Dinoceras.*

By late August, Cope's party was down to four pack mules and three men. As Marsh took to the Bridger Basin, Cope had shifted to the Wasatch Basin. Whether this was by chance or to avoid coming face to face with the Yale party is not clear, but Cope and Marsh did not cross paths. That didn't mean they were unaware of what the other was doing.

One day Cope even watched from afar as Marsh's men worked over a spot, and when they left, he went down to investigate. He found in their excavation the pieces of a weathered skull and some loose teeth. Figuring that his rivals had either overlooked or rejected the fossil, he claimed it and eventually used the material to describe a new species.

But the skull and the teeth were really a mischievous plant by the Marsh men. The fossils were actually from two different animals. It would be almost twenty years before the error would be caught and corrected.[23]

In the Wasatch, Cope found a number of large vertebrate fossils. Again he found the remains—including the skulls—of a massive multihorned animal. This one he called *Eobasileus.* In a letter in early September, from his camp on the Green River, he described it to his father.

"This was a monstorous animal, and Elephantine in size and proportions. Its skull is three-feet long, & the hips five feet across. The head of the femur of one is as large as the top of my hat. It stood shorter in the legs than an elephant, and was proportioned more as in the Rhinoceros, but was twice as large as the largest living of the latter. . . . In a word *Eobasileus* is the most extraordinary fossil mammal found in N. America, & I have good material of illustrating it. Marsh & Leidy have obtained it near the same time & I have no idea whether they have fathered in advance of me or not."[24]

Cope was fairly sure that the animal was a proboscidean, which is to say that it had a trunk. He sketched his vision of the animal for his father—a stocky pachyderm with short tusks and a fat horn over each eye.

Cope closed his letter with more mundane matters. "Annie I suppose has sent thee the cacti," he said. "I will probably remain here for about a week and then close up the expedition and sell out. . . . The season here is autumnal; sometimes ice and snow are not far off."

A week later, however, Cope was still in the field. The nights were getting frosty, and blankets were "none too many." Bacon, beans, bread, and rice were the staples now, with a deer or grouse added to the fare when one of the men made a good shot.

Coming out of the mountains, Cope dropped into the Uinta Basin—the same basin Marsh had discovered and named in 1870. This would be his last stop. Camp life was getting ever more basic. They cooked their meat Indian-style on forked sticks, and at night Cope spread his blankets out under the willow trees and fell "asleep looking up at Cassiopeia and listening to the yelping of coyotes." When he awoke at 5 A.M., the blankets were covered with frost, and the water in his canteen was frozen.

One of the men traveling with Cope, James Manley, wrote to his mother in Ohio of the fossil hunt. "We found many different species of elephants, lions, tigers . . . lizard, one with legs ten feet and tail twenty-five feet long. . . . We found no men or monkey. They did not exist at that period, man has come since. I did the hauling of them to the rail road to be shipped."[25]

On September 18, Cope returned to the post. By this time, both Leidy and Marsh were back east. Cope had a third dispatch ready for the American Philosophical Society. This one announced that the extinct animal found near Black Buttes was a dinosaur. It also reported the discovery of new vertebrate species from the upper waters of the Bitter Creek, including *Eobasileus.* The expedition had been a great success, but Cope came back to Fort Bridger exhausted and with a heavy cold that quickly turned into a bad fever.

Now responsibility for the Cope family fell on Annie, who found herself nursing a sick Edward, mothering six-year-old Julia, corresponding with Hayden to try to get money, and fending off the landlady, a woman of the West, whose ripe and florid vocabulary could blister paint and make a young Quaker wife blanch. Cope's fever was high, and he suffered from delirious dreams in which he saw "multitudes of persons speaking ill of something and all frustrating . . . attempts to sleep."

Cope had been sick for nearly a week, when by a low lamplight—so as not to disturb her sleeping patient—Annie wrote back to Philadelphia.

> *Dear Father & Mother,*
>
> *My dear E came into the post on the 18th having contracted a heavy cold from sleeping out with insufficient covering, which has since been developing.*
>
> *A high fever & some inflammation of the brain for a day or two producing great restlessness, and no sleep, only dozing to frightful scenes, making it most roilsome and wearisome.*
>
> *However, Dr. Corson seems to understand his case, and is most attentive.*
>
> *A blister on the back of the neck has diminished the inflammation, but leaves him in a very weak & helpless condition. The time is painfully long for him from his inability to converse with anyone or see strangers.*
>
> *I had hoped that the worst was over today; but the fever returned this p.m. Dr. applied blisters to the temples, gave him Dorire's powder, and he seems to now be sleeping the first refreshing sleep without nightmares since he has taken sick. Dr. staid with me until a late hour, but things look so favorable I released him and will go to bed myself.[26]*

Since July, when forced to spend a good deal of his own money, Cope had been trying to get some of it back from Hayden. After all, the survey was supposed to provide at least transport and rations.

In a July 21st letter, Cope had outlined all his expenditures, which added up to eleven hundred dollars for two months in the field. Cope assured Hayden, "I have had very good success in this time better than I could have expected & much that is new in spite of Marsh & Leidy's previous work. . . . You see the money is well invested." But Cope pleaded, "I personally have only enough money to put my wife and child through. So imagine about $800."[27] Hayden came through and sent two four-hundred-dollar checks to Annie Cope at Fort Bridger.

Now in September, with Cope seriously ill, money was an issue again, and Annie wrote to Hayden on September 22. "My husband came in to the post on the 18th not well, with mountain fever which has prostrated him very much and renders him unable to write to you at present." Annie went on to give Hayden a brief account of the areas her husband had explored before coming back to the fort.

Four days later, Annie again wrote to Hayden. "Since writing to you . . . my husband has been quite ill, with inflammation of the brain and constant fever for 10 days, which has reduced him extremely weak though the inflammation has been reduced the last day or two he cannot sit up in bed and . . . you might be early apprized of his inability to attend to any finances. . . . It may be some weeks before he is able to attend to business or start for home."[28]

By October 10, Cope had recovered enough to dictate to Annie a letter for Hayden. It outlined his expenses—another $790—and Cope added, "I have spent all my private means."[29]

Two days later, Cope was strong enough to write on his own to his father. "Nothing is left of the fever except the weakness," he reported. "I am favored with a good appetite and my nights are positively happy under the influence of an opiate."

On a more devout note, Cope assured, "I am blessed with cheerful feelings, and sometimes still more so by the nearness of the church's comforter, the Elder Brother and sympathizing Friend, whose service is perfect liberty; and who sticks close to those who endeavour to walk near him."[30]

The following day, in a letter to his mother-in-law, Cope praised Annie. "Thy daughter, my excellent wife has shown the talents of her family for nursing. She tended to me faithfully and saved me much suffering. . . . It has proved a very fortunate circumstance that she accompanied me here. She has also much benefited by the atmosphere; every day I see her do with ease what she could not have done before leaving home."

Cope tallying up his finds in that letter counted a total of sixty-two species of terrestrial animals and about fourteen species of fish. "About a fifth of these were not on the books, and I published their characters with a name for each. Some of them were of the hugest size, while others are not greater than mice. Not a one of them is living yet and nothing like a great many of them has ever been seen by human eyes."[31]

He fretted a bit about his sickness having "caused a great delay" in his work. But he managed to post two more brief papers to the American Philosophical Society, dated October 12, 1872. These were "On a New Vertebrate Genus from the Northern Part of the Tertiary Basin of the Green River" and "Description of New Extinct Reptiles from the Upper Green River Eocene Basin."[32]

A few days latter, Cope wrote to his brother, Philip, "Complaints are diminishing before Dr. Corson's attacks, and the influence of good food. Annie has been indefatigable, and has no doubt hastened my recovery by many days, by her care and skill. It will not be very long before we will leave here, that is as soon as I am strong enough to stand it, as our landlady renders Annie's situation very unpleasant. Her language is not good at the best of times, but now and then she descends to low abuse. . . . We are now looking anxiously to the day we get off."[33]

While Cope was recuperating, incredible accounts reached the fort of the discovery of a diamond-and-ruby mine near the neighboring town of Rock Creek. Soon the news had swept through all Wyoming and created great excitement among eastern investors. A consortium was formed and hundreds of thousands of dollars were raised to finance the mine. Henry Janin, a noted geologist and mining engineer, had verified the extraordinary discovery. Unfortunately for the mine's two developers, Philip Arnold and John Slack, Clarence King's survey was still working in Wyoming.

At the moment, King himself was in the Sandwich Islands strolling the beaches and being smitten with Hawaiian princess Keelikolani. "I like best the primitive state," King would confess to a friend. "Paradise for me is still a garden with a primeval woman."

But when he heard about the Wyoming diamonds, he quit paradise and headed for Rock Creek. In the early autumn, King found the gem field and, using his Yale training, quickly noted that the ratio of rubies to diamonds seemed consistent—twelve to one—wherever he looked. He also found diamonds in crevices where they simply could not have sat for very long. It was easy enough to prove that the mine was a fraud.

Arnold and Slack, it turned out, had bought thirty-five thousand dollars of uncut gems in London and Antwerp and "salted" the cavern near Rock Creek. They had pulled in an estimated six hundred thousand dollars before King exposed them.[34]

Among the dupes had been Horace Greeley and the New York jeweler Charles Tiffany. The *San Francisco Chronicle* proclaimed, "We have escaped, thanks to GOD and CLARENCE KING, a great financial ruin."[35]

It was not until early November that the Copes made their way east, and then it was with some difficulty. Cope had hoped to get back $250 from selling his livestock, but he was unable to find a buyer. On October 30, still at Fort Bridger, he wired Hayden at a Salt Lake City hotel.

"Could not sell stock wintered it so I need the balance two hundred dollars mail to Leavenworth Kansas."[36] There is no record whether Hayden sent the money.

By Thanksgiving, Cope, Annie, and Julia were back in Philadelphia. They had been gone six grueling, expensive months. Cope had spent more than two thousand dollars, two years of salary for a Haverford professor, on his Wyoming expedition and had come home physically exhausted and broke.

Still, scientifically it had been an enormous success. So many new species, so many fossil specimens. Cope was especially pleased with the massive skull of *Eobasileus,* or was it *Loxolophodon* or *Dinoceras* or *Uintathere?* Much would have to be sorted out, and now once again Cope would find himself on Marsh's turf.

Marsh, Dr. Carter told Leidy, "seems hot on the path of Professor Cope, and says he will expose his . . . villanies!! Won't he have a pretty large job for one person?"[37]

Chapter Seven

THE BOX WITH BENJAMIN MUDGE'S fossils was already packed and addressed to Philadelphia when the letters arrived from New Haven. While Marsh had been down on the Smoky Hill, Mudge had found some small, but interesting bones while fossil prospecting along the middle fork of the Solomon River, about fifty miles north of Hays City. These he was now preparing to send to Cope.

But having heard that Mudge was in the field, Marsh wrote to him in early September asking him if he had found anything interesting. Anything in the way of birds? At about the same time, Professor Dana had also written, curious whether Mudge might have something for Yale.

The inquiry from Dana must have been particularly flattering, for after Joseph Henry, Dana was one of the nation's most distinguished scientists. A fixture at Yale for almost three decades, Dana had given American geology its theoretical framework with his studies of mountain building, volcanoes, and the origin of continents. His 1834 *Systems of Mineralogy* and 1862 *Manual on Geology* had become staple texts. A small, spare man, with chronic health problems, the fifty-nine-year-old Dana was a force in American science. He was not only a senior Yale professor, but also editor and coproprietor of the *American Journal of Science.* Mudge wrote a new address label for his box and sent it not to Philadelphia, but to New Haven.[1]

When Marsh opened Mudge's parcel, he thought he had the remains of two animals—the hollow bones of a bird and two jaws from a small reptile. The bird he named *Icthyornis dispar* and the reptile, *Colonosaurus mudgei.* It was only when further work was done on the specimens, revealing a skull, did Marsh realize that he didn't have two animals; he had just one—a bird with teeth.

In February of 1873, he published a preliminary notice on the find in the *American Journal of Science,* remarking that "the fortunate discovery of these interesting fossils . . . does much to break down the old distinction between Birds and Reptiles, which *Archaeopteryx* has so materially diminished."[2]

The huge bird Marsh himself had found that summer on the Smoky Hill he named *Hesperornis regalis.* Initially, he thought it was related to the common loon. But perhaps as a result of the discovery of *Icthyornis,* he worked carefully through the material, and when the chalk was removed from one of the students' specimens, he found a nearly perfect skeleton, with parts of the head and jaw. *Hesperornis* also had teeth. Marsh described it as "a carnivorous swimming ostrich." (Further research would show that this flightless, diving bird was similar in skeletal features to modern loons and grebes.).[3]

Ichthyornis could fly, and Marsh would eventually find another flying Cretaceous bird with teeth in Kansas, *Apatornis.* These two birds Marsh compared to gulls and terns, respectively.

Looking at *Archaeopteryx, Hesperornis,* and *Ichthyornis,* Marsh argued that they were so very different from one another that the evolution of birds must have begun at a much earlier time, perhaps during the Triassic period more than two hundred million years ago, perhaps even at the dawn of the age of dinosaurs.

For Huxley in England, the papers coming out of America were sketchy but very promising. Marsh's toothed bird and Cope's birdlike dinosaur tracks were both useful ammunition in the ongoing battle over evolution and paleontological theory. Too bad all this wonderful material was an ocean away.

It was clear that Marsh had quite enough to do up in New Haven without brooding about Cope and the Philadelphian's Fort Bridger material. But he couldn't help it. It was as if there was a sense of personal injury in Cope's going into the basin and writing up discoveries before Marsh could sort through his booty.

"I do not wonder at your earnest efforts to bring out all your discoveries in view of the fact that Cope and Leidy, both seem to be running a race with you for priority," wrote a sympathetic Spencer Baird in the late summer of 1872.[4]

But when Marsh found out that Cope had sent Baird a manuscript on his Bridger Basin work, he was incensed, and Baird quickly tried to defuse the situation. "I do not want you to think that Cope 'has gone back on you.' . . . The manuscript account of his exploration as far as I can recollect, embraced only descriptions of new fossil fishes. I do not know, indeed, whether he intended it for anything other than my information. It was sent to me from the Academy at Philadelphia without any special intimation as to what I was to do with it afterward, but I sent it back thinking it might be wanted for Proceedings. So far, I have received nothing from Cope in print—on any subject, although you appear to have received . . . Leidy's announcement."[5]

Baird was finding that navigating between Cope and Marsh could be tricky. But clearly, he did not want to alienate Marsh, a man who could mount expeditions big enough to gather duplicate specimens for the Smithsonian, a man who had the resources to buy a tapir skeleton when the Smithsonian was broke, a man who was affiliated with one of the top universities in the country. Baird was among the first scientists to wander into the growing cross fire between Cope and Marsh. Soon he would have plenty of company.

The main target of Marsh's complaint was those damnable papers Cope kept spinning out. It wasn't just that they were inaccurate—at least as far as Marsh was concerned they were—but that they came so fast, if the dates were to be believed. Marsh, of course, didn't believe them.

But the truth be told, the reports coming out of the Bridger Basin were a muddle. There had been too many discoveries, by too many independent parties, in too short a time. This in a day when there were no protocols, no uniform publication standards, and no final arbiter. No one in science had seen anything quite like it before.

❧

The system of naming and classifying species had been established by the eighteenth century Swedish naturalist Carolus Linneaus. Linneaus divided life into two great kingdoms—plant and animal. Within each, every living thing was to be identified by two names—genus, a broad class that shared a number of similarities, and species, a more specific, closely related group within the genus. The genera themselves would be grouped into larger families.

For example, the Australian dingo, red wolf, and a Shetland sheepdog are all members of the family Canidae and the genus *Canis*. But the dingo is *Canis dingo,* the red wolf, *Canis laterns,* and the sheepdog *Canis familiaris.* The person who identifies a new species gets to name it, and his or her own name follows the new name *(Hadrosaursus foulkii* Leidy).

To ensure that each species had only one name, scientists relied on the the rule of priority. The first name published in the literature is the one recognized by the scientific community. Since the chances of two scientists finding and naming the same species on the same day seemed incredibly remote, the system worked fine for more than a century. That is, it worked until Cope, Marsh, and Leidy all turned up in the Bridger Basin.

Consider, for example, the remains of a small fossil lemur with a skull barely three inches long, discovered that summer. This fossil was given a total of seven different names by the three paleontologists—*Notharctus, Hipposyus, Limnotherium, Telmalestes, Telmatolestes, Thinolestes,* and *Tomitherium.* Part of the confusion came from identifications based on fragmentary material, but part of it was the product of the taxonomic three-ring circus going on in Wyoming.

How to sort it all out? Cope argued that his name, *Tomitherium rostratum* Cope, should take precedence over *Limnotherium affine* Marsh, based on his more complete description of the species.

"Professor Marsh states that this species is the one he named *Limnotherium affine* in a paper in the *American Journal of Science and Arts,* the advance copies of which bear the date August 7, 1872. This is also the date of the publication of the paper in which the name *Tomitherium rostratum* was proposed," Cope wrote in the American Philosophical Society's *Proceedings.* Since neither publication states the hour of their appearance, Cope argued, "Professor Marsh's description is extremely brief consisting of five lines and six measurements. . . . My original description was fuller, consisting of seventeen lines." In the end, it would be Leidy's *Notharctus* that would be deemed the first name published and thus the one that would be used in the future.

But the real battleground in this taxonomy war would be those huge, weird, many-horned, tusk-toothed beasts that had captured the fancy of both Cope and Marsh. It was Leidy who first named the animal *Uintatherium* on August 1. Cope named it *Loxolophodon* on August 17. In a bulletin dated August 19, Marsh used the names *Tinoceras* and *Dinoceras* for the same fossil. The very next day Cope sent another dispatch naming his more complete material *Eobasileus cornutus.*

What is interesting is that not only were they giving the same material different names, but that they knew they were doing it. Cope's September letter to his father shows that he knew Leidy and Marsh had found similar fossils, and in his August 28 letter to Marsh, Sam Smith said, "we got one tusk and part of the jaw nearly one foot long, I think the same kind that Prof. Lidy got part of the tusk of hear that he is blowing about."

One might have thought that there would be an inclination to sort out the differences and clean up the nomenclature. That certainly would have been Leidy's preference (not the least because he clearly had priority). But in a sense for Cope and Marsh, this was no longer about some big, old mammal that lived fifty million years ago. There was history, but it didn't go that far back.

After the wrong-headed *Elasmosaurus,* Marsh infiltrating the Jersey marl pits, Newberry's Ohio specimens, Cope presuming to trod into Kansas and Wyoming, countless little cuts and digs, it was as if each man's emotions and ego had been rubbed raw. Any little prod was bound to cause pain and anger. Those huge skulls from Wyoming were, in effect, a big poke in the wound.

The strategy adopted by both men was to defend, deny, and denigrate. The battle would be waged primarily in the pages of the *American Naturalist,* although Marsh would also use the *American Journal of Science* and Cope *Proceedings* of the American Philosophical Society. All in all, it was an unprecedented and ugly spectacle.

But Cope's immediate concern upon returning to Philadelphia was money, and he set about writing atlas and encyclopedia articles that brought him a total of three hundred dollars. He also received a fifty-dollar "New Year's present" from his father, so once again the wolf was kept away from the door.[6]

As 1873 began, the two men were still on speaking terms, although just barely. On January 20, Cope sent Marsh a box of fossils that had accidentally been sent to him in Haddonfield. "I send you some small specimens I recently received from Kansas as having been abstracted from one of your boxes! Of course, they are yours," Cope said. He added, "Your bird with teeth is simply delightful."[7]

Marsh, however, was having trouble maintaining cordiality. In a reply a week later, he wrote:

> *I am glad you fully appreciated my bird with teeth and I hope soon to send you some photographs of it.*
>
> *Your paper on the "Proboscidians" came the 20th inst, with postmark 18th of January, although bearing the date 16th. Why don't you send your papers more promptly, as I invariably do. I am willing to accept as publication even an uncorrected proof (as we agreed). . . . And Leidy promised to do the same. . . .*
>
> *The Kansas fossil you sent came all right, where are the rest? and how about those from Wyoming?*
>
> *The information I received on this subject made me very angry, and had it come at the time I was so mad with you for getting away Smith (to whom I had given valuable notes about localities etc.) I should have "gone for you" not with pistols or fists, but in print. I came very near publishing this with some of your other transgressions including a certificate from Mr. Kinne but my better judgment prevailed. I was never so angry in my life.*
>
> *No don't you get angry about all this, but pitch into me with equal frankness if I've done anything you don't like. In haste yours very truly.*
>
> O. C. Marsh[8]

That letter provoked an immediate, four-page response from Cope. "It is far more irritating to me to be charged with dishonorable acts than to lose material, species, etc.," Cope said. "All the specimens you obtained during August 1872, you owe to me. Had I chosen they all would have been mine. I allowed your men Chew and Smith to accompany me & at last when they turned back discouraged, I discovered a new basin of fossils, showed it to them & allowed them to camp and collect with me for a considerable time. By this I lost several fine things."[9] Cope closed his letter asking Marsh to take back all charges of impropriety.

Marsh replied within days, saying he desired "most sincerely to be on friendly terms" and would "promptly make amends" for any future slight or injustice. But in the present case, he was completely unwilling to budge.

"I feel I have been deeply wronged by you in numerous instances," Marsh wrote. "These wrongs I have usually borne in silence. . . . After the Smith affair last summer, I made up my mind that forbearance was no longer a virtue."[10]

In early February, the two men met face to face in New York City, at a banquet honoring the British physicist John Tyndall. "I meet friends from all parts of the East . . . ," Cope wrote to his father. "Among others Marsh! who stuck to me like a leech and I hope became fully satisfied that I was not a thief. It seems persons had been writing to him and had wronged me greatly. As to dates I said nothing."[11] Cope's hope was in vain, the storm was now just a few weeks away from breaking.

In March, Marsh published an eleven-page article in the *Naturalist* titled "The Fossil Mammals of the Order Dinocerata." In it he claimed priority with *Tinoceras,* which had been named in early 1872. "The Yale Museum contains the remains of many individuals of the order *Dinocerata,"* Marsh wrote. Whereas, Marsh said, Cope had named *Loxolophodon* based on "a single premolar tooth."

Marsh went on to describe the animal. "The horns of the *Dinocerata* were a remarkable feature. Those on the nasal bone were probably short dermal weapons something like those of a rhinoceros, but much smaller. Those on the maxillaries [upper jaw] were conical, much elongated and undoubtedly formed the most powerful means of defense. The posterior horns [on top of the head] were the largest, and their flattened cores indicated that they were expanded and perhaps branched."[12]

In the same article, Marsh went after Cope, charging that *Eobasileus* was "apparently not distinct from those described previously by Dr. Leidy and the writer." He also complained "no less than seven of Prof. Cope's papers are antedated." That was tantamount to calling Cope a cheat.

Marsh went on to list sixteen errors in Cope's description and called his idea that the animal had a trunk "quite erroneous." Some of the mistakes were simply functions of speed and incomplete material. For example, Cope had originally identified canine teeth as incisors. But he was correcting such errors even before Marsh took pen in hand. In addition, Marsh conceded that although he hadn't actually seen *Eobasileus,* "nevertheless, I will venture, with due difference to express my belief he is mistaken."

"Cope's description has to be impossible unless, indeed, this mythical *Eobasileus* under the Professor's domestication, has changed its characters more rapidly than Darwin himself ever imagined. . . . Surely such an animal belongs in the Arabian Nights and out of the records of science."[13]

In the very same issue of the *Naturalist,* Cope had a four-page paper entitled, "The Gigantic Mammals of the Genus Eobasileus." In it, apparently unaware of Marsh's charges, he gave a general description of the animal, saying that its canine teeth (not incisors) were "shorter than the walrus and longer than the saber-tooth tiger."[14] Cope went on to say he was certain that the animal did have a trunk and that none of the distinctions made by Marsh to separate his own animal and put it in new order was "sufficiently important."

The growing spat was beginning to worry Hayden, even as he urged Cope to quickly finish his analyses so they could be printed by the survey. "You must not be alarmed" by Marsh's attacks, Cope assured him." Give him rope & he will hang himself. . . . I have priority of him to a large degree."[15]

But in April, Marsh fired three more volleys. First, in a note in the *American Journal of Science,* he picked apart some of Cope's osteological and anatomical analyses. For example, in a continuation of the trunk debate, he argued, "Prof. Cope is entirely in error in saying the muzzle of this species could not reach the ground by several feet."[16]

Second, he appeared before the Academy of Natural Sciences in Philadelphia and outlined all the problems with the dates of Cope's papers. Joseph LeConte, who was friendly with Marsh and had a distaste for the brash, acerbic Cope, made a motion to set up a committee to investigate Cope's papers. It was defeated.

Marsh also went to the American Philosophical Society and read a list of charges there. In large part, Cope's problems stemmed from the gentlemen's club aspect of the society. The officers were not full-time professionals, and the gaps between receiving communications, reading them into the record, and getting them printed depended on how much spare time busy men happened to have. "I have another lesson of the weakness and depravity of human nature on hand which confirms previous ones," Cope wrote to his father. "The acting Secretary of the Philos Soc not being a paid officer has been careless and indifferent."[17]

As a member of the philosophical society, Marsh pushed a motion to censure Cope and have the society retract the papers. The society balked at that, but did agree to change its procedures and not print any more of Cope's papers on the great Eocene beast.

Cope was ready to battle back, but was finding it difficult. Marsh was outflanking him politically. In an April letter to his father, Cope outlined his problems and asked for help.

> *Dear Father,*
>
> *I have an answer ready for Marsh which will be finished in a few days. . . . I show that but 3 of his changes if necessary have any foundation & 2 others I corrected before he wrote a line, and the other is doubtful. I have certificates from two persons proving the accuracy of my dates, and show his new order is without foundation.*
>
> *Nevertheless, I am in a bit of fix in one respect. The four plates thee has seen . . . of Lox. cornutus were to have been published by the Philo. Society. . . . The lithographer charged $30.00 a piece, so large a sum that the Secretaries withdrew permission & said I must ask the Society. I did so, & some one to whom I had given copies of the paper (Dr. LeConte) asserted that they have already been published. Fraley and others of that stamp then said that it was irregular and threw the whole thing out. I now have to pay the bill for drawing and printing the Society's 1,000 copies. [Cope estimated the cost at $290.]*
>
> *This I will not be able to pay for a long time. The chief regret is that I am not able to publish my plates so as to confront Marsh's statements which are throughout false. Text & assertion may do, but nothing but plates will prove it after such vitriolic assertions. . . . Marsh has always been extraordinarily jealous, and it would seem to have at last developed into insanity. . . . This is the only way in which I can counteract the damage Marsh is trying to do me. Hayden will do nothing, he is a coward. Marsh has now the whole editions of the American Journal of Science & Arts & American Naturalist; probably 10 times that of the Philosophical Society Proceedings.*
>
> *If thee can help me out of this scrape I will be always mindful of it.*
>
> > *With love to Mother I am thy son*
> > *Edward D.*[18]

In an effort to buttress his claims, Cope also got a letter of support from Pendleton King, professor of natural history at the University of Louisiana, and affidavits from the printers who actually set his papers in pamphlet form. (From time to time, Marsh also resorted to this form of self-publication.) But Marsh argued that an unschooled printer typesetting a pamphlet was not the same thing as a scientific body receiving a research paper. "Printing is not publication," Marsh maintained.

Cope also wrote to Hayden for the money to publish his plates. "This attack is made on your survey as well as on me. Marsh told me that your collaborators are a 'bad lot' & I suppose he wants to make me appear like the rest!"[19]

Hayden now found himself in the sniper fire between Cope and Marsh. "I am afraid Cope is going to humbug me," he wrote to Leidy in late April. "He may come out all right, but there is some mischief brewing. I ought to have some hold on him. . . . You know what a mule head he is."[20]

Marsh also had a rebuttal in the May *Naturalist* to Cope's "Gigantic Mammals" article, arguing that it contained "no new facts, but some interesting additions to the long list of errors."[21] The Yale professor insisted that *Eobasileus,* based on a photograph provided to him by Harvard's Louis Agassiz, was merely a *Tinoceras grandis* Marsh.

The Harvard professor, like Baird, had reasons for courting Marsh. Agassiz was building the Museum of Comparative Zoology in Cambridge, but Harvard had no notable vertebrate paleontologist and, as a result, no specimens of the fabulous animals being discovered in the West. Agassiz desperately wanted some of those specimens. "No great museum can be without at least some of the most curious types you have discovered," he admitted to Marsh.[22] (Harvard twice offered Marsh professorships, but he turned them down.)

In that same letter, Agassiz pointed out that Harvard and Yale had actually been the only two bidders in the sale of the German specimen, the Eichstädt pterodactyl. "I am sorry you paid such a stupendous price for it. You might have just as well have obtained it for half the price . . . for I was your only competition," he told Marsh. It had cost Marsh one thousand dollars. Why, if only Harvard and Yale had cooperated.

Agassiz was seeking specimens from Marsh, offering to pay for them. He even suggested that his preparer come down to New Haven and make plaster casts of some of the notable fossil specimens—Harvard would foot the bill—and the two universities would share the casts. But Marsh was apparently reluctant to send fossils to Cambridge, although he did offer Agassiz a tapir skeleton.

So Agassiz was happy to pass along the photographs of *Eobasileus* to Marsh as a gesture of friendship and solidarity. "You are welcome of keep the photographs of Prof. Cope's as long they are of any use to you," Agassiz assured him.

"I have read your reply to his explanation," Agassiz continued. "It is sharp, but he deserves to be treated with even more severity. Your cutting words read like the expression of an honest man who has been wronged."[23]

In that same letter, Agassiz made a pitch for getting at least a piece of Marsh's upcoming 1873 expedition.

"I have long wished for occasion to show you how I truly sympathize with your work & how glad I would be to cooperate. Your statement that you start for the west gives me such a chance. Extensive as your means must be . . . I take it for granted more means would not be objectionable. So I now make the following proposition, if acceptable. I have no desire of acquiring specimens for the sake of describing and publishing, all I am aiming at is to accumulate materials in the museum."

Poor Agassiz, he didn't stand a chance. If Marsh wouldn't let Yale's future president into his treasure room, what odds did a Harvard professor have? Besides, Marsh's goal was to make the Peabody Museum—not the Museum of Comparative Zoology—the greatest in the country.

There was, however, more than just the lust for specimens driving the sympathies and alliances. Baird, Agassiz, and Marsh were all institution builders, members of a growing professional cadre of scientists. They shared a vision of what science could and should be. For them, there was no future in the clubby, gentlemanly science of the society and the academy. Hadn't Cope's recent woes proved that?

In the May issue of the *Naturalist,* Cope responded to Marsh's charges in an article entitled "On Some of Prof. Marsh's Criticisms." After a point-by-point rebuttal, Cope said that Marsh "knows perfectly well that my descriptions antedate his by a month and more, and he is posterior to Dr. Leidy, by at least two months. He is, however, not strong enough to state the nomenclature accordingly, but endeavors to prove something else."[24]

"To sum up the matter," Cope wrote, "it is plain that most of Prof. Marsh's criticism are misrepresentations . . . and his statements as to the dates of my papers are either criminally ambiguous or untrue. I might now proceed to characterize the effrontery of such proceedings in fitting terms, but forbear, believing that with a little change of scene the author of them will be glad to bury them in oblivion as is the writer of this notice."

It was wishful thinking. All Marsh wanted to bury was Cope. In May, Marsh had yet another article in the *Naturalist.* He contended that Cope had now revised and corrected much of his work, adopting "nearly all my views . . . as well as most of my corrections of his errors, although without giving credit in either case."[25] But Cope, Marsh insisted, "still misrepresents the structure of this group on several points and most of his dates are incorrect as before."

So obsessed was Marsh that he wrote to prominent scientists to see if they could confirm or deny Cope's dates. "In regard to the papers of Mr. Cope," James Hall replied from Albany, "I fear I cannot give you any satisfaction. I was absent from the end of July till the end of November. . . . I received nothing between the dates you mentioned." Still, Hall cautioned Marsh from making a judgment based on this "negative evidence."[26] The feud was spilling out menacingly all over scientific society.

A continent away, the personal feud was eclipsed by the tremendous value of the fossil discoveries—and both Cope and Marsh made sure to send their papers to the most influential scientists in Europe.

"I always felt that when Paleontology took root in 'the United States' the energy of your character would give an accelerated impulse to the progress of science," the great Richard Owen told Cope in a note of thanks for some papers. "But," he added, "I could not foresee that your virgin soil would be so productive of [such] strange—and what is better linking—forms."[27]

But Marsh would concede no compliments. He had his teeth sunk deep in Cope and would not let go. He wrote a rebuttal to Cope's rebuttal. But the editors of the *Naturalist* had had quite enough, and in the June edition, they ran this notice:

> "We regret that Professors Marsh and Cope have considered it necessary to carry their controversy to the extent that they have. Wishing to maintain the perfect independence of the *Naturalist* in all matters involving scientific criticism, we have allowed both parties to have their full say, but feeling that now the controversy between the authors in question has come to be a personal one and that the *Naturalist* is not called upon to devote further space to its consideration, the continuance of the subject will be allowed only in the form of an appendix at the expense of the author."[28]

Marsh paid for a nine-page appendix in that June issue, his longest, most caustic attack. He called Cope's May article "a slcight-of-hand performance with names and dates" and a "tangled web of misstatements and misrepresentations." He went on to rebut and reject every statement, every piece of evidence, every defense Cope had offered up. He ridiculed Cope's ability as a paleontologist, dredging up *Elasmosaurus platyrus.* "After the investigation of a very perfect specimen for months, he placed the *head on the end of the tail,* and restored the animal in the position as the type of a new order," Marsh taunted.

"Prof. Cope's errors will continue to invite correction," Marsh continued, "but these, like his blunders, are hydra-headed, and life is really too short to spend valuable time in such an ungracious task.

"The present controversy," he concluded, "was forced upon me by Prof. Cope's misstatements and mistakes, which I had borne for years in silence, if not with equanimity."[29]

Although he had been relentless and quite merciless, Marsh could ring no concessions from Cope, even though the battle had surely taken its toll. In the July issue of the *Naturalist,* Cope offered his final rebuttal, also in a paid appendix. It was a brief, one-paragraph statement: "The recklessness of assertion, the erroneousness of statement and the incapacity of comprehending our relative positions, on the part of Prof. Marsh render further discussion on the trivial matters upon which we disagree unnecessary; and my time is too fully occupied on more important subjects to permit me to waste it upon personal affairs which are already sufficiently before the public. Professor M. has recorded his views 'oere prenne,' and may continue to do so without personal notice by E.D. Cope."[30]

Through the entire battle, Cope continued to turn out papers and articles on a wide range of other topics, for he simply could not rein in his active and curious mind, which danced over subjects as varied as the intelligence of monkeys, the coloration of fishes, life on the plains, and the consequences of evolution.

While this war raged on, noticeably absent from the action was Leidy. Such a vengeful fight was clearly contrary to both his personal and professional approach to science. Leidy had been delighted with his trip to Fort Bridger, until he returned to Philadelphia and the brewing war between Cope and Marsh.

"I think I shall take another trip to the west next summer," Leidy told Hayden. "However, as Marsh and Cope are now working actively at the Bridger tertiary, to avoid the excitement of competition, I shall go no further with it."[31]

But poor Leidy could neither avoid the race nor keep the pace. "In my absence," he told Hayden, "Marsh has described many new species and genera, and I am told that Prof. Cope has descriptions of new species constantly being published to which I have no access. . . . You will perceive how many errors may be made.

"We have no doubt in some cases described the same things under different names and thus produced some confusion, which can only be corrected in the future."

Try as he might, Leidy could not escape the battle. In April, Marsh wrote to him, complaining about one of his papers. "I am a little troubled about the dates of Cope's which you virtually adopt in your synopsis and fear you may decide the question by tacitly admitting them," Marsh said. The Yale professor suggested putting a question mark next to each of challenged dates.[32]

A few days later, Marsh was still lobbying for the question mark notation and added, "I hear that Cope's 'Reply Broadside' will come out in the Am. Naturalist for May. If he states anything that is not true or fair I shall go for him hard next time."[33]

Of course, putting a question mark next to Cope's dates was really endorsing Marsh, so Leidy tried to compromise by suggesting that it be noted that the dates were "disputed" by Marsh.[34]

But another reason that the Bridger battle pushed Leidy further away from paleontology was a financial one. Both Cope and Marsh were already spending large sums on exploration and the purchase of fossil material. As a university professor, with no other resources, Leidy simply didn't have the money to keep up.

"Formerly every fossil bone found in the States came to me, for nobody else cared to study such things," Leidy explained to a British colleague, "but now Professors Marsh and Cope, with long purses, offer money for what used to come to me for nothing, and in that respect, I cannot compete with them."[35]

It was obvious to those who had seen the competitors. "There's no use contending against the machinery Prof. M employs, i.e.—$'s and cts. His expeditions and his employees left in the field may reasonably be expected to clean up this country," Dr. Carter told Leidy.

For a few years, Leidy would try to keep up and then finally decide to withdraw from the field almost entirely and spend the remainder of his career studying tiny aquatic animals under a microscope.

There may have been another reason for Leidy's retreat: The very nature of the science was changing. Cope and Marsh were pushing the bounds of interpretation and publishing papers at a speed that was more attuned to Huxley than Leidy. The quiet, methodical, descriptive Lcidy approach had already come in for criticism. In any case, Leidy vacated his title as America's Owen and left it to Cope and Marsh to fight over the crown.

And speaking of fights, who really won the battle of the Bridger Basin?

Assessing the combat with the long lens of historical perspective, University of North Carolina paleontologist Walter Wheeler calculated that "from August 1872 to June 1873 Cope and Marsh each published 16 different articles on *Uintathere*. Neither one paid any attention to the priority of the other's scientific names, and they both virtually ignored the priority of Leidy's. The result was nomenclatural chaos."[36]

Nevertheless, Leidy's name was first, and the beast is now called a *Uintathere*. It turned out that both Leidy and Marsh had obtained specimens of *Uintatherium* from the lower Eocene beds. But Cope's animal came from the geologically younger Wasatch Basin—which is upper Eocene—and so eight to ten million years separated Cope's animal from Marsh's animal.

Cope's specimen was a more developed, larger species. It was, in fact, the largest of all the uintatheres, and, as such, it retained the name *Eobasileus*. Much of the arguing and confusion came from the fact that Cope and Marsh thought they had the same species, when they didn't.

Marsh's name for the beasts—*Dinoceras*—was clearly late, what taxonomists call a junior synonym. But as in the cases of fossil horses and birds, Marsh displayed a penchant for collecting, and only he gathered enough fossil remains over the years—more than two hundred individuals—to write a comprehensive monograph on the animals. His 1884 *Dinocerata* ran 237 pages and included fifty-six lithographs and two hundred woodcuts.

"During the Mesozoic period, all the mammals appeared to have been small, and it is not probable that any of large size existed, as reptilian life then reigned supreme," Marsh wrote. "With the dawn of the tertiary a new era began, and mammalian life first found the conditions for its full and rapid development. . . . *Dinoceras* and its allies, in the middle Eocene, were much larger, and were clearly the monarchs of the region in which they lived."

The reason for their disappearance, for a Darwinian like Marsh, was "not difficult to find." He suspected that their "small brain, highly specialized character and huge bulk rendered them incapable of adapting themselves to new conditions. . . . Smaller mammals with large brains and more plastic structure readily adapted themselves to their environment and survived or even sent off new lines."[37]

In deference to this massive work, Marsh's name, Dinocerata, is used in some modern classifications as a group name for uintatheres, although the genus it was based on, *Dinoceras,* is never used. Marsh was also right about the uintathere's trunk—or lack thereof. The animal simply didn't have one.

Lost in the heat of battle over this single fossil was the fact that once again Cope and Marsh had done much to exhume not just a few species, but an entire ancient habitat. For just as they had reconstructed the Cretaceous seashore that once was Kansas, now they had rediscovered the humid, lush forests of subtropical, Eocene Wyoming, a land of lions, camels, crocodiles, rhinos, and turtles as big as grizzly bears.

✣

The fight in the journals had run right into the 1873 collecting season, and Cope, Marsh, and Leidy were all making plans to return to the West.

Marsh had rustled up a party of thirteen students. His plan was to return to Fort McPhearson and, once again, head through the Sand Hills to search the Niobrara River valley, the region denied to him two years earlier by a Sioux wildfire. Then they would head for Fort Bridger.

Cope was planning to ride the new Northern Pacific Railroad, yet another rail line pushing west, out into the Dakota badlands. But the menace of Sioux was palpable that year. "I do not know that I shall get West this summer," Cope lamented to his father in May. "Hayden objects to the expense of sending me . . . but he is a wire puller, and I suspect other reasons. I can never rely upon him." Cope still had his wagon, harness, horse, and two mules at Fort Bridger. "So," he said, "that part of the cost is already defrayed."[38]

Cope lobbied Hayden, telling him that a full-scale expedition was essential and that he was "compelled to employ the manner of Prof. Marsh. It is useless to compete with him successfully without *money.*"[39]

Hayden did ante up $250 for the season, but instead of the Dakotas, Cope went to Greeley, Colorado, about forty miles north of Denver. From there, he headed east across the northern plains of the territory—this was the very same region in which Marsh made his 1870 badlands discovery. In early July, Cope was just one hundred miles southwest of Marsh's party in Nebraska.

Cope, like Marsh, found titanothere fossils, including a new species he dubbed *symbrodon.* Cope had a small party of hired men, but no military escort. "Without the good effects of Grant's peace policy [with the Indians] the exploration I do not hesitate to say could not have been made," Cope wrote to his father.[40]

When Ulysses S. Grant had become president a year earlier, he had set no great goals for his administration or the nation. He would administer the laws—whether he agreed with them or not—and pay the national debt, in gold if need be. The only issue he stepped forward on was a call for a new, less militaristic, less exploitative Indian policy.

"The proper treatment of the original occupants of this land—the Indians—is one deserving of careful study," he announced in his first inaugural address. "I will favor any course toward them which tends to their civilization and ultimate citizenship."

Grant's policy of appeasement and negotiation—which included replacing politically appointed Indian agents, mainly spoilsmen and entrepreneurs, with representatives of religious missionary groups—played well in the East, where people were war weary, reluctant to finance the military, and increasingly sympathetic to the plight of the "noble savage."

Out west, homesteaders, politicians, army officers, Sitting Bull, and quite a few other Indians remained dubious about Grant's policy. Still, Cope thought it was safe enough to have Annie join him for a few weeks while he went fossil hunting.

But even though Cope had come to Colorado in search of fossils, his sharp eye could not help but take in all forms of nature and life—even tiny animals living in a rain puddle. He found that rain pools lasting only a few days on the Kansas and Colorado prairie teemed with worms, small crustaceans, insect larvae and adults. In a single puddle, no deeper than a foot or longer than thirty feet, he counted three species of worms, six insects, eight crustaceans, and one spider.

"The insects," he reported in a paper on the subject, included "a bluish fly . . . a slender beetle . . . [and a] cosmopolitan boatman who swims on his back, the hemipterous notonecta."[41]

Meanwhile, up on the Niobrara, Marsh was collecting more Pliocene mammals, especially fossil horses. The trek through the Sand Hills had once again been hard. One day, the party was left wet and bruised by a ferocious hailstorm. After twelve days of collecting, Marsh headed back to the Fort McPhearson and boarded the train for western Wyoming.

From his camp on Pawnee Creek, near the Wyoming border, Cope made his way up to the Union Pacific tracks to catch the train at Pine Bluffs for a quick trip to Cheyenne for supplies and mail. When the train pulled into Cheyenne and the passengers got out of the coaches, Cope looked down the platform, and there was Marsh. He was, Cope reported to his father, "running about in great excitement. . . . He is said to be going west to Bridger."[42]

The Yale party reached Fort Bridger on July 25 and spent ten days collecting around Grizzly Buttes and Henry's Fork. They harvested five tons of material. "Among its prizes were a perfect *Dinoceras* skull," one of the students reported. Then it was on to Salt Lake City, where they received an unexpectedly cordial welcome—and a special interview with Brigham Young himself.

"After the conversation opened, Brigham Young bent his inquiries especially to the subject of fossil horses," according to a *New York Tribune* story.
"He made it a point to ascertain minutely where fossil remains of the horse
family were found; he asked particularly as to the facts respecting this peculiar group. . . . When at length his curiosity on all these points was satisfied,
Brigham Young explained its cause. Some years ago, during a public discussion in London, the point was raised against the authority of the Book
of Mormon, as revelation, that it spoke of horses existing in America in the
prehistoric era. . . . It is well known that there were no horses in this country at the time of its discovery, and that the Spanish first introduced these
animals.

"So it seems that while most theologians are regarding the developments
of the natural sciences with fear and trembling, the chiefs of the Mormon
religion are prepared to hail the discoveries of paleontology as an aid to their
peculiar belief. . . .

"And thus Prof. Marsh, one of the warmest advocates of the development
theory, is raised to the ranks of defender of the faith."[43] Young gave Marsh
a Bible as a memento of their meeting.

From Salt Lake City, some of the students went to the John Day Basin in
Oregon to collect fossils. The group reunited in San Francisco and headed
east, with a brief stop in Kansas. They returned to New Haven in the late fall
with forty-nine crates of fossils.

Meanwhile, after collecting on the northern plains, Cope had gone
south to Pueblo, Colorado, and then finally in early October, about the
time the Yale Party was in Kansas, he reached Fort Bridger. A check for two
hundred dollars from his father was waiting for him. He was also able to
finally sell his stock and wagon. He spent several days collecting and got
some valuable material. "Among others," he told his father, "another cra-
nium of *Loxolophodon cornutum.*"[44]

"I find Marsh at a discount out here where his manners have produced
the same impression they have back East," Cope wrote in the same letter.
The two men remained very much in each other's thoughts. Marsh, it
seems, continually fretted about Cope's whereabouts and activities.

"I know nothing of Cope," Dr. Carter reported to Marsh in August. "A
letter in his hand writing reached here five days ago addressed to Sam
Smith . . . addressed from Greeley, Colo. I scarcely think he intends coming
here."[45] But Carter was "able to learn" that his instructions to Smith
focused on the Bitter Creek region.

Marsh had again hired Smith and Chew to collect for him that summer
in the basin, and Carter served as Marsh's agent. In November, Carter tal-

lied up the bill for the summer's work. It came to $2,218.51. It was so detailed that it listed items such as two pairs of moccasins for $4.50 and the purchase of pears ($0.60), jam ($0.75), and coffee ($0.50).[46]

Leidy also spent July at Fort Bridger, but he reported to Hayden that his trip, unlike the "eminently successful" expeditions of Cope and Marsh, hadn't been particularly fruitful. Leidy had met Cope in Denver. "He told me he had explored a new field east of Denver and south of the U.P.R.R. and had discovered a multitude of fine fossils," Leidy wrote.[47]

But Cope's behavior and attitude clearly bothered Leidy, who complained to his friends at Fort Bridger that Cope was "overzealous in science and does no scruple to take advantage of his opportunities."

❧

At the outset of the summer, Cope had considered riding the new Northern Pacific Railway to the Dakota badlands, but by September the Northern Pacific had ground to a halt and was on the verge of financial collapse, and the entire economy of the nation was tottering. The reason—the Franco-Prussian War.

Back in the summer of 1871, when Marsh was on his first expedition and the war in Europe had just broken out, a cavalry soldier in North Platte, Nebraska, had declared with "forcible profanity" how little he cared about some foreign war. But what he and everyone else had learned by late 1873 was that the nations of the world were now more closely knit than ever before. Incredible as it was, a German siege of Paris was now affecting American railroads, western settlers, and Sioux Indians, not to mention the American economy. It even determined where paleontologists went looking for fossils. Yes, the world was more tightly hitched and firmly cinched than ever.

The day the crash of 1873 began—September 18—could hardly have started more agreeably. After spending the night at Jay Cooke's fifty-two-room Philadelphia mansion, Ogontz, President Grant breakfasted on eggs and kippers with his host and returned to Washington. Cooke, one of the great financiers of the day, went to the offices of Cooke and Company.

It was Cooke who helped finance the Union effort in the Civil War by brokering bonds abroad. The war had left Cooke a wealthy and honored man. Why, when somebody was really rich, folks would say he's "as rich as Jay Cooke."[48]

After the war, Cooke switched to financing a second transcontinental railroad, the Northern Pacific. Building railroads demanded huge quantities of money, more money than was to be had domestically, particularly with the federal government still struggling with Civil War debts. So Cooke aggressively marketed railroad bonds in Europe, and the money poured in. By 1890, roughly a third of all American railroad stocks and bonds would be held by Europeans.

The outbreak of the Franco-Prussian War, however, forced a large number of German investors to redeem their bonds. At the same time, interest rates in England rose, putting further pressure on the American market.

The Northern Pacific had millions of dollars in overdrafts when the run on the bonds started. Then rumors of Northern Pacific mismanagement bubbled to the surface. The run turned into a stampede. Just before eleven o'clock on the morning of September 18, Cooke and Company shut its doors. By that afternoon, thirty-seven banks and brokerage houses in New York City had also closed.

By the end of the week, work on the Northern Pacific had stopped in the Dakota Territory, and as cash dried up, eighty-nine other railroads from Maine to California defaulted on their bonds. Five banks in Chicago went under, and within a few weeks, five thousand commercial businesses went bankrupt.

The crash of 1873 lead to a depression that dogged the country for the rest of the decade, leaving three million unemployed, breadlines in New York and Boston, farmers burning unsold crops, and doctors and lawyers forced to cut their fees by half.

The building of the Northern Pacific had been creating new pressures and tensions with the Sioux. At first, War Department officials thought the default would at least reduce the strain and buy them some time for dealing with the problem. But instead it created an atmosphere in which Indian resentment would build and find focus in leaders like Sitting Bull and Crazy Horse, and its ultimate expression at a place called the Little Bighorn.

Yes, it had come to the point where even in North Platte, Nebraska, one had to pay attention to distant wars fought by armies that couldn't speak English. As for Jay Cooke, he was forced to move from Ogontz to a tiny cottage.

⚜

Back east, the battle of words between Cope and Marsh continued to rage on and continued to draw other scientists into the fray. "Your note on Dinocerata came early this week and is already set up for an art. in the

October no., of the *Journal of Science,"* Dana wrote to Marsh in September.
But he warned Marsh, "I cannot give a full list of species without putting in
also all of Cope's and so making a muddle of it." Dana suggested that
Marsh included "only a few of the prominent types."[49]

In the midst of the duel, Buffalo Bill and his Wild West show arrived in
New Haven and played the Music Hall for two days. Bill tried to see
Marsh, even left a free ticket for him at the box office, but the two never
connected. "Should you visit Nebraska," Bill wrote in a good-bye note,
"call and see your old guide. Major North and myself are in the cattle business 60 miles north of North Platte on the Dismal River."[50]

Marsh's obsession with Cope continued on every front, as he now tried
to suppress Cope's papers for the Hayden Survey. Late in the year, Marsh
was pressing Hayden to muzzle Cope, and Hayden once again found himself navigating those dangerous shoals between the two paleontologists.
Marsh wrote a detailed, seven-page complaint. "I ask you only for simple
justice," he said.[51]

Writing from Washington, D.C., in early December—on Department of
the Interior stationery—Hayden carefully laid out his position.

> *I have consulted with Prof. Baird and Mr. S. H. Scudder who happened
> to be here and they both agreed with my own decision that I can do noth-
> ing in the case except where Prof. Cope uses personalities. I insisted on and
> obtained a promise to that effect, and I do not now know of a single per-
> sonal allusion to you that could be offensive in the report for 1873. As to
> dates, claims for species or discoveries, those matters should be settled by the
> parties and they will be undoubtedly in due time. I do not consider myself
> competent to decide disputed claims. . . . [Cope's] The Cretaceous of
> Kansas will appear first, but as long as he does not allude to you person-
> ally in an offensive way, I can do nothing. If he claims your species you
> must reclaim them and present your evidence.*
>
> *Prof. Cope is one of the collaborators of the Survey, you are not, and
> have refused to become such though requested by me to become so many
> times within the last three years. You call upon me to decide against Cope
> in a matter which Cope claims to be as much in the right as yourself, and
> which must be settled by experts. Gill and Leidy should take the matter
> up and investigate all the circumstances and their opinions placed on paper
> would forever settle the difficulty. I am sorry, of course, but the above view
> is the only one I could take under the circumstances. . . .*
>
> *Now in this matter you must take any course you see fit. My course is
> as plain as anything can be. Your disputed scientific claims must be wholly*

settled between yourselves (Cope and Marsh) and such experts as you can agree on. There is no need for haste so far as the other publications are concerned. The whole affair is a struggle in which I wish you well, but can do nothing more than I have done.

Sincerely,
F. V. Hayden[52]

Cope might have seen Hayden as a "coward" and a "wire puller," but Hayden had backed him up. Of course, if Marsh had agreed to collaborate with Hayden's survey, the story might have been different, with Cope joining Newberry, Hall, and Leidy as a Hayden castoff. But now the two men were allies, and as far as Marsh was concerned, those that gave aid and comfort to his enemies were enemies as well. Hayden had become a target, and when Marsh got a clear shot, he would take it.

Knowledgeable scientists sympathized with Hayden. "Cope is a man of great learning & ability and were he not in so burning haste would always do splendid work," Dana told Hayden in the fall of 1873. But he assured him that he had been right to use Cope for his survey.[53]

"Marsh could [do] no service to you," Dana wrote. "I wish they would stop their race and work quietly. I have told Marsh more than once that it would do more for his reputation among zoologists to describe one species thoroughly than to be the one to *name* a hundred. . . . Insufficient descriptions make an earnest zoologist curse American science."[54]

Still, Marsh was haunted by Cope and fretted about his success in the West. He had hired another collector, Ervin Devendorf from Greeley, to cover pretty much the same Colorado territory Cope had explored and was constantly badgering Devendorf, fearful of Cope's coming away with something good.

"You mentioned *Cope's* getting 8 or 9 of those large heads are you *positive* that he did. I myself rather doubt it," Devendorf tried to assure Marsh on December 12.[55]

A few days later, he wrote to Marsh: "I have been making inquiries as regards Cope's successes. . . . Found you were misinformed by someone. . . . Cope said last summer that he had knowledge in Nevada, Wyoming and the grounds where *we* were this fall. . . . I discerned *marks* distinctly made I presume by Cope, so I judged he could strike certain places next spring. Those marks are now defaced by the sole of my boot, but I know where they were."[56]

Chapter Eight

ON APRIL 22, 1874, Marsh received a telegram from John Newberry. It read, "Elected triumphantly to the Academy today." A few days later, Marsh received an official letter from Theodore Gill, a zoologist and assistant librarian at the Smithsonian, informing him that at its spring meeting, he had been elected—almost unanimously—as a member of the National Academy of Sciences.

It was, on the one hand, an honor. All the top scientists—Hall, Dana, Hayden, Meek, Newberry, Leidy, and Cope—were members. But on the other, it really didn't mean much, for the academy was a moribund, and some might say bogus, body.

The academy had been the pet project of the "Lazzaroni," an exclusive and informal scientific coterie that reigned from the 1840s to the end of the Civil War. The Lazzaroni—the name was used to describe Neapolitan beggars and riffraff—included Henry, Dana, Agassiz, and the brilliant Harvard mathematician Benjamin Pierce. The group's ringleader was Alexander Dallas Bache—the superintendent of the U.S. Coast and Geodetic Survey and the great-grandson of Benjamin Franklin. In 1828, Bache had, at the age of twenty-two, become professor of natural history at the University of Pennsylvania, and fifteen years later, with Henry's help, he took over the coastal survey—one of the major federal scientific agencies. In turn, four years after that, Bache was instrumental in getting his good friend Henry his position at the Smithsonian.

The Lazzaroni's stated aim was "to eat an outrageously good dinner together." But the subtext was to set American science policy. The "Lazzaroni agenda" included developing scientific standards to separate "charlatans" from "real working men of science"; raising the status of scientists; increasing support; recruiting good men; and enlisting government in the cause.[1]

One desire they nursed was for a more elite group to counter the American Association for the Advancement of Science—an organization that anyone, anyone at all, could join. On a visit to England, Henry had been impressed by the "aristocratical" nature of the British association. It was run,

Henry noted, by "those who have some reputation for science. . . . The great body of the members have no voice."

But it was precisely that kind of scientific elitism that engendered suspicion among congressmen and Americans in general. So perhaps it wasn't surprising that it was late at night, during the closing, chaotic hours of the 1863 congressional session, with the nation in the throes of a Civil War, that a bill creating the National Academy of Sciences, legislation masterminded by Bache, slipped through both houses.

The legislation created an academy of fifty members that would, at the request of the government, "investigate, examine and report upon any question of science or art." Any future openings in the academy would be filled by a vote of its members. The Lazzaroni had created its self-perpetuating, elite club, with Bache, of course, as its president.

At the time, there were not many scientists in America. *The Dictionary of American Biography* listed only 370 in 1876, but perhaps that made selection or exclusion from the academy's fifty that much more intense. Baird wasn't a charter member because Agassiz was displeased with him. George Bond, the director of the Harvard Observatory, was blackballed by Gould, Pierce, and Bache. Cope became a member soon after returning to the States from Europe, but Marsh—still pretty much unpublished—had to wait.

After the first meeting of the academy, Leidy, who was a charter member, wrote to Hayden saying that the body "appears to me to be nothing more than the formation of an illiberal clique, based on Plymouth Rock." In another letter, Leidy called it "a grand humbug."[2]

The scientists might have had their elite academy, but that didn't necessarily mean the government was much impressed. Other than advising the administration on some wartime technology, the National Academy of Sciences had not been asked to do anything of consequence for more than a decade, and its only published works were a few memoirs by members. When Bache died in 1867, the academy might have died with him.

But Henry—in deference to Bache's memory—took on the presidency, and he set about reorienting the academy from the role of policy adviser to an organization promoting research by issuing grants and prizes funded by a legacy Bache had left the academy. Henry also slowly began to increase the size of the group—despite the resistance of his Lazzaroni friends. By the end of the 1870s, membership had doubled to one hundred. "His cautious policies had saved the organization and allowed new blood to enter it at the cost of its position as an active adviser to government," said science historian A. Hunter Dupree.[3]

And so Marsh was now poised to become one of the select. Although even here the tensions of the paleontology wars surfaced. Two days before his election, Marsh received a note from Hayden in Washington.

"Your name is being used extensively here at this time by certain parties to sanction a statement that the survey of which I have charge is a fraud, etc. It is working to your disadvantage. Is the use of your name in such a connection authorized by you? Please write or telegraph me on receipt of this at my expense. I wish to make use of your reply for your own good."[4]

Hayden was thin-skinned and insecure enough to fret about bad words behind his back at any time. But that spring was a particularly difficult time. By 1874, the federal government was funding six different surveys. There were two geological surveys under the Army Corps of Engineers. The Interior Department had two civilian geological surveys (Hayden's and Powell's), plus a civilian homestead land-parceling survey. The U.S. Coast and Geodetic Survey, under the Treasury Department, was developing detailed maps of the nation's coastline.

There had even been clashes between surveying parties. Lieutenant George M. Wheeler, head of the army's survey, had accused Hayden of poaching on his land in the Arkansas River basin. The two surveys collided again in Colorado. Hayden's and the other War Department's survey, being conducted along the fortieth parallel by Clarence King, also overlapped in Utah. John Wesley Powell noted that he and Wheeler duplicated work along the Colorado River.

At a congressional hearing that spring on the state of the surveys, the competition exploded into a sharp rancorous exchange between Hayden and Wheeler. The outburst was so bad that the chairman of the Committee on Public Lands chided both men for "ill-judged and hasty expressions which good taste would have withheld."

Wheeler presented one deposition that quoted Hayden saying that if Wheeler engaged in "attempts to interfere with me or my survey in any way, I will utterly crush him—and I have enough Congressional influence to do so, and I will bring it to bear."[5]

Powell testifying at the same hearing was more measured, but he noted that Wheeler had gone over an estimated twenty-six thousand square miles of Colorado River territory already done by his survey.

Both Cope and Marsh were linked to the surveys because of their interests in western fossils. Cope had become a valued scientist for Hayden, but he would also use the resources of Wheeler's survey. Marsh was already receiving specimens from both Powell and King.

There was, however, a growing feeling in Washington that the surveys should be reformed. Some in Congress simply wanted to cut costs. Others mainly wanted to improve the surveys. "We are inviting thousands of foreigners to come here," Joseph Henry said in an address to the National Academy of Sciences, "and we ought to be able to tell them what we have to offer." But that would mean that somebody's survey was going to be shut down. It was in this atmosphere that Hayden heard that Marsh was reportedly bad-mouthing his operation.

It isn't clear what kind of response Hayden anticipated, but it is fair to say that it wasn't the missile hurled back at him from New Haven, for Marsh sat down, grabbed a pencil, and angrily scrawled a reply.

"Your letter of the 20th came duly, and I regretted extremely to receive it. Your language could admit of only one interpretation, and that was an implied threat, that if I did not at once endorse your survey, I should suffer for it at the Academy. As no personal considerations whatever, could induce me to yield in such a case, I made no reply, leaving it for you to act as you saw fit. As the Academy will probably adjourn before this reaches you, I now answer your letter, with the same candor, but hardly with kind feelings, that I should have done had you written me a straightforward letter about the rumors you allude to."[6]

Hayden did not vote against Marsh's candidacy to the academy. Still, the battle lines were becoming more pronounced. The vote was thirty-seven to one. The lone opponent to Marsh's membership was Cope.

In the meantime, Hayden was gathering support from the scientific community for his survey, warning that it would be "crushed out" under the military. "I received a splendid memorial from Yale College," he told Leidy, "signed by all the Professors . . . except Marsh."[7]

The science community wanted a reformed survey in the hands of civilians, like Hayden or Powell, but Grant, being an old soldier, was reluctant to deal the army out of the business. "The President has leaned strongly toward the War Department . . . ," Hayden told Leidy. "It is a case of life and death for the survey. The struggle is a desperate one. Now is the time for scientific friends to indicate what they will do. . . . Marsh is working the other way."[8]

But Grant's backing of the army against the push by reformers and scientists for a civilian survey led to a political stalemate, and that was the end of reforming the surveys.

✤

Summer was now approaching and with it another collecting season. Cope hopped from Hayden to Lieutenant Wheeler and arranged to tag along with one of his mapping parties in New Mexico. This was virgin territory, a part of the country not yet explored by Leidy or Marsh. There were other reasons for changing surveys. "The points Hayden had in view are too near the hostile Indians to be safe," he explained to his father.[9]

Marsh had considered making a trip into the Dakota badlands and had gotten the support of E. P. Smith, the commissioner of Indians Affairs. Smith even wrote to Spotted Tail, a chief at the Whetstone Indian Agency, to explain that some of the Great Father's "white children want very much to learn about the buffalo and other great animals, which used to range over the hills and valleys. . . . They want to find some of the bones of these animals. . . . The teacher of these white children whose name is Professor Marsh has told the Great Father than they cannot learn about these things without coming out upon the plains."[10]

But Marsh was now much too busy in New Haven to go west. The Peabody Museum was finally under construction, and he and his Yale students had already gathered so much material over the past four years that it demanded sorting.

Besides, boxes were still coming in pell-mell. After losing his professorship at the Kansas State Agricultural College in a political fight, Benjamin Mudge had become a full-time collector for Marsh. Marsh would finance Mudge with one thousand dollars in 1874 and in return would receive thirty large boxes of fossils from Kansas.[11]

In July, George Custer invited Marsh to accompany him on an expedition into the Black Hills of Dakota, but Marsh passed. Instead, he sent George Bird Grinnell.

Then in the fall came a letter, an enticing letter, from General Ord. He wrote to Marsh saying that "a vast deposit of fossil remains of extinct marine and other animals has been discovered ten miles north of the Red Cloud Agency covering an area six miles square."[12] The bones were just lying there across an immense stretch of the plains. Marsh was persuaded to make a quick trip for a quick look. He had little idea of the maelstrom of politics, prejudice, corruption, and violence he was about to enter. For unlike Cope, who had steered clear of Indian territory, Marsh was heading into its very heart.

From the time Marsh got off the train at Cheyenne, the news was ominous and as he rode to Fort Laramie, it got no better. Times were bad at the Red Cloud Agency. There was trouble in the Dakotas.

Just two weeks earlier the agency had been in turmoil over the "the flag pole incident." The Indian agent, J. J. Saville, had ordered his men to erect a flagpole in the agency stockade. But the Sioux protested, saying that they did not want an American flag flying at their agency, on their land. This was not an army post. Saville paid little attention to the complaint.

The next day, however, a band of braves appeared in the compound—armed and covered with war paint. When the agency men went to work on the pole, the braves let out war hoops, scared away the laborers, and set upon the flagpole with axes and tomahawks, chopping it to pieces. One of the agency clerks quickly rode to nearby Fort Robinson for help.

Lieutenant Emmet Crawford was dispatched with twenty-six men. But by the time he arrived at the agency, there was a huge crowd of several hundred braves facing his detachment, yelling and firing guns into the air.

Crawford and his men advanced while the Sioux encircled them. The army unit was close to being overwhelmed by the crowd, when some of the Sioux formed a wall between their tribesmen and the soldiers, enabling the cavalrymen to withdraw to the stockade, where they waited until the crowd disbanded.

On November 4, Marsh arrived at the agency with several wagons, a detachment of soldiers, and four officers, who had volunteered to help search for fossils—a testimonial to how popular fossil hunting had become. He arrived the very day a critical council of chiefs was under way.

The Marsh party pulled up to the agency compound—eleven rough-hewn buildings surrounded by a ten-foot-high stockade—which sat on the banks of the narrow, serpentine White River. The compound was dominated by a large barn and warehouse. All around, the plains were dotted with clusters of teepees, thousands of teepees. "The whole vicinity was alive with Indians, their families, and their ponies . . . ," according to one press account. "It was impossible to move even a few paces without encountering Indians. Indians were everywhere."[13]

The tribes of the reservation had gathered for the annual disbursement of goods. But the atmosphere hadn't cooled since the flagpole incident, and the day Marsh arrived, the council of chiefs rejected a Bureau of Indian Affairs demand for a census of the Sioux. Saville warned that rations for the tribes would be withheld until they capitulated.

Saville had tried to count lodges when he first arrived at the agency a year earlier, but a band of braves blocked his way and briefly held him hostage. The braves said he was under "arrest." This time, the chiefs had held council for a week before calling Saville in to give him a dressing-down. The agent replied that there would be no beef, no flour, no tobacco, nothing, if there was no census. Considering everything that had happened since he had arrived in August of 1873, it was with some apprehension that Saville delivered this ultimatum. Expecting trouble, he sent a message to the commandant of the neighboring army post, asking him how many soldiers he had on hand.

All Marsh wanted was safe passage to the Dakota badlands, some sixty miles to the northeast, for a few days' collecting. This, however, was not going to be a simple request, for the paleontologist had unwittingly walked into the middle of a conflict that had been festering for six years—a struggle pitting the Sioux against the Indian Bureau, the white settlers, the railroads, and the army.

The area of interest to Marsh—the sprawling, desolate White River badlands—was not technically tribal land, for not even the Sioux wanted it. But it was close enough to Sioux territory, and times were tense enough, that Saville urged Marsh to get both the permission of the council of chiefs and a Sioux escort for his collecting trip.

Saville called the council together, and Marsh put his case to the chiefs, who were immediately suspicious. Collecting old bones in the badlands as winter threatened to sweep across the plains? It sounded far-fetched. What seemed more likely was that Marsh was planning to slip into the nearby Black Hills to look for gold. That was something the white man would do.

One chief, White Tail, jumped up, interrupted Marsh, and delivered a long litany of the abuses and misfortunes the Sioux had suffered, and flat out accused the Yale professor of being a gold thief. Undaunted, Marsh, speaking through an interpreter, did his best to ease the chiefs' fears. He tried to assure them that bones were all he was interested in, that he would pay for the services of the Sioux braves who accompanied him. Sitting Bull, who was at the council, even though he wasn't a reservation chief, proposed that the braves each be paid $5 a day. After some bargaining, Marsh agreed to $1.50 a day, which was still 50 percent more than the daily rate Cope had paid his men in the Bridger Basin.[14]

Marsh also said he would serve as an emissary for the tribes, taking their complaints about the Indian agency back to federal officials in Washington. It seemed Marsh had won the day. It was agreed that the party would leave the next morning.

But it snowed the following day, and with the snow came a change in the Sioux. The departure was delayed, and in the next few days—facing the harsh realities of winter—the tribes capitulated, and the census was done, revealing that twelve thousand Ogalala Sioux were now gathered on the banks of the White River. Camped north of the river, not far from the agency, but outside its orbit, were another three thousand "northern" Minoconjous, Sans Arcs, and Hunkpaps. While refusing to live on a reservation, these tribes, led by chiefs such as Sitting Bull and Crazy Horse, were not adverse to showing up when supplies were distributed and getting some of the Great Father's gifts. (The Indian bureau estimated that there were a total of fifty-three thousand Sioux in 1874, with seven thousand to ten thousand thought to be hostile.)

When the weather cleared, Marsh was ready to start and arrived at the agency with his wagons, military escort, and fossil-hunting army officers. But the sight of the soldiers, coupled with lingering bad feelings over the census and inferior rations, left the Ogalala restive and undermined Marsh's agreement.

A throng of Sioux braves carrying rifles and revolvers massed around the party and its wagons. One of the chiefs blocking Marsh's path was Sitting Bull, who told him the Ogalala braves were afraid to go because of the northern tribes across the river. Red Cloud, perhaps trying to save face, once again accused Marsh of seeking gold. The charge drew shouts from the crowd. "The white men are going into our country to find gold," shouted Chief Little Crow. "We must stop them at once." The women and children in the crowd scattered as guns were drawn. Any attempt to move forward would now set off gunfire.

A badly rattled Saville, who in the last year had seen his brother-in-law and a cavalry office killed by Sioux, urged Marsh and his party to leave the agency as fast as they could. The wagons and the soldiers retreated to Fort Robinson, about a mile and a half down the road. They were followed all the way back by a swarm of Sioux that pinned them in on both sides of the trail. Marsh was frustrated, but there was no simple solution.

The Yale professor had walked into a thicket of problems that were supposed to have been settled by the 1868 treaty between the U.S. government and the Sioux nation. The treaty, however, had begun to unravel almost as soon as it was signed. The agreement had given all of South Dakota west of the Missouri River to the Sioux as a "permanent reservation." This included the sacred Black Hills, which were absolutely off limits to white settlers. The region north of the North Platte River and the Bighorn Mountains was called "unceded Indian territory." The Sioux maintained that this still-disputed land stretched all the way to the Yellowstone River in Wyoming.

There was a bitter argument among the tribal chiefs as to how they would respond to the treaty. Sitting Bull, Crazy Horse, and Gall led thousands of Sioux who refused to abide by the terms and continued to roam the plains, particularly in the area around the Powder and Little Bighorn Rivers. These "northern" Sioux remained free, obstinate, and combative, engaging in skirmishes with army patrols, railroad-surveying teams, and settlers.

Red Cloud, however, had already waged an unsuccessful war against the white soldiers, and he dutifully led his and allied tribes to the new reservations, where they would be recipients of government aid. But the move proved no solution for Red Cloud's tribe.[15]

After the Civil War, white settlers felt that the Sioux's very presence was an impediment to progress, as well as a source of fear and hate. To many, the solution was simply to kill the Sioux and dissolve the Indian bureau. Dakota settlers paid bounties for Indian scalps, fed them poison bread, and organized Indian-hunting parties. The *Army & Navy Journal,* in an 1878 article titled "Governing the Indians," said, "The rough and ready settler looks upon the Redskins as varmin that ought to be exterminated."

Ignoring the treaty, the Dakota territorial legislative assembly passed a bill in 1872 calling for the Black Hills to be opened to settlers. The legislators sought Secretary of the Interior Columbus Delano's support. Delano, rather than pointing out that the United States had a sovereign treaty with the Sioux, simply indicated that if the Indians' acceptance could be won, Washington would go along with it.

Such an agreement was not forthcoming, but the idea of it incited the settlers to keep pushing. The Red Cloud Agency was first established in 1871 on the North Platte River near Fort Laramie in eastern Wyoming. Two years later, responding to complaints that the Sioux had too much land, the agency was relocated to the eastern corner of what is now Nebraska. It would be moved yet again, in another two years, to South Dakota.

The greatest pressure on the Sioux, however, came not from the government or the settlers, but from the railroads. One of the goals of the 1868 treaty was to keep the tribes well away from the Union Pacific Railroad to the south. By 1871, however, the new Northern Pacific Railway had pushed as far as Bismarck, and surveyors—with army protection—were moving steadily across the Dakotas, across Sioux territory.

It seemed there was nothing either the government or the Sioux could do about the ever-lengthening iron rails. Laying rails was the great American exercise of the second half of the nineteenth century. In 1850, there were 9,000 miles of track in the nation. Ten years later, the figure was 30,000, and by the 1880s, it had reached nearly 116,000 miles, with some eighteen thousand locomotives hauling fifteen billion tons of goods.

"Through its energetic railroad development, the country was producing real wealth as no country ever produced it before," proclaimed Charles Francis Adams Jr., the railroad reformer and president of the Union Pacific.

Of course, financing railroads was such an all-consuming effort that Adams's brother Henry, a Harvard historian and chronicler of the era, lamented that his generation was "already mortgaged to the railways, and no one knew better than the generation itself."

It wasn't, however, just a question of money and development. The railroad was the emblem of the time. "There is more poetry in the rush of a single railroad train across the continent than in all the gory story of the burning of Troy," wrote the western poet Joaquin Miller.

Even scientific discovery was dictated by the rails. It had been at Antelope Station, Nebraska, that Marsh had gotten his first "hat full" of western fossils, and for the next thirty years, names associated with the railroads, like Buffalo Park, Kansas, Golden, Colorado, and Como Bluff, Wyoming, would also be closely linked to paleontology. Neither the Sioux nor the *Brontosaurus* could withstand the railroads.

For the tribes of the plains, their fate was sealed even before the railroads brought settlers, for first came the buffalo hunters, who exterminated an estimated ten million bison roaming the prairies. The bison were wiped away to feed railroad work crews, to make the plains safe for speeding trains, and to enable the transformation of the land into farm fields. But as the buffalo vanished, so did the plains Indians' very way of life. What could the Sioux possibly do to stop such a force?

In the early 1870s, the federal government sent a delegation to persuade the tribes to allow the railroad to cross their territory and floated the idea of purchasing the Black Hills from the Sioux. The tribal chiefs were unanimous in their refusal. The delegation didn't believe this was a severe impediment, reporting back that the Indians would not be able to present any serious "combined resistance" as they had "neither ammunition nor subsistence to undertake a general war."

Still, the Sioux had won at least a brief respite from the "iron horse," thanks to the Franco-Prussian War, and those in the Grant administration trying to defuse tensions along the frontier also welcomed the hiatus. Yet it seemed that it was impossible to untangle the western plains from the industrial economy and speculative markets. One result of the depression that followed the crash of 1873 was a craving for more gold to meet debt payments—particularly to foreign investors—in "specie." And that, once again, would prompt white men to eye Sioux territory.

George Armstrong Custer contributed mightily to this problem. In August of 1874, he was dispatched from Fort Abraham Lincoln, on the banks of the Missouri River, to make an expedition into the Black Hills. It was a direct violation of the treaty. But the general feeling was that military, railroad, mining, and development interests all needed a better grip on the potential resources of the hills the Sioux called their sacred *Pa Sapa*. It was this trip that Custer had invited Marsh to join.

Even though the expedition was a clear breach of the treaty, there was nothing clandestine about Custer's approach. He left Fort Lincoln with twelve hundred troops, including ten companies of the Seventh Cavalry, one each of the Twentieth and Seventeenth Infantry, a detachment of Indian scouts, 110 wagons and ambulances, three Gatling guns, three newspaper correspondents, one photographer, four scientists, including Grinnell; President Grant's son, Colonel Fred Grant; and Laurence Barret, an actor friend of Custer's from New York City. There was also a full military band, mounted on white horses. This parade departed Fort Lincoln on July 1, 1874, and nineteen days later crossed the Belle Fourche and headed into the hills.[16]

It is little wonder that the Black Hills inspired awe and reverence from the Sioux, for they rise up, like a mystical island, out of a sea of bleak, relentless prairies. The coat of thick forest turns the hills black against their gray, granite cliffs, and once inside this domain, the world is magically transformed.

The Custer party—and "party" is probably the correct word—found the Black Hills luxuriant in knee-deep, fresh grasses. Wild cherries, blueberries, and gooseberries abounded. Cavalry soldiers would scoop up wildflowers—daisies and violets—as they rode along to weave into garlands that they draped on their horses. Streams ran cold and clear. The air was filled with "sweet, wild odors." Game was plentiful.

One day Custer led a hike up Harneys Peak—the tallest mountain in the Black Hills—for luncheon at the summit. Back at camp, the enlisted men played baseball. The score that day was recorded as eleven to six, with the Actives defeating the Athletes. "In the long evenings, we'd make a great campfire," recalled Sergeant Charles Windolph, "and almost every night there'd be a band concert. . . . It was something to stretch out before a big open fire and listen to the music. Soldiering wasn't half bad those times." Windolph described the expedition as a "long picnic party."

Custer's reports praised the hills as perfect for timbering, grazing, and farming. But the key dispatch was his August 2 communiqué, which announced that there was gold in the Black Hills. "Gold has been found in several places," Custer said. "It is the belief of those who are giving their attention to this subject that it will be found paying in large quantities."

In a dispatch two weeks later, he wrote "on some water courses almost every pan full of earth produced gold in small yet paying quantities." Miners, Custer said, even found "gold among the roots of the grass." Why, men with no experience mining were finding it "at an expense of but little labor."[17]

Press reports of Custer's findings immediately touched off a scramble among prospectors and would-be prospectors to get into the Black Hills. That in turn led Lieutenant General Philip Sheridan, the commander of the Department of the Missouri, who had ordered the Custer reconnaissance, to wire new orders from Chicago. General Alfred Terry was directed to place his forces along the Missouri and stop prospectors, seize and destroy wagons, and "send the argonauts themselves under arrest to the nearest military post." It would, however, be a losing battle. Custer returned to Fort Abraham Lincoln on August 30, but the damage was done. By the next summer, some eight hundred prospectors would be working the hills. The following winter, there would be fifteen thousand.[18]

The Sioux called Custer's expedition the Trail of Thieves. It is little wonder that when Marsh turned up in October with his story about wanting to go into the badlands to search for bones, the chiefs were suspicious.

If the conduct of the railroads, the settlers, and the army wasn't enough to anger the Sioux, the behavior of the Indian bureau was more than sufficient to incite them. The reservation tribes were constantly being short-changed on supplies, and those that they did receive were often of inferior quality.

As early as 1871, an investigation by the Board of Indian Commissioners—a civilian oversight group created by President Grant—discovered widespread cheating by a group of bureaucrats and supply contractors dubbed the "Indian Ring."[19]

The board's secretary, James Walker, found at the Red Cloud Agency, for example, that J. W. Bosler, of Carlisle, Pennsylvania, had a contract for beef at the rate of 6½ cents a pound when the going rate was 4½ cents. The total contract had been worth $756,700.

Another contractor, D. J. McCann, of Nebraska City, had overcharged the government $15,000 for freight hauling, and G. M. Dodge, of Council Bluffs, Iowa, had a contract to provide corn at the hundred-weight price of $2.26 while the going market price was $1.50.

A few of the more rapacious contractors—like Bosler—were banned from obtaining government contracts. McCann was actually prosecuted and sent to jail for six months for his role in gouging the government. But retribution was limited. "Let us be charitable in regard to the past," the board concluded, "and more watchful in the future."[20]

When Walker's report became public, Secretary of the Interior Delano sent his own commission, led by Episcopal Bishop W. H. Hare, to the agencies in 1873. The Hare report was largely a whitewash, blaming most of the problem on the Indians and commending the agents for generally doing a good job under difficult circumstances. Hare said the "wilder spirits" among the agency Indians and the recalcitrant northern Sioux were the real problem. "The government owes it to its agents to save them from the necessity of being the toys or tools of lawless savages," the Hare report stated, and it went on to describe rebellious Indians getting supplies by intimidation, war parties running off entire herds of cattle, and teamsters and soldiers being shot.

"These gentlemen have performed their duties at a time of great trial . . . with great energy, honesty, and entire fidelity to the interests of the government and the Indians," the report said of the agents.[21] One of the agents Hare exonerated was J. J. Saville, which may not be so surprising considering that Hare had recommended his appointment in the first place.

But Saville, who was Marsh's primary contact at the Red Cloud Agency, was a man deeply and desperately in over his head. An ordained Episcopal minister, Saville arrived at the Red Cloud Agency on August 8, 1873, just as it had been moved from Fort Laramie to an isolated spot on the banks of the White River.

Upon his arrival, the former agent, J. W. Daniels, and his clerk left without providing any documents, records, or instructions. The agency office was a tent, and all the supplies were piled on the ground under tarpaulins. Saville faced some eight thousand unhappy Sioux. "Inexperienced," he wrote in his first annual report, "it was a complicated business."[22]

Saville set about hiring clerks, constructing permanent buildings, and dispensing the rations for the tribes. Here again he ran into trouble. Drifting down to the reservation were a large number of the northern Sioux. "They flocked in and doubled the numbers claiming rights and rations beyond the supplies available," Saville said in his annual report. "They were unused to the agency, vicious, insolent and demanding."

Throughout the winter, tensions grew. On the night of February 8, 1874, Frank Appleton, an agency clerk who also happened to be Saville's brother-in-law, was shot dead right in the compound. "The Indian who shot Appleton was a Miniconjou named 'Lone Horn of the North,' " Saville said in his report.

The Appleton shooting was followed by a demonstration during which more than three hundred Sioux braves, in battle regalia, besieged the still-unfinished stockade, singing and shooting off their rifles. Saville asked for help from the army, and General John E. Smith arrived from Fort Laramie with six companies of cavalry, eight of infantry, and a wagon train. Eventually, Smith was to set up a small army post within sight of the agency. It was named Fort Robinson, in memory of a cavalry officer recently killed in the region by the Sioux.

✤

It was into all this that Marsh had plunged with his innocent request to take his small party into the badlands. Perhaps facing the hostility, the danger, and the welter of political and social issues, it might have been wise to just turn around and go back to New Haven. But once Marsh got started on something, it was awfully hard for him to stop.

After Marsh's first failed attempt to leave for the badlands, Saville suggested that he hold a feast for the chiefs in an effort to make peace. The banquet was held in a large tent, and the assembled party of fifty included Sitting Bull, Red Cloud, Pawnee Killer, Pretty Crow, and Young Man Afraid of His Horse. They dined on meat, rice, and dried apples while Marsh gave a speech. Again the chiefs gave their consent, and Red Cloud's son-in-law, Sword, was appointed to lead the party. Marsh was warned that he had to avoid the northern Miniconjous across the White River, for they would surely massacre the entire party.

The next day, Marsh sent word that his party was ready to move. But once again his Sioux escort balked at leaving camp. Infuriated, Marsh would delay no more. A little after midnight, he took his wagons and headed for the badlands. The procession had to snake close by some of the Sioux camps, since there was only one ford in a fifteen-mile stretch of the White River. Dogs barked, the wagons rumbled, but there was no effort to stop Marsh.

Then it was out onto the huge swells of buffalo-grass plains, wave after wave of gold prairie capped with patches of snow. This was a land so vast that anything human was reduced to nothing more than a speck.

As the party moved north, the smooth prairies began to be broken by rocky outcrops. As the miles passed, the rocks got bigger and bigger, until buttes, showing stripes of cinnamon, green, and gray, started to stud the landscape. Off in the distance, the badlands loomed.

One soldier, protecting railroad surveyors, described it this way. "A day or so before we reached the Badlands, we could see them in the distance, and a pretty sight it was. It looked like a great city in the distance, great sand buttes looking like buildings, castles, forts, everything about a great city."

Awesome and terrible in their other-world countenance, the White River canyons were the greatest and most spectacular of western badlands. It was fantasy terrain seventy million years in the making. The oldest rocks formed during the Cretaceous, when that vast inland sea stretched across the continent. As the sea drained, it was replaced by a swampy plain, which was home to the first species of the dawning Age of Mammals.

The area eventually dried into a vast savanna. There was little vegetation due to sparse rainfall. This left the land open to the forces of erosion: the relentless winds and the rare, but intense bursts of rain. Deep canyons began to be cut into the plains. Cliffs and parapets were sculpted by wind and water, and eventually the process laid bare layers of gray and green sands, blue clays, yellow and pink gravels, dark volcanic ash, light buff-gray shales, and brown sandstone.

The final product was a labyrinth of multicolored hard-rock canyons, cliffs, buttes, and bluffs, with little vegetation and virtually no drinkable water. (What pools there were were heavily alkali.) The Indians called the region *mako sicha,* meaning, "bad land." The French Canadian trappers turned that to *mauvaise terre.*[23]

But also exposed in those rocks were millions of years of life, captured in fossils. There was the *Pteranodon,* a winged, hang-gliding reptile that snatched fish from the Cretaceous sea, as well as the *Plesiosaurus,* the giant sea turtle *Archelon,* and the *Ammonitids,* with their strange coiled shells.

Then thirty million years ago, *Archaeotherium,* a giant pig, and *Mesohippus,* a fox-size, three-toed ancestor of the horse roamed the land. There was also the *Brontotherium,* a rhinolike animal almost fourteen feet long and seven feet high.

The White River badlands were one of the first fossil fields identified in the West, the earliest fossils having been collected there in 1843. Ten years later, the Smithsonian and the Philadelphia Academy of Natural Sciences financed Hayden's exploration of the area.

"I think it must be the greatest cemetery in the world for Eocene mammalia," Leidy wrote to Hayden in 1851. "You can have no idea how much my mind has become inflamed upon this subject. Night after night, I dream of strange forms, Eocene crania with recent eyes in them." These were the treasures that Marsh now sought.

When the Marsh party reached the edge of the badlands, they set up camp in an area screened by ravines and started collecting. The fossils were scattered over a ten-mile circuit, and the weather was so intensely cold that everyone worked hard just to keep warm. Icicles formed on Marsh's beard, and he had to chip them off so he could eat dinner. Each morning, he had to thaw out his boots before he could get his feet into them. The group quickly built a large pile of fossils. Meanwhile, on the nearby buttes, Sioux sentinels monitored the Marsh party. Surprised by the fact that Marsh seemed to truly be collecting no more than rocks and bones, they dubbed him the "Big Bone Chief."

Marsh had always expected the expedition to be a brief one because it was so late in the season, and the threat of snowstorms hovered over the party every day. But the prospect of another menace abbreviated the work even more quickly. Sword and Red Cloud's brother, Spider, came riding into camp one day to warn Marsh that the Miniconjous had sent their women and children to the Black Hills and were preparing a war party to attack the paleontologist's group. The attack might come that very night.

This created a dilemma. Hastily throwing the fossils into the wagons and dashing across the prairie would mean that all the specimens would surely be broken to bits. They could try to pack through the night, but that would necessitate using lanterns in one of the tents, which would create a beacon and an easy target for any war party in the vicinity. Marsh decided to spend one more day packing. Then with some two tons of fossils, the Marsh party moved out less than a day before the Miniconjou war party passed through the area. Not finding Marsh, they apparently decided not to try to follow him back to the Red Cloud Agency and Fort Robinson.

Marsh returned with a great cache, especially a large number of bronothere bones, which would enable him to add this beast, like the earlier uintathere, to his detailed description of early mammal life.

✤

Meanwhile, Cope was in an entirely different part of the country, exploring an entirely different niche of ancient history. In fact, Cope had made perhaps the most important discovery of his career, the Puerco formation in northern New Mexico. The Puerco turned out to be the oldest formation in the country with significant mammal fossils—the true beginning of the Age of Mammals.

Cope's challenge in New Mexico was keeping the army from getting in his way. Unlike Hayden, who fancied scientific work, Lieutenant Wheeler, a by-the-book West Point graduate, was focused almost exclusively on topography and geology. Making maps is what the army survey was about, and the thirty-two-year-old Wheeler, who had graduated first in his class in engineering and mathematics, was determined to churn out maps. Technically, Cope was there as a geologist for the army.[24]

"It is absurd to order stops here where there are no fossils, and marches there where fossil abound!" Cope wrote to his father. "We are breaking through this, however, and will lay it aside before long."[25]

Lieutenant Wheeler had placed zoologist H. C. Yarrow in charge of Cope's group, but had been quite specific about his orders. This left

Cope totally frustrated. Yarrow, Cope told Annie, "was not courageous enough to disregard these [orders] and I can not regard them and succeed in my work."[26] As irritating as things were, Cope particularly asked Annie not to mention his complaints to anyone, "especially of Hayden's people."

But Cope was so determined and so difficult that Yarrow was ready to resign as leader of the group. Yarrow and Cope went to Santa Fe and put the issue before the regional commander, General Gregg. "To my delight," Cope reported, "the Gen. at once took my view of the case and set the Dr. at liberty to violate and disregard the points I had found so objectionable."[27]

The party headed over the jagged crest of the Jemez Mountains, west of Santa Fe, where Cope found a Pliocene badlands, with marl "as red as blood" and "moderately rich" in the fossils of camels and horses, mastodons, and weasels.

Orders had the party then heading to Pagosa Springs, Colorado. Yarrow and Cope fought again. "Knowing that to obey orders was to kill the expedition I resolved to risk a violation of them and took guides, Mr. Shedd and a pack animal and left the concern with rations for 4 men for 7 days. We traveled through beautiful and mountainous country," Cope wrote.[28]

They crossed over the mountains into the San Juan basin and discovered a harsh, rolling plain of gray and green rock, which had been created as the streams from the surrounding ancient mountain ranges carried mud and sand down onto the basin's older Cretaceous strata.

When Cope surveyed this barren expanse, it looked to him like the Eocene badlands of Wyoming, and when he began to find some of the same sorts of fossils, he knew it was Eocene. Still, everything he found in the San Juan badlands was "rare and strange." Cope suspected he had a formation even older than the Bridger. "My dream was realized," he said, "and we hunted awhile and then rode to our camp in the narrow canyon in high spirits."

It was, Cope thought, "the most important find in geology I ever made, and the paleontology promises grandly." The next day he wrote to Lieutenant Wheeler, asking that the men and wagons be sent to him.

Meanwhile poor Yarrow was facing virtual mutiny—the teamsters and cook had balked at going any farther with him—so he, too, wrote to Wheeler asking him to settle affairs. On September 13, Cope received a message from Wheeler summoning him immediately to Tierra Amarilla. Cope cached his fossils and left early the next morning. He rode all day and reached the little town at five in the afternoon, just as Wheeler was about to leave. It turned out that Yarrow had decided to quit the surveying team altogether and return to Washington, D.C.

The other professional in the group, topographer P. R. Ainsworth, had been killed when his revolver accidentally went off. So Wheeler put Cope in charge of the party. This suited Cope just fine.

The one setback was the fact that Wheeler could only give Cope half of his salary. "I cannot therefore send thee the $125 thee kindly lent me until the end of the season," he told his father. "Wheeler complains of Gov't stringency and I can hardly get enough for the commonest wants."

As precious as the San Juan basin was, a few weeks later, Cope would make an even more valuable find. In late October, a few days before Marsh was preparing to leave New Haven for the Red Cloud Agency, Cope discovered another new formation near the Rio Puerco and not far from the northern New Mexico town of Nacimiento (later to be known as Cuba). He didn't have much time to explore that season, but it was clear this layer, below the San Juan and above the Cretaceous, was the oldest Eocene rock he had ever seen. Cope would send collectors back to the Puerco, and over the next decade, he would describe 107 Vertebrata it contained, including 93 mammalian species. (In time, paleontologists would realize that the Puerco was not Eocene, but part of the even older Paleocene epoch, a time sixty to sixty-five million years ago, just after the last of the dinosaurs had died out. The formation would also be renamed the Nacimiento.)

In 1877, Wheeler would publish a fine volume on his survey's paleontology; the second part of this work was Cope's 364-page report, illustrated by eighty-three plates. It detailed dozens of fossil fish, reptiles, birds, and mammals from the New Mexico formations, as well as an astounding array of carnivores, some weasel size, others as large as a jaguar.[29]

All in all, Cope had a fine time in New Mexico, delighting in the strangeness of the Southwest. "This is to an American . . . a foreign country," Cope wrote to Annie from Taos. "I rather like these Spanish Americans. . . . They are lively and pleasant. The chief fault in their expression is an absence of intelligence. I am agreeably disappointed in them. The signoras and signoritas are often handsome and only need intelligence to bring out real beauty. The churches are great piles of mud!"[30]

It was a long letter, running more than six pages, in which Cope confessed, "I am somewhat homesick," and asked Annie to *send me one of thy photos. . . . I wish I had some more $ to send thee.*

"The Indians are often in our camp," Cope wrote to his daughter, Julia. "They live in queer houses which Mamma will show thee photographs of; the

little round things like bee-hives in front are ovens, where they bake bread. . . .
All the houses are made of blocks of mud, which are dried in the sun."[31]

The Indians were "very friendly," Cope noted. "They use Spanish as well
as their own tongue so we can get along with them very well. They come
to sell milk, eggs, fish, etc. In a short time we hope to see some of their mysteries in their council chamber."[32]

Cope did not neglect his own "mysteries," holding his own tent-side
Sunday services, reading one Sabbath St. John's story of the miracle of the
loaves and fishes. "I always feel the love of God after those services," he told
Annie, "and sometimes during them."

❖

While Marsh's trip to the Dakotas may not have been such an easygoing
travelogue nor his fossils as valuable as Cope's, he did manage to get out of
the White River badlands with his bones—and his scalp—and that had to
count for something.

Meanwhile, between the friendly Pueblo in the Southwest and the
restive Sioux in the Dakotas, the army was engaged in a full-scale military
campaign against the Kiowas, Comanche, and Cheyenne in the "Red River
War" of northern Texas.[33]

Red Cloud's effort to warn the party left Marsh more sympathetic to the
Sioux's complaints than perhaps he had been in those first frustrating days
at the Indian agency. "We escaped a war party of Indians in consequence of
warning and assistance sent by Red Cloud . . . ," Marsh was to explain.
"This act of kindness led me on my return to the agency to make further
investigation. . . . I soon found reason to believe their charges of mismanagement and fraud were essentially true."

Marsh found the pork "rusty stuff," the coffee beans green, the tobacco
"vile" and runny with a dark viscous liquid, the flour "dark in color and
sticky to the touch." The cattle being driven into the agency were scrawny,
and the contractor was still Bosler, even though he was supposed to have
been banned. Marsh went into the warehouse and found eighteen bales of
blankets, where there were supposed to be thirty-five.

He even used an odometer to measure the distance between the Red
Cloud Agency and Cheyenne, suspecting that the government was once
again being overcharged for hauling. He left the Dakotas armed with samples of the inferior supplies and the stories of both the Sioux and soldiers—
neither of who had much use for the Bureau of Indian Affairs or its agents.
Marsh promised Red Cloud that he would take his complaints to Washington.

Red Cloud didn't place much faith in Marsh's promise to plead the Sioux's cause in the far-off capital. Of course, Red Cloud could not know that Marsh was a white man cut from a different cloth. P. T. Barnum could have told him that. Cope could certainly have told Red Cloud that and more. Pretty soon both Red Cloud and Ulysses S. Grant would learn the same.

Chapter Nine

ON FRIDAY EVENING, APRIL 23, 1875, Buffalo Bill and Kit Carson took the stage of Ford's Theater in their box-office triumph *Life on the Border*. The Washington playhouse, which ten years earlier had been the scene of the greatest of American tragedies when John Wilkes Booth pumped a bullet into Abraham Lincoln, was packed this night with army officers and a "large representation of the best theater going circles." Everyone was anticipating the "bear fight" finale, which the newspapers said was absolutely thrilling.

Marsh was also in town and also thinking about life on the border, although he apparently wasn't in the theatergoing circle. The National Academy of Sciences' spring meeting—Marsh's first—was the reason for his visit. But as well as his scientific papers, he carried the flour, tobacco, and sugar he had taken away from the Dakotas five months earlier. It was time to make good on his promise to Red Cloud.

Just one block away from Ford's Theater, and a few hours before the curtain went up, Marsh met with Commissioner of Indian Affairs E. P. Smith. He told Smith his story and showed his samples, but Smith's response was far from satisfactory. The commissioner suggested that the samples might have been picked over. He intimated that the spoilage, particularly of the flour, might have occurred after it was in the possession of the Sioux. The Indians, he explained, were not accustomed to using flour.

Then Marsh raised the issue of Saville's incompetence, and Smith allowed there might be some problems. But he pointed out that at a salary of fifteen hundred dollars a year, it would be hard to get anyone better. "The inferior rations I exhibited were plausibly explained and the damaging facts I had observed were of little consequence," Marsh would recount of the meeting.

Totally dissatisfied and deeply irritated, Marsh sought out Marshall Jewell, the postmaster general and a former governor of Connecticut, and asked him to arrange a meeting with President Grant for the very next day. Marsh was determined to make his point, but what he failed to realize was that he was now entering a Badlands of an entirely different sort from those he had known out west.

Washington in those postwar years was still a small, unfinished place that barely covered a patch thirty blocks by twenty-three blocks. Many of the "streets" were merely dirt lanes, lined with vacant lots grazed by cows, pigs, and sheep.

The Capitol, with its grand white dome, had recently been completed, but the Washington Monument was only half built and looked like a smokestack surrounded by shanties and livestock. Mark Twain called it the "memorial Chimney." Behind the Capitol, in the swampy southeast section of town, sat the jail, poorhouse, and the congressional cemetery.

The heart of American government was still a backwater, yet, as the nation was changing, so was the town. A civil war, growing international trade, and the emerging West were all forces demanding and transforming national governance and creating, in the words of Henry Adams's 1880 novel, *Democracy,* a "clash of interests, the interests of forty millions of people and a whole continent, centering at Washington."

The city had become a magnet for all sorts of political aspirants. "Every individual you encounter in the city of Washington, almost," wrote Mark Twain and Charles Dudley Warner in *The Gilded Age,*" . . . from the highest bureau chief, clear down to the maid who scrubs Department halls, the night watchmen in public buildings and the darkey boy who purifies the Department spittoons—represents Political Influence. . . . They have gathered from every corner of the Union."[1]

This was a Washington of "appalling contrasts," said historian Allan Nevins. "Shining carriages laden with sealskins and diamonds stuck in mud holes of unpaved streets. Mansions resplendent with crystal chandeliers, mahogany and silver stood beside Negro shacks."[2]

There were really several Washingtons. There was the Washington of the clerk, living in a rooming house and eating in a twenty-dollar-a-month dining salon. There was the Washington of the parvenu in his townhouse, gulping oysters and washing them down with champagne. There was the Washington of the recently freed slave, living in a shanty on a dirt path.

And then there was the "old Washington," the quiet, refined society that had existed in the city's somnolent antebellum days. "Old Washington preferred evenings spent in Professor Henry's parlor at the Smithsonian, where young scientists and scholars recently arrived in government service might also be found."[3]

Henry also presided over the biweekly meetings of the Washington Philosophical Society, hardly the place one would expect to find members of the Grant administration or Congress.

Yet another Washington was now emerging, the Washington of government science, which was growing "bolder in the new era of governmental activism."[4] The surveys were hiring large numbers of researchers, and each year their annual reports were filled with important scientific papers. And despite initial political opposition, the Smithsonian and the Naval Observatory, created in 1842 to measure latitude and longitude but also the source of important works on astronomy, had both become solid, established scientific institutions.

Since the birth of the nation—even before that—Philadelphia and Boston had been the paragons of American scientific society, and for a time, Philadelphia had been preeminent. But now thanks to men like Henry, Baird, Bache, and Pierce (who succeeded Bache at the U.S. Coast and Geodetic Survey), there were reasons for scientists to come to Washington, besides the biannual National Academy of Sciences meetings.

Still, it was politics that built Washington, and politics still ruled. On Saturday, Marsh accompanied by Jewell went to the White House on his very political mission. Carrying his samples of flour, sugar, and tobacco, the professor met the president.

The story of the Red Cloud Agency must have been particularly painful to Grant. The one and only thing he had truly sought to do in his administration was to fashion a new and more humane Indian policy. And now here was this Yale professor coming to tell him even that wasn't going well.

As a young and lonely captain posted to the Pacific Northwest in 1850s, Grant had seen Indians sorely treated by the army and the settlers, and it had touched him. "This poor remnant of a once powerful tribe," he wrote in 1853, "is fast wasting away before those blessings of civilization 'whiskey and small pox.'" He came away from the Northwest with this melancholy vision and a drinking problem of his own. Now he felt he had a chance to do something for those once powerful tribes.

Grant had launched a two-pronged policy of negotiation and appeasement in an attempt to diffuse the massacres and skirmishes flaring up all across the West. First, the political operators and spoilsmen were replaced as Indian agents with representatives of religious groups. "I have attempted a new policy," Grant explained in his first annual message to Congress, "toward these wards of the nation. . . . The Society of Friends is well known as having succeeded in living in peace with the Indians in early settlements of Pennsylvania . . . [this] induced me to give the management of a few reservations of Indians to them."

Although it was immediately dubbed the "Quaker Policy," politics being what it was even among the pious, Grant had to provide reservations for all the denominations doing missionary work. Soon there were Dutch

Reform reservations, Presbyterian reservations, and Episcopalian reservations, like the Red Cloud Agency.

The other part of Grant's plan was the "Peace Policy," which sought to end the treaty system that recognized each tribe's sovereignty and instead emphasized the treatment of Indians not as tribal members but as individuals responsible for their own welfare. It sought the establishment of reservations where the Indians could receive economic, educational, and cultural support. There was, of course, some confusion embedded in the policy, which simultaneously saw Indians as independent individuals but still required them to stay on tribal reservations. Nevertheless, the main idea was to replace military confrontation with a program that would make the "original occupants of this land" civilized and Christian.[5]

The men Grant picked to implement this plan were Jacob Cox, an urbane, reform-minded Ohio legislator as secretary of the interior, and Ely S. Parker as commissioner of Indian affairs. Parker was a Grant crony from army days, but he was both educated and a full-blooded Seneca.

William Welsh, a Philadelphia businessman and crusader for Indian rights, also persuaded Grant, within the first weeks of his administration, to establish an independent board of Indian commissioners. Grant made Welsh chairman of the new watchdog agency.

But the policy sputtered from the start. First, humanitarians, like Welsh, saw Parker as a hack and politico, not their idea of a noble savage, and they heavily lobbied against him. This led to a political standoff. The initial investigations by the board into the Indian Ring were done as much to get at Parker as the suppliers who were bilking the government.

Parker finally gave up and resigned, but for Welsh it was a Pyrrhic victory. He and his entire board became so frustrated with the unremitting corruption, they resigned en masse in 1874. Grant appointed a whole new board. Welsh would ultimately give up the idea of civilian administration of reservations and become an advocate of the army overseeing the Indians.

Parker's boss Cox fared no better. A supporter of Andrew Johnson's moderate reconstruction policy toward the South, he already had many Washington enemies, and his unwillingness to do business in spoils, patronage, and insider deals made the list even longer. When Cox attempted to thwart mineral claims on public lands, which he called a transparent fraud, the chorus against him became strong enough to convince Grant that his administration was being dragged down. Cox resigned.

Now Marsh had come to the White House to tell Grant that the problems in Indian territories were only getting worse. A front-page story in the *New York Tribune,* the Monday following Marsh's meeting, reported that

"The President expressed very positively his desire that the Indians should be fairly dealt with, and that promises to them should be directly kept." But his advice to Marsh was that the Yale professor go and see the secretary of the interior.

By this time, the Interior Department was the domain of Columbus Delano, an Ohio criminal lawyer and political operator. "A dry, baldish, clerical-looking man, with a sly contriving air," Delano had parlayed a seat in Congress into the directorship of the already tainted Bureau of Internal Revenue in 1869 and then secretary of the interior a year later. "His appointment marked a sad step in the deliquescence of the Administration," said Nevins, in his classic work *Hamilton Fish—The Inner History of the Grant Administration*. The Bureau of Indian Affairs was now headed by E. P. Smith, who was a Congregational minister. Not a political hack, but certainly no more capable.

Unlike his predecessor, Delano set about helping the railroads press claims for large federal land grants, even where titles were dubious. Delano's son, John, was perpetually involved in land schemes and scams in the West, until his behavior became a subject at cabinet meetings.

Treasury secretary Benjamin Bristow, the most zealous reformer in the Grant administration, had received a letter and canceled checks that showed John Delano was obtaining partnerships in surveying contracts, which the surveying companies could not have received without political help. But Grant was reluctant to confront Delano. Meanwhile, Delano and Orville Babcock, Grant's opportunistic and shady private secretary, were actively trying to oust Bristow from the cabinet. Assistant Secretary of the Interior Cowan explained that if a reformer like Bristow looked into the Interior Department, he'd find it "rotten from top to bottom." Failure to derail Bristow would soon have dramatic repercussions.

Before Marsh could see Delano, he was summoned, on April 28, to New York City to meet with the Board of Indian Commissioners at the Fifth Avenue Hotel. Perhaps already sensing the futility of going through official channels, Marsh appeared at the evening meeting with his evidence and something new—a newspaper reporter, Frank Wyckoff of the *New York Tribune*.[6]

The commissioners were dismayed to see the reporter, and before the meeting even started, they questioned Marsh's intentions. Marsh countered that he had no reason to believe the meeting was private, and as it turned out, Wyckoff's story was the only record of the session, for the commission made no transcript or report available. Marsh was learning.

Marsh once again displayed the evidence, and the board was more impressed with the problem than Smith had been. "Something must be done to reform this business, even if it is necessary to put a special agent on every barrel of flour!" one commissioner exclaimed. "You forget," replied another, "that he would eat up the flour on the way."

Another commissioner said that in his experience the "Sioux were the worst Indians." Marsh took exception and said he had found in the Sioux a "higher order of intellect. . . . Among their chiefs were many of marked intelligence."

The commissioners and Marsh discussed the problem of the incompetence of agents, particularly those appointed by the religious denominations. "Do you mean they become dishonest?" a commissioner asked.

"I do not say that," Marsh said, "but I do say that the kind of men that can be hired to take their life in their hands . . . for $1,500 a year, is not the kind that should be trusted without watching them when, as at the Red Cloud Agency, they have to distribute more than $400,000 annually. They may not be dishonest, but they are likely to be lacking in business capacity for such trust."

Wyckoff's story appeared in the *Tribune* on April 30 under the headline:

INDIAN MISMANAGEMENT
PROF. MARSH BEFORE THE INDIAN COMMISSIONERS

The paper had already written front-page stories about Marsh's meetings with Smith and President Grant, and it would continue to write vigorously about the issue. It was an ideal story for the *Tribune*. Horace Greeley's old paper was opposed to the Grant administration, and several of the men on the paper's editorial board were Yale graduates. Republican newspapers like the *Springfield Republican* and the *Washington National,* as well as the *New York Times,* did not initially pay much attention to Marsh's story. The *Tribune* and Marsh, however, maintained a steady drumbeat.

Then the counterattack against Marsh began. On May 4, Wyoming Congressman W. R. Steel asked to meet with the Indian commissioners to rebut Marsh's charges, contending that the wide-eyed academic had been taken in by wily savages. "Red Cloud lied to him every morning for seven months," Steel said. He explained that the helter-skelter distribution of supplies Marsh had witnessed was the result of the threats of Sioux violence. It was done to "preserve order" and avoid riots. Steel also took offense at Marsh's charges about unscrupulous contractors, since many of them were constituents of the congressman's Cheyenne district. Marsh sent off a letter to the editor of the *Tribune* rebutting Steel, who replied in kind with a letter to the editor of the *Times.*

Back in Washington, Delano was grumbling that these charges were being made to the president, the Board of Indian Commissioners, and even the press, but that no one had come to see him. Still, on May 10, he got into the act by writing to Clinton Fiske, chairman of the Board of Indian Commissioners, announcing his desire to appoint a special commission to investigate "certain reports put in circulation by a Mr. Marsh, relative to the Indian service." Delano asked Fiske to recommend three candidates for this commission.

Delano's reference to "a Mr. Marsh" was certainly a backhanded slap at the distinguished Yale professor, and it sent up the hackles among Marsh supporters. The *Tribune* immediately demanded the secretary's resignation.

But on May 10, it was the "Whiskey Ring," not the Indian Ring, that was worrying the Grant administration. Distillers in St. Louis, Chicago, Milwaukee, Peoria, Indianapolis, and other cities had been systematically defrauding the federal government of excise revenues that added up to millions of dollars. Along the way, legions of bureaucrats and elected officials, leading right to the White House, had been bribed and bought. The ring had been broken by an investigation spearheaded by Treasury secretary Bristow.

As big as the Whiskey Ring was, it marked only the crest of the wave of corruption washing over the nation. Rings, kickback plots, and market conspiracies seemed to permeate the life of the country. In the general scheme of things, Marsh's concern for a bunch of Indians in the middle of nowhere hardly registered. The entire annual budget for Indian programs was about $1.5 million. In 1874, distillers in St. Louis alone had defrauded the government of an estimated $1.2 million in revenue.

The very day Delano was writing his letter to the Board of Indian Commissioners, government agents were moving in to seize records, papers, and whiskey stills in cities across the nation. The *Tribune*'s lead story on May 11 said, "Officers of the government today made battle upon dishonest and cheating distillers in St. Louis, Milwaukee, Chicago, Evansville and several other cities in the West and the South."

The Whiskey Ring trail led right to the White House and Babcock. Grant's brother Orvil and son Fred were also implicated, but it was the handsome, ruddy-faced, Babcock, with his auburn mustache and shining smile, who was the ultimate intriguer and perhaps greatest symbol of venality in a hopelessly venal age. Sitting in the anteroom just outside Grant's office, opening the president's mail, screening the president's visitors, the thirty-nine-year-old Babcock had become a power in his own right.

Bristow's Whiskey Ring investigation would result in dozens of businessmen, bureaucrats, and elected officials being found guilty of defrauding the government and accepting bribes. In early 1876, Babcock went on trial in St. Louis, and testimony showed that he had actively helped managed the ring and tried to thwart federal investigators. Grant's personal secretary, however, was acquitted. A key element in his defense was a deposition from the president in support of his secretary. To convict Babcock would have been much the same as calling the president a liar. Babcock went back to his job in the White House for a month and then was made inspector of light-houses. A few weeks later, he was arrested on burglary charges.

The Whiskey Ring was neither the first nor the last frisson of corruption to shake government, and, in all fairness, it wasn't limited just to the Grant administration. Government—city, state, and national—had become a cash-and-carry business. Things got so bad up on Capitol Hill that to be sure of buying a vote, the bribe had to be the biggest and the last. "Honesty" in politics simply had to be redefined. An honest politician, explained Pennsylvania senator Simon Cameron—the man who once told Joseph Henry how tired he was of this "thing called science"—was basically "one who will stay bought when he is bought."

And if the Grant administration didn't have enough trouble, there were more press reports about Delano appearing. "Corruption has at last been traced to the bosom of the Secretary's family," the press announced. Grant still would not consider firing Delano. "If Delano were now to resign, it would be retreating under fire and be accepted as an admission of charges," Grant explained.

So it is clear that Marsh and Red Cloud were not the only headaches tor-menting Delano and the Grant administration as spring slid into summer in 1875. Marsh, however, was not to be deterred. Even if he was a minor headache, he would be incessant.

Scandals or no scandals, the Grant administration still had to deal with the issues of the day, and the fate of the Black Hills was once again a growing problem. Miners and settlers were still pressing in on the hills, so the admin-istration brought a delegation of Sioux chiefs to Washington to consider a new proposition. The federal government offered the tribes twenty-five thousand dollars for their hunting rights along the Platte River in the hopes that this would relieve some of the tensions by keeping the Sioux and set-tlers apart.

On May 18, the Sioux chiefs, including Red Cloud and Spotted Tail, met with Commissioner Smith at the Interior Department. Smith welcomed them and then dispatched them to see the marvels of American ingenuity at the Patent Office. The next day, they would go to the White House and see the Great Father.

Marsh also returned to Washington, and after the Sioux had been sent sight-seeing, he and Smith had another meeting. Marsh then tried to meet with Red Cloud and Spotted Tail, but the two refused to see him, newspaper accounts said, because they had been told not to speak to anyone unless Smith or Delano were present. Marsh, in a letter to the *Times,* said that the meeting was actually blocked by Saville, who was acting as a chaperon for the chiefs.

The next afternoon, the Sioux, in "full paint and feathers," paid a call on Grant at the White House. The chiefs' tomahawks were decorated with ribbons, and someone had stuck a "Grant & Wilson" campaign flag in the bowl of a peace pipe. There were those in the administration who still had hopes that Grant, despite all his travails, might win a third term.

Red Cloud, speaking through an Indian bureau interpreter, reminded the president that he had been told to come to the Great Father when he had complaints to make, and he now had complaints. Grant urged the chief to talk to his "two great chiefs," Smith and Delano.

Spotted Owl told Grant that he had talked with those chiefs. They had made promises to him that had not been fulfilled. They had lied to him, and he did not want to have more talks with them. It was a passionate speech, but according to the *Washington Republican National,* it lost a great deal in the translation. "When the interpreter gave Grant Spotted Tail's speech," the paper's story said, "he left out the charge that the Secretary and the Commissioner had lied . . . in deference to the President."

The interpreters were not the only clamps that the Indian bureau placed on the Sioux chiefs. Reds Cloud and company were being billeted at the Tremont House Hotel, a respectable hostelry, where neither whiskey nor women were available. This was a disappointment, since earlier visits to the capital had involved both. It took the chiefs several days to figure out how to get from the Tremont House to the bawdier Washington Hotel. But they managed.

On May 28, the chiefs asked to see Grant about the Black Hills. The president sent word that he would meet with the delegation at Delano's office at three o'clock. But when the Sioux arrived, neither Grant nor Delano was there. Instead they found Assistant Secretary Cowan, Smith, and Marsh. Red Cloud complained about the rations being issued to his tribe, but under questioning, the chief became evasive. Smith would later use these equivocal statements by Red Cloud to counter Marsh. Red Cloud blamed the confusion on the interpreters.

The chiefs refused to sign the concession on hunting rights and left Washington in late May. The *New York Times* in an editorial titled "The Dying Race" concluded that "any question relating to the Indians is now popularly regarded as a bore. . . . The national faith has been pledged and broken again and again and so it will be until the end."

Marsh stayed on to meet with government officials, including Delano. He was to recount sarcastically that Delano "was especially interested in the efforts to Christianize and civilize these wards of the nation; and he earnestly entreated me to aid him in this enterprise. His appeals in behalf of his noble work—of which so much is said in the East and so little is done in the West—move me deeply."

On May 31, Marsh paid another visit to the White House for another interview with Grant. What could anyone make of the president? "He was a deeply affectionate man, and he was surrounded by low-hangers-on," said General James Harrison Wilson, a former Grant cavalry commander and brother of Grant's vice president, Bluford Wilson.

But a frustrated Congressman James Garfield, when watching Grant confronted with still more scandal, said, "His imperturbability is amazing, I doubt whether to call it greatness or stupidity."[7]

"The progress of evolution from President Washington to President Grant was alone evidence to upset Darwin," bemoaned Henry Adams. "Darwinists ought to conclude that America was reverting to the Stone Age."[8]

Another stop Marsh made in Washington was at the auditor's office in the Treasury Department. At the Red Cloud Agency, he had seen cattle being driven in that Saville was recording as "averaging" 850 pounds per head. Marsh was convinced that the animals weighed no more than 750 pounds each. But in going through the invoices, he discovered that the government was being charged 1,040 pounds for each steer, and just that past March, Commissioner Smith had concluded still another new contract with Bosler!

In early June, Delano announced the appointment of his three-man commission—all current or former elected officials—to look into Marsh's allegations. Later that month, Saville chimed in. In a letter to Smith, he offered his resignation and demanded an investigation of the charges against him.

Marsh once again tried to strike first. On July 13, he sent a letter to Grant and five reform-minded cabinet officers, accompanied by a thirty-six-page pamphlet detailing the charges and evidence at the Red Cloud Agency. He also sent copies to the newspapers and fifteen hundred prominent citizens across the country.

In the cover letter to Grant, Marsh wrote, "I was impressed with your earnest desire to do justice to the Indians." The problem, Marsh explained, was that he had "no confidence in the sincerity of the Secretary of the Interior or the Commissioner of Indian Affairs . . . because I have reason to know that they have long been aware of these abuses.

"The evidence now in my possession reflects unfavorably on both Secretary Delano and Commissioner Smith," Marsh said. "You alone have the will and the power to destroy that combination of bad men, known as the Indian Ring, who are debasing this service, and thwarting the efforts of all who endeavor to bring to a full consummation your noble peace policy."[9]

The pamphlet, which ran eight full newspaper columns, set off another storm of public indignation, and Delano once again began circling his political wagons. Marsh met with Grant, on July 14, at the president's seaside vacation home in Long Branch, New Jersey. But Grant still took no action.

Marsh's pamphlet caused "a great fluttering" at the Interior Department, according to the *Tribune*. Smith issued a statement emphasizing that a special commission had already been established to look into Marsh's charges. On July 21, the commission heard testimony from Marsh in New York before heading to Cheyenne to hold additional hearings.

Later that summer, another pamphlet, titled "Documents Relating to the Charges of Prof. O. C. Marsh," surfaced in Washington, D.C., and became part of the debate. It was a diatribe against the Sioux and Marsh. It was, Marsh believed, the work of Delano and the Department of the Interior.

The broadside charged that "Red Cloud exhibited the usual grumbling and complaining propensity of his race in regard to the assistance he received from the Great Father." Marsh, the document argued, was merely trying to ingratiate himself with Red Cloud to gain access to the badlands. "A man of limited general business experience, whose speciality is scientific research . . . might be easily misled," it said.

Marsh, the pamphlet insinuated, had gotten his appointment at Yale mainly due to the generous endowment his uncle, George Peabody, had made to the university and also noted that it had taken him five months to bring his charges. It discounted the critical testimony of several army officers. "It is well known that the younger officers of the Army are generally unfriendly to the civilian management of the Indians," the pamphlet said. It also charged that the *Tribune* was simply using the accusations as a way of throwing mud at President Grant.

As for the June meeting between Marsh and Delano, the pamphlet's version was decidedly different from Marsh's caustic account. "How the Secretary could have proceeded with greater evidence of candor and fairness is difficult to see, but in doing this he seems to have given offense to Prof. Marsh and his friends."

Marsh received reports from Washington that Delano had sent a "secret agent" on to Cheyenne ahead of the commission to lay the groundwork for the hearings, and, in late August, Colonel T. H. Stanton, who had helped collect fossils in the badlands, wrote to him saying that he had encountered the commission on its way down to the Red Cloud Agency. The investigators were being guided by Saville and Bosler. Stanton said he "thought it a little singular that the court and the prisoners should be such good company. . . . Look for a first-class white-wash."

The personal attacks and the cover-up left Marsh chafing and ready to fire off another volley, but his friends now urged him to bide his time. "My first advice holds good. *Keep Still,*" wrote Isaac Bromley, a member of the *Tribune*'s editorial board, on August 23. "It is no longer your fight. You can't improve it by rushing into print to answer Saville, Smith, Delano and that crowd."

Besides, the fracas had drawn old warriors back to battle. Both Welsh and Samuel Walker, who had been instrumental in the 1871 investigation of the Indian Ring, surfaced to write letters to the newspapers and lobby the Board of Indian Commissioners.

While Marsh was doing battle in Washington, Benjamin Mudge was once again leading an expedition on the Kansas plains for Yale. Cope had tried to hire him away, but Mudge told him that he was "engaged for" Marsh.[10] He would spend nearly six months in the field, at a cost to Marsh of $1,793.17. But despite repeated requests for some opinion on the material sent to New Haven, Mudge could get no reply.

"I think you are doing a good thing to fight the Indian Ring," Mudge wrote in July, "but hope it will not interfere with the examination of fossils." Along with the letter, he sent two boxes of specimens weighing a total of 590 pounds.[11]

Mudge also asked Marsh to hire one of his students, twenty-four-year-old Samuel Williston. "He excells in Mathematics and the Natural Sciences," Mudge assured. Williston—who was to become a valued aide, a noted paleontologist in his own right, and one day a great enemy of Marsh—went on the payroll.[12]

In Haddonfield, Cope, too, followed the Indian Ring controversy with avid interest and read of the attacks on Marsh, undoubtedly with great relish. Perhaps he showed too much sympathy for Delano and the Indian Ring, even if they were enemies of his enemy. "I do not admire Wm.

Welsh's language to Pres. Grant," he wrote to his father in late August, "and the Interocean [newspaper] gives him a severe overhauling for it. The Indian business is mixed between false charges on honest men, and true charges against the speculators; & the excessive zeal of some well intending men & malice of others. The truth is hard to get at."[13]

But public opinion—at least enlightened public opinion—was now firmly behind Marsh. "When charges of fraud began to be made against them . . . ," the Nation noted that same month, "Commissioner Smith fell back on his Christian character, and Mr. Delano tried to discredit his assailant."

On September 9, the investigating commission was back in Washington and heard a nineteen-page rebuttal statement from Marsh, in which he dealt with the "falsehoods" that had surfaced that summer. There had been, Marsh told the commission, a systematic "policy, long continued of meeting evidence . . . by misrepresentations."[14]

The following morning, a little before eight o'clock, Marsh walked into the dining room at Wormley's—one of Washington's foremost hotels and watering holes—for breakfast. Sitting reading a newspaper at the next table was Columbus Delano and his son, John.

Delano turned. "Is this Mr. Marsh?" he asked.

Marsh got up, offered his hand, and said, "Good morning, Mr. Delano. It is a pleasant morning."

When Marsh had again sat down at his table, Delano, with a smile, asked, "When are you going to stop investigating me?"

"I really don't know," Marsh replied.

"When," and now Delano's voice was louder, "are you going to stop assaulting me?"

"Probably when you stop attacking me," Marsh shot back.

His voice rising even louder now, Delano insisted that he had done nothing of the kind, and Marsh came right back at him. The Yale professor said that since the commission started its investigation, he had "not said a word considering the case," but Delano's department continued to attack him.

Delano jumped to his feet and called Marsh a "liar" and a "poltroon," repeating the insults several times, as he stood "pale and quivering" over Marsh's table. For a moment, Marsh thought of getting up and leaving, but then pulled a pencil and orange envelope from his jacket and starting writing down the incident.

Delano sat down at his own table, muttering. In a few minutes when things had cooled down, Marsh turned and told Delano that he had simply been obliged to defend himself.

Delano exploded, again calling Marsh a liar and some other choice things.

"You have set Welsh, Walker, and the other hounds on me," he shouted.

"I do not intend to be insulted at my breakfast by the secretary of the interior or any other man," Marsh responded. "I have treated you as a gentleman should."

"I don't know what a gentleman is," Delano snapped, and he got up and stalked out of the dining room.[15] Somehow, the incident found its way into the September 16 edition of the *Nation*.

The real drama, however, had already been played out. Delano had tendered his resignation to Grant two weeks earlier, although it would not be official until October 1. By year's end, Smith's resignation would follow.

In early October, the peripatetic George Armstrong Custer knocked on the door of Marsh's New Haven apartment. The professor wasn't in. "I simply desired to take you by the hand and thank you for the considerable and disinterested service you have rendered the government and the country . . . by your exposing the well known frauds and irregularities of the Indian Ring," he explained in a note.

The "Red Cloud Agency . . . ," Custer assured Marsh, "is not an isolated instance. I know that the Indians at other agencies are the victims of similar mistreatment."[16]

On October 18, the commission issued a 929-page report. "The results of our investigation," the report stated, "fully sustain the allegations of Prof. Marsh that the agent is incompetent and unfit for the position which he occupies; that he should be removed without delay."

The commission went on to describe Saville as having "a nervous and irritable temperament, inordinate loquacity, undignified bearing and manners, a want of coolness and collectedness of mind." Saville resigned and moved to Omaha, where he died in 1922.

The report also recommended that some contractors be excluded from further federal business and suggested a number of administrative changes in the bureau. It was highly reminiscent of the recommendations proposed four years earlier. The commission found no evidence that either Delano or Smith were implicated in the Indian Ring.

It was, for the most part, a victory for the forces of reform. "Professor Marsh let daylight into a section of this department . . . ," wrote the Boston *Transcript*. "It was his trenchant criticism which forced the Government into an investigating mood." Grant's Peace Policy, however, was in shambles. During Grant's time in Washington, there would be more than two hundred battles with Indian tribes, and the Northern Pacific Railway was once again pushing west across the prairies.

On November 23, Grant met with Generals Sheridan and Crook, Secretary of War Robert Belknap, Smith, and the new interior secretary, Zachariah Chandler. It was decided that the army would turn a blind eye toward the miners burrowing into the Black Hills and that it was time for the army to chase those recalcitrant northern Sioux back to the reservations. Crook would lead an expeditionary force that spring to do just that. One of his officers would be Custer.

Whatever progress had been made in cleaning up the Department of Interior, the "frolic of corruption," as Nevins called it, continued. The Whiskey Ring trials were not even completed when it bubbled to the surface that Secretary of War Belknap, or more accurately his wife, had been arranging for kickbacks from the awarding of western trading-post contracts. Orvil Grant was also implicated. Was there no end?

"The continent spills its riches for everybody; everybody is grabbing his share; 'I must get mine'—so men argued," lamented Secretary of State Hamilton Fish, the most venerable member of Grant's cabinet. "Why be over-scrupulous in making money when it is so plentiful? Why should politics be more honest than business, or business than politics, or Tom than Dick and Harry?"

And speaking of riches, at the close that that year, money was suddenly no longer an obstacle for Cope. In December of 1875, Alfred Cope died, at the age of sixty-nine, and Edward received an inheritance of nearly a quarter of a million dollars.[17] It was a small fortune gathered not from speculation and manipulation, but slowly and rigorously by the Protestant work ethic and Quaker thrift.

It is difficult to plumb the depth of loss Cope must have felt. The father had been the son's greatest confidant, but also his greatest nemesis. Cope had to have been deeply saddened. And yet, now he was released both from his financial constraints and the personal constraints of acting as he thought his father wanted him to act. Within little more than a year, Cope would leave the Quaker Meeting for good and become a Unitarian. The resignation, he said, "cost me a pang." His "personal religion" was, he promised Annie, still intact, but he had come to serious differences of doctrine with his Quaker brethren, and so he went his own way.

Unburdened at last, and with his inheritance wisely invested, he should have had an ample annual income and a free hand to pursue the scientific road that he had fought so long to attain. But this was the Gilded Age.

As for Marsh, he returned to New Haven to continue opening crates from the West and oversee the new Peabody Museum. He concerned himself no more with spoilsmen and politicians. Perhaps the impact of his efforts had already been buried by new waves of Washington corruption, but twelve hundred miles away in the Dakotas, what he had done was not forgotten.

In January of 1877, Marsh received a box from Fort Robinson. In it were a peace pipe from Red Cloud and a letter from Lieutenant Carpenter, one of Marsh's fossil-hunting minions, which read:

> *I send by express, Red Cloud's pipe and hope it will arrive all right.*
>
> *Mr. Red Cloud came to my quarters and said he wanted to give it to you, and wished me to, at the same time, to tell you something. This is his speech, as translated by an Interpreter. "I remember the wise chief. He came here and I asked him to tell the Great Father something. He promised to do so, and I thought he would do like all white men, and forget me when he went away. But he did not. He told the Great Father everything just as he promised he would, and I think he is the best white man I ever saw. I like him. I want you to tell him this."*

Chapter Ten

 WHEN NEWS OF THE MASSACRE at the Little Bighorn finally reached New Haven, Custer had been dead and buried in a shallow grave for eleven days. Sitting Bull and the Sioux had done on the Montana plains what the entire Confederate Army had not been able to do in five years of war. The bold, black headline in the July 6, 1876, edition of the *New Haven Palladium* declared:

AN INDIAN MASSACRE
GENERAL CUSTER & HIS
COMMAND ENTIRELY
CUT TO PIECES

They were so entirely cut to pieces—an estimated 265 soldiers dead—that it stood as the single worst defeat the army had ever suffered at the hands of Indians and raised the specter of worse things to come. Still, Custer retained some of that luck and charm that, at the age of twenty-six, had vaulted him from a lieutenant to a brevet major general. For instead of being reviled as the commander of the most catastrophic episode in Indian fighting, he was wept over and mourned as a fallen hero. Walt Whitman was so moved, he dashed off a poem for the *New York Tribune* about the "dusky Sioux" and "a trumpet note for heroes."

The plan for the army to chase the unruly Sioux back to their reservations was quickly coming undone. It soon became clear that in addition to Custer's massacre, General George Crook's command had also been repulsed by the Indians. The fear rose that instead of being shooed back onto the reservations, the tribes might actually have the upper hand and that all the Indian nations were amassing for a grand and final assault against white settlers and the army. It looked as if Grant's negotiators for the rights to the Black Hills had been dead wrong when they had assumed that the Sioux had neither the food nor ammunition to offer any "serious resistance." By the middle of July, the *Palladium* was ready to exclaim, "The Sioux. A General Indian War Threatened."

For Marsh, the news was of more than casual interest, having crossed paths with both Custer and Sitting Bull. Only a few months earlier, Custer had tried to pay Marsh a visit in New Haven, but the professor had been out. Now, there would be no more pleasantries between the paleontologist and the Indian fighter.

The western news Marsh was most interested in, however, came not from Montana, but Kansas, as once again Benjamin Mudge and Samuel Williston were out scouring the Cretaceous beds for Yale. The news from Kansas was good. Soon box after box began to arrive in New Haven filled with hard Kansas clay. Mudge and Williston even telegraphed the news of discovering new *Hesperornis* specimens.[1]

Of course, Cope was always on the mind. "Cope's man Sternberg is in the vicinity . . . ," Mudge reported. "If he gets anything it will be by accident."[2] Since Marsh was mainly interested in reptiles and birds, Williston joked that they were taking "pains to leave . . . plenty of fishes" for Sternberg to spend his time gathering.

Marsh also had another collector, David Baldwin from Canon City, Colorado, working in those Eocene beds of New Mexico discovered by Cope in 1874. "I heard that Cope is coming," Baldwin wrote from Santa Fe, "but he hasn't appeared."[3]

Yes, it promised to be an interesting and busy summer in the inner sanctum of the Peabody Museum, provided Indians didn't become too much of a problem. Marsh, however, briefly had put aside his fossils and any concerns about the Sioux to receive the most important guest he had ever entertained.

⚜

As the steamer *Germanic* pulled into New York City harbor, on the morning of August 5, the distinguished, middle-age man with the prominent nose, mutton-chop whiskers, and sharp black eyes stood at the ship's rail, gazing at the city that rose up before him.

What, he asked, were the tall building with a cupola and the tower that loomed over the skyline? When told that he was looking at the New York Tribune and Western Union Telegraph buildings, Thomas Henry Huxley exclaimed, "Ah, that is interesting. That is American. In the Old World, the first things you see as you approach a great city are steeples; here you see first centers of intelligence."

The fifty-one-year-old Huxley was primed for America, and America was certainly ready for Huxley. The curator of paleontology collections at the Royal School of Mines, the naturalist for the British Geological Survey, and the author of *Man's Place in Nature,* Huxley was arguably the most famous scientist of the day. A measure of Huxley's renown came from his own creative work, which included writings on vertebrate paleontology and marine biology. A larger share came from his role as a great interpreter of science for the layman. In classic lectures, such as "On a Piece of Chalk," which he delivered to the Workingman's Association of Norwich, Huxley was able to take something as common as a morsel of blackboard chalk and use it as a foil to explain the geological and biological forces that shaped the world. "A great chapter of the world's history is written in chalk," he told his audience.

Huxley had the gift of making even the remote and elusive vivid. He could give a listener the feel of the ocean floor by conjuring up a wagon ride across its slopes and valleys or make him see a microscopic fossil by describing it as "a badly grown raspberry." It was, however, as Charles Darwin's alter ego, an attack dog for the theory of evolution, that Huxley gained his greatest notoriety.

The shy, retiring Darwin had avoided publishing his *Origin of Species* for nearly two decades because he knew how controversial it would be. Darwin was an ailing recluse and such a gentleman as to display differential respect and politeness toward even his most strident critics. Huxley, by contrast, was a superb public speaker and relished the limelight, almost as much as he savored a good fight. "I am sharpening my beak and claws in readiness," he assured Darwin.

Huxley's scientific knowledge and ability to craft presentations for the public at large made him a formidable ally. Indeed, after reading a set of Huxley's general lectures on evolution, which had been printed in pamphlet form, Darwin said, "What is the good of my writing a thundering big book, when everything is in this green little book, so despicable for its size?"

Darwin was, of course, simply praising Huxley with faint damnation. Darwin knew that he was fortunate to have Huxley in his camp, for just as he had suspected, when, in the fall of 1859 *Origin of Species* was published, it caused a furor.

Darwin had gotten his first inkling of the process of evolution when he served as a naturalist on the HMS *Beagle*'s five-year voyage, which ended in 1836. For the next twenty-three years, he diligently pursued the trail, doing extensive studies on species as disparate as pigeons and barnacles.

The idea of evolution had been kicking around since the ancient Greeks. Even Darwin's grandfather, Erasmus Darwin, had written a highly speculative study on the subject titled *Zoonomia*. But until the nineteenth century, theorists lacked two important elements to make the theory work: time and a mechanism or reason for the process. These were provided to Darwin by two of his century's most provocative minds.

It was Sir Charles Lyell who gave Darwin enough time for evolution. At the beginning of the century, it was still generally accepted that all species were the distinct, all-in-a-moment creations described in Genesis and that Earth as calculated by the generations of the Bible was only fifty-eight hundred years old. To be precise, Irish archbishop James Ussher, working back generation by generation, had calculated that Earth was created on Sunday, October 23, 4004 B.C.—at 8 A.M. That simply didn't leave enough time for evolution to work.

But Lyell looked at Earth's geological processes—erosion from the forces of weather, earthquakes, volcanoes, rivers carrying silt—and he saw a slow, ongoing, perpetual-motion machine.

If mountains were slowly raised and then slowly worn away by natural forces, geological time had to be much, much longer than man had thought. If one calculated how slowly the forces of erosion worked in the modern world, it was clear that something like a river cutting a canyon through hard rock must have taken hundreds of thousands or even millions of years. Earth had to be considerably older than the biblical calculations.

All well and good. But why does evolution take place, and what is the mechanism that drives it? The answer to that came not from a scientist, but the political philosopher and cleric, the Reverend Thomas Malthus. In his *Essay on a Principle of Population,* Malthus argued that population pressures increase geometrically, while food supplies increase only arithmetically. The result is that there are always too many mouths to feed. That leads to a "struggle for existence" in which wars, plagues, and famine cull the populace.

Malthus wrote his tract as a conservative argument in political economics to explain why trying to improve the lot of poor was pointless, perhaps even counterproductive. But in this vision, Darwin found his mechanism for evolution—natural selection.

All organisms in the biological world are in a competition for food and living space. Those that have some advantage—a longer beak, stronger hind legs, sharper teeth—gain an edge, even if it is only a slight one. Over time, these attributes would be reinforced. Similarly, those individuals with handicaps would be eliminated.

Over much more time, this process of natural selection would lead to the evolution of new organs and organisms that heighten the advantages. Thus, the lump of light-sensitive nerves in an eel is refined into the complex optical organ of the eye.

"Nothing at first can appear more difficult to believe," Darwin conceded in *Origin of Species,* "than that the more complex organs and instincts have been perfected, not by means superior to, though analogous with human wisdom, but by the accumulation of innumerable slight variations, each good for the individual possessor."

Darwin's theory was doubly damning to the conventional orthodoxy. Not only did it challenge the idea of the Bible's individual creation of each plant and animal, but it substituted a chaotic, indifferent, amoral process for any rational or guiding hand in the development of life on Earth. If that wasn't enough, it linked man into the chain of animal life on the planet, placing him merely one step above the ape rather than as the divine creation of God. And that is why *Origin of Species* was quickly dubbed "the most dangerous book in the world."

When Huxley read it, however, he had quite a different reaction. "My reflection," he said, "when I first made myself master of the central idea was, 'How extremely stupid not to have thought of that.' "

So while not the author of the theory, Huxley launched himself into the defense and dissemination of the concept, as the shy and sickly Darwin retired to his comfortable country home in Kent.

In June of 1860, seven months after the book's publication, the first great battle over Darwin's theory erupted at the British Association for the Advancement of Science's annual meeting in Oxford. The Darwinian forces were represented by Huxley and the noted botanist, Sir Joseph Hooker; the opposition was led by Sir Richard Owen and the bishop of Oxford, Samuel Wilberforce. While there were several skirmishes during the first two days, the main event shaped up at the Saturday session. Huxley had planned to leave for London on Friday evening, having no desire he said to be "episcopally pounded" by Wilberforce. He was, however, persuaded to stay.

The Saturday session drew a crowd of more than seven hundred, forcing the gathering to be moved to the library of the university's museum. Ladies in bright summer crinolines lined the windows, black-frocked clergymen occupied the center of the room, and behind them sat a small, boisterous group of undergraduates. All had been drawn by the debate over the "monkey theory," as it had come to be called. To this packed house, the purple-vested Wilberforce, whose lush oratory had earned him the nickname "Soapy Sam," fired away. He spoke for more than a half hour attempting to ridicule and dismiss Darwin rather than address his theory.

At one point, the bishop turned to Huxley and "begged to know was it through his grandfather or his grandmother that he claimed his descent from a monkey?" As Wilberforce, quite content with his barb, returned to his audience, Huxley is supposed to have slapped his knee and softly exclaimed, "The Lord hath delivered him into mine hands."

In a dark coat and white collar, Huxley must have looked much the cleric himself as began his address. His words, however, were far from ecclesiastical. He began by saying he had no shame in having an ape for a grandfather. "If there were an ancestor whom I should feel ashamed on recalling, it would rather be a man of restless and versatile intellect, who not content with an equivocal success in his own sphere of activity, plunges into scientific questions with which he had no real acquaintance, only to obscure them by an aimless rhetoric . . . and skilled appeals to religious prejudice." This was merely the beginning of Huxley's attack. Lady Brewster fainted and had to be carried from the room.

The real challenge to Darwin's theory, however, came not from the Wilberforces, but from scientists such as Owen, Germany's Andreas Wagner, and America's Louis Agassiz.

Indeed, while Darwin knew that his theory would be controversial, he was unprepared for the criticism that his work—particularly his methods— received from the most distinguished scientists and philosophers of the time.[4]

The eminent physicist and philosopher John Herschel found the processes of natural selection too random, too hit or miss, too far from the elegance of Newtonian physics. He called Darwin's theory "the law of higgledly, piggedly." Owen dispatched it as "just one of those obvious possibilities that might float through the imagination of any speculative naturalist."

Owen, however, was more than simply dismissive. He could not abide Darwin's theory, and as director of the British Museum, Hunterian professor at the Royal College of Physicians, a protégé of Prince Albert, the country's most distinguished paleontologist, the "English Cuvier," he presented a serious challenge. After all, it was Owen who in 1841 created the new order—Dinosauria—to counter evolutionary ideas.

Owen had created dinosaurs to rebut the theory of evolution proposed by Jean Baptiste Lamarck, which had been popular before Darwin came on the scene with natural selection. Lamarckian evolution held that forms tended to move from the simple to the complex and that attributes gained along the way from use and environment—a neck stretching to reach leaves, as in the case of the giraffe—could be passed from one generation to the next. There even seemed to be a bit of that in Darwin's example of light-sensitive nerves evolving into an eye.

But if evolution tended to move from the basic to the sophisticated, then clearly dinosaurs stood the theory on its head. The huge reptiles had more refined organs—such as four-chambered instead of three-chambered hearts—and greater size than the modern-day crop of reptiles. Clearly, Owen argued, this wasn't evolution!

Huxley and Owen had been acidly sparring over vertebrate paleontology, the relationship of man and apes, and the general direction of English science since 1856. So *Origin of Species* just added fuel to their fire. Despite Owen's position as the most honored and senior paleontologist in the country, Huxley was unimpressed, declaring that Owen was "not so great as he thinks himself."

Owen might be Huxley's rival, but that didn't necessarily make him the enemy of all Darwinians. No, Owen still had prestige, power, and respect in scientific circles, and Marsh, for one, did his best to ingratiate himself with the elder paleontologist. In addition to naming a pterodactyl after Owen, Marsh made sure he posted all his important papers to the British Museum. "Let me congratulate you on returning from your last foray west with your scalp," Owen enthused in one letter, "and next thank you for . . . *The New Order of Ecocene Mammals.*"[5]

There was, however, only one scalp Huxley wanted and that belonged to Owen. At Oxford, the two sharply squared off on the topic of whether an ape's brain is closer to that of a human (Huxley) or a lemur (Owen). American mathematician Benjamin Pierce, who was at the session, was shocked at what a "very sharp pass" the two Englishmen had. And so across Europe the Darwinian and anti-Darwinian camps drew their battle lines.

The America Huxley sailed to in the summer of 1876 had reacted much differently to Darwin's theory. It really had not been until after the Civil War that the nation's intellectual and public discourse could turn to new scientific theories, and when it did, there was much more acceptance, at least of some parts of Darwinian evolution.

It was, to be sure, anathema to the clergy. The Reverend Dewitt Talmadge of Brooklyn, aping Wilberforce, attempted to disprove the notion of the survival of the fittest by asking whether the generals who died in the Civil War had not been as good as those who survived? In 1874, Charles Hodge, a professor at the Princeton Theological Seminary, wrote a small volume titled *What Is Darwinism?* His answer was that any theory that propounds "the denial of design in nature is virtually the denial of God. . . . What is Darwinism? It is Atheism."

The church, however, held less sway in America than in Europe. There was no state religion, and, even without "Darwinism," the old Protestant denominations were already having trouble responding to the changing American scene. "Never before had the church been materially more powerful or spiritually less effective," observed Henry Steel Commager in *The American Mind.*

In American scientific circles, Darwin's theory received a fair reception. Upon reading *Origin of Species,* Joseph Leidy immediately sent Darwin a letter of congratulations and a few of his own articles that tended to support the theory. In a show of solidarity, he also arranged to have Darwin voted a member of Philadelphia's Academy of Natural Sciences. At Harvard and Yale, and in the scientific societies in Philadelphia, New York, and Boston, the theory received a generally open hearing. Marsh immediately understood the power of Darwinian evolution and adopted it as the organizing principle for his work.

When *Origin of Species* was first published, Darwin's greatest American opponent had been Harvard's Louis Agassiz. For the Swiss-born Agassiz, the study of nature was an exploration of God's handiwork, and he considered Darwin's theory "merely conjectural." In a letter to Cope, he dismissed it as "ingenious but fanciful." Agassiz, like Cuvier, believed that periodic catastrophes wiped out species, which were then divinely replaced.

Agassiz's Harvard colleague, botanist Asa Gray, was Darwin's chief American ally. In fact, Darwin had sought Gray's expertise on some issues dealing with plants. When Alfred Russel Wallace proposed much the same idea of evolution in 1858, a letter to Gray, dated 1857, was a key to Darwin's ability to prove his priority in developing the theory.

As in the case of Huxley and Owen, there was no love lost between Gray and Agassiz. In part, it came from Agassiz's popularity and his ability to translate it into big donations for his Museum of Comparative Zoology, while Gray struggled to keep up his Harvard herbarium going.

"Agassiz cannot abide it [Darwin's theory] . . . and so has publicly denounced it as atheism, etc., etc.," Gray wrote in early 1860. "I am bound to stick up for its philosophy, and I am struck with the great ability of the book and charmed by its fairness. I also want to stop Agassiz's mouth with his own words, and show up his loose ways of putting things. He is a sort of demagogue, and always talks to the rabble."

Darwin in an 1860 letter wrote, "I am amused by Asa Gray's account of the excitement my book has made amongst naturalists. . . . Agassiz has denounced it in a newspaper, but yet in such terms that it is in fact a fine advertisement!"[6]

Two of Agassiz's arguments were that some life forms like trilobites—an ancient lobsterlike arthropod—were more complex than some modern arthropods. Yet they appear early in the fossil record and then disappear. Another was that some marine organisms found in the fossil record can still be found today—unchanged and therefore, untouched by evolution.

Agassiz flatly denied the process of evolution. Many other American scientists were not so sure. They could see hints of evolution in the fossil record, but were still reluctant to subscribe to Darwin's vision. This was the predicament Cope faced. He simply could not accept natural selection as the sole evolutionary force because it seemed to harbor terrible religious, moral, and social implications.

Embedded like a black seed in the heart of Darwin's theory was Malthus's bleak economic and political vision of society. By adding the force of nature to it, Darwin had amplified its power. It challenged the idea of "free will" and seemingly sanctioned "the slaughter of innocents."[7] It was destined to be turned back upon society and enlarged yet again, rippling out to touch a myriad of social and political shores. Ultimately, Darwinian evolution would be used to denigrate the poor, celebrate the rich, praise nationalism, and extol war.

This road was too severe, too hopeless for some scientists. Natural selection was useful as far as it went, but for Cope it simply didn't go far enough in explaining the reasons for evolution. The key to evolution was in variation, but from where did that variation come? Any theory of evolution that didn't explain variation, Cope had once told his father, was "incomplete." The answer for Cope was that those variations were part of a design.

In 1869, he made his first attempt at reworking the theory of evolution in an eighty-page pamphlet titled *Origin of Genera*. In it he argued that variation was created by the "acceleration or retardation" of characteristics, and this force was internal and part of an overall design.

After all, Cope asked, what were the odds of good things happening by chance? "Since the number of variations possible to an organism is very great," he argued, "the probability of the one admirably adaptive structure . . . having arisen by chance is extremely small."[8]

Cope also resurrected the Lamarckian belief that environmental adaptations could be passed from generation to generation. All in all, it was a masterful and heartfelt effort to imbue what was clearly a remarkable pattern of change in the fossil chronicle with spirituality and morality. Variation was part of a design, a plan; and hard work and achievement by the father could be passed on to the son. This was a kinder, gentler evolution. So much so, that Cope was able to proclaim "the science of evolution is the science of creation."[9]

This became the foundation of the neo-Lamarckian school of evolution, a uniquely American reaction to Darwin's theory and one that managed to simultaneously deal with the emerging fossil record and still shelter some of Victorian society's most cherished tenets. Cope, A. S. Packard, and John Ryder were its main leaders. For a time, their ideas held broader sway in America than those of Darwin and Huxley.

The problem was that this theory required a set of forces that were impossible to measure or demonstrate. Still, the neo-Lamarckian dressed them up in scholarly Greek. There was, for example, the so-called growth force, "bathmism," and variation through stimuli, or "epigenesis," and the transmission of growth force from generation to the next, or "perigenesis."

For Cope, it was a life's work. His *Origin of Genera* was followed in 1886 with a series of essays titled *The Origin of the Fittest* and ten years after that by the voluminous *Primary Facts of Organic Evolution*. This effort would, according to Harvard paleontologist and science historian Stephen J. Gould, make Cope "America's first great evolutionary theoretician."

Primary Facts was a monumental effort to take the known material—particularly in the fossil record—and organize it into a neo-Lamarckian framework. "The present book," Cope explained, "is an attempt to select from the mass of facts accumulated by biologists, those which, in the author's opinion throw light upon the problem of organic evolution."

In some five hundred pages, Cope sifted through a massive amount of data, but his conclusion wasn't different than it had been twenty-seven years earlier. "It has been proved, as it appears to me, that the variation which has resulted in evolution has not been multifarious or promiscuous, but in definite directions."[10]

American scientists weren't the only ones trying to take the fossil record and make a sense out of it that was different from Darwin's. Owen, who so intensely disliked both Darwin's theory and its champion, Huxley, had been working on the idea that there were developmental "archetypes."[11]

There was, for example, a vertebrate archetype of which all creatures with backbones were merely variations. There had been a divine blueprint. Huxley ridiculed Owen's approach as misguided romantic Platonism—not science.

What Cope's arguments, as well as the Owen-Huxley and Agassiz-Gray battles, underscored was something that Darwin had been acutely aware of—the proof or refutation of the theory lay in the fossil record. Evolution moved far too slowly to expect to see it or verify it in the modern world. But if these transformations did occur, somehow they had to be preserved among the fossils.

Darwin realized this but feared that the fossil record was too incomplete and fragmented to be of much use. In *Origin of Species,* he devoted an entire chapter to "the imperfection of the geological record.

"What an infinite number of generations, which the mind cannot grasp, must have succeeded each other in the long rock of years!" Darwin wrote. "Now, turn to our richest geological museums, and what a paltry display we behold!" The fossil record was very weak. "This is perhaps the most obvious and gravest objection which can be urged against my theory," Darwin conceded.

A year after *Origin of Species* was published, the bizarre *Archaeopteryx* had been discovered in the fine limestone of Solnhofen, Bavaria. This creature with the bony tail and long claws of a reptile and feathers of a bird was clearly a link between the two forms. It was, at the time, the most valuable of all fossils, the single greatest piece of evidence for Darwin's theory.

When a German specimen came on the market, Baird, the inveterate but poor collector, urged Marsh to buy it. "Now is your chance," he wrote, "regardless of cost."[12] Marsh passed. The fossil sold for ten thousand dollars.

Huxley was also delighted with *Archaeopteryx.* But opponents, like the University of Munich's Andreas Wagner, argued that the feathers were coincidental and nothing more than "peculiar adornments." He renamed the fossil *Griphosaurus,* or griffin lizard. "Darwin and his adherents will probably employ the new discovery as an exceedingly welcome occurrence for the justification of their strange views upon the transformation of animals," Wagner said. In that case, he demanded, where were all the intermediates between this link and the true bird?

There was the challenge again, and neither Darwin nor Huxley had a full reply. The gap in the fossil record was their missing link, their Achilles' heel. The *New York Times,* in an 1876 article discussing Darwin's theory, clearly stated the problem. "When it is urged against the evolutionists that during enormous periods of time, we see no development in a given organism, or but the slightest change, the reply is made that we must go further back to the limitless period beyond, when there is time for any evolution. In some degrees, it is a response *ad ignitum. We* know nothing of the 'past eternity' and cannot answer."

So this was the dilemma as Huxley disembarked in New York City on an August summer's day. The theory of evolution by natural selection had come to permeate every aspect of intellectual life, forcing responses from theologians, philosophers, scientists, politicians, and educators. It was debated, praised, and condemned. It had been held up as justification for the laissez-faire economy, social policy, and even war. But it remained merely a theory.

"In spite of twenty years labor," noted historian David Hull, "Darwin had failed to provide any proof of his theory of evolution by natural selection." Huxley had now been defending the theory for another seventeen years, and he had only bits of proof, like *Archaeopteryx*. But Huxley had heard that in America there might be proof, not buried in massive rock strata but rather waiting in New Haven, Connecticut.

Two days after arriving in New York, Henrietta Huxley, who was accompanying her husband on his American tour, went north to the summer resort at Saratoga, with its mineral springs and racetrack. Huxley boarded a special, private parlor car provided to him by the New York Central Railroad and headed for New Haven.

❧

Marsh was waiting as the 1:10 P.M. train from New York pulled into the station. After settling themselves in a carriage, the Yale professor proposed a short tour of the university buildings. "Show me what you have got inside them. I can see plenty of bricks and mortar in my own country," Huxley replied. And with that, they were off to that Victorian temple of bones—the Peabody Museum.

Like a rug merchant unfurling his wares, Marsh placed before Huxley pterodactyls, mosasaurs, plesiosaurs, and the fossil remains of many other long-vanished species. Huxley was delighted. It was, the Englishman told his wife in a letter, "the most wonderful thing I ever saw."

Bones were not, however, the only entertainment Marsh was to provide. Huxley was wined and dined and feted at a string of teas and dinners. One dinner was held with some key scientific men—including Leidy and Clarence King. The governor of Connecticut came to visit and told a reporter that he was delighted to find that Huxley was not a "highfalutin" philosopher, but rather had the sensibilities of a "commercial or mercantile" man. Obviously, a high Yankee compliment. Huxley took it as such. "That is something I did not know and I am rather proud of it," he wrote to his wife. "We may be rich yet."

Huxley and Marsh drove up and down the elm-canopied streets of New Haven, like scientific royalty. "I can assure you I am being 'made of' as I thought nobody but the little wife was foolish enough to do," he wrote to Henrietta.

The news from the West continued to be menacing. On the day before Huxley arrived in town, the *New Haven Evening Register* carried this dispatch from St. Paul: "The steamer Carroll arrived this morning from General

Terry's camp having brought General Forsythe and 20 sick and wounded soldiers. The Carroll was on her way up when near the mouth of the Powder River Indians on both sides of the river kept up a running fire upon the boat."

Washington was still obsessed with scandal; this time it was the courtly secretary of war, Robert Belknap, who was brought down in a kickback scheme involving supply contracts for western forts. On August 1, Belknap had narrowly escaped being tried on impeachment charges by the Senate, which had voted thirty-five to twenty-five for the trial to proceed. The vote, however, clearly showed there was not enough support to reach the required two-thirds for conviction. Belknap had already resigned, so the case was dropped.

How much these current events intruded into the daily life of Huxley and Marsh is difficult to say, although it is clear that as his visit to America progressed, the Englishman was becoming a perceptive critic of American foibles.

What is certain is that Marsh and Huxley plumbed the depths of time at the Peabody Museum. Each day from nine to six, with a break for lunch, a drive around town, and tea at the end of the day, the two worked their way through Marsh's treasures—particularly one set of fossils that the Yale professor very much wanted Huxley to see—his collection of fossil horses.

At the end of his tour, Huxley was to give a series of lectures on evolution in New York City, and Marsh knew that he intended to speak about the genealogy of the horse. It was a subject Huxley, and Russian paleontologist Vladimir Kovalesky, had both written on based upon European specimens.

"My own explorations had led me to conclusions quite different from his," Marsh wrote, "and my specimens seemed to prove to me conclusively that the horse originated in the New World, not the Old, and that its genealogy had to be worked out here. With some hesitation, I laid the whole matter frankly before Huxley, and he spent nearly two days going over my specimens with me and testing each point that I made."

As early as 1870, Huxley had offered the horse as a potential example of evolution and had focused on four fossil species and the changes in their teeth, feet, and ulna, or forelimb bone, over a thirty-million-year period. "The process by which the *Anchitherium* has been converted to *Equus* is one of reduction and specialization," Huxley wrote in his essay "Paleontology and Evolution."

Marsh had come across some horse fossils, by chance, back in 1868 on that first stop at Antelope Station, Nebraska. Since then, in his relentless, methodical, acquisitive way, he had continued to collect as many horse fossils as he could lay his hands on. It had become a unique collection.

Marsh had pieced together a sixty-million-year story of the horse and its transformation from the fox-sized, four-toed *Hyracotherium vassaccus* to the donkey-sized *Merychippa sejuntus,* and finally the modern horse, *Equus complicatus.* In all, Marsh documented thirty different species in three families that lead from *Hyracotherium* to *Equus.*

This story was sketched in teeth and femurs and jawbones rescued from the fossil beds across the West, and through these fragments, one could see how the tooth of *Hyracotherium,* really no bigger than that of a child, slowly evolved to the tooth of *Mesohippus,* which is comparable to an adult human's molar, and finally to the huge, flat, three-inch-long tooth of *Equus.*

This was not just a tale of the evolution of anatomy but of the transformation of Earth itself. It told of how the West in Eocene times was a thick forest, where the foxy *Hyracotherium* was well adapted and how it became vast prairies by the Pleistocene where the larger and swifter *Equus,* with hooves made by the fusing of the toes and large teeth for grazing on tough grasses, was better equipped. It was not simply a story of specialization as Huxley had thought, but rather one of the complex interrelationship between environment and species, and also a tale of trial and error.

Huxley, however, was reluctant to give up his notions and challenged Marsh time and time again. With each challenge, Marsh dispatched an assistant to fetch the appropriate box containing the appropriate evidence. "I believe you are a magician," Huxley finally declared. "Whatever I want, you just conjure up." At the end of the two days, Huxley had capitulated.

"He then informed me," Marsh wrote, "that all this was new to him, and that my facts demonstrated the evolution of the horse beyond question, and that for the first time indicated the direct line of descent of an existing animal."

The Darwinians had steered clear of arguing too robustly that the fossil record could prove the theory of evolution because they had feared that it would be impossible to fill in all the gaps, that too many links would be missing, and that their absence would offer an easy target for the critics. But Marsh, with his uncompromising, obsessive attention to detail, had missed no links, left no holes. Here for the first time was physical proof of evolution.

"No collection which has hitherto been formed, approaches that made by Professor Marsh, in completeness of the chain of evidence by which certain existing mammals are connected with their older tertiary ancestry," Huxley later wrote to a colleague.

And if that was not enough, Marsh offered Huxley a peek at his work on the Kansas birds with teeth. Birds with teeth! Why, if Marsh could do with birds what he had done with horses, he would not only have shown the evolution of a species, but of one order of animals into another. Who could argue with Darwin's theory then?

Marsh assured Huxley that somewhere out there in the West must be the fossil remains of an even older, five-toed horse, which might have trotted among the dinosaurs. In a giddy moment, Huxley doodled for Marsh his impression of that very first horse, which he dubbed *Eohippus*. Marsh said the horse ought to have a rider, and so Huxley created *Eohomo*. The cartoon, still among Marsh's papers, shows a smiling horse—with five toes—and a smiling, hairy, simian jockey.

On August 16, Huxley left New Haven to join Alexander Agassiz, the son of Louis Agassiz, in tony Newport, Rhode Island. The great Agassiz's son was also a Harvard naturalist, but he was a Darwinian. The day after his departure, Huxley wrote to Marsh, "My recollections are sorting themselves out and I find how rich my store is." A few days later in a letter to Clarence King, Huxley simply stated, "There is no collection of fossil vertebrate in existence, which can compare with it."

Huxley rejoined his wife, and they then went on to the annual meeting of American Association for the Advancement of Science in Buffalo. They toured Niagara Falls and visited Huxley's older sister and nephew in Nashville, Tennessee. From there, Huxley faced his two major speeches of the trip—the inaugural address for the new Johns Hopkins University, in Baltimore, and his lectures on evolution in New York City. The Baltimore and Ohio Railroad provided another plush, private parlor car for the journey from Tennessee to Maryland.

One the morning of September 12, the Baltimore Academy of Music was packed with a standing-room-only crowd of more than two thousand people as Huxley took to the stage. By that time, he had seen a good deal of America and Americans, and while impressed, he was also troubled.

Although his speech was titled "University Education," Huxley concluded by raising questions about where the nation was heading and challenging its values. "I cannot say that I am the slightest degree impressed by your bigness, or your material resources. Size is not grandeur, and territory does not make a nation. The great issue, about which hangs a true sublimity, and the terror of overhanging fate, is what are you going to do with these things? What is to be the end to which these are the means?"

America was young and fresh, in Huxley's eyes, but he knew that it risked all the political and economic problems that were already wracking

Europe. "You and your descendants," he told the audience, "will have to decide whether shifting corruption is better than permanent bureaucracy; and as the population thickens in your great cities and the pressure of want is felt, the gaunt specter of pauperism will stalk you."

Still, he held out hope. "Truly America has a great future before her; great in toil, in care, and in responsibility; great in true glory if she be guided in wisdom and right; great in shame if she fail.

"I cannot understand," Huxley continued, "why other nations should envy you or be blind to the fact that it is for the highest interest of mankind that you should succeed; but the one condition of success, your sole safeguard, is moral worth and intellectual clearness."

Huxley did not know to what ends American wealth would be put nor how it would fashion the worth and clarity he believed the nation needed to make its contribution to the world, yet even as he spoke, answers were being forged. The very university rising in Baltimore was part of that answer. Unlike previous American universities, Johns Hopkins—built with the legacy of railroad and shipping money—was geared to the sciences, advanced graduate education, and research.

Slowly, America was committing a larger and larger portion of its burgeoning wealth to science. At Harvard, textile money had financed the Lowell Scientific School, and at Yale, railroad and cotton money built the Sheffield Scientific School. George Peabody's mercantile largess had created the Peabody Museum. Why, in the 1880s, even P. T. Barnum would contribute one hundred thousand dollars to Tufts University for what would become the foundation of its biological sciences program

The emerging land-grant system of universities, while at the outset offering a decidedly applied and agrarian bent, was also turning American land into American science.

The eight-year-old Cornell University was perhaps the best example of the new American university. Started with a federal land grant, the fledgling institution also became the recipient of an endowment from Ezra Cornell, the founder of the Western Union Telegraph Company. Cornell would teach agriculture, engineering, and science, and teach it to both men and women. (In 1872, it had become the first American university to open its doors to female students.)

This was a far cry from the classical academy. This was not education for the elite; it was education in the service of democracy and industry. "The emergence of science and the subsequent development of industry and vocation" were seen as ways of building the nation and fostering equality.[13]

Within a few years, the German electrical engineer and industrialist Werner von Siemens would warn the Prussian government, "Recently England, France, and America, those countries which are our most dangerous enemies in the struggle for survival, have recognized the great meaning of scientific superiority . . . [and] have zealously striven to improve natural scientific education through improvements in teaching to create institutions that promote scientific progress." For a worried German to mention the United States in the same breath with France and England was surely a measure of progress.

Siemens, of course, was right. America was beginning to erect a superstructure of science that would not be rivaled in the century to come. Huxley could not foresee how American science would completely eclipse the Europeans—and the world. Yet it was already happening.

And even if he could not see it, as he went on to New York City to give his lectures on evolution, he had already felt the force of the change in the basement laboratory of the Peabody Museum.

❖

On the way to New York, the Huxleys stopped in Philadelphia to examine the fossil treasures of the Academy of Natural Sciences and to visit the Centennial Exhibition. Although Leidy had always claimed that he was "too busy to theorize," Darwin's *Origin of Species* had been for him "like a meteor [that] flashed upon the skies." He offered the Huxleys an enthusiastic welcome and a tour of the academy, which had just moved into its new building on Logan Circle. The academy's new home had reading and lecture rooms, laboratories, and an "apartment" for artists copying natural objects. The library had grown to thirty thousand volumes, and the birds collection was now the largest in the world.[14]

Huxley had to be impressed with the huge *Hadrosaurus* restoration of his fellow countryman, Benjamin Waterhouse Hawkins. Surprisingly, when the Huxleys went across the Schuylkill River to the Centennial Exhibition, which sprawled across the flat fields of Fairmount Park, they encountered yet another *Hadrosaurus.*

This one was in front of the Smithsonian Institution's exhibit, a project that Spencer Baird had put tremendous effort into because in it was the promise of finally obtaining his long dreamed of museum.

Just a few years earlier, it had been doubtful whether the United States would even have a centennial, and perhaps that trauma made the celebration that much sweeter, that much grander. Collectively, city, state, and federal governments had raised nearly six million dollars to create this first American world's fair. An estimated ten million people flowed through the exhibition gates that summer—equal to one out every five Americans.

Congress had advanced Philadelphia more than a million dollars in loans for the exhibition. Many doubted whether any of that money would ever be paid back, but the Smithsonian was told if Philadelphia did make good on the loan, a portion of the returned money would go to building a national museum.[15]

Baird mobilized his forces and even persuaded employees to work late and on weekends—for no extra salary—to put together the best possible exhibit. He wanted a good show, but at first he wasn't certain mounting the *Hadrosaurus* was such a good idea. It was, of course, an issue upon which Cope and Marsh would thoroughly disagree.

Cope had been one of the original proponents of the idea. "It would be a great feature for the Exposition . . . ," he told Baird. "It would give great impetus to scientific study among the people—which is sadly wanted." Cope added this was especially important in Philadelphia, where he said "science is rather on the decline."[16]

Baird, however, was uncertain about the idea and unsure of anyone's "ability with the materials on hand to make these restorations." He sought Marsh's advice. "We have had a great preference brought to bear upon us to expend a portion of our centennial appropriation in employing Water-house Hawkins to make restorations of some prehistoric animals for the Philadelphia exhibition, the backers being LeConte, Cope, Guyot, & other gentlemen. Prof. Henry is inclined to accede," Baird wrote to Marsh in November of 1875.[17]

Marsh thought it all a bad idea. "I do not think it possible to make restorations of any of the more important extinct animals of this country that would be of real value to science," Marsh told Baird. Of course, Marsh thought that fossils were for scientists, not for the public.

Such a narrow view, Cope thought. Certainly there were scientific limits, but could they not see the public-relations value and how restorations were "especially appropriate for a great popular exposition." Yes, it was true that they weren't "appropriate for a scientific museum," but this was America's first world's fair.[18]

Cope prevailed, and a *Hadrosaurus* was built to celebrate the American centennial. It turned out to be a worthy competitor to Corliss's steam engine, Otis's elevator, and Bell's telephone, all of which made their debuts at the fair. The *Hadrosaurus* was such a hit that it was moved to Washington, where it stood outside the Smithsonian until time and weather eventually claimed it.

After a day of sight-seeing in Philadelphia, where *Hardosauri* just seemed to abound, Thomas and Henrietta Huxley got on the train once more and headed to New York City, the last leg of their journey.

❖

On Monday evening September 18, Huxley again faced a standing-room-only audience. This time there were more than thirteen hundred people packed into Chickering Hall, the Fifth Avenue recital auditorium, to hear the first of Huxley's three lectures on evolution. At five dollars a seat, a "highly respectable crush" filled the hall. The city's Social Register was well represented and so were the urban cognoscenti, like Peter Cooper, the elderly inventor, philanthropist, and builder of the Tom Thumb locomotive.

Huxley's talk dealt with geological and biological predicates to evolution. It left the *New York Times* correspondent disappointed, and he noted Huxley had been "comparatively indifferent to the imaginative and poetic side of his subject."

In his second lecture, again given to an overflowing hall, Huxley discussed transitional forms of life and how they tended to point to evolution. Huxley ended by announcing, "In my next lecture, I will take up what I like to call the demonstrative evidence of evolution."

On Friday, September 22, he delivered his final lecture. Once again the hall was packed, and when Huxley was finished, the speech became the lead story in the next morning's *Times*.

THE THEORY OF EVOLUTION
PROF. HUXLEY'S FINAL LECTURE
THE DEMONSTRATIVE EVIDENCE IN FAVOR OF
THE EVOLUTIONARY THEORY—SIMILARITIES
BETWEEN MAN AND THE HORSE
THE CHAIN OF EQUINE EVIDENCE

"The horse is in many ways a most remarkable animal in as much as it presents us with an example of one of the most perfect pieces of machinery in the animal kingdom," Huxley told his audience. "And as a necessary consequence of any sort of perfection . . . you find that he is a beautiful creature."

Huxley admired the animal's hooves and powerful legs, which were clearly built for speed, and its mouth and teeth, an exceptional "apparatus for providing the mechanism with the fuel which it requires." How had the horse come to this perfection?

Huxley then set about answering that question. He discussed his own work and that of other Europeans on the genealogy of the horse. And then he turned to America.

"You are all aware that when this country was discovered by Europeans, there were found no traces of the existence of horses in any part of the American continent. . . . Nevertheless, as soon as geology began to be pursued in this country, it was found that remains of horses, like horses existing at the present day, are to be found in abundance in the last superficial deposits." Then as bone hunters probed deeper in the tertiary deposits, new and curious animals were found.

"But it is only recently that the very admirably continued and most thoroughly and patiently worked out investigation of Prof. Marsh have given us a just idea of the enormous wealth and scientific importance of the deposits," Huxley announced.

"I have had the advantage of glancing over his collections at New Haven, and I can undertake to say that so far as my knowledge extends, there is nothing in any way comparable to them for extent, and the care with which the remains have been got together or their scientific importance." This drew a round of applause from the audience.

Using sketches provided by Marsh, Huxley walked his audience through the remarkable evolution of the horse. The assembled New Yorkers again responded with applause.

"That is what I mean, ladies and gentlemen, by demonstrative evidence of evolution," the English scientist concluded. "An inductive hypothesis is said to be demonstrated when the facts are shown to be in accordance with it. If this is not scientific proof, there can be no inductive conclusions, which can said to be scientifically proved and the doctrine of evolution at the present time rests upon as secure a foundation as the Copernican theory of the motion of the heavenly bodies." Again, the audience applauded.

Huxley received forty-eight hundred dollars for the three lectures and the next day boarded a ship to return to England. "I had," he announced, "a very pleasant trip in Yankee-land." Upon his return to England, Huxley wrote to Marsh, "I am thinking of discoursing on the birds with teeth. Have you anything new to tell on that subject? I have implicit faith in the inexhaustibility of the contents of those boxes."

Huxley's faith was not misplaced, for he had been in back in London just seven weeks when word reached him that Marsh had indeed found the five-toed dawn horse, *Eohippus*. It has not been hiding out west, but rather in an unopened crate in the Peabody Museum. "I had him 'corralled' in the basement of our Museum when you where there," Marsh wrote to Huxley, "but he was so covered with Eocene mud that I did not know him from Orohippus. I promise you his grandfather in time for your next Horse Lecture if you will give me proper notice."

Marsh himself also became a great champion of evolution, and in a keynote address before the American Association for the Advancement of Science's annual meeting in 1877, he proclaimed, "To doubt evolution today is to doubt science, and science is only another name for truth."

Still, doubters remained. Princeton professor Arnold Guyot, an ardent creationist, who never cared much for Marsh after the Yale professor had finagled him out of a mastodon skeleton that had been bought and paid for by Princeton, wrote to Marsh after his speech.

"You truly say that *Science* is another name for *Truth*.

"But was it *Science?* Is not this the same question as what is truth?"

⚜

After Huxley left New Haven, Marsh returned to the task of dealing with the steady stream of boxes from his fossil hunters in Kansas. Crate after crate came filled with specimens of mastodons, pterodactyls, dinosaurs, and Jayhawk clay. By early August, the party had sent more than twenty crates to New Haven. "We are up to our knees in Eocene mud," Marsh exclaimed.

Mudge and Williston kept Marsh informed of the events in their day-to-day lives. "We bought a horse to replace the one that was drown," Mudge wrote. "The thermometer seldom gets more than one or two degrees above a hundred," Williston noted.

"A party of teamsters & desperadoes murdered a man at the station yesterday morning attempting to steal his horse," Williston wrote. "A special train brought up a sheriff and men from Hays who captured them all last night with a large amount of plunder and they are now on the way to the station. There were 14 of them, but with one for whom there was a standing reward—there was an exchange of 'compliments' with the sheriff. His funeral services will be very short!!"

But the most interesting piece of gossip came late in the summer in a letter from Mudge, who wrote, "I have just learned from Mr. Sternberg, brother to the Chas. Sternberg who has been in the employ of Prof. Cope that Cope and his brother Charles have gone to Dakota. So I think he will not trouble us here."

Cope had gone into Sioux Country where Sitting Bull's band was now being chased by thousands of U.S. soldiers. How foolhardy. How typical. Well, perhaps Sitting Bull would perform a service for Marsh and lift Cope's chestnut scalp from his skull.

Chapter Eleven

THE SPRING OF 1876 had also been a busy time for Cope. He had been working fourteen-hour days to finish a volume on Cretaceous life for the Hayden Survey, and at the same time, he found himself having to fend off charges of improperly keeping fossils that had been donated to the Academy of Natural Sciences.

The charge had been leveled by a Mr. Gaskill, of New Jersey, who had sent several fossils he found to Cope for the academy. Gaskill had been told by a visitor that the fossils had never reached Philadelphia. And who was that visitor? O. C. Marsh.

Still, Gaskill's complaint had to be addressed. Cope insisted that he had handed over the specimens, and a search of the academy collections proved him right. "It seems possible," the academy minutes concluded, "that this grave charge against the corresponding secretary might have its origins in personal hostility secretly indulged rather than in facts." Marsh!

While Cope was work bound in Philadelphia, he had hired a lone fossil hunter, young and inexperienced, to try to match Mudge and Williston on the Kansas plains. It was a gamble. Ambitious, but green and untested, there was no way of knowing how this new agent would fare. Cope, however, had a bit of the gambling man in him.

Before long, the bet would more than pay off as Charles H. Sternberg proved himself an extraordinarily adept fossil hunter and a Cope loyalist. And perhaps the best part of it was that Sternberg had been within a hairs-breadth of working for Marsh.

In the winter of 1875, Sternberg, the son of a Lutheran minister, was studying at the Kansas State Agricultural College, in Manhattan. Mudge, who was once again a professor there, was putting together that summer's expedition with Williston. The twenty-six-year-old Sternberg tried to win a spot in their party, begged for one, but failed.

He turned to Cope. "I put my soul in the letter I wrote him, for this was my last chance," Sternberg says in his memoir, *The Life of a Fossil Hunter.* "I told him of my love for science, and my earnest longing to enter the chalk of western Kansas . . . no matter what it might cost me in discomfort and danger. I said, however, that I was too poor to go at my own expense."[1]

Cope soon replied. Sternberg was too nervous to open the envelope. When he did, a three-hundred-dollar bank draft fluttered to his feet. "I like your style," Cope's note read. "Go to work." In June and July, Sternberg feverishly searched the Kansas deposits, but without the success of Mudge and Williston. The young man worked himself sick, and then Cope arranged for J. C. Isaac to come from Wyoming to help. But at the end of July, Cope decided to put aside his manuscripts and specimens and go west himself. He informed Sternberg that they would abandon Kansas altogether and head for Montana.

✤

Cope arrived in Omaha on August 1. Isaac and Sternberg were waiting for him on the railway platform. It was the first time the three had ever met. Sternberg was shocked when Cope emerged from a coach exhausted and staggering, helped along by his wife, Annie. How, he wondered, could this man ever survive the rigors of the frontier?

Cope seeing that Sternberg nursed a limp—the result of a childhood fall from a hayloft—had similar doubts. "Can Mr. Sternberg ride a horse?" he asked Issac.

"I've seen him mount a pony bareback and cut out one of his mares from a herd of wild horses," Issac replied. Cope seemed satisfied. The trip from Omaha took them west past Montana to Ogden, Utah, where Annie Cope left the party to return to Philadelphia. At Ogden, they took the narrow-gauge Utah Northern Railroad north to Franklin, Idaho. This circuitous route was designed to make the final leg of the journey—the stagecoach ride—as short as possible, for there was no more tortuous mode of transportation than the Concord coach.

There was, however, hardly any other way to get to Montana, the most remote and inaccessible corner of the United States. With no railroads and just a trickle of river and stagecoach traffic into the territory, it was easier to get from Philadelphia to London or San Francisco than to Helena. The *Bozeman Times* lamented that the region was "dull, monotonous . . . cutoff from civilization." It wasn't surprising that the bloodiest of battles between the white man and the Indians had been fought in this most isolated part of the country.

Cope, Sternberg, and Isaac arrived at Franklin on August 9. They camped on the train platform that night, and the next morning, along with the other passengers, they climbed aboard the morning stage. With a snap of the reins and the swaying of the coach, they started the four-day trip to Helena.

On the barren plains of eastern Idaho, the six-horse team kicked up huge clouds of fine dust that coated the coach and, in Sternberg's words, "penetrated our clothing and filled our eyes and ears, and, sticking to the perspiration that oozed from every pore, soon gave us the appearance of having jaundice."

The eight passengers—seven men and one woman—were packed into a five-foot-wide by six-foot-long wooden gondola suspended on thick leather braces that did not so much absorb the shocks and jolts of the steel-rimmed, wooden wheels as amplify and wildly distribute them.

At a twelve-mile-an-hour clip, the coach moved along morning, afternoon, and night. "If worn out from continued loss of sleep," Sternberg wrote, "we dozed for a moment, a sudden lurch of the coach into a chuck hole would break out heads against a post or a neighbor's head."

In an attempt to enable Cope to get some sleep, Sternberg cradled him in his arms one night. Such a round-the-clock marathon was always vulnerable to sweltering days, chilly nights, bandits, and Indian attacks. (As a precaution against highwaymen, Cope had sewn most of his money into his pants legs. This was called "banking.") When they came to steep hills, the passengers had to get out and walk behind the coach.

The only respite was the changing of horses and drivers at way stations, where one could buy a meal of hot biscuits, black coffee, bacon, and mustard for one dollar. Perhaps there was a time that such rigors might not have seemed so very hard, but when compared with the railroads' sleeper cars— all polished wood, art murals, fresh towels, and pillows—and dining cars, in which one could have *"salmon de grenoville à l'espagnole"* and for an extra fifteen cents, a glass of French wine, stagecoach travel had become absolute torment.[2]

The stagecoach companies were unapologetic. Why, they even expected the passengers to follow *their* rules—dictums like the ones nailed to the wall at every Barstow and Helena Stage Company way station.

- Abstinence from liquor is requested, but if you must drink share the bottle. To do otherwise makes you appear selfish and un-neighborly.
- If a lady is present gentlemen are urged to forgo smoking cigars and pipes as the odor of same may be repugnant to the gentler sex. Chewing tobacco is permitted but spit with the wind not against it.
- Buffalo robes are provided for your comfort during the cold weather.

Hogging robes will not be tolerated and offenders will be made to ride with the driver.

- Don't snore loudly while sleeping or use your fellow passenger's shoulder for a pillow. He (or she) may not understand and friction may result.
- Fire arms may be kept on your person for emergencies. Do not fire for pleasure or shoot at wild animals as the sound riles the horses.
- In the event of runaway horses remain calm. Leaping from the coach will leave you injured, at the mercy of the elements, hostile Indians & hungry coyotes.
- Forbidden topics of discussion are stage coach robbers and Indian uprisings.
- Gentlemen guilty of unchivalrous behavior towards lady passengers will be put off the stage. It is a long walk back.

And after three days and two nights of this ordeal, Cope and his fellow passengers faced one last obstacle—"Whiskey Jack." Jack was to drive the last leg of Cope's stagecoach journey, but he was loudly, aromatically, splendidly drunk. Cope was incensed, but the issue wasn't simply one of morality, although doubtless the Quaker still in him was deeply offended, but rather one of practicality. Riding in a stagecoach was bad enough with a sober driver. With one that staggered like a souse and smelled like a whiskey bottle, who knew what would happen?

"I strongly protested going with such a man . . . ," Cope wrote in a letter to his wife. "We refused to go without another man. So they gave us a messenger of the Express Co. to ride with him, although 'Whiskey Jack,' as Issac knew him still drove. And driving it was."[3]

Jack was notorious for his drunken driving, having once actually fallen right off a coach. Fortunately, the horses knew the route and ran past the next way station. A rider galloped after the coach and brought it back.

Each time the stage company appointed a new superintendent, there was speculation that Jack would be sacked, but he boldly and repeatedly swore to shoot dead any superintendent that tried to do it. It would take more than Cope's protests to get Jack out of the driver's seat. The express company's man rode up top with Jack to make sure that he at least did not fall off the stage. And so, while Marsh and Huxley were spending their time poring over fossils, having tea with the governor, and trotting around the sylvan streets of New Haven, Cope was being tossed around by Whiskey Jack.

"There was no sleep that night," Cope wrote. ". . . We rushed and tore and jumped and bounded and as the other man afterwards told me, we would have most certainly been wrecked had it not been for his exertion."

By the following morning, Whiskey Jack was dead tired and could hardly keep his eyes open. The express company employee was spelled from riding shotgun by one of the passengers, Judge H. W. Blake, who was on his way to Helena to conduct the territory's supreme court. Jack, however, stayed behind the reins. Without the judge, Cope said, the stage "would have been wrecked in broad daylight." Blake saw at least one positive aspect in Jack. "His breath," the judge said, "scared the road agents off." Cope was furious. "I was and am very indignant," he wrote to Annie, "and will report the affair." It did no good. Jack never missed a run until the railroad finally put the stagecoach out of business.[4]

On August 14, Cope arrived in Helena, the new, bustling capital of Montana. Just that winter, the territorial legislature had met for the first time in a brick building next to the Belmont Saloon, and in the spring, a local Methodist minister, W. C. Shippan, chopped down the hanging tree in Dry Gulch, the scene of vigilante justice. Shippan saw it as an act of progress, but pretty soon the sentiment around town was that Helena had lost an important part of its heritage.

Cope's arrival was front-page news in the *Helena Daily Herald*. "Professor Edward D. Cope, eminent in the science world, is in the city with several aides, *en route* to the mouth of the Judith River, a section of the country he seeks to explore in the interest of science," the paper announced.[5]

But it was talk of Indians, not scientists, that hummed in Helena. "The Indian situation is the absorbing topic of conversation in every place—the street, the saloon, the hotel, the family, church. It is upper most in everybody's thoughts," the *Helena Independent* had written toward the end of July.[6] But unlike Walt Whitman and his fellow easterners, most western settlers couldn't muster much sympathy for Custer, the army, or the Sioux. The military had simply bollixed up killing the enemy. The *Fort Benton Record* contended that if Custer had not died, he would have been court-martialed, and the *Helena Daily Herald* agreed, noting, "It was Custer's rashness that precipitated the disaster."[7]

Perhaps Elizabeth Chester Fiske, the wife of the *Helena Daily Herald*'s editor, captured the sentiments of westerners best when she wrote: "Any one of those brave men who was sacrificed . . . was worth more than all the Indians in the country, and yet every year thousands of just such men are slain and our 'Indian Policy' remains not unchanged, but ever changing for the worse. The only comfort and only safety, of the extreme West lies in the total extermination of the savage."[8]

Cope was urged not to push on to the Judith River. It remained too dangerous. But after a couple of days' rest, the stubborn Cope, with Sternberg and Isaac in tow, boarded a stage to head north for Fort Benton.

❧

On August 17, Cope and his men arrived at Fort Benton on the back of a buckboard wagon. They had been forced to hitch a ride when their stage-coach busted a wheel on its way to this last outpost of civilization (though it was a stretch to call this bustling, surly river port civilization).

The town owed its existence to the mountain snows that, with each spring thaw, raised the level of the Missouri River just enough to make it the most western navigable point on the waterway. Thus, in railroadless Montana, for a few months each year, Fort Benton became the territory's biggest mercantile port.

Cope and company came down Front Street, the heart of the town. On one side of the broad, dusty thoroughfare were the docks, heaped with barrels, crates, piles of logs, pipes, tarps, and general chaos. Tied up along the riverbank were rear-paddle-wheel steamers—like the *Rosebud, Far West, Nellie Peck,* and *Yellowstone.* These fifty-foot-long boats, three decks high, with tall, black smokestacks, were the town's lifeblood, bringing goods upriver from St. Louis and carrying back furs, hides, timber, and gold. A one-way trip would take seven to fourteen weeks, depending on the height of the river, the number of stops, and the availability of wood for fuel along the way.

On the other side of the street was a line of stores built of rough timber, their pitched roofs hiding behind false facades, their wood-planked sidewalks gap-toothed and coming apart. At the far end of Front Street was the small, wooden army compound, home to the one company of infantry that gave the town its name. The soldiers, however, were not there to guard the citizenry or fight Indians, but rather to protect the merchandise.[9]

The avenue between the docks and the stores was crammed with Conestoga freight wagons and coaches that created traffic jams and shouting matches. The fifteen-foot-long Conestoga wagons, operated by hauling companies, like the Diamond R Bull Train, would load up with as much as two tons of goods at the docks to be carted across the territory by teams of sixteen to twenty oxen. Dogs and pigs ran through the traffic and happily picked through the trash and debris littering the dusty street, which with just a touch of rain would turn to a muddy soup.

The sidewalks and saloons were inhabited by gamblers, prostitutes, outlaws, trappers, hunters, bullwhackers, river men, whiskey traders, miners, and mule skinners. There were more than a dozen saloons—a robust number for a town of seven hundred hundred souls and just four streets—with names like the Jungle, the Board of Trade, Break of the Day, and the Medicine Lodge.

The Occidental Saloon was touted as the "toughest joint in the West," at least until its proprietor, Nick Welch, came out one morning and much to his dismay found neither a corpse nor a drunk sprawled before his establishment. "I'm hitting the trail further west," Welch announced. "This dump is getting civilized."[10]

T. C. Power and I. G. Baker were the mercantile princes of the place, receiving and distributing dry goods across the territory. Welch and his fellow saloon keepers dispensed Fort Benton's bawdier products—whiskey, women, and cards. Both endeavors were important to the economy. "The gambling business is as openly conducted as the dry goods stores," an 1885 history of Montana said of Fort Benton. "In fact more so, since the stores do close up once in awhile, which is more than can be said for the 'tiger dens.' "[11]

Faro, roulette, and poker were the preferred games of chance, with bets ranging from the two bits plunked down by street urchins to the twenty-dollar gold pieces of "strike-it-rich" miners. Upstairs, some of the saloons had "handsomely appointed apartments" for high-stakes games.

Selling whiskey to the Indians was another lucrative, if illegal, part of Fort Benton's economic life. Those in the Grant administration and on Capitol Hill who were trying to fashion a conciliatory Indian policy were frustrated by the whiskey trade and sought to have it choked off.

But in a report to Congress, D. D. Mitchell, the superintendent of Fort Benton, said, "The avenues through which whiskey can and is being introduced among the Indians are so wide and so numerous that all the troops on the service could not prevent its introduction." Sternberg described the place as a "typical frontier town . . . streets paved with playing cards and whiskey for sale in open saloons and groceries."

So it was here amid this hurly-burly that Cope would have to find the supplies and men he needed to set out for the wilderness. It would not be an easy or inexpensive exercise. This was a long way—in every way—from Philadelphia.

And now Sitting Bull had really whipped up the town and put a crimp in Fort Benton's business. Out there in northwestern Montana, all by itself, 133 miles from the territorial capital Helena, the community felt vulnerable and was unnerved by the prospect of a couple of thousand Sioux warriors passing through town.

Again, Cope was advised against going out into the Missouri River valley. There were more than two thousand Sioux braves out there somewhere, and thirty-six hundred soldiers chasing them. There were also an estimated fifteen thousand Crows, Blackfeet, and Assiniboines along the Missouri. This summer, fossil hunting could be an extremely dangerous proposition.

Right after the massacre, the great fear was that the Sioux, chased by the army, would move west and toward the populated settlements along the Missouri and that other tribes—Santees, Assiniboines, Cree, and Blackfeet—would be inflamed by Sitting Bull's success and rise up, too.

But as the weeks passed, alarm faded. No one was sure where Sitting Bull and Crazy Horse were, but it seemed that towns like Helena and Butte were safe. The one exception remained the area around Fort Benton, which sat in the most likely path for the Sioux to take if they tried to escape to Canada.

"The Professor was strongly advised against the folly of going into the neutral ground between the Sioux and their hereditary enemies, the Crows," Sternberg said. "A member of either tribe might kill us, and lay our death on the other tribe."

Cope reasoned, however, that all the Sioux braves were now massed with Sitting Bull somewhere in south-central Montana. Until the Sioux were pressured to move north by the army, perhaps making a dash to Canada, Cope guessed the river valley would be safe. He bet that there were at least several weeks, perhaps a month, of peace in the valley.

The residents of Fort Benton were less confident. "The rumors coming in from the north are sufficiently alarming," a Fort Benton correspondent wrote to the *Helena Daily Herald* at the end of July. "I am not disposed to excite unnecessary alarm, but as I said before, the news is sufficiently exciting to keep our people wide awake to possible danger."[12]

This was not simply a case of hysteria or melodrama. In northern Montana, whites and Indians had long been living in an atmosphere heavy with animus and violence. Since 1870, at least thirty people in the area had been killed by Indians. (The records of Indians killed were not so meticulously kept.) Just that April, two whiskey traders were found murdered near the Bear Paw Mountains—right in the vicinity where Cope planned to search for fossils. They were victims, it was suspected, of Assiniboines.

J. J. Everson, who carried the mail from Fort Benton to Cypress Hills, would have been yet another casualty if he hadn't managed to outrun a band of Santee Sioux on July 8. The mailman "returned in an exhausted condition to Brown's ranch, on the Marias River, last Monday," the *Fort Benton Record* said. "He reported a war party of Santee Sioux, numbering about 100 warriors, chased him from Lonesome Prairie to within a few miles of the Marias River. Everson is ill from the effects of the chase, but offers to resume his route at once if furnished with a suitable escort."[13]

In late July, there was news that Indians has been spotted in the Missouri River valley and that Unpacas were seen, several times, around Fort Peck—another river port two hundred miles to the east. They appeared to be waiting for an opportunity to attack. Somebody had, at the same time, been killed and scalped down at Fort Laramie.

Even the Little Bighorn battle had palpably touched the town, as one of its sons—twenty-year-old Billy Jackson—had signed on as a scout for Custer. Everyone must have figured Billy a goner. Jackson, however, had been lucky. When Custer split his four hundred men, Billy went with Major Marcus Reno instead of Custer. Reno was supposed to attack the Sioux encampment of two thousand lodges from the east while Custer looped around and attacked from the other side.

No sooner had Reno begun his charge than he realized he was over-matched. The troops either withdrew or ran, depending on who tells the story, splashed across the Little Bighorn River, and scrambled up a hill from which 150 men held off the Sioux until a relief column arrived. Custer's group, of course, was entirely cut to pieces.

Billy Jackson was one of a group of scouts who stood their ground on the near bank of the river to give fire cover to the retreating soldiers as they crossed the water and scrambled up the hill. "We had time for a shot before the Indians were on us," Jackson recounted in an oral history. "My horse was killed beneath me and in falling it fell in a manner that partly covered my body. This fact is what saved my life for the running Sioux never checked their charge but ran their horses right over us."[14]

Crawling through the melee, cloaked by the clouds of dust and gun smoke, Jackson made his way to the riverbank and hid in the bushes. There he found three of his comrades. But they were cut off from Reno's hill by the river. Crossing it in the daylight would have been a quick way to die. So the four scouts waited. "All day long we lay in the heavy underbrush just 300 yards from Reno and his men where they were entrenched behind their dead horses and in rifle pits," Jackson said.

At about midnight, Jackson stole out of the brush, picked up some blankets from dead Sioux warriors, and disguised as Indians (Jackson spoke Sioux), they made their way across the river and to Reno's camp.

For a while there was even talk in Fort Benton that Madame Moustache was coming back to town to organize a citizen militia to defend the town. The madame—and she was, among other things, really a madam—was already a great legend across the West.[15] She first appeared in 1854 as a young, petite, and engaging dark-haired girl in Nevada City, California. She called herself Madame Eleanor Dumont of San Francisco. There was no Monsieur Dumont. She rented a small storeroom in the mining town and opened a vingt-et-un game. The madame gave her place an air of style and those who had them would get out their stovepipe hats and fancy clothes to lose their money at Madame Dumont's game.

The madame deftly rolled cigarettes, drank champagne, and dealt cards.

Her place was a big success. Toward the end of 1855, mining waned in Nevada City, and the gaming competition was stiffer. So she broke camp and spent the next two decades wandering from mining town to mining town trying to repeat her success.

By the time she turned up in Fort Benton in 1870 to take over the Jungle, she had been through several fortunes. She had been a prostitute and a madam, as well as a gambler and saloon keeper. (Calamity Jane had been one of her girls.) She was also heavier, a bit coarser, and the down on her upper lip had thickened enough to give her the nickname "Madame Moustache," although no one ever used it to her face.

Her reputation preceded her, but what really endeared her to the citizens of Fort Benton was the day she heard that a steamer with passengers suffering from smallpox was approaching town. Madame grabbed a pair of six-shooters and went down to the landing. She fired several shots at the boat and warned the captain not to dock lest he lose his life. It was the kind of civic responsibility that counted in a place like Fort Benton. In 1875, she sold the saloon and moved on to the Black Hills.

But after the Custer massacre, the pistol-toting madam seemed just what Fort Benton needed to organize the town's defense. At the time, however, Dumont was in the brand-new and very raw mining town of Deadwood, where Wild Bill Hickock had just been shot in the back while playing cards.

So instead of Madame Moustache, Fort Benton got Edward Cope. The rough-hewn town did not know what to make of "Professor Shoup and his bottle of bugs" as the *Record* described him. But they knew what to do with him.

"The professor had difficulty in securing an outfit without paying an exorbitant price for it. They knew him to be a stranger and they 'took him in,' " Sternberg wrote. Cope had to spend nearly fourteen hundred dollars for seven horses, a wagon, supplies, and the services of a cook and a guide for three months.

"My only trouble is getting men," Cope wrote to his wife. "Poor men are plenty, but good men are very dear asking $100 per month, which I will not give." Eventually he had to relent and pay the $100 a month—all three months in advance—to a cook, Austin Merrill, and a guide, Jim Deer. (That was more than three times as much as he had paid for help in the Bridger Basin.)[16]

Finally, on August 19, Cope and his four-man party set out for the Judith River. Before leaving Fort Benton, Cope wrote a letter to Annie assuring her that only "cock and bull stories about the Sioux have been published in

the Helena and other papers. . . . Everyone considers them false. . . . Everybody including Captain Williams who is commandant at the fort says there
is no danger in the region to which I am going."

✦

They traveled across the rolling, wind-swept high plains for nearly five days.
This was truly a land of big skies and of a bareness only broken by the distant, indigo mountain peaks. The Bear Paw Mountains—where the two
whiskey traders had been killed that spring—loomed up before them in the
east. One day, it poured, and the wagon stuck fast in the gray prairie mud.
Cope draped a pup tent over a carbine rifle and a pick handle and hunkered
down for a wet and wind-lashed night.

At last, the party dropped down into the deep Missouri River valley—a
dazzling contrast to the dry, windy plains. The river snaked through a valley
of soaring limestone cliffs, parapets, and columns in varying hues of beige,
rose, and ocher. The river was lined with groves of willows, box elder, ash,
and cottonwood trees, and spreading away from the banks were green
meadows studded with yellow and red wildflowers. Higher up, the hills
were fringed with forests of jack and ponderosa pines. When Meriwether
Lewis and William Clark first paddled up the river in 1804, in search of a
northwest passage to the Pacific, they thought the place "romantic."

The sediments that made up the rock strata had originally been laid
down in broad layers as the prehistoric inland sea ebbed and flowed across
the region. Sediments deposited on the ocean floor became the shale that
dominates the region today. At the edges, as the sea migrated due to climatic
conditions, the sandy coasts were turned into sandstone.

Then these deposits were subjected to faults, upheaval, volcanic activity
and glaciers. Finally, the Missouri River cut a surgical incision through the
layers, revealing millions of years of geological history. It was this incision
that Cope wanted to explore. He suspected that one stratum—the Hell
Creek formation, created seventy million years ago, when the inland sea was
in retreat near the end of Cretaceous—might be a fossil storehouse.

Cope made his first camp on the northern side of the Missouri opposite
the mouth of the Judith River. He was not far from a river trading post run
by I. G. Baker—three log cabins with the overly ambitious name of Fort
Claggett. Here the prices were even higher than they were in Fort Benton.

Behind Fort Claggett, hard, white, river bluffs rose almost one thousand
feet. It was these cliffs Cope first began to explore. The stratum of interest,
being relatively recent in geological time, was high on the bluffs. To get to

it required a good deal of climbing, and slipping, and banging away with a pick in one hand, while holding on to a rocky precipice with the other. What the fossil hunters gleaned from this hard and dangerous work was primarily fossilized teeth.

Contrary to Sternberg's fears, camp life and fieldwork agreed with the Philadelphia naturalist, who seemed to get stronger each day. "Since my last from Benton, I have got to working in regular style," Cope wrote in a letter home. But neither the work nor his frontier surroundings would keep him from his daily devotions.[17]

"We have just had a reading of the bible & prayer," he noted in the same letter. "I took Ephesians IV and part V, which is a practical kind. Sternberg is a very religious character & Isaac is a good fellow and I am fortunate in having secured a very satisfactory man for cook. They behave differently from my Colorado party who scraped their teeth and chopped wood when I read."

The portion of the river valley Cope was exploring was so fertile and filled with game—buffalo, elk, and bighorn sheep—that it was a neutral hunting ground for many tribes, even the Sioux and their blood enemies, the Crow.

There was a large Crow camp on the opposite bank of the river. This created some anxiety among Cope's men, particularly Isaac, who had recently saved his scalp by outriding a war party in Wyoming. Isaac insisted that they set a watch through the night. Sternberg took the first turn, Isaac second. But when Cope was roused for his watch at four in the morning, he announced that his Spencer carbine was packed in the bottom of his trunk. He then rolled over and went back to sleep.

In the middle of the night, a Crow chief named Beaver Heart and his squaw wandered in, giving Isaac a scare. Beaver Heart had hoped Cope and company were whiskey traders. After disabusing them of the notion, Cope suggested they sleep under the wagon and join him for breakfast in the morning.

The next morning, Cope was washing his dental bridge in a basin of water, when some of Beaver Heart's fellow chiefs—Wolf Bow, Horse Guard, Spaniard, Enemy Hunter, and Two Bellies—came along to join the breakfast party. Cope quickly slipped his teeth back in. The Indians were amazed.

"Do it again. Do it again," they demanded. Cope obliged. The Indians tried to do the same with their own teeth, but naturally failed. They asked Cope for an encore. It was a trick he would perform several times. "They were greatly amused to see me take out my teeth & put them back in; one man rode several miles to see it," he recounted to Annie.[18]

The breakfast was a big success. "They behaved with perfect food manners using the fork, spoons for everything," Cope told his wife. "I showed them your photo at which Beaver Heart said 'pretty good' & [I told] the squaw that thee cried when I was away."

Cope crossed the river and visited the village, which he found to be composed of about 110 lodges and more than one thousand Indians, mostly River Crows, with a few Piegans and Montana Crows. The Cope party had no other contact with the Indians, who broke camp the next day to follow the buffalo.

Using a flat-bottomed scow, Cope and his men now transported their equipment to the south side of the valley to explore the Judith River and neighboring Dog Creek. The Judith was a line of demarcation in the valley. West of the Judith, the river plains were fecund, filled with groves and grassy meadows. But east of the Judith's picturesque and winding valley began the badlands, a maze of barren, black rock canyons, devoid of water and vegetation. This harsh and unforgiving land ran along the valley for the next forty miles, until Cow Island, where the river steamers stopped when the Missouri was no longer navigable to Fort Benton.

Each morning, with the first hint of dawn Cope, Sternberg, and Isaac were up. They had breakfast, packed a lunch of cold bacon and hardtack in their saddlebags, gathered their picks and collecting bags, and rode out of camp.

The work was hard, the days hot, and the three were constantly plagued by swarms of gnats that got under their hats and shirt sleeves and gave them sores that ran pus and produced thick scabs. The gnats also got under the saddles, causing the horses great irritation. The men tried to combat the bugs by covering their faces and arms with bacon grease and rubbing the stuff under the collars and saddles of their horses. Despite the pests, they worked the badlands tenaciously. "Cope traveled the country as no man has since," wrote western historian Dan Cushman. "He crossed it from ridge to ridge, across the grain, as the Western saying went. Even today no roads come close to Cope's course."[19]

One day, Sternberg slipped from a high ledge and thought he was about to crash to his death on the boulders below. His life flashed before his eyes. "My mother seemed to stand out more prominently than anyone else," he wrote. And then suddenly he found himself back on the ledge. "I do not know how I escaped," Sternberg said.

Another day, Isaac disappeared in the badlands canyons. Sternberg and Cope realized the risk of getting lost themselves while searching for him, and so they entered a ravine here and there yelling for him. It was nearly dark when Cope found him. "The lands are very confused & are a labyrinth of gorges & precipices & I found that he had fallen down and injured himself," Cope wrote. The injuries apparently were not serious, for Isaac was out fossil hunting again within days.[20]

One evening, returning to camp, Cope's horse suddenly balked in the dark. Cope gave him the spurs, and the animal sprung into the air. Isaac, who was following, did the same. The next day, they saw that they had come upon a ten-foot wide gorge and save for the strength and keen eyesight of their horses, Cope might have ended up a mangled mass, a hundred feet below.

At the end of each day, the trio dragged themselves back to camp, exhausted and thirsty. In the badland canyons, there was only poisonous, alkali water, which Cope described as "mawkish of color, bitter of manganese & salt . . . the worst water I ever saw."[21] Now Austin Merrill and Jim Deer did their part. "My hunter James Deer has brought in ducks, fish, sage hens & our cook is a good one & makes us all sorts of dishes," Cope wrote.

And then bed. Cope's fertile imagination, however, seemed unable to stop working. In his dreams, the ancient beasts he was exhuming would come to life and torment him. "Every animal of which we found traces during the day played with him at night, tossing him into the air, kicking him, trampling upon him," Sternberg wrote. "When I would awake him, he would thank me cordially and lie down for another attack." The next day, they were up at sunrise and soon riding out into the badlands or up the steep slopes to the prairie.

As for the fossil hunting, Cope had been right in his suspicions about the Hell Creek formation. Some areas were layered with bones, but often only the teeth had been resistant enough to withstand time. Upon his return to Philadelphia, Cope was able to identify twenty-one fossil species, including several dinosaurs, from just this cache of teeth.

Among the animals the team unearthed were the kangaroo-like *Iguanodon,* an *Adocus,* which had four hundred teeth arranged in magazines, so that as one set wore out, another replaced it, and the raylike *Myledaphus bipartitus,* whose teeth worked like a whirring mill.

Cope's greatest find of the expedition, however, was the skull of *Monoclonius crassus,* the first known horned dinosaur. "We are succeeding very well in our enterprise . . . [many shells and small fish] . . . but some gigantic monsters," Cope wrote. "The climbing is perfectly hard work. The badlands are the steepest I have seen. The ravines and canyons are 1,000 feet deep near the Missouri River and down to 600 feet off from it. They are so steep that in many localities we cannot collect at all.

"I feel as though I have been a long time from home & wish to see you very much," he wrote to Annie in early September. "I look at your photographs as the best I can do. Tell Julia I am going to write to her & hope she will write to me. Now I close with the best love to you both. Thy affect. husband, EDC."

Cope wrote no more of Sioux braves on the warpath, but his men continued to fret over the Indians' whereabouts. Merrill and Deer became particularly anxious as the days passed. Even if Cope had been correct in his analysis, with each day, the likelihood that the Indians would move toward Canada became greater. It was now only a matter of time. Still, Cope continued searching for fossils.

On a Tuesday afternoon toward the middle of September, Cope, true to his word, sat down and penned a letter, gentle and sweet, to ten-year-old Julia.[22]

> *Dear Daughter,*
>
> *When we first reached here three weeks ago or more, we found a great camp of Indians of the tribe of River Crows. The day after we came they packed up and went away. They took down their tents, piled the furs & skins on their horses and set the children on the piles & strapped them on so that they should not fall off. Think of tying little 2 or 3 year olds on top of wild Indian ponies! But they are not afraid and learn how to ride very early.*
>
> *I have four ponies and one I ride is not four years old. He is a very good pony but is a little timid sometimes and jumps a little; but I am training him so that he behaves better and better.*
>
> *We have wild animals near the camp such as coyotes and deer. The wild sheep are common in the rough banks of the rivers and the hunter for my camp brought one in the other day. We have it boiled, roasted and fried and broiled and it was very good. We see them almost every day when we go out to find fossils.*
>
> *We find in the high rocks there are many bones & teeth of huge fossil reptiles like Laclafis and Hadrosaurus. I have found four new kinds of <u>Laclafis</u>, which ate meat and several kinds that ate leaves and wood.*
>
> *They were as large as elephants but their teeth are very small, no larger than the end of my little finger. One kind had more than four hundred in his mouth at once, of which one hundred were in use at once. The rest coming in from below to take their place as soon as they were worn out. This kind is called <u>Cionodon</u>.*
>
> *My Camp is on Dog Creek ten miles from the mouth. We moved there*

*since I wrote Mamma. It rained two days ago and we had to stay in the
tent and wagon. The creek rose very high and the water got so muddy that
we had to boil it before we could drink it. Then the high, bare badlands
bluffs got slippery as soap so that we could hardly hunt for fossils, but slid
about and got all muddy. But the creek is down and the bluffs are dry.*

*Now, farewell. Read & learn all thee can, for the more thee know the
more useful thee will be. So say thy loving*

Papa

By the end of September, Cope had decided that it was time to break
camp and move up the river toward Cow Island, where the last steamer of
the season would soon depart. Cope and Jim Deer went down to the island
to make arrangements, while Isaac, Sternberg, and Merrill were left to
move the camp.

Now getting out of river valley was a good deal more difficult than getting into it. Here the bluffs were steeper, and in addition, they had collected
twelve hundred pounds of fossils. The three men left their supplies at Dog
Creek as they first attempted to get the wagon out of the valley.

Facing a steep ridge covered with loose shale, Merrill balked at even trying to get the wagon up the slope. An impatient Isaac took the reins and
urged the horses on. He had gotten about thirty feet up the incline when
gravity got the better of the rig and pulled it over. Isaac, horses, and wagon
rolled over and over and over. When they reached the sandstone ledge from
which they had started, the wagon landed upright, and the horses ended up
on their feet, unharmed. Incredibly, Isaac was still in one piece.

The three men then tried a different approach. They constructed a
windlass to drag the wagon up the slope to the prairie. Then all the bones,
goods, and supplies followed. They were reassembling the gear when they
saw one horseman approaching from the south and another from the east.

The southern rider turned out to be Jim Deer. The eastern horseman was
Cope. Deer announced that Sitting Bull was rumored to be within a hundred miles and heading in their direction. The guide said he had already seen
signs of Sioux scouting parties. Deer said he was clearing out. When Merrill heard the news, he also grabbed his bedroll and headed after the depart-
ing guide. "The scout and our valiant cook had concluded that their
precious scalps were too valuable to risk," Sternberg said disparagingly.

Everything now dictated that the Cope party move quickly. Not only was
there a possibility of the Sioux appearing, but there was only one more boat
heading downriver this season—the *Josephine.* They had only a few days to
reach Cow Island. If Cope failed to reach the boat, at best his fossils would

be stranded in Montana for the entire winter; at worst they would meet Sitting Bull.

Under the twin threats of the Sioux and the *Josephine*'s pending departure, Cope, Sternberg, and Isaac put in a fourteen-hour day to haul the bones across prairie and badlands. It was late at night before they stopped for a supper of bacon and hardtack and a few hours of sleep. At daybreak, they set out again.

Late on the second night, they reached a ravine leading back to the Missouri River, twelve hundred feet below. They were just three miles above Cow Island. The steamer could come upriver this far, load the bones, and they would be off. The wagon was unloaded and lowered down to the valley floor using an improvised block and tackle. Then the baggage was lowered. Again, it was after midnight when they sat down to supper.

Cope and Sternberg now rode back to Cow Island to be sure the steamboat would come upriver to fetch the precious crates. On the way, however, Cope could not resist stopping in the badlands for one last fossil hunt. The two men separated, agreeing to rendezvous at four that afternoon. The hours passed, and the sun was sinking. Sternberg could do no more than watch the sun and wait. Finally, Cope finally came galloping out of a badlands coulee.

It would now be impossible to reach Cow Island before sunset. Sternberg pleaded with Cope to spend the night on the prairie and not try to cross the badlands in the dark, where a single misstep could lead to death. Cope paid no attention. He was determined to get to Cow Island. But perhaps having learned a lesson from his blind leap over a chasm earlier in the trip, he dismounted, cut a stout stick, which he used like a blindman's cane, and tried to tap his way to the riverbank. The black rock valleys had the power to soak up whatever starlight and moonlight was in the air and close out all but a sliver of sky. In that blackness, Cope tapped and tapped and tapped. Time and time again, he and Sternberg would follow a trail through the mountains and along ledges only to reach a point where his cane tapped on nothing but thin air.

Once, they actually reached the river, only to find a cliff walling them off from reaching Cow Island downstream. All through the night, Cope and Sternberg felt their way through the badlands. Just before daybreak, they stood on the bank opposite Cow Island.

"I have never known another man who would have attempted this journey. It was both foolhardy and useless," Sternberg wrote, "but we could say that we accomplished what no one else ever had in reaching Cow Island through the Bad Lands after dark."

Cope called out for the army squad billeted on the island to send a boat to ferry them across. But in the early morning fog, the two men could not be seen, and the sergeant feared this might be some Indian trick. Exhausted and chilled, Cope and Sternberg paced back and forth on the shore until the fog lifted. Realizing his error, the sergeant hurriedly dispatched a boat, which promptly capsized. A second boat was sent to rescue the first and then retrieve Cope and Sternberg.

At last, they reached the island and were given a warm pot of beans and some hardtack with strawberry jam. Then a warm nest of blankets was made under a tarpaulin covering a shipment of gold. Cope and Sternberg slept with the gold all that day and through the night.

The following morning, they sought out the steamer captain. "I am Professor Cope, of Philadelphia," the paleontologist told the captain. "I have a four-horse wagon at a steamboat snubbing-post three miles below. I would like you to stop there on your way down and carry my outfit to this side. My baggage and freight are also there, and I want to take passage for Omaha."

"Well, sir, I am the captain of this boat," the skipper replied. "If you want to go downriver, you must have your baggage, freight, and self at this landing before ten o'clock tomorrow morning, when I leave for downriver points."

So, it had come to this. Cope had a little more than twenty-four hours to get the fossils to Cow Island. There would be no time to retrace their steps through the badlands. Instead, Cope purchased an old sand scow and set off up the river to Isaac and the bones. (He had tried to borrow it, but the owner, having heard the conversation with the captain, knew there was a buck to be made.)

Cope and Sternberg rowed back to camp. Isaac wasn't there. With no time to lose, they started packing and loading the scow. Just before they were ready to shove off, Isaac, who had gone searching for them in the badlands, turned up. The three men swam the horses across the river and then started for Cow Island.

A towline was attached to the most dependable of the horses—Old Major—and the animal began the slow journey downstream, pulling the scow. Sternberg rode the horse; a couple of mountain men, whom Cope had met at Cow Island, stood on either bank with long poles to keep the boat from turning in to shore.

Isaac and Cope had the toughest duty—sitting in the scow and unraveling the towline when it got snagged on a rock or a branch. Such a hitch would immediately build tension in the line and releasing it was like setting off a spring or more accurately, a catapult. Each time Cope or Isaac freed the line, they were pitched into the cold, shallow river.

The sun was setting when the scow came in under the hull of the big steamer. The deck was filled with curious passengers watching the progress of the little boat. Cope was covered with mud from head to foot. His clothes were in tatters. His fossils, however, were intact. In his next letter to Annie, he proudly announced that he had collected twelve hundred pounds of fossils and added, "We had a lively time getting them to the boat."[23]

The October nights were already getting chilly, so the lady passengers were wearing furs and the men were sporting ulsters. Cope, however, had forgotten to bring any winter clothes, so after removing his muddy rags and washing up, he emerged from the sergeant's tent with hair combed, mustache trimmed, dressed in a summer suit with a linen duster.

The next morning, true to the captain's word, the *Josephine* weighed anchor and headed downriver. The steamboat did not get very far before its voyage was checked. At Fort Buford, on the North Dakota border, General Hazen commandeered the steamer, prepared to unload all the passengers and cargo, and fill it with soldiers to head back up the Missouri.

The Sioux had finally made their dash toward Canada and crossed the river not at Fort Benton, but at Cow Island. A brief battle occurred, and five soldiers were killed. After a day's consideration, however, Hazen decided to use another boat, and let the *Josephine* go. But further down the river, at Fort Lincoln, the boat was stopped again and used this time to ferry soldiers— fresh recruits for Custer's Seventh Cavalry, with their new saddles and horses—to join the chase. "The officers' wives watched from our steamer, none knew that they would see their husbands again," Cope wrote in a letter, "but were cheerful, some too much so, but some showed their feelings." So as Cope moved east, a small army was rushing into the valley. The paleontologist's timing had been impeccable.

LEFT: Edward Drinker Cope, at the age of 30 in 1870. The scion of a wealthy Philadelphia Quaker family, Cope was determined to be a scientist even though his father wanted him to become a farmer. (American Museum of Natural History)

BELOW: Edward Drinker Cope at 55. By 1895 Cope had run through his fortune, become the most prolific scientist in America, and he was still ready to do battle with Marsh. (National Academy of Sciences)

ABOVE: O.C. Marsh in London in 1865 at the age of 34. Born on a small farm, Marsh had been contemplating a career as a carpenter or country school-teacher until his rich uncle, George Peabody, staked him to a university education. (Peabody Museum of Natural History, Yale University)

RIGHT: O.C. Marsh was the most prominent paleontologist in the country by 1897. But financial setbacks and health problems were already beginning to sap the 64-year-old's strength. (National Academy of Sciences)

ABOVE: Joseph Leidy was the dean of American paleontology. In 1869, Cope was one of the students in the famous anatomy course at the University of Pennsylvania medical school. (Academy of Natural Sciences of Philadelphia)

ABOVE: Cope's vision of the *Elasmosaurus*, a giant ocean reptile from the Cretaceous, put on canvas by Charles Knight in 1897. (American Museum of Natural History)

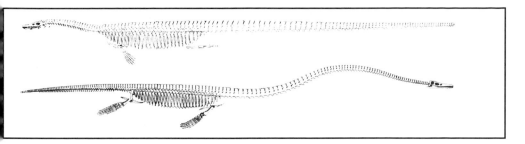

TOP: When Cope reconstructed the *Elasmosaurus*, he thought it had a long tail and a short, flexible neck (top skeleton). But Marsh discovered that Cope had mistakenly placed the skull on the wrong end. The animal had a long neck and a short tail (bottom skeleton). Cope was deeply embarrassed. (Academy of Natural Sciences of Philadelphia)

ABOVE: Cope, Marsh, and Leidy all discovered kulls of the same animal in Wyoming's Bridger Basin. Each gave the animal a different name. Cope thought the animal had a trunk and ketched the beast for his father in this letter rom the plains. (American Museum of Natural History)

RIGHT: Cope with the skull of the controversial ossil, which is now called *Uintathere*, the name Leidy gave it. (American Museum of Natural History)

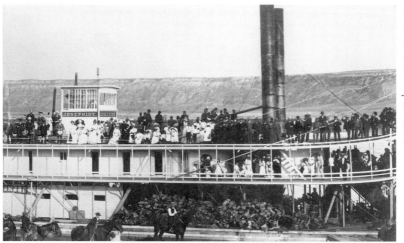

LEFT: Cope and his men had to hurriedly haul bones down the Missouri River to catch the *Josephine*–the last steamship of the season. (Montana Historical Society)

RIGHT: The first of the big, western dinosaur quarries was found near Morrison, Colorado, by Arthur Lakes, a local school teacher. Lakes was also an amateur painter and this watercolor shows Benjamin Mudge sitting on a vertebrae and examining an *Atlantasaurus* bone. (Peabody Museum of Natural History, Yale University)

BOTTOM: Cope tried increasing his fortune through mining and was even briefly president of the Sierra Apache Mining Company– his signature is on the stock certificate. (R. Eveleth, New Mexico Bureau of Mines)

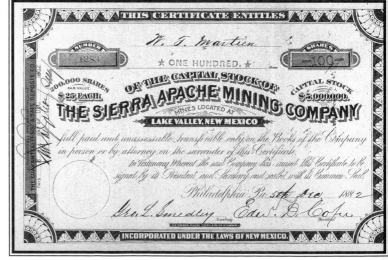

ABOVE: In the 1870s, both Cope and Marsh made Fort Bridger, Wyoming, a base of operations for searching the fertile Eocene fossil beds that surrounded the fort. (Wyoming Division of Cultural Resources)

BELOW: Front Street, Fort Benton. Since the territory had no railroads, bull trains carrying goods from the Missouri River steamboats were Montana's lifeline in the 1870s. Cope turned up in Fort Benton a few weeks after Custer had been massacred and ignored warnings not to venture into the river valley. (Montana Historical Society)

RIGHT: Marsh and Chief Red Cloud. The portrait was taken during Red Cloud's 1883 visit to New Haven. (Peabody Museum of Natural History, Yale University)

BOTTOM: Cope allied himself with Ferdinand Hayden's U.S. Geological Survey. Hayden led teams of surveyors and scientists into the field through the 1870s. His survey also published much of Cope's work. This 1870 team is near Red Buttes, Wyoming. The bearded Hayden is seated at the head of the table. (U.S. Geological Survey)

LEFT: Clarence King, on the right with the geological hammer, also led a major survey. King and Marsh had been classmates at Yale's Sheffield Scientific School and the King Survey published Marsh's study on "birds with teeth." (U.S. Geological Survey)

BOTTOM LEFT: Cope's study at 2102 Pine in Philadelphia. The cluttered townhouse filled with bones had become the politically and financially beleaguered naturalist's last refuge. (American Museum of Natural History)

BOTTOM RIGHT: The Smithsonian's Spencer Baird (The Smithsonian Institution Archives)

LEFT: John Wesley Powell (U.S. Geological Survey)

BELOW: Cope protégé Henry Fairfield Osborn (American Museum of Natural History)

BELOW: In 1870, Marsh led his first Yale expedition onto the western plains. Marsh's band was composed of fresh-faced Yalies looking for adventure as well as fossils. (Peabody Museum of Natural History, Yale University)

Chapter Twelve

 ON A SUNDAY AFTERNOON in March 1877, Arthur Lakes and his friend, retired navy captain Henry Beckwith, were out for a ramble among the humpbacked hills just west of Denver, when they stumbled across something quite unexpected.

Lakes, an Oxford-educated Episcopalian minister, schoolteacher, and amateur geologist, was hunting for fossil leaves and measuring geological strata along Bear Creek when he and Beckwith came upon what looked like a fossilized tree trunk. But as the Englishman examined the specimen, he realized that it was too smooth to be a tree, and then he noticed "little patches of purplish hue," which he recognized as bone. It was a truly immense bone of some unbelievably gigantic animal.

They started searching for the rest of the beast and came upon a "monstrous vertebra" etched in the sandstone. It was almost three feet in circumference. "It was so utterly beyond anything I had ever read or conceived possible that I could hardly believe my eyes," Lakes would recall.[1]

The two men stood there in silent astonishment and then threw their hats up in the air with a cheer. A few minutes later, Beckwith found another huge bone, a "Herculean warclub" ten inches in diameter and two feet long. Lakes suspected it was a leg bone. "Why this beats all!" Beckwith exclaimed.

The two men collected the bones and with the help of a local blacksmith (it took all three of them to lift the vertebra), carted them to the nearby town of Morrison. Then Lakes left for Golden, about ten miles to the north, where he taught at Jarvis Hall College, a small, private school. But the next weekend, he was back searching for and finding more bones, including one that looked like "the stump of a large tree." What sort of titanic animal possessed such bones?

On April 2, Lakes wrote a letter to Marsh. "A few days ago . . . I discovered in company with a friend, Mr. Beckwith of Connecticut, some enormous bones apparently a vertebra & a humerus bone of some gigantic saurian in the upper Jurassic or lower Cretaceous."

Lakes included sketches of the bones and a geological cross section of the hills with the letter and said, "I anticipate that a good many more bones will be added to those already found." The schoolteacher said if the fossils were of "sufficient interest" to Marsh, he would be "glad to communicate . . . & receive any instructions or directions from you in regard to the bones."[2]

And what was Marsh's reply to such provocative news and such a promising offer? Silence.

But Lakes was undaunted. He set up a little tent camp on the banks of Bear Creek and with the help of a couple of former students, continued to comb the hills, and he continued to find huge bones. Lakes's bones became the talk of Morrison. When he came riding into town with his cargo, a procession of the curious would follow the wagon down the street and gather around it.

Everybody wanted to help unload the bones and carry them into the empty office being used as a storeroom. But Lakes was mortified when "a young fellow grabbed hold of the beautiful smooth polished shaft" only to have it "crumbled like a biscuit in his hands." The bones were set out on the floor of the office, and the townspeople crammed the room, debating the nature of the animal that would leave such remains. Some still doubted whether they were bones at all.

Lakes wrote to Marsh again, on April 20, informing him that he had collected more bones, including a femur fourteen inches across its base. This led Lakes to calculate that the animal was "not less than sixty to seventy feet" in length. Marsh's response to this news? Silence.

By the end of April, Lakes had ten crates of bones, each averaging nearly two hundred pounds, sitting in the office. By the middle of May, the cache had grown to more than a ton.

Lakes, spurred by the excitement of his find, was not put off by Marsh's apathy. On May 19, although unencouraged and unbidden, the Colorado schoolteacher shipped a ton of bones to New Haven. He also asked Marsh for remuneration, pointing out that it had been necessary to hire a laborer and a wagon, and he was doing all this on a teaching salary that was "extremely small."

At about the same time, doubtless prompted by Marsh's apparent indifference, Lakes also sent some vertebrae to Cope in Philadelphia. Lakes had no idea what he had done. Dr. Carter up at Fort Bridger could have told him what was afoot. Spencer Baird might have warned him. Hayden would have known that "some mischief" was brewing. But Lakes innocently made the offer to both men to collect and sell the bones to whomever was interested in them. His offer was about to set off the largest scramble for dinosaur bones in history, the paleontological equivalent of the California gold rush of 1849.

It took almost a month for the bones to make it New Haven. But Marsh's intentions still weren't clear, and on June 15, Lakes wrote a letter that upped the ante. His eight-page dispatch detailed all the material he had found and included numerous sketches. He closed the letter saying, "If you wish to secure the further remains of these specimens as well as those that have already got out I hope you will write soon about it as offers have been made me & I should feel inclined to part with them to the highest bidder."[3]

When the bones arrived in Philadelphia, Cope took a quick look and wrote almost immediately, asking Lakes to send the skull and teeth that went with the vertebrae. He also offered "pecuniary aid in continuing the work."

But Cope said that he couldn't make "an intelligent offer" on the skeleton unless he could see more of it, particularly the skull. Lakes readied the skull for a trip to Philadelphia.

Meanwhile, Marsh had finally sent a letter and a one-hundred-dollar check to Lakes on June 9, but they didn't reach him until June 20. "Despairing of hearing from you," Lakes explained, "I was on the look out for anyone who would help me or make some sort of an offer to purchase the specimens. Prof. Cope having written me two or three letters on this point, offering to aid me in my research."[4] Just a few days earlier, Lakes had sent two skulls and some teeth to Cope. "I reproach myself for having been too hasty," Lakes said.

The imminent threat of Cope getting the Morrison bones was enough to prod Marsh into real action. He immediately telegraphed Lakes. He also sent a telegram to Mudge, who was fossil hunting for Yale in Kansas, directing him to leave for Colorado without delay.

It wasn't until June 27 that Lakes received Marsh's telegram. (It had been sent to Golden, not Morrison.) Lakes informed the Yale professor that it was too late to stop the skulls from going to Cope but assured Marsh that his understanding with Cope was that "the final disposition of the creature should be subject to my order."[5]

But Lakes added that even if Cope was to get this particular skeleton, he had five or six other creatures, of which at least some parts were already in the boxes sent to New Haven.

Lakes went on to say that Cope had offered him "further inducement" by indicating that there might be two or three months' work for $150 to $175 a month. "I have not concluded any arrangement with him until I should hear from you," Lakes assured him.

Marsh wanted it all. All the bones, all the skulls. He would hire Lakes. He would have Mudge supervise the quarrying. He wanted those bones that were sent to Philadelphia as well. He also wanted Lakes to keep the whereabouts of the quarry secret. But Lakes replied that it was too late for that. There had already been a newspaper article, "The Bones of Monsters," in the *Colorado Springs Gazette,* announcing the discovery.[6]

Two years earlier, Mudge had been ready to send the remains of *Icthyornis* to Cope, when a couple of well-timed letters had enabled Marsh to bend fate. It looked like he was going to do it again. But what he could not know was that Lakes's discovery was merely the first call in what would become the greatest surge and the most productive years in all of dinosaur hunting. Cope would still have his chances.

✤

It might seem surprising that Marsh was so deeply indifferent to the big bones, until one remembers that dinosaurs, at that moment, weren't the hot battleground of paleontology and evolutionary theory. Marsh's greatest successes had come from his Eocene horses and Cretaceous birds. Those were the things, not Jurassic dinosaur bones, that had dazzled Huxley.

Dinosaurs had been fodder for Huxley and Owen in their tit-for-tat war. Owen had created dinosaurs to debunk evolutionary ideas, and Huxley had turned them around, offering the thesis that dinosaurs were ancestral forms of birds. But by and large, most naturalists still considered dinosaurs merely fascinating oddities. Marsh possibly felt his time would be better spent in the pursuit of fossil mammals and birds.

Indeed, of the nineteen papers Marsh published between 1874 and 1876, twelve dealt with prehistoric mammals, such as uintatheres, brontotheres, and horses. Two were on birds with teeth, and two on pterodactyls. Other prehistoric reptiles, including dinosaurs, were barely in Marsh's field of vision. The fact was that material was still so rare and fragmentary on these odd beasts that it was difficult to say much about them.

But the merest hint of Cope arriving on the scene was enough to change that, and although neither man intended it, they were on the threshold of propelling dinosaurs to a more central role in the analysis of the evolution of life on the planet.

Many dinosaurs were big. *Hadrosaurus, Agathaumas sylvestris, Laelaps* were all large animals. But the beasts Lakes was beginning to dig out of the hard Colorado sandstone dwarfed them all. Animals that large had never been even imagined. At first, it wasn't clear what such animals were or ought to be called. Some paleontologists didn't think they were dinosaurs at all. Indeed, there was only one animal they could be compared to, Richard Owen's *Cetiosaurus.*

In 1841, Owen had looked over the fossil remains of an animal that was so huge that the most likely model was neither the elephant nor kangaroo, but rather the whale. Owen dubbed it *Cetiosaurus,* or "whale lizard." At first, he thought that like the whale it had to be a strictly aquatic creature. How could anything that large have made its way on land?

But some thirty years later, when a more complete skeleton was unearthed, Owen conceded that it appeared the *Cetiosaurus* might have spent at least some time on dry land. Huxley, of course, argued that Owen had got it wrong. *Cetiosaurus* wasn't some aquatic lizard, but rather a huge dinosaur, the biggest dinosaur ever. That's about as far as the argument had gone. Now Marsh and Cope were going to settle it.

Their answers were to be found in the pastel gray, green, and mauve rock of what would soon be dubbed the Morrison formation. The Morrison—three hundred feet thick in some places—was easily visible in those hump-backed hills that Lakes was exploring. The hills, known as Dakota hogbacks, stood as a series of parallel ridges and shallow valleys along the eastern front of the Rocky Mountains. The Morrison sediments had been there even before the Cretaceous sea flooded the middle of North America.

The Morrison, embedded in the hillsides, dated back to the middle of the Jurassic, 140 to 200 million years ago. The rock formation was a sequence of weathered shale, limestone, and sandstone that collected when the region was a broad plain covered by small lakes and rivers.

Just as Cope and Marsh had journeyed back in time to the shores of Kansas's balmy Cretaceous sea and then into the lush, subtropical forests of Eocene Wyoming, now they were on their way back to the African-like savanna of Jurassic Colorado.

On June 29, Lakes was at his Bear Creek camp when "a little old gentleman rode up on horseback."[7] Benjamin Mudge had arrived. He promptly hired Lakes for the summer at $125 a month, Lakes's student helper for $10 a month, and a "strong, good man" for $2 a day.[8]

That past winter Marsh, Mudge, and Williston had worked up a code for telegrams to guard against the Cope forces learning their plans: "Ammunition" was money, "health" was luck, and "B. Jones" was Cope. Now Mudge sent Marsh a wire: "Have made satisfactory arrangements for two months. Jones cannot interfere."

Mudge also had Lakes write to Cope, and a few weeks later, he was able to send another telegram to New Haven. "Fossils sent Cope are yours.

Lakes sends order for them." Marsh didn't wait for Cope to comply. He dispatched his most trusted aide, Thomas Attwater Bostwick, to Philadelphia to collect the bones in early August. "Please say to Prof. Cope that the fossil are now the property of Yale College," Marsh instructed.[9]

Bostwick telegraphed the next day from Philadelphia to assure Marsh the bones were packed. Everything had worked out admirably. Mudge was able to report that he had struck a deal with Lakes that "cuts off Prof. C. and all others from obtaining his aid in any way."[10]

Marsh had won this round.

In the July 1 edition of the *American Journal of Science,* Marsh published a one-page article, "Notice of a New and Gigantic Dinosaur." He said, "The Museum of Yale College has recently received from the Cretaceous deposits of Colorado a collection of reptilian remains of much interest. Among these specimens are portions of an enormous Dinosaur, which surpasses in magnitude any land animal hitherto discovered." Marsh estimated it was fifty feet long. He named it *Titanosaurus montanus.*[11]

A week later, Mudge wrote to Marsh, "the more I see of the vertebrates the more I am impressed with the value of the 'find,' and equally impressed with bad condition of the bones."[12] They were massive, but they tended to "crumble like biscuits."

By July 14, Mudge and Lakes had gathered another twenty-five hundred pounds of bones and shipped them in ten boxes to New Haven. The size of the finds continued to be extraordinary. Mudge, for example, had worked for a day and half to free from the sandstone a humerus that was fifty-five inches long, twenty-five inches wide at its widest part, and ten inches thick. In early August, they unearthed the remains of a dinosaur that was even bigger than *Titanosaurus.* Marsh named it "deceptive lizard"—*Apatosaurus.*

Mudge and Lakes quickly became friends. "The more I see of Prof. L the more I like him. I am confident he will be straight forward and honorable," Mudge told Marsh. "Professor Mudge we found to be quite an acquisition to our party," Lakes wrote in his journal. "He appeared to be about sixty years of age but was lithe and active as a boy and full of interesting information besides being a perfect gentleman."

Three years earlier at Wyoming's Black Buttes, Cope had found *Agathaumas sylvestris.* At about six tons, it had been the most massive animal known to have lived in North America. Marsh's *Apatosaurus,* when alive, weighed more than thirty tons and was better than fifty feet long.

Summer came to the mountains. The sun's heat bounced off the metallic sandstone, and so did the men's picks and hammers. Despite misgivings, Mudge agreed to use gunpowder to blast loose the sandstone caps and split the rock walls.

As the work proceeded the quarry trenches got deeper and deeper. Lakes's first quarry—thirty feet long, fifteen feet deep, and ten feet wide— had been buried one rainy night by a massive sandstone boulder. He moved along the side of the hill and started again, but slides and cave-ins became a recurring problem. One rock slide buried a spot under a ton of sandstone just a few hours after men stopped work. One day, a clay wall gave way, knocking down one of the laborers.

Those weren't the only risks the fossil hunters faced. Lakes and Mudge were chiseling a smooth bone from an overhanging ledge, one day, when Mudge got in the way of Lakes's hammer. "I hit him a gentle tap behind the ear and knocked him over with an exclamation of Oh! on his part and apologies on mine," Lakes said.[13]

Another time while watching two men go at the hard rock with a heavy sledge, Lakes was struck between the eyes by a flying rock fragment, leaving him stunned. Lakes left the quarry each week to preach at the Episcopal church in Idaho Springs. That Sunday, he delivered his sermon from behind a pair of black eyes.

However great the risks, the prize was even greater. Lakes and Mudge were finding a unique array of fossils—and they were all Marsh's. But then came some troubling news. In early August, Mudge wrote, "I learned last evening that Cope had a friend in Denver, who was making inquiries about the Canon City fossils, apparently with the idea of sending some one there for them: and to collect more."[14]

Canon City was about one hundred miles to the south of Morrison, on a spot where the Arkansas River flowed out of the mountains and onto the plains. What was Cope doing down there? What had he found? Marsh was going to have to find out.

Marsh wired Mudge and told him to go to Canon City. Mudge left the very evening the telegram arrived.[15]

Upon receiving Lakes's fossils, Cope had quickly set out to write a paper about them and delivered remarks before the American Philosophical Society on July 20. Cope withdrew the paper when Lakes directed him to send the fossils on to New Haven. It must have been galling.

But soon Cope was able to soothe his wounds with a balm of his very own Colorado fossil bones. Back in March, at about the same time Lakes first wrote to Marsh, Cope received a letter from O. W. Lucas, a schoolteacher in Canon City and amateur botanist. Lucas was out collecting plants on Oil Creek, a few miles north of Canon City, when he stumbled on some fossil fragments. He sent them to Cope for identification, and eventually Cope and Lucas struck a deal for the purchase of fossil bones at a rate of ten cents a pound.

Up in Morrison, the fossil-bearing rock stratum was a hard sandstone layer on a steep hillside. This had led to much banging and blasting, the menace of rock slides, and crumbling bones. The same geological horizon down in Canon City was nearly horizontal and had huge soft areas. The digging was easier, and the bones were in better condition.

Lucas started shipping bones to Philadelphia, and in August, Cope published his own paper, with his own new great dinosaur, the *Camarasaurus,* which he proclaimed "the largest or most bulky animal capable of progression on land, of which we have any account." In his paper, Cope noted that the Canon City vertebrae were larger than the one he had seen from Morrison (and then had to send to Yale) and so concluded "this remarkable creature . . . exceeds in its proportions any other land animal hitherto discovered, including the one found near Golden City by Professor Lakes."[16]

Cope, however, wasn't satisfied with merely having a bigger dinosaur than Marsh. In his paper, he argued that Marsh's brief July paper had failed to give an adequate description of his animal. How was it different from, say, Owen's *Cetiosaurus?* One couldn't tell from the Marsh report. Besides, Cope archly noted, the name *Titanosaurus* had already been used. A few months later, Marsh was forced to rename the dinosaur *Atlantosaurus.* But he was able to take a measure of revenge by pointing out that the name of Cope's famous, first dinosaur find—*Laelaps*—had also been used before. Marsh renamed Cope's dinosaur *Dryptosaurus.*

Still, as far as Cope was concerned, he had won. He had found and named the most gigantic animal ever known to man.

Cope was fascinated by the construction of his great beast, particularly by the hollowed or chambered vertebrae, which helped lighten the load of the immense frame and also interlocked with one another to strengthen the trunk portion of the backbone. It was from these vertebrae Cope got the name for the animal—"chambered lizard."

But when Cope looked at the overall makeup of his new dinosaur, he did not see a whale, like Owen, who was still insisting the *Cetiosaurus* was primarily an aquatic creature. No, with its long forelimbs and neck, Cope said, it "suggests a resemblance in form and habits between those huge reptiles and the giraffe." Cope envisioned his *Camarasaurus* grazing the treetops. Another animal model had been added in the effort to imagine the life of dinosaurs.

Lucas's next shipment brought Cope an even more towering beast, which he named *Amphicoelias.* Based on its fossil vertebrae, Cope calculated that the animal perched on its hind legs would have reached more than 130 feet into the air. *Amphicoelias* would be the tallest dinosaur ever found. Now it was Marsh's turn to squirm.

Mudge arrived in Canon City on August 11 and immediately started scouting out the scene. One night, he managed to gain entry to the storeroom where Lucas was preparing to ship bones to Cope and by dim lamplight examined the treasures.

"Very few of the bones have any familiar shape . . . ," Mudge told Marsh. "All are a larger scale than T.m. [*Titanosaurus montanus*] from 10 to 30 percent." A year earlier, Marsh had hired a Canon City man, David Baldwin, to collect fossils for him in southern Colorado and New Mexico. Baldwin apparently had mentioned the local bones to Marsh, telling him that they were sold in curio shops as petrified wood. But no interest had been expressed.

After seeing the fossils, Mudge said, "I exceedingly regret that Baldwin did not secure them for you, as he might when they were first discovered." Mudge tried to get back into the storeroom to see more of the bones, but "the man in charge did not appear willing."[17]

Marsh wrote and scolded Baldwin, who was becoming increasingly irritated with Marsh's imperious behavior and tardy payments. "I had found bones in the Jurassic in several places before Lucas," Baldwin replied in his own defense, "but did not dig them up on account of not hearing from you."[18]

Canon City was another of those booming western towns that at the beginning of the 1870s barely had a main street, but by 1877 had dozens of blocks, with more being added each year. The town sat at the Royal Gorge, the imposing chasm where the Arkansas River emerged from the Rockies. It was a transportation center for traffic to Santa Fe, Kansas City, and the home of the bountiful Bull-Domingo silver mine.

But it was the decision the town fathers made in 1868 that set the tone for the place. In that year, the territorial legislature gave Canon City the choice of becoming the site for a university or a prison. The town leaders chose the prison, believing that it would be more "permanent."[19]

Mudge hired a wagon and began exploring Garden Park, the area north of town where the bones were being found. Mudge also worked his charm on young Oramel Lucas, who was having second thoughts about his agreement with Cope.

"He feels that he has sold his big bones too cheap to Cope," Mudge reported, "and we can secure his good will in the future by a little kindness and good treatment. He is a young man trying to obtain an education."[20]

Lucas, however, believed he and Cope had made an honest bargain, and he was determined to hold up his end. Still, Mudge persuaded him that while his big bones had to go to Cope, anything else might be sold to Marsh. Through this bit of sophistry, Mudge obtained "some bones which look . . . like birds." These bones came from a sandstone layer about ten feet above where the big dinosaur bones were being excavated. "Whatever it is he will sell it when you have decided what it is. . . . At any rate it looks to me to be new and valuable."

Marsh immediately wired Mudge: "Purchase specimen if possible. Jones has violated all agreements. Answer."[21]

Mudge procured the skeleton, and three days later Marsh sent another urgent telegram: "Lucas specimen received. Important pieces missing. Send every fragment."[22]

Mudge provided details on how the bones had been arranged when they were found and sent along some fragments that he had not considered "worth sending by express." Mudge and Lucas returned to the site where the skeleton was discovered, but they could find nothing more.

The reason for Marsh's excitement was that Lucas had provided the bones of not a bird, but a small dinosaur. Marsh named it *Nanosaurus agilis*. And so, among Cope's behemoths, Marsh had been able pluck another of the provocative and diminutive birdlike dinosaurs. Meanwhile, Mudge reported, "Lucas is still at work on the skeleton for Cope. He sent last week 600 lbs for express & 3,000 lbs by freight."[23]

Lucas continued to send "all important bones of his large Dinosaurs to Cope," Mudge reported, but added that the young schoolteacher "promised me the refusal of anything new which he may find."[24] That wasn't good enough. Marsh needed more manpower in Canon City. In early September, he sent another telegram, this one to Samuel Williston in Kansas.

❖

While the battle of the big dinosaurs was being fought along the front range of the Rocky Mountains, both Cope and Marsh still had parties pushing the competition on the Kansas and Nebraska plains.

After Mudge had left, Williston was in charge of Marsh's Kansas operations, and Sternberg—recently returned from a winter in Philadelphia—was Cope's man on the prairie.

If Sternberg had not been bound to Cope before his time in Philadelphia, he was a total loyalist after the visit. The barn at Cope's Haddonfield home had been turned into a workshop, and Sternberg roomed there with young Jacob Geismar, Cope's preparer and sole employee.

Sternberg had a standing invitation for Sunday dinner with Cope, Annie, and Julia. "The food was plain but daintily cooked, and the Professor's conversation was a feast in itself . . . ," Sternberg wrote in *The Life of a Fossil Hunter.* "He used to sit with sparkling eyes, telling story after story, while we laughed at his sallies until we could laugh no more."[25]

He was invited to dinner parties the Copes gave, and Annie included him in luncheons she held for the young men that came to hear Cope lecture. At one Philadelphia lecture, Cope asked Sternberg to stand up so that he be given credit for his work in the Judith River badlands.

By the early spring, Sternberg was back in Kansas, and Cope had moved from Haddonfield to a pair of townhouses on Philadelphia's Pine Street—one for the Cope family, one for the Cope fossils. For the first part of the season, Sternberg worked the Smoky Hill River region collecting fossil shells and fishes.

Also out on the plains was Professor Snow, the Kansas State University chancellor and entomologist, and one day Sternberg had the chance to see the Wild West and science cross paths.

A group of cowboys driving a herd of cattle north on the Chisholm Trail passed Professor Snow and his students running across the prairie waving big mesh nets in the air "like men possessed."

At the nearby town of Buffalo, the owner of the Texas herd asked a storekeeper, "What are those men doing?"

"Catching bugs," was the clipped reply.

"I don't believe it," said the cowboy. "They are grown men."

"All right, you can find out for yourself, if you want to," the shop owner said.

The cowboy went out and spoke to the professor, who happily took his visitor to his tent and showed him hundreds of mounted insects.

"Well, did I tell the truth?" the storekeeper asked.

"That man," the cowboy said, "is the smartest man I ever saw. He knows the names and surnames of all the bugs in this country."

Sternberg and his four-man party had to deal with the seemingly endless litany of western woes, including rescuing the team and wagon from quicksand, outrunning a tornado, and fighting a squall to keep their tents from being blown away.

In July, Cope directed Sternberg to head north to the Niobrara region in Nebraska. It was there along the Loup River that Sternberg found the fossil of a great land turtle—nearly three feet long and two feet wide. Cope was to call it *Testudo orthopygia*. They also found the remains of the ancient rhino, *Aphelops megalodus,* and the mastodon *Trilophodon campester.* Both new species, both named by Cope.

Williston was also scouring the plains for fossils and trying to keep his eye on Sternberg and Company. "Send hundred ammunition. Health poor. B. Jones nothing going south," Williston had wired New Haven in April.[26] Three months later, Williston sent Marsh a letter from Buffalo, announcing that he was sending on a pterodactyl skull. "I know just what Sternberg has shipped," he also reported, "1 bird, 19 pterodactyls, 38 saurians, 5 turtles and 210 fishes, in all 15 boxes."[27]

But on September 13, Williston received Marsh's telegram directing him to head for Canon City. The following day, he was ready to catch a train. He also sent Marsh an itemized bill for expenses in Kansas, which came to $781.

When the train to Denver pulled into Monument Station, Williston climbed aboard. He entered a coach and sat down. It took him a little while to realize that sitting there in the same coach was Sternberg. Sternberg had received his own telegram from Cope.

Williston went over to chat. "Where was Sternberg going?" he wondered. Sternberg was thinking the same about Williston. They rode over the prairie together, amiable enough. "He was greatly astonished, thinking I was on his trail," Sternberg recounted. "He tried to find out my destination, but failed." Sternberg was curious too and asked the conductor if he knew where Williston was headed.

The two young men spent the evening together in Denver and then went their separate ways. The following day, Williston wrote Marsh from the Grand Hotel in South Pueblo, Colorado. "I met Sternberg *going to a new region* . . . I could not find out where he was going, but he took a northern train at Denver and was preparing for a long journey so that I think he is going up into the Dakota region where he was last year. . . . Has Cope himself left Philadelphia?"

Sternberg was not going back to the Dakotas. Cope had directed him to head for the John Day River Basin in Oregon—and, coincidentally, into the middle of the Bannock Indian War. As for Cope, he had left Philadelphia himself, but not for Colorado, not for the Dakotas, or for Oregon. Cope was in Texas.

The same day Williston was fretting about his whereabouts, Cope was being given a tour of San Antonio by General Ord. "I find the place worth staying in," he wrote to Annie, "with its winding river, its piazzas, catholic churches, and mixed population of Americans, Mexicans, Germans and Poles, together 20,000 people."[28]

When Williston arrived in Canon City, Mudge was out of town. So Williston eagerly went right to work, but could find no location that yielded bones comparable to those of Lucas. "I am very sorry to find that Cope is getting by far the best lot of fossils. . . . I think there must be a number of new species of those dinosaurs if we only get good bones," Williston lamented.[29]

Five days later, Williston expressed some hope to Marsh saying that they were beginning to get "some things . . . that I think you will like." One find Williston was particularly proud of was the hind leg, pelvis, and tail of a monumental dinosaur all neatly arranged in hard sandstone.

The problem, Williston said, was that the bones were "broken into innumerable pieces." Most of the material couldn't be saved, but Williston saw that the vertebrae had peculiar chevrons unlike any that he had ever seen. So he salvaged what he could by protecting them with strips of paper dipped in flour paste.

The bones, however, were few and far between and not in as good condition as those going to Philadelphia. On October 8, Mudge wired New Haven saying, "Unless luck better . . . I am sending Williston to Morrison."[30] Marsh finally had to concede that Cope had won the second round. Mudge went home to Kansas, and Williston left Canon City for Morrison.

⚜

In early September, after spending August exploring middle Colorado with some eastern entomologists, Lakes started working the Morrison quarries again and uncovered some unusual, large, pointed, dorsal spines. Lakes said they looked like "the ends of spearheads or long spikes." When Marsh finally pieced together the animal that owned those spines (helped enormously by some better specimens Williston had culled at Canon City), he would find an animal about twenty feet in length and weighing two tons. It had a series of armor plates along its backbone and spikes on its tail. Marsh decided to call it the "armed roof reptile"—*Stegosaurus.*

Blazing autumn was coming to the mountains, and Lakes wrote, "It was not long before our camp was invaded by ladies on horseback from the hotel at Morrison who came up to gather the leaves to paste up in graceful festoons around their rooms in Denver. Sometimes these ladies would stop and partake of a cup of coffee or a glass of lemonade at our tent."[31]

Lakes also spent part of his time painting watercolors of the bluffs and quarry sites. Perhaps Lakes had a future as a schoolteacher, preacher, or fossil collector, but he certainly didn't have one as an artist. Still, in a day where photographs were hard to come by, and were only in black and white, Lakes's flat, primitive portrayals of the fossil expedition were unique. In one painting, Mudge, in a jacket and bowler hat, is sitting on an *Atlantosaurus* vertebra examining a huge leg bone. A field hand is swinging an ax just behind him.

Williston arrived at Morrison and was pronounced "a very pleasant fellow" by Lakes. They started working some of the old quarry areas, as Marsh wanted more *Apatosaurus* bones. The quarries still had to be dug deep into the hill, and the sandstone overhangs were pronounced. Soon the leaf ladies were gone, and the snows had come. The day after one snowstorm, the temperature rose, and everything began to thaw. At the end of the workday, Lakes, Williston, and the rest of the crew laid their tools in the quarry hole and left.

"About midnight one of our men was walking through the village when he heard a roar like thunder from the cliffs above as if the whole hogback was coming down. Next morning we came as usual to our hole when lo there lay the whole ledge fallen in and filling the excavation with the weight of rocks of over 100 tons. . . . Had this fallen when we were there our entire party would have been crushed to atoms," Lakes wrote.

The snowstorms became more frequent. Williston, weary and ill, left Colorado and returned to his home in Kansas. By the end of the year, Marsh decided to close down the quarry. He asked Lakes to come and spend the winter at the Peabody Museum, but Lakes declined and returned to Jarvis Hall in Golden.

⚜

This fossil-hunting season also brought another big change in the battle between Cope and Marsh. A new competitor had entered the field— Princeton University. Well, perhaps it was overly grand to say that the university had entered the fray. More accurately, two nineteen-year-old undergraduates had boldly marched into the fossil war.

William Berryman Scott and Henry Fairfield Osborn decided that they'd have a western adventure and go collect fossils. They innocently sought Marsh's advice on where to hunt, but he wouldn't even see them.

Then they went to see Cope, who received them, but was both wary and cagey. What about the Bridger Basin, they asked, were there fossils there? "Well, there were before I got there," Cope replied. Frustrated by their reception from the nation's eminent paleontologists, Osborn and Scott set off for the West on their own.

When news came to Marsh from both Sam Smith and James Van Allen Carter that Scott and Osborn were hunting around in the Bridger Basin, it had to have been a source of irritation. Carter was trying to keep an eye on the boys, but had to report to New Haven that "the Princeton party has given us the slip."[32]

Carter was probably more concerned by the news that the army had decided to decommission Fort Bridger. Judge Carter was thinking of buying up the buildings. Everyone else was thinking of moving on.[33]

Scott and Osborn returned from their western expedition completely and totally enthralled with paleontology, and when Cope realized that they weren't Marsh agents, his entire demeanor changed. He gave them a full run of his collections. The young men started making frequent trips to Philadelphia to consult with both Cope and Leidy. Cope even went up to Princeton to help them classify and arrange their Bridger Basin finds.

But when the two young men made a formal request to see Marsh's Bridger Basin material, the Yale professor only grudgingly agreed. He ordered his staff to cover all other material in the Peabody workshops, and when the two arrived, Marsh put on a pair of carpet slippers, so as not to make a sound, and lurked in the corners, keeping an eye on the Princeton students.[34]

The result of all this was that Osborn and Scott became deeply committed to paleontology and to Cope. Scott would go on to become a professor at Princeton. Osborn would hold a professorship at Columbia University and head the American Museum of Natural History. Both men would adore Cope and see Marsh as their archenemy.

This would not be good news for Marsh. It already wasn't. Within a few months, Lakes was to tell Marsh that Princeton had also offered to hire him and to purchase his fossils, and added, "It is hopeless to attempt to keep the secrets of the bones from general information."[35]

In 1877, Leidy was also back in Wyoming, but now he had abandoned the Bridger Basin. In a move that was almost symbolic, he had gone up into the Uinta Mountains, where he was studying microscopic organisms at high elevations. No more bone battles with Cope or Marsh for the gentle Philadelphian.

✣

While Lakes, Mudge, Williston, Lucas, and Sternberg dashed across the West digging up fossils from Kansas to Colorado to Oregon, Cope and

Marsh were busy in their workshops separating bone from rock, sorting, analyzing, and naming.

In the basement rooms of the Peabody Museum, Marsh had already started to assemble the most able staff in the country. The highly trusted Thomas Bostwick, who had come into Marsh's employ right out of grammar school, kept the records and did the packing. The artist Frederick Berger sketched illustrations of bones and fossils, and William F. Hopson turned them into engraving plates. Adam Herrman was Marsh's restorer, and Tobias Kappeler made plaster casts of important and interesting bones.

George Bird Grinnell was also at the museum on a part-time basis, while working on his doctoral dissertation. Oscar Harger was Marsh's intellectual alter ego and his first permanent assistant in paleontology. A graduate of Yale College, who also studied at the Sheffield Scientific School, Harger was scholarly and creative. Marsh was happy to have his ability at the museum, but absolutely forbade Harger to publish any of his own papers or analyses on vertebrate paleontology. Marsh was also very stingy in giving anyone credit in his own work. The poor and sickly Harger needed the Peabody position, but his brilliance and Marsh's hard-fisted ways would eventually clash.

Against this small army, Cope and Geismar worked in the Philadelphia townhouse that had been turned into a paleontological studio. Geismar did the unpacking, the preparing, and the recording keeping. Cope did the detail work, the drawing, and the analysis.

The townhouse had quickly became cluttered with crates, bones, books, and workbenches. But the elegant dwelling had not been designed to be an atelier. When Cope and Geismar wanted to reconstruct the leg of the *Camarasaurus,* they had to hang it down the stairway between the second-floor bedrooms and the first-floor parlor.

Now, from Pine Street and the Peabody came a parade of dinosaurs unlike anything the world had ever seen. Marsh was to announce the discovery of six new genera of dinosaurs, and what an incredible range of creatures he had found in the Colorado hills. There was the huge *Apatosaurus,* fifty feet long and thirty tons; the giant carnivorous *Allosaurus;* the cat-sized *Nanosaurus;* and the spiked and armor-plated *Stegosaurus.* Cope would piece together five different dinosaurs, including the towering *Amphicoelias,* bulky *Camarasaurus,* and slender *Dystrophaeus.*[36]

Cope was fascinated with the architecture of the huge beasts. "The species of *Camarasaurus* and *Amphicoelias,* which attained to the most gigantic proportions, are remarkable for the light construction of the vertebrae . . . ," he observed. "They are also remarkable for the enormous elevation of the superior arches . . . the result of which is to give the ribs an unusually elevated basis. . . . On the other hand the bones of the tail and the limbs are solid or nearly so, in great contrast with some of the *Dinosauria* of later geological periods."[37]

At the end of the year, Cope made a bold move to help counter Marsh's special relationship with Benjamin Silliman's *Journal*. He bought the *American Naturalist* for fifteen hundred dollars. It was his first major gambit using his new fortune. Marsh was furious.

"I suppose you have heard that Cope has bought the copyright," he wrote in a letter to Leidy. "There is a strong feeling at Cambridge and elsewhere that this is a swindle and Alexander Agassiz has drawn up a protest. . . . I think all the prominent naturalists will sign it."[38]

Cope wasn't worried. He was too busy sifting through the fossil fishes and turtles sent to him by Sternberg and his own fossils gleaned from later Pliocene beds in Clarendon, Texas. He wrote a total of thirty-three papers that winter on fossil fishes, amphibians, reptiles, mastodons, crocodiles, oreodonts, and rhinos—as well as on his colossal dinosaurs.

Up in New Haven, Marsh was pondering the nature of the Jurassic giants and saw a number of shared characteristics: They had four feet, long necks and tails, small heads, five-toed "hands and feet," and they were plant eaters. Marsh decided that they formed a distinct group among the dinosaurs and proposed calling them sauropods, or "lizard-footed" dinosaurs, because of their five toes (bipedal dinosaurs had three toes). The name stuck.[39]

All in all, it had been an extraordinary year. But as incredible as it was, 1878 held even more promise. Marsh had been contacted by two new fossil collectors who had also found big bones. By now, he was no longer casual about such information, and he quickly made efforts to lock up the collectors, ascertain the value of their site, and above all, keep it secret.

This he had managed to do, and the first reports coming back from this new site were that it was much better than Morrison, even better than Canon City. Things looked very promising for the coming season.

But then came the news that was surely going to change the landscape of American science. Joseph Henry—the president of the National Academy of Sciences, the secretary of the Smithsonian, the nation's preeminent scientist—was dead.

Chapter Thirteen

ON MAY 13, 1878, after a sterling career spanning nearly half a century, Joseph Henry died from a liver infection at the age of eighty. No death would so profoundly touch America's fledgling scientific community as this one, for, as his obituary in the *Nation* noted, Henry had been the one person "who during the present generation has exerted the most enduring and widespread influence upon the progress of American science."[1]

Henry's "departure," J. H. Coffin, the home secretary of the National Academy of Sciences, wrote in a letter to Marsh, "creates a void in our Washington circle and in all the scientific associations in the land."[2] It was a moment that marked the passage from one era of American science to another. It was a time of change.

The day after Henry's death, Cope was packing to attend the funeral in Washington and calculating on the possibilities at hand. "His death will leave a vacancy in the Smithsonian," he said in a note to his wife. Cope knew that Spencer Baird—Henry's deputy for eighteen years—was the most likely replacement at the Smithsonian. Still, he could hope. "Some years ago Prof. B. told me that he would rather that I should have that position than any other person and I may get it," Cope wrote. "But the events of the Marshian controversy may have weakened me, there, so that everything is very uncertain. It is best to be *on the spot.*"[3]

Henry had done an extraordinary job in creating the Smithsonian and piloting it through scientific shoals and political rapids. Despite Congress's initial reluctance, he had created an important scientific institution out of a piece of serendipity that American leaders hadn't wanted at all.

When the U.S. government was first informed in 1836 that it had inherited the equivalent of five hundred thousand dollars from an obscure British chemist named James Smithson, it was totally unenthusiastic about the bequest.

Smithson, the bastard son of a British noble, had spent most of his life in France. When he died a bachelor in 1829, his will directed that when his last living relative, a third nephew, also died, the whole of his property should be given "to the United States of America, to found at Washington, under the name Smithsonian Institution, an Establishment for the increase and diffusion of knowledge among men."

The prospect of this huge legacy set off a howling debate in Congress. States' rights advocates, such as Senator John C. Calhoun of South Carolina, questioned whether the government even had the power to accept gifts from foreign individuals. It was, Calhoun argued, "beneath the dignity of the United States to receive presents of this kind from anyone." Calhoun's greatest fear was that the money would be used to create a central national university—an idea that had faced consistent states' rights opposition since the time of George Washington.

Congress eventually voted to accept the gift, but vacillated on what do to with the money. Finally, in 1844, with criticism rising and the value of the legacy falling, the Smithsonian was created although Congress still wasn't sure what the institution ought to be. The bill creating it provided for a library, museum, art gallery, lecture rooms, and a chemical laboratory. The new institution would be overseen by a board of regents.

When that board met in late 1846 to select the institution's first secretary, it decisively, though not unanimously, chose Henry. Instrumental in the selection was Alexander Dallas Bache, a regent and the new superintendent of the U.S. Coast and Geodetic Survey.

Henry quickly saw that the Smithsonian could not be all things, and to avoid running afoul of Congress, it would have to live largely within the monies created by the interest on its endowment. He decided that in its first three years, the Smithsonian would "ask nothing from Congress except the safe-keeping of its own funds." He would steer clear of controversy and appropriation hearings.

To do this, he quickly pared down the new institution's goals to "facilitating and promoting the discovery of new truths" and the publishing of those results. Thus, its aim was research and publication. The Smithsonian, he said, would only do those things "which cannot be produced by existing institutions in our country."

The Smithsonian had nurtured scientific research and become a Washington beacon for scientists across the nation. But now, someone else would have to take over its leadership.

The names most often mentioned for the job were J. E. Hilgard, the director of the Naval Observatory, Clarence King, and, of course, Baird. Cope was not really on the list, but he increasingly craved some post, position, or title that would give him greater standing. A few months earlier, he had tried for election to the vice presidency at the Academy of Natural Sciences in Philadelphia, but lost. "He wants badly to be Prest. of the Am.

Assoc. Adv. of Sc," Joseph LeConte reported to Marsh, "but I hope his character is sufficiently known to prevent such a disgrace."[4]

The secretaryship of the Smithsonian would also elude Cope. On May 19, the day after Henry's funeral, the Smithsonian regents unanimously chose Baird for the post. Here was the first small shift in the constellation. Finally, Baird, the ferocious worker, who would spend as much as fifteen hours a day at the institution, could bring his specimens up from the basement and make them the Smithsonian's centerpiece.

His ambition, which historian Robert V. Bruce described as "imperial," was to make those natural history collections preeminent. The Smithsonian would become more of a museum. The promotion of research would increasingly pass to universities and other government science agencies.

Within a year of taking over, Baird would obtain a $250,000 appropriation from Congress to erect the museum building that Henry had always balked at pursuing. To fill it, Baird would be far more involved in politicking and deal making with his fellow scientists than Henry would ever have entertained.

After Henry's funeral, Cope returned to Philadelphia, recording no note of disappointment, and began preparations for a trip to Europe. He had been invited to attend the annual meeting of the British Association for the Advancement of Science to be held in Dublin. With the situation so fluid at home, it was not the best time for a trip, but Marsh was on the continent at that very moment. "On some accounts it is not convenient to go—but I must counteract the Marsh mud, which appears to have stuck over there in several places," he told Annie.[5]

Marsh's continental visit, however, was about to be cut short—as a direct result of Henry's death. One of Henry's other important positions had been president of the National Academy of Sciences, and just that past April, Henry had gotten a new vice president—Marsh. The Yale professor had only been an academy member for only four years, but he had a knack for getting elected to things. Suddenly, he was the academy's "interim" president.

With Marsh's possession of the academy gavel, the relationship between government and science was also about to change, much as Baird's ascension at the Smithsonian would change that institution.

Even though Henry had rescued the academy from its moribund state, the government still had not sought its advice. Part of the reason was the austere Henry himself and his determination to keep the academy scholarly, impartial, and apolitical. This made it an oddity in backslapping, logrolling, deal-making Washington. If Congress asked a question, Henry was prepared to give an honest answer. That's probably why legislators never asked.

But the interim president was a man not cowed by Washington politics, a man capable of wading into the fray, a man comfortable wielding power and making deals. He was also a man who congressional reformers believed they could count on.

After eight years of Grant and his venal entourage, the idea of reform was much in vogue. There were those that said the new president, Rutherford B. Hayes, had stolen his election, stuffing ballot boxes in the South. But now that he was in Washington, Hayes was committed to reform, and his new interior secretary, Carl Schurz, was one of the most ardent members of the movement.

Soon after getting into office, Schurz focused on the problem of the six overlapping surveys, a situation that had not gotten any better since the 1874 hearings. The Treasury Department's survey was still mapping American shores, but it was nearing the end of its task, quickly running out of coast to survey.

The War Department still had Lieutenant George Wheeler making military maps, although he was now doing it without Cope's help. After creating so many problems down in New Mexico in 1874, Cope was never invited back by the army survey.

Clarence King had completed his fieldwork for the survey of the fortieth parallel and retired to New Haven, where he was turning out volumes of impressive reports.

In Schurz's own Interior Department, the General Land Office was still surveying and distributing land to settlers, while Ferdinand Hayden continued to mount large geological and scientific expeditions to the West, and John Wesley Powell explored the mountains and rivers of the central Rocky Mountains.

So much uncoordinated work. Something really had to be done, and done now. The economy had not recovered from the crash of 1873, with 1877 and 1878 particularly bad years. Congress was desperately searching for ways to cut the budget.

There was still another impetus for streamlining the surveys. The settling of the West was no longer the nation's future. It was, at that moment, America's present. The Indian wars were over. The railroads were running. The land had to be settled, plowed, timbered, and mined. It was already happening, as fast as locomotive and wagon would allow. At the end of the Civil War, there had been 3.6 million people living in the territory west of the Mississippi. By the spring of 1878, there were more than 13 million—a fourfold increase in a little more than ten years. But the assessing, parceling, and settling of the land was a haphazard, often chaotic, exercise. The cartographers and surveyors had barely been able to keep up.

In such a confused atmosphere, it was easy for graft and corruption to flourish, and increasingly large chunks of the American West were falling into the hands of banks, corporations, and large landholders. There was a feeling that a better understanding of the nation's resources and a more efficient method of surveying and distributing land was needed. The surveys had to be merged and reformed. The question was how it would be done?

The nation's scientific community was not an impartial bystander in this debate. Dozens of prominent naturalists, botanists, geologists, and paleontologists received grants and specimens from the surveys and, at government expense, had their reports and papers published. And no two scientists were more intimately involved with the surveys than Cope and Marsh. In fact, their "paleontological war was indirectly sustained and abetted by the chaotic state of the geological work done by the agencies of the U.S. government," according to Princeton paleontologist and Cope protégé William Berryman Scott.[6]

Cope had received support from both Lieutenant Wheeler's survey of the hundredth meridian and Hayden's survey of the Rocky Mountains. It was Hayden's survey that published the bulk of Cope's work.

King's survey published Marsh's key paleontological works on the evolution of horses, and birds with teeth, while Powell's Second Division of the Rocky Mountain Survey sent all its fossils to New Haven.

If the surveys were to be merged, there would clearly be winners and losers in the nation's scientific community. So congressional politics wasn't the only politics at play, and perhaps that is why it was all the more remarkable that the Republican reformers and the scientific politicos decided to use the National Academy of Sciences as the agent to decide the fate of the surveys.

This was what sent Marsh scurrying home from Europe.

It was to be the first major battle among scientists over government funding in America, and they would reveal themselves to be as vicious and petty as any machine politician or lobbyist. And once again, right in the middle of the fray would be Cope and Marsh.

It officially began on the afternoon of June 20, 1878, just a little more than a month after Marsh assumed presidency of the academy. Rep. Abram Hewitt of New York—a friend and club mate of Marsh's—rose in the House of Representatives and proposed an amendment to the Sundry Civil Expense Act, asking the academy to:

take into consideration the method and expenses of conducting all surveys of a scientific character under the War or Interior Department, and the survey of the Land Office, and to report to Congress as soon thereafter as may be practicable a plan for surveying and mapping the Territories of the United States on such general system as will, in their judgment, secure the best results at the least possible cost.

The scientific community through its most elite organization would have the first chance to propose reforms. The fate of the surveys was in large part in the hands of O. C. Marsh. Clearly, this was not a good thing for either Hayden or Cope.

⚜

From the nation's birth, the vastness of the continent inspired dreams, schemes, and hopes. It also demanded exploration and settlement. Who knew what was out there? When, in 1803, Thomas Jefferson sent Lewis and Clark to find a Pacific northwest passage, he also hoped that they would discover dinosaurs, mammoths, and other strange beasts still living in the interior of the great continent. "There is surely space enough . . . for mammoths and megalonyxs who may exist there," he said.[7] It would turn out that all that was left of the woolly mammoth and the other exotic, ancient animals were the fossils waiting for Cope and Marsh.

Many followed Lewis and Clark. John Fremont mapped the Oregon Trail, and Charles Wilkes surveyed the Columbia River basin. In 1850, Secretary of War Jefferson Davis commissioned a series of surveys to find the best transcontinental rail route, and numerous land surveys cut up the Midwest, like a large a birthday cake, so pieces could be handed out to settlers.[8]

That parceling of homesteads was in the hands of the Interior Department's General Land Office, which in turn relied on eighteen regional surveyors-general. The surveyors-general themselves depended on contracts let to private surveyors. It was these contracts with which Columbus Delano's son, John, was so deeply and questionably involved.

Under the 1862 Homestead Act, the land was to be divided into quarter sections—160 acres—free to those who could hold the land and improve it. But the surveying and quartering often could not move as quickly as the squatters spilling into the West. By 1878, there had been 2.5 million entries under the Homestead Act—a total of four hundred million acres transferred from public to private hands in sixteen years. The same year that Congress passed the Homestead Act, it also approved the Pacific Railroad Act, which gave the railroads alternate sections of lands on each side of their tracks, which they could sell to offset their capital expenses in building the railway.

There was a tremendous amount of land being doled out, and the problem was that this was being done in an atmosphere of confusion and corruption. Fraudulent land claims were common. One popular scam involved the "homesteader" who carried a moveable shanty and barrel of water on a wagon. Plunking down the shanty and pouring water on the ground was close enough to building a home and irrigating the land to claim a quarter section. Then this homesteader would turn around and sell his claim to a speculator or a corporation and move on to his next homestead.

But even those quarter sections taken by hardworking farmers seemed to end up in the hands of the banks and syndicates. Two-thirds of the homesteaders failed, with banks seizing their land for unpaid mortgages. The banks then put the land on the market where it would be snapped up by speculators and ranching consortiums. "In the end," said Wallace Stegner, "the Homestead Act stimulated the monopolizing of land that its advocates had intended to prevent."[9]

And if that wasn't bad enough, Congress was still devising ways to turn over public lands to private individuals and enterprises. Since the Homestead Act, Congress had passed the Timber Culture Act in 1873, the Desert Land Act of 1877, and in 1878, it was already debating the Timber and Stone Act.

From the point of view of the Republican reformers, something had to be done, not only to improve the disbursement of land, but to enhance the government's understanding of the resources that were actually out there.

The question was how could the surveys do the job? The problem was that each of the four main surveys exploring western lands had looked at different things, from different vantage points. This was due to the interests and natures of the men who led the surveys and the government agencies that financed them. The result was a very imperfect picture of the West.

George Wheeler, a thirty-six-year-old ramrod, serious army career officer, focused on the military goal of describing terrain and making maps. The War Department wasn't interested in farming or mining. While Wheeler did produce some good science reports, the scientists were definitely subordinate to the soldiers.[10]

For Clarence King, mining was the single the most important thing. The Sheffield Scientific School graduate, who was the same age as Wheeler, was simply engaged in the Gilded Age hunt for riches. King's survey paid close attention to the mineral resources in the one-hundred-mile band that ran along the fortieth parallel—and the transcontinental railroad tracks. Farming, timbering, and settlement, however, didn't much interest him either.

John Wesley Powell's initial exploration of the Colorado River and Grand Canyon had been as much an adventure as a scientific expedition. Since then, Powell, forty-five, had done some good geology and mapping. But his survey's most singular contribution remained in the exploration of rivers and the study of the ethnology of Indian tribes of the Colorado River basin.

At the age of fifty, Hayden was the dean of the survey leaders, having started his explorations in the 1850s. His survey was the most wide ranging, dealing with everything from prehistoric animals to the assessment of coal deposits. The Hayden Survey did far more natural history research than any other, publishing papers on locusts in Colorado, snakes in Montana, butterflies in Utah, fish in the Rio Grande, as well as minerals in Nevada.

Hayden also had scientists look at two of the great myths powering western development. The first was the tenet that settlement changed climate, making arid regions wetter. This was commonly known as the theory that "rain follows the plow." The second notion was that a vast coal deposit, the "Great Lignite," underlay the West.

Even if Hayden's survey didn't prove these beliefs, so dear to those touting western development, just having them examined seriously added legitimacy. It also made Hayden a favorite in Congress. (Hayden's strategy of passing out copies of W. H. Jackson's beautiful western photographs and hiring legislators' kith and kin for summer work also bolstered this congressional goodwill.)

There was much good work in the surveys, but clearly there were holes in some places, and redundancies in others, and always conflicts. It took vision and determination to mount a survey and struggle with the wilderness. Such men weren't going to yield to one another easily.

But as big as the West was, it couldn't accommodate so many individual visions. Well, at least, the nation couldn't. Just look at the mapping mess created by the independent surveys. Between 1867 and 1877, the government spent nearly $1.9 million mapping the West, with Hayden getting a little more than a third of the money, Wheeler about a quarter, King a fifth, and Powell a seventh. All the surveys produced maps, but they used different scales and techniques.

Wheeler and Hayden were mapping at eight miles to the inch, while King was using four miles to the inch. Wheeler used crosshatches to show mountains. King used contour lines. Powell had started at eight miles to the inch, but eventually switched to the more detailed technique. (The fact that King lent him some of his maps might have been the reason for the switch.) The result was there were no comprehensive maps. Confusion continued to reign west of the hundredth meridian.

Something had to be done. The new secretary of the interior was going to see to that.

✤

Carl Shurz had arrived in the United States in the early 1850s, escaping the Prussian crackdown that followed the democratic, romantic, and unsuccessful revolutionary movement of 1848. He quickly applied his idealistic politics to America. He fought in the Civil War, won election to the Senate from Missouri, opposed Grant, supported civil service reform, and became a central member of the Republican reform movement, which included Congressman James Garfield of Ohio, New York's Abram Hewitt, and *Nation* editor Edwin L. Godkin.

Not long after arriving at the Interior Department, Schurz began to look at the survey question. Since three of the surveys—King's, Wheeler's, and the coastal—were in other departments, Schurz focused on Powell, Hayden, and the General Land Office. The new secretary asked Powell and Hayden for their thoughts.

Powell began 1877 feeling extremely vulnerable. His survey was the runt of the litter, having received annual appropriations ranging between ten thousand and forty-five thousand dollars, a half to a fifth of what Hayden received.

It was also the survey that had produced the fewest works. Wheeler had made by far the most maps. King was in the process of turning out seven volumes of the finest geology, cartography, mineralogy, and paleontology studies ever produced in America.

Hayden's survey had been the most prolific. Hayden cultivated a broad range of scientists who analyzed specimens and sometimes traveled with his surveying parties. He provided an umbrella and a press for their work. When all his survey's works were finally published, there were twelve volumes of annual reports, six volumes of bulletins, twelve volumes of miscellaneous publications, thirteen volumes of monographs, and seventeen volumes of unclassified publications. There were seven volumes on paleontology—five written by Cope.

In the budget-cutting atmosphere of 1877, Powell was worried that Congress might not give him any appropriation at all. He begged for help from John Strong Newberry, who had left Cleveland and medicine and was teaching geology at the Columbia University School of Mines, in New York City.

Newberry wrote to Garfield and Hewitt—both members of the House Appropriations Committee. In those letters, Newberry not only praised

Powell, but also blasted Hayden. "Hayden has come to be so much of a fraud that he has lost the sympathy and respect of the country," Newberry said. "The most important contributions lately made to science through his agency are papers on Paleontology prepared by experts from materials obtained through his collectors. These, however interesting to scientists, seem hardly to belong in the category of necessities for which the expenditures of government should be chiefly made in these hard times."

Here was the blueprint for the coming fight. Attack Hayden's character and discredit the work of his survey. Still, Congress gave Hayden seventy-five thousand dollars, while cutting Powell's appropriation from forty-five thousand to thirty thousand dollars. At least Powell's survey was still alive.

In May, Powell and Hayden exchanged heated words in Schurz's office with charges of duplication, backbiting, and waste being hurled around the room. Schurz had to be chagrined.

Three days after that scene, Powell wrote a long, reasoned letter to Schurz proposing a compromise. Hayden would report on natural history (which Newberry was already arguing the federal government shouldn't fund), and Powell would take ethnography. Powell was searching for some way to institutionalize his weaker survey.

Hayden replied that was fine with him, as long as his survey also did all the geology and geography. That, of course, would leave Powell with hardly any survey at all. Hayden could act that way because at the moment he held better—if not all—the cards. But the forces to overturn him, though just eddies at the moment, were already at work.

First, over the years, Hayden had made himself a fair number of enemies, including highly influential men like Newberry and Albany's James Hall. Second, being a politician-scientist, Hayden had cultivated the corrupt Delano when he headed Interior. This was a strike against him with Schurz. Third, his enemies had found a useful line of attack in dismissing much of the survey's work as impractical and not worthy of federal funding.

Finally, there was Hayden himself with his temper, insecurities, and as one employee put it, "those old fires of jealousy and suspicions that ever smolder."[11]

This was the stage that had already been set when Joseph Henry passed away.

But the decision to use the National Academy of Sciences was a new wrinkle and one that depended exclusively on O. C. Marsh being at the academy helm. Congressman Hewitt may have been the author of the resolution asking the academy's advice, but the forces behind the resolution were none other than Powell and Clarence King.

"The four [survey] chiefs maintained their rivalry in camp and in Congress," King wrote in a third-person autobiography. "Amongst them King and Powell felt most strongly the evils of the want of correlation . . . and it was mainly through their combined influence that the conduct of the surveys [again] became a matter of Congressional investigation, and the National Academy of Sciences was drawn in as an advisor. . . . Powell led this movement."[12]

The Marsh academy was a perfect vehicle with its intersecting interests and liaisons. King and Marsh were friends, former classmates at Yale's Sheffield Scientific School, and collaborators on King's survey. Powell and Marsh were kindred spirits. Both had campaigned for Indian rights, and both had been enemies of Delano. Since 1872, Powell had also tried to ingratiate himself by sending any fossils his survey happened to find to Marsh.

But perhaps most important, King and Powell were well aware of Marsh's intense dislike for Hayden and Hayden's top collaborator Cope.

Hewitt was a reform-minded Republican from New York, whose family was in the iron business. This gave him an interest in the development of western mining resources. He was also, incidentally, partners with King in a western cattle venture. King, Marsh, and Hewitt were all members of the tony Century Club in New York City.

Marsh was an ocean away when Henry died and the reformers made their opening gambit to use the National Academy of Sciences. But as soon as he heard what was afoot, Marsh immediately made plans to leave Europe for home. His departure had to wait, however, until he paid a visit to Charles Darwin at his country home. Still, even before leaving England, Marsh began sending letters to key scientists and preparing a committee to look into the merger of the surveys. Powell was already mailing Marsh material.

Twenty-six years earlier, when Marsh was a student at Phillips Exeter Academy, one of the school's greatest honors was the presidency of the debating club, the Philomathean Society. It was a plum traditionally reserved for a senior.

But seizing on the unpopularity of an upperclassman's candidacy, Marsh was able to inveigle his way toward the prize. "Marsh organized the middlers with great skill, held the class firmly together," W. E. Park, a classmate and friend, remembered, "picked up loose votes lying around the school, and defeated the senior candidate by a majority of one. The excitement in the school was tremendous, and Marsh became a great hero."[13]

Cope might not know how to win elections, but Marsh certainly did. The Yale professor was in his element, and Hewitt, Garfield, and Schurz doubtless knew that they could count on the academy and Marsh for the right kind of solution to the survey problem. Now it was Hayden who was worried. "I do not feel assured of prolonged existence," Hayden confided to a friend.

In the 1878 appropriations bill, the same to which Hewitt's National Academy of Sciences' rider was attached, Congress gave Powell his largest grant ever—fifty thousand dollars. Hayden's appropriation was held at seventy-five thousand dollars. The tide had turned. But that summer, Powell had more at stake than money, for he alone of the survey chiefs had a vision, a daring and radical vision of America. For Powell, the stakes in the coming struggle were nothing less than the very future of the American West.

His enemies called him—among other things—a "revolutionist," and what an odd revolutionist he was. He had neither the training of university-bred Marsh and King nor the eastern affluence and propriety of Cope. He was not a medical man like Leidy, Hayden, and Newberry. Powell was unique.

The son of Wesleyan abolitionist preacher, Powell grew up in villages and farms dotting Ohio, Illinois, and Wisconsin. He had a "home-made" education, which included a few sporadic semesters at Wheaton and Oberlin Colleges. He had gathered enough learning, however, to become a high school teacher. Then came the Civil War.

Powell entered as a private. Within three months, he was a lieutenant and in another five, a captain. On April 5, 1862, at the Battle of Shiloh, a minié ball shattered his right arm. Army surgeons had to amputate it above the elbow. Powell returned to duty, became an artillery officer, and rose to the rank of major.

After the war, he landed a position as professor of geology at Illinois Wesleyan University, and then he moved to Illinois State Normal University. Like Hall in Albany and Mudge in Kansas, Powell lobbied the state legislature for funds to support scientific activities. Then he tried doing the same with Congress.

In 1868, Powell led his first expedition—composed largely of students and family members—to the West. The following year, he made a name for himself with his descent of the Colorado River, and from that point on, he had been squeezing small appropriations from Congress to keep his exploration going. Among his earliest supporters in the capital were Joseph Henry and James Garfield.

But unlike any of the other survey leaders, Powell had fashioned a complete vision of the West and a theory on how it should be developed. Just
twelve weeks before Hewitt had offered his resolution asking the academy's
advice on the surveys, Powell delivered a bureaucratic bomb to Schurz.

Powell sent the secretary his *Report on the Lands of the Arid Region of the
United States, with a More Detailed Account of the Lands of Utah*. Powell's bold
study began:

> The Physical Conditions which exist in the arid lands, and which
> inexorably control the operations of men, are such that the industries
> of the West are necessarily unlike those of the East, and their institu-
> tions must be adapted to their industrial wants. It is thus that a new
> phase of Aryan civilization is being developed in the western half of
> America.

In this report, Powell offered a revolutionary view of the future settlement
of the West. In essence, he said that the land west of the hundredth meridian simply received too little rainfall to be cut up in rectangular quarter sections, as had the fertile and moist Midwest. Similarly, traditional approaches
to water rights, timbering, and grazing also could not be used. Everything
about the West, the report argued, was different and needed a different
development approach, one more attuned to the hot, dry land.

What would be needed were homesteads of up to twenty-five hundred
acres, village cooperatives, large-scale government irrigation projects, and
areas simply blocked off from development.

It also called for more rigorous and comprehensive surveys and assess-
ments of natural resources before development could take place. Powell
wanted to abolish the surveyors-general and the surveying contracts. He
wanted the government do all the measuring and mapping.

Arid Region instantly made Powell a pariah with western political and
economic interests. They saw the report as a threat to private development
and the heavy hand of the federal government in local affairs. Editorials in
western newspapers excoriated Powell for trying to halt progress.

Representative Thomas Patterson of Colorado called him a "charlatan of
science and intermeddler in affairs of which he has no conception." Powell, the critics argued, had based his report on bad science and faulty rea-
soning.

In August, Marsh handpicked a committee to review the problem of the
surveys and make a recommendation to the academy. His selection was
pure craftiness, as a majority of the group were either opponents of Hayden

or supporters of King. Among the members were Newberry, a true Hayden enemy, and William Petit Trowbridge, a former Yale professor, now a colleague of Newberry's at Columbia.

Alexander Agassiz was also asked to serve. King had named a mountain after Agassiz, and Agassiz had invested in King's cattle venture. Simon Newcomb, the mathematician, astronomer, and director of the Nautical Almanac, was also a member. Newcomb was one of Marsh's key sources for Washington gossip and had been a supporter of King to fill Henry's post at the Smithsonian.

The group was rounded out by two of the most distinguished names in American science: James Dwight Dana from Yale and William B. Rogers, a geologist and founder of the Massachusetts Institute of Technology. Marsh served as member ex officio, a practice started by Henry.[14]

Hayden could not have been happy with the composition, but General Andrew A. Humphreys, chief of the Army Corps of Engineers, was furious. The committee was a bunch of academics; there were no representatives from the government services—especially the military. Scientists had always chafed when working under military surveys. Now that the Indian wars were over, it was clear that the intention was to place the future survey in civilian hands.

As soon as the Hewitt rider passed, Powell sent copies of *Arid Region* to Marsh with the request, "I beg you to distribute [them] among the gentlemen who may be appointed members of the committee of the National Academy of Sciences."

By September, Marsh had a draft report he was circulating among the committee members, and in early October, he wrote to Schurz outlining the committee's tentative findings. Schurz passed the letter on to Powell.[15] The secretary also asked Powell and Hayden to submit formal statements to the committee.

Powell, who had stayed in Washington that summer, engaging in a lively round of correspondence and lobbying, provided a sixteen-page response titled "Report on the Methods of Surveying the Public Domain." In it he strongly criticized the General Land Office, Wheeler, and Hayden, and once again brought up the argument that zoology and botany as branches of general science are "poor subjects of government patronage." Unless, like locust and cotton worms, they "may suddenly affect the national welfare."

Hayden was indecisive. "I am asked to make a reply," he wrote to Leidy, "I do not know what to say. Think something up for me." Finally, he offered a hopelessly lame statement. "In reply, I beg to say that any plans which I could offer for the survey of the Western Territories would naturally be based upon the organization now under my charge."

Hayden was playing right into Marsh's hands.

✤

Both Hayden and Cope had displayed extraordinarily bad timing. Just as the intrigue was afoot, Cope left for Europe, and Hayden went west to Wyoming. Hayden's decision was at least in part prompted by his failing health. He might even have been suffering from the onset of the syphilis that would eventually claim his life. (In May, Hayden's wife, Emma, wrote to a friend, somewhat cryptically, that "all disappointments seem trivial compared to the great one—I could not trust myself to allude to it when I wrote you, for it was the one of the hardest trials I have ever known.")

One of Hayden's Washington employees, F. W. Pearson, did keep his boss posted on developments back east, where the news was ominous. "Powell is in town," he reported in late July. "I see him frequently driving up and down the street industriously."

A few weeks later came the report, "I have been up and around Powell's office quite frequently, and he appears to have a pretty good force of men at work. . . . He may be doing something on the quiet. I can see or hear nothing." But Hayden lingered out west, and his letters to friends back east seem noncommittal and unenthusiastic.

And what of Cope? At about the same time Hayden went to Cheyenne, Cope boarded the SS *Elysia* headed for England. His ultimate destination, however, was Trinity College in Dublin and the annual meeting of the British Association for the Advancement of Science.

From London, Cope took the mail train—"The Wild Irishman"— which barreled through Rugby and Chester at speeds of up to sixty miles an hour. He found Dublin "generally good looking" and reported to Annie that "the ladies and girls are often very good looking, handsomer than the English as one would expect."

Cope brought with him drawings of *Camarasaurus* and his other dinosaurs, done by fellow Philadelphian John Ryder. They "attracted great attention" as did his paper on the new dinosaurs, and plates and charts from the Hayden Survey. "The Hayden Survey I find to be very popular, and many persons exceedingly regret that there should be any opposition to it," he reported.[16]

Cope had a fine time. "The only traces of Marsh's handiwork I could discover was in the indifference of Huxley's which I ascribe to that source. He took no pains to see me or hear any of my papers—a coolness I suspect he would not have shown to friend Marsh. I however introduced myself and I think we should have had some pleasant conversation."[17]

The best entertainment was a party given by the College of Surgeons, which was attended by the Duke and Duchess of Marlborough. It was at this soiree that Cope was smitten by the wife of one Dr. Traquair, a Scottish expert on Paleozoic fish. Cope and Mrs. Traquair danced and danced. She was, Cope told his wife, "rather petite (for Ireland) and a very pleasant and sensible young lady. She has a rather wide face, but good red lips. Her husband . . . was rather jealous and I finally had to exchange her for someone else."

Then it was on to Paris and the meeting of the French Association for the Advancement of Science, and another round of dinners, banquets, and parties. "There was a grand entertainment . . . ," Cope wrote home, "at the Department of Arts and Measures (Patent Office) where everything was gorgeous with illumination, music, etc. with free refreshments."[18]

Again Cope displayed Ryder's drawings of the new North American dinosaurs, and again "they excited a great deal of interest." Cope was nominated to membership in the French Geological Society. He worried about Marsh criticism, but was told by "one person of importance . . . that the criticism of a certain person *ne fait rien.*"[19]

Cope enjoyed France, but like many a tourist found it an expensive place. "I have spent a good deal of money here and could not stay longer if I would," he told Annie. "I got thee a silk dress which is reposing in the bottom of my trunk. I could not get a very plain one, but this is not extravagantly gay. In looking over the ladies dresses (a new business for me!) I saw some very beautiful things in silk and others so ornamented as to be ugly."[20]

Cope made another purchase while in Paris, an extensive and expensive collection of Pleistocene fossils from the Argentine pampas. The collection—worth tens of thousands of dollars—had been shown at the Paris Exposition. It was a costly acquisition, but after all, wasn't this what having means was all about?

Cope returned to London and met with Richard Owen and Harry Seeley, who was one of the most prolific and cantankerous of the English paleontologists, something of a British Cope. (By 1878, Seeley himself had already identified more than a dozen new dinosaurs.[21]) "Mr. Seeley has always been my fast friend thro' evil as well as good report and is so still. His wife too is a delightful woman about thy age . . . ," he wrote to Annie. "Seeley has to work hard; delivers 1000! lectures in a year for which he is poorly paid."[22]

Cope closed that letter to his wife, "I am wanting to get back to you as this life does not suit me very well. I cannot live without a family and you are the point of attraction wherever I go."

By early November, after nearly three months abroad, Cope returned to Philadelphia.

But while Cope had been dancing, partying, and shopping, Marsh had been calculating and crafting. At about the same time Cope was arriving in the States, Marsh was putting the finishing touches on a plan that would satisfy the reformers and his own interests as well.

❖

On November 6, the National Academy of Sciences gathered in New York City, at Columbia University, to consider the report on merging the surveys prepared by its special committee.

The meeting began at 11 A.M. with Marsh presenting the report calling for the merging of the existing surveys into a single U.S. Geological and Geographic Survey. The report suggested that disbursement of land be done by the General Land Office, but that mapping and surveying be under the supervision of the U.S. Coast and Geodetic Survey. All three agencies, the report said, should be placed under the Interior Department. It suggested the creation of a public lands commission to codify public-land laws. All these ideas were in Powell's original *Arid Region* document.[23]

"I see the Academy has made its report," Powell's secretary James Pilling wrote to his boss, "and it sounds wonderfully like something I have read—perhaps written—before."

But Marsh made some additions. For example, the report proposed a requirement that all collections made by the surveys be deposited in the national museum. This was aimed directly at Hayden and Cope. Hayden often circulated collections made by his survey and allowed researchers to retain part of the material in exchange for their work. The requirement would also apply to scientists, like Cope, who accompanied surveys and collected material, even if they traveled at their own expense.

The report was discussed for three and one-half hours and then voted on. Hayden found himself in an awkward position of not liking the document, for the merger of the surveys could end in him losing his entire operation, but being unable to strongly oppose it. He said nothing during the discussion. Cope, however, launched an attack. The final vote was thirty-seven to one. Cope was once again the lone dissenter. When informed of the decision, General Humphreys of the Army Corps of Engineers was so angry that he resigned from the academy in protest. The general, mused mathematician and Marsh confidant Simon Newcomb, "opens the fight by a sort of hara-kiri."

The report went to Congress, and now the reformers did their part. Instead of being referred to the Committee on Public Lands, the report became the property of the more sympathetic Appropriations Committee, where Hewitt, Garfield, and committee chairman John D. C. Atkins, of Tennessee, could keep an eye on it.

Ten days after the academy session at Columbia, another notable meeting took place, this one in the parlor of Powell's M Street home in Washington. For a good many months, Powell had entertained a Saturday night gathering of scientists, politicians, and men of letters. It had started out as a few of Powell's intimates having a couple of drinks together. But as the intrigues of Washington multiplied, so did the attendees.

This night, the gathering included Harvard historian Henry Adams, mining engineer Fred Endlich, and cavalry officer Clarence Dutton. The issue before the group was forming a new club. They decided to call it the Cosmos Club and to rent rooms in the Corcoran Building. The Cosmos Club would become one of the most prestigious and elite clubs in the capital, and Powell that night was elected its first president. The rough-hewn, midwestern outsider, the little man with a straggly steel-wool beard, slightly cross-eyed gaze, and just one arm, had become the consummate Washington insider.

Now the real political battle was under way. Western interests were opposed to the academy proposal as undue federal influence in the development of the states and territories. Colorado's Patterson ridiculed the report and called its authors "theorists who knew nothing about the practical problems or the public lands."[24]

Cope argued in the *American Naturalist* that while he supported the unification of all the mapping and geodetic work, and the reform of the General Land Office, he believed that when it came to the geological work, "there is no such reason for consolidation. If the work be well done, it matter not how many organizations it be confided in, provided it not be duplicated."[25]

"It seems the fight has begun," wrote Wolcott Gibbs, the Harvard chemist and Marsh ally. "You might if possible . . . be in Washington to help Hewitt out. . . . Why has Gen. Humphrey's resigned from the Academy?"[26]

Now Powell was truly a man in motion, hustling from newspaper office to newspaper office with his "propaganda," then hiking up Capitol Hill, buttonholing congressmen and senators in the hallways and lobbying hard in the committee rooms.

He had good reason to expend such energy. His *Arid Region* report had been transformed into the National Academy of Sciences' recommendation, and the entire academy plan had pretty much been turned into House Resolution 6140. He was that close to victory.

At the final hearing on the legislation, the heads of all the surveys were asked to testify. In an account of the hearing, Joseph Stanley-Brown, one of Powell's secretaries, said, "Lt. Wheeler was dignified and indifferent. Clarence King being friendly did not put in an appearance. Dr. Hayden spoke impassioned and bitter words."

All this time, Powell paced the back of the committee chamber, his good hand grasping the stump of his right arm behind his back. Then came Powell's turn. He spoke, laying before the committee "in an impersonal calm and lucid manner the details of his scheme. It was plain to see the day had been won." Perhaps the day, but not the battle.

❖

On the evening of February 18, 1879, the members of the U.S. House of Representatives took up H.R. 6140—for the final time. They had been debating the bill for almost nine days.[27]

At the outset of the debate, Hewitt had couched the issue by asking his fellow members:

> What is there in this richly endowed land of ours which may be dug or gathered, or harvested, and made part of the wealth of America and the world, and how and where does it lie? These are the questions which the enterprise, the capital, and the labor of the United States are engaged in working out. . . . And it is to the solution of these questions, the greatest of all national problems, that the scientific surveys of the public domain should be directed.

Representative Atkins moved that the legislation be approved. But California's Horace Page, while supporting the survey consolidation, made a motion that would have removed the General Land Office and the surveyors-general from the bill.

Dudley Haskell from Kansas raised an even more sweeping objection, contending that while the bill was based on the National Academy of Sciences' report, not all scientists agreed with that document. "Now sir," Haskell said, "I hold in my hand a letter from one of the prominent members of the Academy of Sciences. He goes on in the opening to the letter to criticize the whole scheme of consolidation."

Dudley went on to read the letter's concluding passage. "As a member of the National Academy, I take the liberty of stating that there is much opposition to it among its members. The names of Baird (Secretary of the Smithsonian Institution), of Leidy (University of Pennsylvania), of Lesley (head of geological survey of Pennsylvania), Guyot (professor of geology Princeton) shows that opposition springs from the strongest men."

Of course, none of those men had actually voted against the academy's report. Still, the letter touched off a tempest on the House floor.

"Who is the author of that letter?" demanded one congressman.

"Let the whole letter be read," said another.

"I have read all that I think is necessary," Haskell replied.

"Let us know the name of the author," a lawmaker insisted.

"I am not to receive instruction . . . ," Haskell said, refusing to divulge the name. "I will say that the letter was sent to a member of this House, the gentleman from Pennsylvania [Representative Freeman] and that it is written by a member of the board in Pennsylvania."

Who could it be but Cope?

That night, however, the real battle came down to the issue of the surveyors-general and control of the land. The politicians didn't like the idea of a single, big survey, but they were more concerned with who would control the distribution of land to settlers and businesses.

Disbursement of land simply could not go to a single federal survey. "Centralization of all the machinery here in Washington would necessarily subject the actual settler to vexatious delays and increased expense," one Ohio congressman warned. "The greater facilities you furnish the settler in the way of perfecting his title, the more rapidly you settle our domain."

Another opponent argued that "this vast scheme of scientific exploration conducted by the government is in little harmony with the character of our institutions or the genius of people."

Finally Colorado's Patterson rose and charged that the proposed reform bill "is not the recommendation of practical men but of visionary scientists and men who are blinded by political prejudices."

Page's amendment removing the General Land Office from the survey merger bill passed ninety-eight to seventy-nine. But Atkins was able to preserve most of the other elements of the academy's recommendations.

A few days later the appropriation bills were approved with the rider consolidating all the scientific surveys, except the U.S. Coast and Geodetic Survey, under the Department of the Interior. It also established the Public Lands Commission to review federal land laws. The Hayden, Powell, Wheeler, and King Surveys would be officially abolished, and in their place would stand the U.S. Geological Survey. But the surveyors-general and the

General Land Office and their way of doing business remained intact. Powell's vision of a more orderly method of western development had been thwarted, but at least the scientific work would be integrated and organized. It was half a victory.

The bill then went to the Senate, where Hayden's longtime lobbying strategy had earned him stronger support. Now the battle was truly joined. "The fight will commence in the Senate," Newcomb wrote to Marsh. "There is where we will want King."

King, who had left most of the battle to Powell, now hurried to Washington, carrying letters of introduction to the president from novelist and *Atlantic* editor William Dean Howells, and from Mrs. Howells to her "Dear Cousin Lucy," the president's wife. King's only fault, Howells informed the president, was "that a man who can give us such literature should be content to be merely a great scientist."

Mrs. Howells told dear Lucy that King was simply "the most accomplished man of his age in the country."

Wormley's Hotel became headquarters for King and Hewitt, as they burned the gaslight in late-night strategy sessions. Initially, Hayden's Senate allies tried to gut the House bill, virtually undoing the merger. Now King bent his inimitable charm toward wooing senators, and Hewitt managed a compromise in the joint conference committee that basically saved the half victory. The surveys would be merged.

But for Marsh and Powell, that still wasn't enough. They also needed control of the new survey. It was clear that Powell was far too controversial a figure to ever win Senate confirmation as the new agency's director. Indeed, the reform forces had foreseen this and included a twenty-thousand-dollar appropriation for the preparation of studies on North American ethnology under the Smithsonian Institution. Powell would have his little sinecure. As for the director of the U.S. Geological Survey, the natural and logical alternative was Marsh's good friend King.

If Powell began as an outsider, Clarence King was the ultimate insider. He had gone to Yale. He was a member of the Century Club in New York City and the Union Pacific Club in San Francisco. He was a confidant to intellectuals and opinion makers like Henry Adams and the author, diplomat, and secretary of state John Hay. His book, *Mountaineering in the Sierra Nevada,* classed him with serious western writers like Bret Harte.

Hay simply called King "the best and brightest man of his generation," and Adams's praise was even more enthusiastic. "He knew America," Adams wrote, "especially west of the hundredth meridian, better than anyone; he knew the professor by heart, and he knew the Congressman better than he did the professor. He knew even women; even the American woman; even the New York woman, which is saying much. . . . One Clarence King existed only in the world."[28] Handsome, charming, witty, King was able to win over even the most hard-bitten politician.

When King began his survey in 1869, he was just twenty-seven. The survey of the fortieth parallel cut through the Rocky Mountains from California to Colorado, following the route of the Central Pacific Railroad. The surface of the region had pretty much been mapped by the railroad, so King set out to determine what natural resources along the route could be exploited. The War Department initially financed the work, but then Congress asked him to continue his survey through Utah and as far east as Wyoming.

From the outset, the university-trained King used the finest European surveys as his standard, and he produced high-quality maps and analyses. The survey focused on topology, geography, surface geology, and mineralogy.

The actual surveying had taken from 1869 to 1872. King spent the rest of the decade in New Haven working on the survey reports. When completed in 1880 there were seven volumes (including two by Marsh), and the total bill had been $386,711.[29]

King and Marsh were more than collaborators. They were also friends. King teased Marsh about the size of his growing fossil collection, warning him that shipping so many fossils east to New Haven could tip the earth's center of gravity. He assured Marsh that come judgment day, the Angel Gabriel would start at Yale. "Think of the time he could save by starting there," King quipped.

He also chided Marsh about his bachelorhood, saying that it was strange that among so many bones, Marsh "never got a rib." But King supposed that for an inveterate collector like Marsh "only a harem would do."[30]

While Marsh and Powell were now anxious for King to take over the new survey, King was surprisingly less enthusiastic. He was, after all, a man of his age, and his age was gilded. The truth was that while he was blessed with riches in intellect, looks, and personality, King was not a wealthy man. In fact, he had grown up in that genteel poverty that sounds picturesque, but really isn't.

His father had died on the other side of the world in the China trade, and King was raised by a beautiful, but penniless mother, amid the splendor of Newport, Rhode Island. And so, while being dashing, literary, and scientific, King was also looking to make a buck.

At the same time Powell and Marsh were promoting him to head the new survey, King had promised a New York publisher a novel, and he was trying to persuade Hewitt to throw in with him on a scheme to break Alexander Graham Bell's patent on the telephone. There was money to be made in talk. "We will whisper around the world," King enticed. Then there was, of course, his western cattle venture, and perhaps some Mexican gold mines, too.

The law creating the U.S. Geological Survey provided for a director's salary of six thousand dollars a year. But the law specifically said that "the director and members of the Geological Survey shall have no personal or private interests in the lands or mineral wealth of the region under survey, and shall execute no examinations or surveys for private parties or corporations." This would seriously hamper the bold Mr. King. Still, even he couldn't help but enjoy the race, particularly since Hayden hadn't completely given up.

"Hayden is moving Heaven and Earth to get the President's support, but I think I have the inside track," King confided to Marsh as early as January 1879.[31]

Powell was not so sure. "The most vigorous efforts are being made by Hayden to get the appointment under the bill . . . ," Powell wrote to Marsh in late February. "Can you not get letters from Michigan University, Rochester, and from scientific and public men in addition to what has already been obtained. Dr. Hayden is collecting from every source—Europe and America."[32]

Hayden had gathered together all the testimonials he had garnered over the years and now issued them in a pamphlet form. The effect was to suggest that this broad array of scientists and politicians were supporting his bid to become the first director of the U.S. Geological Survey.

Not that Hayden didn't have real support. He had the distinguished English botanist Joseph Hooker; John William Dawson, head of the Canadian Geological Survey; Archibald Geikie of the British Geological Survey; Princeton's Arnold Guyot; and from Harvard, botanist Asa Gray and entomologist Samuel Scudder.

Hayden had also sought—and received—the help of his old Oberlin College classmate Jacob Cox, the interior secretary before Delano, who had been too upstanding for the corrupt Grant administration.

A few days later, Powell wrote to Congressman Atkins asking him to speak to Schurz and President Hayes about the post. "If Dr. Hayden is appointed, all hope of further reform in the system of land surveys is at an end or indefinitely postponed," he warned.

In a memorandum to Garfield, which gained some circulation on Capitol Hill, Powell charged Hayden with wasting "splendid appropriations upon work which was intended purely for noise and show—in photographs—[and] in utterly irrelevant zoological works."

The Hayden forces could play just as rough. A rather defamatory report on King and Powell also surfaced on the Hill. Cope wrote to Schurz charging King with being improperly involved in mining ventures and accepting private consulting fees while in the government's employ

In early March, Cope and Guyot traveled to Washington to do a little lobbying. "Guyot and Cope have been here for Hayden, and interviewed the President," Newcomb reported to Marsh. "The latter is, I think, only prevented by Schurz from tendering H. the appointment owing to overwhelming preponderance of *numbers* in his favor. It is therefore extremely desirable that [Massachusetts Institute of Technology's] W. B. Rogers and President Porter [of Yale] come as soon as practicable. The same remark applies to Newberry."[33]

Harvard's President Eliot also sent President Hayes a note that said, "Dr. Hayden, who is said to be with Congressmen, the leading candidate for the position, does not command the confidence of men of science. I have often heard Dr. Hayden discussed among scientific men, but have never heard either his attainments or his character spoken of with respect. In the contrary, I have often heard his ignorance, his scientific incapacity, and his low habits when in camp, commented on with aversion and mortification." One wonders which scientists Eliot spoke to, considering that two of his foremost professors—Scudder and Gray—were Hayden supporters.

Hayden's old mentor, James Hall, chimed in from Albany. "I did not think it possible that so notorious a charlatan in geology and so positively dishonest a man could have any chance when coming into competition with such a man as Clarence King," the crusty Hall wrote.

Marsh went to see the president about a week after Cope. Powell went to see the president, too, and so did Newcomb. When Newcomb found out that President Hayes—the former governor of Ohio—would put great weight in the opinion of Newberry—the former Ohio state geologist—the mathematician immediately wired New York City. A prompt visit to the White House was arranged.

Schurz pointed out to the president that Hayden had been an intimate of Columbus Delano. Garfield, Atkins, and Hewitt also expressed their belief that Hayden was not qualified to implement their reforms.

On March 20, Schurz announced that President Hayes had decided to forward to the Senate Clarence King's nomination as the first director of the U.S. Geological Survey. On April 3, the Senate confirmed King.

While King supporters and friends rejoiced, the new director hurried off to drive one more load of beef down the Oregon Trail before becoming a bureaucrat. "Our fight ended so satisfactorily that we shall never be happy till we've had another and got licked," Henry Adams exulted to Marsh. Marsh wrote to Powell on April 6 saying, "Now that the battle is won we can go back to pure science again." Perhaps.

Lieutenant Wheeler was now out of the survey business. Hayden had to accept a minor position under King. Cope still had a series of pending survey publications that he would have to speak to the new director about. But his days tagging along with Wheeler or Hayden teams and drawing army supplies were over.

Powell was also out of the survey business, at least in theory. He would now head the Smithsonian's American Bureau of Ethnology. The legislation also provided for the creation of the Public Lands Commission to codify land law, and Powell was appointed as one of the three commissioners.

Still, Powell alone of the former survey chiefs would have access to the new survey. "It will be one of my greatest pleasures to forward your scientific work and to advance your personal interests," King assured Powell in an April letter. Yes, Powell would have an inside track at the U.S. Geological Survey. So would Marsh.

Things had worked out admirably from Marsh's point of view. He had bested Hayden and Cope in Washington, and he now hoped to be doing the very same out west. For when a second great cache of western dinosaur bones had come to his attention, he had moved swiftly and secretly to lock up the boneyard and cut Cope off. Or so he thought.

Chapter Fourteen

 AFTER THE THUNDEROUS cave-in at the Morrison quarry, a weary and ailing Williston had made his way home to Manhattan, Kansas, in early November of 1877. But there would be no rest. A late-night telegram arrived from New Haven just days after his homecoming. Marsh had been trying desperately to get in touch with him for days. He had wired Morrison, only to find Williston gone.

Marsh wanted Williston back in the field—and fast. But not in Colorado, now he was to go to Wyoming, and he was to go in secret. "I shall start back as soon as possible," Williston assured him. "It is impossible almost to keep my movements here unknown. . . . I shall give it out I am going from here to Oregon!"[1]

The true destination, however, was Como Bluff, Wyoming. During the middle of the Colorado dinosaur frenzy, Marsh had received a cagey, but tantalizing, letter from the Union Pacific Station agent's office in Laramie. It read:

> *July 19, 1877*
> *Prof. C. Marsh, Geologist*
> *Yale College*
>
> *Dear Sir:*
> *I write to announce to you the discovery not far from this place of a large number of fossils, supposed to be those of the Megatherium, although there is no one here sufficient of a geologist to state for certainty. We have excavated one (1) partly, and know where there is several others that we have not, as yet, done any work upon. The formation in which they are found is of the Tertiary Period.*
> *We are desirous of disposing of what fossils we have, and also, the secret of the others. We are working men and not able to present them as a gift, and if we can sell the secret of the fossil bed, and procure work in excavating others we would like to do so.*
> *We have said nothing to anyone as yet.*

We measured one shoulder blade and found it to measure four feet eight inches 4 ft. 8 in. in length.

One joint of the vertebrae measures two feet and one half 2½ in circumference and ten inches (10) in length.

As proof of our sincerity and truth, we will send you a few fossils, at what they cost us in time and money in unearthing.

We would be pleased to hear from you, as you are well known as an enthusiastic geologist, and a man of means, both of which we are desirous of finding—more especially the latter.

Hoping to hear from you very soon, before the snows of winter set in.

> *We remain,*
> *Very respectfully*
> *Your Obedient Servants*
> *Harlow and Edwards*

It was a letter with as much error as truth in it. The strata at issue really weren't Tertiary, and the bones weren't from the Cenozoic ground sloth known as *Megatherium*. But then Harlow and Edwards weren't Harlow and Edwards, either. Marsh couldn't be certain what it was his two mysterious fossil hunters were talking about, but after having been almost too casual with Lakes, this time he took no chances.

He urged Harlow and Edwards to ship him the bones. But the men didn't get around to sending the fossils until September 17, and they didn't arrive in New Haven until the middle of October. When Marsh opened up the crates, he found about a dozen large vertebrae, pieces of claws and teeth, and some truly monumental leg and shoulder bones. He knew once he was again looking at the remains of huge dinosaurs.

Harlow and Edwards had also sent another letter announcing they had an additional fifteen hundred pounds of bones. "Besides this," they said, "we have discovered the bed of two more animals which we judge to be of the same kind. But which we have not done any work upon yet, and shall not until we hear from you and learn whether they will pay us."

On October 20, Marsh telegraphed his two stealthy and avaricious collectors. "Bones came today. Send rest with all small pieces." He also mailed them a seventy-five-dollar check, along with detailed instructions on how to collect bones and some questions about how and where the bones were found.

Harlow and Edwards were digging at Como Bluff about sixty-five miles west of Cheyenne. It was a place Marsh had actually stopped in 1869 to collect some rare salamanders—*Siredons*—that live in Como Lake, a flat, reedy disk of water at the base of the bluff.

There was a chance Marsh had come upon another major dinosaur graveyard—perhaps as good as Canon City. So it isn't surprising Harlow and Edward's next letter caused tremors in New Haven. "We are keeping our shipments of fossils to you as secret as possible," they wrote, "as there are plenty of men looking for such things and if they could trace us they could find discoveries which we have already made and which we have no desire to have known."

That's when Marsh began telegraphing Williston, and that's why Williston left immediately for "Oregon." On November 14, Williston climbed down from a rail coach at Como Station—two red buildings and a water tower surrounded by endless prairies and low bluffs. He met with "Harlow and Edwards" and immediately wrote to Marsh.

"I arrived here a few hours ago . . . found Messr. 'Harlow and Edwards.' (Reed and Collins) Mr. Collins is the station agent and Mr. Reed the section foreman. They used those names to conceal their identity. . . . I have seen a lot of bones they have ready to ship and they tell me the bones extend for *seven* miles. . . . I go out in the morning."[2]

The two would-be fossil collectors turned out to be William Edward Carlin (not Collins) and William Harlow Reed, two railroad men who were expecting to make a good deal of money from their discovery. But their first seventy-five-dollar check couldn't be cashed because Marsh had made it out to the nonexistent Harlow and Edwards. They mailed it back to the professor.

Two days later, Williston happily reported, "Canon City and Morrison are simply nowhere in comparison with this locality both as regards perfection, accessibility and quantity." The bones, Williston said, were "magnificently preserved and scattered for 6 or seven miles." Williston chose for his first quarry a site near the northwest shore of the lake, about a mile and a half from the station. Because of the protection of the bluffs, the men hoped to be able to work through the winter.

But Williston warned that "there will be great danger next summer of competition. At present but *seven* persons here have seen or know about the fossils but it will be almost impossible to prevent others to know in the spring."[3]

Williston struck a tentative agreement with Carlin and Reed for a salary of seventy-five dollars a month, but Carlin was planning to visit family in Washington, D.C., and decided that he would also stop in New Haven to negotiate directly with Marsh.

"W. E. Carlin will see you in about three weeks," Williston wrote. "He thinks he [has a] right to make considerable money out of the bones."[4] Everybody now knew that the bones, which just a few years ago were sent to Leidy for free, were worth real money.

✢

The Wyoming prairie between Laramie and Rock Creek was studded with bluffs. From the windows of a Union Pacific coach, rumbling across the flat, dry, sage-covered plain, they slid by on either side, huge humps of red, cream, and gray rocks, with clouds, as light and white as whipped cream, topping the most distant ridges.

As bluffs go, Como is nothing special. It is approximately ten miles long and one mile wide, running northwest to southwest. What made it so valuable was that exposed along this hillside were—in various places—the Jurassic Sundance formation, Jurassic Morrison formation, Triassic red beds, as well as Cretaceous formations, such as the Cloverly Sandstone and the Mowry Shale. It was this singular geology that would make Como Bluff perhaps the greatest dinosaur boneyard of all time.[5]

The bluff and the station got their name from the spring-fed lake at the western end of the hill. It, in turn, was named for Lago di Como in the Italian Alps. What made early settlers compare the thin, alkali pond with the cool, deep Alpine lake is hard to see. It was probably just wishful thinking. But it was the lake that first drew scientific interest to the area because of a peculiar tiger salamander that lived in it.

The animal was known as the "devil fish" or "the fish with legs" because of its little understood metamorphosis. It was for specimens of this salamander that Marsh stopped in 1868. Carlin, who was stationmaster at the time, also showed Marsh some fossils, but apparently they didn't interest him.

But now, nine years later, Marsh was most interested. Carlin and Reed were interested, too, interested in money. On November 17, Marsh hastily wrote up a three-page agreement hiring Carlin and Reed each at ninety dollars a month. Marsh also agreed to a bonus "proportionate to the importance of any new fossil found during the work." The men were required to "take all reasonable precautions to keep all others not authorized by Prof. Marsh out of the region." Marsh also retained the right to have his own "two superintendents" at the site.[6]

But Reed demurred at signing any agreement or doing any major work until Carlin had his little chat up in New Haven. Marsh found himself faced with the twin pressures of trying to lock up Como and haggle with Carlin.

Negotiating with Marsh turned out to be an ordeal. He would not budge. "I have argued with you and did everything in my power to come to an understanding and am tired of the whole business," Carlin wrote to Marsh from Washington, D.C., the day before Christmas.[7]

Late in December, a snappish Marsh warned Carlin, "I want the bones *promptly* or not at all."[8] By then Williston, still ailing and longing for home, quit Como and returned to Kansas, leaving his brother Frank to keep an eye on the bluff. But Como's great fossil cache was really in Reed's hands. Marsh's interests were hanging in the balance, but he would not compromise.

First, Reed unhappily capitulated. "It is a very poor way of doing business and I do not approve of it," Reed told Marsh in a letter.[9] Then, Carlin followed. By January of 1878, they had both agreed to Marsh's terms. That month, the first ninety-dollar payments were made to each man. Marsh had won, as he usually did. But he had also sown the seeds of discord and bad feeling that once again would cause him trouble in time to come.

The men used a tent to cover the quarry face, offering them some additional protection from the wind, snow, and cold, and as they worked, the tent moved along the quarry floor with them. Still, it was a hard, Wyoming winter, and there were days it was impossible to make the mile-and-a-half journey from the station to the quarry because of roaring winds or blinding snow.

Before Williston arrived, Carlin and Reed had excavated a considerable amount of material, but it had been the haphazard work of amateurs. Williston organized a systematic program designed to provide Marsh with an orderly flow of fossils.

The bones coming out of Quarry 1 belonged to several large sauropod dinosaurs, but they were so mixed up it was hard to tell exactly what went with what. Out of the jumble, Marsh named a new dinosaur *Morosaurus impar.* Marsh would use that name to describe several specimens. But eventually it would become clear that Marsh's *Morosaurus* was nothing more than Cope's *Camarasaurus,* and Cope had named the animal first.

Still, Como was so rich there would be plenty of important discoveries. One day, not long before he left, Williston was scouting areas just outside the quarry when he came upon the remains of a tiny dinosaur, with vertebrae less than an inch long. The next day, it snowed. "The small saurian I have not yet sent," Williston reported to Marsh, "and cannot for a few days till the snow blows off so that *we can find it.*"[10] When Marsh finally did get the animal, he found that he had yet another small, bipedal dinosaur, which he named *Laosaurus gracilis.* (Its name would eventually be changed to *Othneilia rex* in honor of its discoverer.)

When Williston left, the excavation was pretty much in Reed's hands. Born in Hartford, given a smattering of grammar school education, Reed had been roaming the West since his wife's death in 1871, working as a scout, hunter, and guide. He had landed at Como, where he was the section boss, responsible for keeping a stretch of the Union Pacific tracks in good order.

Reed took his fossil-hunting job seriously and was anxious to provide good results. When the first quarry seemed played out, he moved. But his second site yielded little. His next try—a patch a little more than a mile east of Quarry No. 1, and three miles from the station—yielded a bounty of bones. Out of it came yet another new dinosaur, the carnivorous *Allosaurus fragilis,* as well as another good specimen of *Laosaurus.*[11]

And then he struggled again, finally having to go to an area five miles away from the station. "I had the worst time finding a good quarry," he wrote to Williston in March, "but I wish you where here to see the bones roll out and they are beauties. . . . I think this quarry equal no. 1 for good bones."[12]

Marsh apparently remained testy and demanding, and in early April, Reed wrote to him. "I should be glad when you get your men here as you seem to doubt everything we do and I do not like it." Another thing that Reed didn't like was that Marsh was chronically late with his pay.[13]

Then in an early spring shipment, Marsh found a tiny jaw, and he quickly wired Williston—who had returned to Como "in a furious storm of snow" on April 18—to find more remains of the animal. By June, Marsh was to have enough material to report that he had found the oldest mammal on the North American continent. He called the opossum-sized Jurassic animal *Dryolestes.* It wasn't as grand as a sauropod dinosaur, but it was quite a paleontological coup.

Como Bluff was a wonderful treasure trove and was bound to create anxiety among Marsh and his men about competitors, especially E. D. Cope. "I am sorry to say that Cope knows of this locality and the general nature of the fossils," Williston reported as early as December 9, 1877. "A miner found some vertebrae here last spring and wrote to the Smithsonian describing them. Baird sent the letter to Cope and both replied. He (Brown the miner) was here last week and I read Cope's letter who seemed very anxious to get 'some teeth' or 'joints of the back bones!' "

Marsh was falling farther behind on his payments, and Reed and Carlin were both restive. "I have been looking anxiously forward for a letter containing a remittance of wages due a month ago. But I have been for some reason disappointed," Carlin wrote to Marsh in late March. "We are shipping bones as fast as we can get them for what money we make and should receive our wages promptly when due," he complained.[14]

Carlin, who proved to be less industrious and less dependable than Reed, began using the ever-present threat of competition to prod and pressure Marsh. On April 1, he sent a newspaper clipping to New Haven with a note that said, "I inclose an item clipped from the 'Daily Sentinel' a paper publish in Laramie in regard to our discoveries.

"I think it would be well to hasten operations as much as possible as it will probably be included in the Associated Press Repts from that City and it may be difficult to keep parties out."[15]

The article, titled "The Como Crocodile," reported there had been "frequent rumors of this discovery [of an ancient mammoth beast], but the affair was kept so dark a secret we could obtain nothing definite."

But now the paper announced that it had interviewed a "man familiar with the discovery, and every detail of the subsequent operation." The article named Carlin and Reed, saying they had extracted a forty-six-foot-long animal from the bluff and sent eight thousand pounds of fossils to New Haven.

It also said that they had already received "the handsome sum of $2500 for their labors" and that they were on salary of $130 a month. Of course, Carlin and Reed were making only $90 a month and hadn't received half as much money as the newspaper story indicated. It is a fair bet that Carlin was the newspaper's source, and his aim was shaking more money out of Marsh. Coincidentally, Williston's return to Como came hard upon Marsh's receipt of Carlin's little missive.

When Williston arrived, he had more bad news for Marsh. "One of Cope's men was here . . . ," he wrote with alarm. "He first purported to be selling groceries!! Gave his name as *'Haines,'* thick heavy rather portly man about 40, shaven except moustache and whiskers. Made some botanical collections & was very anxious to learn as much as possible about the fossils & *whether I* was coming out here. They said he walked a little lame. You may perhaps recognize him. He is certainly some man from Phila. or Washington."[16]

To say that Williston was obsessed and uneasy is no understatement, for a few hours later, he wrote Marsh another letter. "I have been talking further with Carlin about this man 'Haines.' There is no doubt but that he is direct from Cope. There is no man in America that knows as much about fossils outside our museum."[17]

Carlin thought the man was Cope himself, but Williston knew that wasn't the case because he had seen a note from Haines. The man, Williston said, "wrote in a very neat fine and legible hand and I've seen Cope's writing!" Cope's hand was a near-illegible scrawl that sometimes defied even his fondest correspondents. Apparently that finger, which led to a poor penmanship grade as a boy at the Westtown school, never got better.

Haines, Williston continued, "didn't mention Cope's name, but yours frequently *rather* disparagingly." When Carlin called Cope "a damned thief," Haines just sneered. "If you recognize him let me know as soon as possible & I will have a little fun at his expense," Williston said. "If you telegraph it, please chose simple words—*the initials of which will indicate the name.*" But the true identify of Haines was never established, and in a few weeks, he was gone.

By this time, the three men had opened four quarry sites. The first pit, Quarry No. 1, had been as rich as Williston predicted. But Quarry No. 2 yielded little. Quarry No. 3 had been very productive, and Quarry No. 4, while not great in quantity, had a good diversity of bones. But Quarry No. 4 was on the far side of Rock Creek, which meant having to haul the large, heavy bones across the creek by hand and then carry them to the railroad tracks. Once at the tracks, the men were able to use a railroad handcar to transport the fossils to the station.

After *Dryolestes* had been found, all other work was brushed aside, and everybody searched for more small mammal bones. Soon a fifth quarry was opened, which was, Williston reported "most productive in small saurians." It was in all likelihood in this area that *Dryolestes* probably was first found.[18]

And so the summer passed. Reed, Carlin, and their hired man, Vincent, searched Como Bluff for fossils, with the specter Haines—whomever he was—hovering about. In July, Williston left for New Haven and a post at the Peabody Museum.

At the end of August, Marsh stopped all collecting. By then Carlin and Reed were at odds with Marsh over wages and between themselves over work. Marsh was months behind on payments, and Reed felt that Carlin wasn't doing his fair share. Carlin wrote to Marsh in September, threatening legal action "to procure what you cannot deny to be a just debt."[19]

The stationmaster had had enough of Marsh. He decided he would become a freelance bone hunter. "It will not be safe to let Carlin know there is something in the quarries you want," Reed warned Marsh.[20] Of course, Reed hadn't been paid either, and he was stuck at Como until November, when Marsh finally got around to sending a check. He then returned to his home in Central City, Nebraska.

♣

Marsh had spent part of the year in Europe, and then was busy engineering the merger of the geological surveys in Washington. Cope was dancing and flirting his way through Europe. But that didn't mean the hunt for dinosaurs in the workshops had come to a halt.

When Williston arrived in New Haven in June of 1878, one of the first things he did was to show Marsh the Canon City dinosaur whose remains he had held together with paste and paper.

The young field hand had been right. He had found a new dinosaur and a huge one at that. Marsh named it *Diplodocus longus,* and with a body length of about eighty feet, it truly was long. The chevrons that had caught Williston's eye gave the dinosaur's backbone a V shape. Over time, paleontologists would come to see that this was a common characteristic of the large sauropod dinosaurs, and they would suspect that a ligament running from the head to the tail fit into the groove to help support the beast's weight, making it a sort of walking suspension bridge.

Among the other dinosaurs marching out of the Peabody Museum that year was the *Allosaurus lucaris,* a large, fierce, two-footed carnivore that may have hunted in packs, and the *Dryosaurus,* a twenty-foot-long, two-footed herbivore.

Cope, being Cope, also managed to turn out a series of papers on the discovery of new dinosaurs somewhere in between dancing with Mrs. Traquair and lobbying President Hayes. Among the dinosaurs that had taken up residence at 2102 Pine Street in Philadelphia were *Symphyrophus musculosus* and *Epanterias amplexus.* (It turned out these dinosaurs were the same as Marsh's *Camptosaurus* and *Allosaurus,* and to Cope's chagrin, Marsh's names would have priority.)

But this flood of new, old bones was confusing as well as exciting—as illustrated by the story of another 1878 dinosaur, Cope's *Thecodontosaurus gibbidens.* This animal, it was believed, was even older than the Jurassic dinosaurs, coming from the Late Triassic, more than two hundred million years ago. It was a time that reptile life was branching in several evolutionary directions.

Richard Owen created the group Thecodontia in the 1840s to try to describe certain animals from this time period. The distinguishing characteristic for these animals was teeth set in deep sockets. The group initially included just three genera—*Palaeosaurus, Thecodontosaurus,* and *Cladeiodon.* These were all dinosaurs or dinosaur-like animals. But as the pace of discovery quickened, Owen ended up adding other animals because they had the characteristic socket teeth, animals that clearly weren't dinosaurs. Socket teeth, it turned out, was too general an attribute. Soon it became clear that Thecodontia wasn't going to hold up as a concept. It was just a grab bag.

Almost thirty years after Owen, Cope again tried to make sense out of these finds by constructing another classification, which he called the Archosauria, or "ruling reptiles." In Cope's view, the similarities that caused confusion in Owen's *Thecodontia* were the result of sharing common ancestry. Owen simply hadn't drawn the circle big enough or looked back far enough.

Cope listed about six characteristics in jaws, skulls, and vertebrae that these animals shared. Even with that, it still included a broad sweep of animals. "The order embraces that large series of forms seen to be equidistant between all extremes of the Reptilian type. It is therefore not a strictly homogeneous group," Cope explained.[21]

From early Triassic archosaurs, Cope reasoned, had come a variety of forms—dinosaurs, crocodiles, birds, mammals—each evolving and each branching off on the tree of life. That is why the group seemed so large and varied. Rather than trying to lay down the material along static formal lines of anatomy, Cope was beginning to articulate a more supple vision of evolutionary relationships. At that time, however, paleontology had neither sufficient fossil material nor scientific techniques to pursue and clarify this vision. Over time, paleontologists would refine Cope's *Archosauria,* but the idea and name, unlike Owen's *Thecodontia,* would remain.

But as fascinating as Cope's dinosaurs were, the Philadelphian's most important discovery that year was a huge, finned reptile that lived 250 million years ago during the Permian period. Cope had unearthed the animal on his Texas trip and named it *Dimetrodon.* It was about ten feet long, and had a fin that stood as tall as a man. What was so interesting about it was that it shared characteristics with early mammals. It was a "mammal-like" reptile.

Working one hundred million years later in the Jurassic, Marsh had found *Dryolestes,* a "reptilelike" mammal. Although neither man realized it, they were beginning from opposite ends to construct an evolutionary bridge that would span millennia.

All in all, 1878 was another extremely productive year. Marsh named ten dinosaur species, and Cope named eight.

Some of those names, and even animals, would disappear as the science of paleontology kept shifting, sorting, revising, and correcting. But for the moment, the two Americans commanded the heights. In England, Cope's good friend Harry Grovier Seeley had named two new dinosaurs and was also becoming increasingly embroiled in a paleontological squabble with Huxley. The reasons were varied, but they may have had to do as much with the fact that Seeley was cranky and Huxley popular as any bit of scientific theory.

Cope still led in the race to identify dinosaurs, but Marsh was catching up. And with the 1879 collecting season approaching, the Yale professor was poised to take over first place. But Cope now knew about Como Bluff. In fact, he was planning a visit.

✤

In February of 1879, Reed returned to Como Bluff. By now, he and Carlin were openly on the outs. The atmosphere at the station was downright unfriendly. Reed moved to a spot on Rock Creek, near Quarry No. 4, and set up a tent camp.

"I am home sick, it is a feeling I never experienced before. I do not mind it trough the day but when the night comes and I get in the tent and think how white people live it is meerly H . . . , H . . . , H . . . , and if the prof wants to keep me in this country he wants to keep me busy," Reed wrote to Williston in early February.[22]

One Saturday night, Reed went down to the station for a little socializing, but the mood was strained. Then he tried to go into the freight room. Carlin told him it was locked. If Reed wanted anything in there, Carlin said he'd get it for him. Reed left and returned to his campfire "in a very bad humor."

In the days that followed, Reed, with the help of a railroad worker named Edward Kennedy, began lugging bones down from the bluff to the tracks and then to the depot, where Reed, however, was no longer allowed to bring his bones inside the station house. While Carlin was working away in the freight room, Reed had to crate his specimens outside on the platform in the bitter cold.

A couple of weeks later came the news that Marsh had been dreading for months. Carlin was going out to the hills "a good deal," Reed reported, and sending "a leter to Prof. Cope nearly every day." It was this, Reed suspected, that led to his chilly reception at the station. "I am going to find out where he is to work if it is possible," Reed said. "He is not in any of the old quarries for I went all along the bluff yesterday."[23]

Now, those old questions hovered over Como Bluff. Where was Cope's man digging, and what was he finding? Was Marsh going to have to start worrying about being beaten again? This problem was surely more pressing since Cope had control of the *American Naturalist.*

Carlin had set up a new quarry not far from the area where Williston and Reed had found *Dryolestes,* and he was making regular shipments to Cope. Reed took off a day from digging just to spy on Carlin. "I don't know what he is getting, but he brings a good deal of stuff to the station," Reed wrote. Reed himself was working in Quarry No. 4, without great success. "I do not expect the box will give satisfaction," he wrote of a shipment, "but I have done the best I could."[24]

Marsh ordered Reed to close down Quarry No. 4 and to recover all the fragments from the rich No. 1 and No. 3 quarries. But before leaving No. 4,

Reed reported that he had "taken the liberty to demolish to the best of my ability [all remaining bones] as there are other parties in the field collecting." Years later, after his break with Marsh, Williston told Cope that it was actually Marsh who encouraged such measures.

"Professor Marsh did once indirectly request me to destroy Kansas fossils rather than let them fall into your hands," Williston wrote Cope. "It is necessary for me to say I only despised him for it."[25]

Sometimes with Kennedy's help, but most often alone, Reed worked the two quarries and sent his letters from the address "Camp Misery." In the middle of March, a spring thaw came, and Reed sent his letter from "Muddy Camp."

"I am still alive and sprawling around in mud knee deep. I never saw it so warm in this country this time of year. The snow is nearly gone and the mud looms up. . . . Kennedy says Carlin is cursing Cope now and I say let him rip he has used me prety mean and I hope he has got his match this time."[26]

For a moment, Reed had the hopeful news that Carlin had been assigned to a new station at Coopers Lakes. "I for one am not sory he has the big head the worst you ever saw," Reed wrote to Williston. But two weeks later, he reported, "Carlin has quit the railroad and is doing a big thing in bones." Carlin was shipping hundreds of pounds of fossils to Cope, and the word around the station was that Cope was paying him $130 a month.

But Cope and Carlin were no longer the only competition; Como Bluff had gotten a reputation. On April 16, Reed told Williston of his encounter with two fossil hunters, one of them "Brown," the miner who had sent fossils to the Smithsonian a year earlier.

Peace and harmony does not prevail here to any extent there are two more men here hunting bones they came up from rock creek last weak they came in the evening and said they wer going to work in quarey no. 1. . . . So I went down the next morning and got there as soon as they did. . . . I asked them what they wer goind to do they said dig for bones I told them they could not get any bones there they said they would see I went the top of the back wall with a pick and commenced to let down dirt and rocks they told me to leave but I was not quite ready to go and I staid with them 4 days I have got a big pile of dirt in that hole in the ground more I think than they wil want to dig out."[27]

Reed hired three men to work Quarry No. 3 with him, and they began sending shipments back to New Haven. But clearly the situation at Como was more volatile and competitive than it had ever been. Marsh needed reinforcements. He wired Arthur Lakes in late April, instructing him to head for Wyoming.

It was about eight o'clock in the evening on May 14 when Lakes reached Como Station. He surveyed the desolate spot and thought that the water tower looked like "a huge coffee pot." He entered the station and found half a dozen men smoking and playing cards.[28]

"Is there a Mr. Reed here?" he asked.

"That is my name," said a tall, swarthy man, in buckskin and a broad, white-felt hat, with the front brim held back against the crown with a gun wad punch. The rocky partnership of Messrs. Reed and Lakes was about to begin.

The next day, Lakes explored the bluff, which he described it in his field journal, with the eye of a painter, as being "composed of ashen gray and variegated red and purple clays and shales with some of them layers of sandstone. . . . The upper strata consists of these ashen and greenish strata passing down to a belt of salmon red and purple clays and shales. The reddish portion is banded with variegated belts and presents a handsome appearance from a distance."

Lakes joined in on the work in Quarry No. 3, and the men found bones of a *Camarasaurus* and an *Allosaurus*. Lakes also joined Reed in his tent camp, pitched in a ravine thick with sagebrush. After a day's work, they would dine on a supper of antelope steak (Reed did a fair bit of hunting), smoke their pipes, talk, and watch the stars fill the black sky. Then it was off to bed in a rough wooden bunk.

Reed was a fount of Wild West stories that delighted Lakes. He pointed out a nearby railroad trestle and told the Englishman how a gang of bank robbers, including Frank James, had camped beneath it, planning to rob the No. 3 Union Pacific train. They were going to stop the train by removing a section of the rail.

The scheme, however, was found out, and a posse was raised to chase the robbers. Deputy Sheriff Robert Widdowfield of Carbon, Wyoming, and Union Pacific detective Henry Vincent were ambushed, and killed while tracking the gang. About four months later, one of the gang members, "Dutch Charlie" Bates, was captured at Green River and sent by train to Carbon for trial.

But when the train pulled into Carbon, a band of two dozen masked men—identified in the local press as citizens and miners—boarded the coach and seized Bates. The prisoner was stood on a barrel, a noose around his neck, the rope draped over a telegraph pole. He admitted his role in the deaths of Widdowfield and Vincent, and his body was left swinging from the pole until the next afternoon.

The train was delayed just thirteen minutes, and the *Cheyenne Daily Leader*'s article was headlined, "Lynching Last Night: 'Dutch Charles' Takes His Last Dance in a Hemp Necktie, with a Telegraph Pole for a Partner." Ever since that episode the ravine under the trestle at Como was known as "Robber's Roost."

In early June, Marsh came to inspect Como Bluff himself. On June 5, Marsh, Lakes, Reed, and some hired hands climbed aboard a pair of railroad handcars and headed down the tracks. Marsh inspected Quarry No. 3 and the new Quarry No. 6, which had been discovered just a few days earlier. This new site, about five hundred yards away from No. 3, was yielding bones of mammals, a crocodile, and what they thought was an *Ichthyosaurus,* an aquatic reptile resembling a huge shark. They had brought a picnic lunch and used the handcar as a sideboard.

The next day, they were on the bluff again. This time they lunched under the cottonwood trees in Robber's Roost. Working their way through the ravine, they found some small, delicate reptile bones. "This led to an eager search," Lakes recounted. ". . . Professor Marsh was full of excitement and enthusiasm leading the way."[29] Soon more small bones were found. They had discovered what would be Quarry No. 7, also known as the "Three Trees Quarry," for three isolated fir trees near the site.

Marsh left on June 6, confident that his crew had plenty of work to do. Soon, the Three Trees Quarry would yield another new dinosaur, *Laosaurus consors.* Indeed, once the *Laosaurus* remains were found, Marsh insisted that they be removed quickly. (About a century later the name of this dinosaur would be changed to *Dryosaurus altus.*)

Reed and Lakes, with the help of some railroad hands, had moved their camp closer to the station to be part of the little Como community, now more agreeable with young David Chase as the new station agent. Still, Lakes felt he was very much laboring on the edge of the great wilderness. One day, the tent was knocked down and torn up by strong winds. Another day, they were pelted by hail "the size of hen's eggs." Campfire dinners featured freshly killed wild game, garnished with canned oysters and strawberries. Reed would spin his tales of desperadoes and Indians. Then came the nights, inky dark, save for the light of the moon and the stars, and filled with skitters and howls of the prairie.

And yet right next to them were the train tracks. Lakes, dusty and weary, could watch the first-class coaches flash by, with their frosted lamps, wood paneling, and enameled decorations. He could see the men in frock coats, waistcoats, and cravats, and women in silks and bustles. He watched them barreling across the wilderness in their capsule of civilization. And then they were gone, and he went back to digging in the clay for bones.

Carlin's departure in late June, to return to railroad work, made life even more agreeable at the Como Station. "Carlin is gone. . . . Mr. Cope's quarry has played out and they are hunting a new one and we are keeping a good look-out for our own discoveries," Reed told Marsh, and by the end of the month his crew had opened still another site—Quarry No. 8.[30]

Lakes, too, had done some Cope field reconnaissance and noted in his journal, "passed beneath Prof. Cope's quarry, which appears to be much in the same horizon as our *Morosaurus* No. 3."[31]

In July and early August, Quarry Nos. 9 through 12 were opened. But of all these, it was Quarry No. 9 that proved to be the jewel of Como Bluff. It was filled with fossils of small reptiles and amphibians, but more than anything else, there was the most bounteous array of Jurassic mammalian diversity ever found on the continent.

Of the roughly two hundred Jurassic mammal specimens currently known in North America, the vast majority were collected at Como Bluff, and all of these, except the jaw of *Dryolestes* and two isolated teeth from Quarry No. 1 and Quarry No. 11, were recovered from Quarry No. 9.

In late June, Marsh asked Lakes to send him maps of the area showing the position of the boneyards. Lakes trekked the bluff and ravines. On climbing to the ridge over the quarries, he found "a pile of stone laid there by Clarence King's survey" some seven years earlier. King had been that close to the great treasure chest of bones, but, of course, he was interested in different kinds of riches.

Lakes spent increasing amounts of time sketching and also doing watercolors of Como Bluff and its inhabitants, including Reed, Kennedy, and even Marsh. While these quarry sketches and landscapes would have great value in time, Reed, for one, thought that Lakes was dawdling when he should be digging.

❖

Carlin's departure didn't mean that Cope was also gone from Como. Carlin's brothers-in-law, the Hubbell boys from Howell, Michigan, had taken over the Cope interests on the bluff. Yet even though they were competitors, relations between the Hubbells and Marsh men were amiable—at least around the station.[32]

When Reed made a trip to the town of Medicine Bow, everyone at Como came to see what he had brought back. "As I am writing this," Lakes scribbled in his journal, "Reed the hunter is lying full length stretched smoking on the bed in the tent. Cope's men and three or four other railroad hands and the station master are also lying around on the grass smoking or trying to extract a tune from some vile musical instrument resembling a pandean pipe with two Jews harps Reed brought with him last night from Medicine Bow."[33]

Upon on the bluff, it was a different story. In early July, Reed reported to Marsh that "the hubbells are running the bone business for Cope and are doing very litle they say that they are going to sue Cope . . . if he does not pay them soon. I guess the work for them is nearly played out we are finding new deposits of small boness nearly every day."[34]

But the very next day, Reed heard that not only had Carlin and the Hubbells finally gotten paid, but that Cope was planning to visit Como. "So," Reed said, "that makes a change in our expectations, but we are corelling everything we can."

Although the survey battle had come out badly for Cope, at least it was behind him. He, too, could, as Marsh had put it, "return to pure science." One of his top priorities for that summer was to check out the fertile Colorado and Wyoming boneyards.

Cope first made his way to Canon City, by way of Denver, which he told Annie "looks like an Eastern city, brand new buildings are going up everywhere." He arrived in Canon City on July 25.

"Canyon City is new and rather rough town of small size," he wrote home. "The scenery is fine. I found Mr. Lucas the discoverer of all the huge saurians, an agreeable young man, and a strict presbyterian. He lives with his father's family, the father himself having died this spring. Seventh day I made a complete survey of the Saurian beds and excavations which commenced 7 miles from town north and extend 7 miles farther. There are signs of many others in the rocks."[35] In his little leather-bound field journal, Cope made notations of seven possible locations for dinosaurs.

One of the other pieces of business Cope concluded in Canon City was to strike a deal with one A. M. Cassidy for exclusive rights to excavate fossils from a tract along Oil Creek. The agreement was drawn up on hotel stationery.

The little health problems that always seemed to dog Cope found him in Canon City. "I felt I was going to have one of my attacks of fever and yesterday I had it sure enough. I slept much and took acconite every hour night and day. Today I am much better . . . ," he assured to Annie. "I had the tooth ache & sore throat as usual, but fortunately no other complications." After recovering from his maladies, Cope headed for Wyoming.

On an early August evening, the Union Pacific train pulled into Como Bluff. Lakes was just coming back from bathing in the lake, and he watched as a "rather interesting young man stepped out of the coach and introduced himself." Edward Drinker Cope had arrived at Como Bluff.

The next morning, Lakes and Cope had "a pleasant chat" at breakfast about England. Then Cope went off to explore. He met the Hubbells and told Julia that they were "good young men from Michigan." Cope concluded that Como's "rocks and fossils are nearly the same as those at Canyon City." In his field journal, Cope noted "three localities of large bones" and made detailed sketches of the Como rock strata.[36]

He told Julia he had seen "the bones of a *Camarasaurus* sticking out of the ground" and that "the boys have dug out a huge flesh-eating saurian which they send off this morning."[37]

That evening, Lakes again dined with Cope, and they discussed geology. Lakes was amused by Cope's singing of a comic song with a refrain at the end "like the howl of a coyote."

The following morning, Cope was on the westbound train. After leaving Como, Cope had to make a decision on whether to stop at old Fort Bridger, which two years earlier had been decommissioned as an army post. "Although the Fort is gone Judge Carter remains, & has charge of the buildings. The place is still a good deal of a watering place & I have learned that Dr. Corson & wife are there on a visit. Dr. C. is now stationed at Ft. Yuma Ariz," he wrote in a letter home. Cope decided to keep moving west.

"The Monstrum horrendum Cope has been and gone," Lakes wrote to Marsh, "and I must say that what I saw of him I liked very much his manner is so affable and his conversation very agreeable, I only wish I could feel sure he had a sound reputation for honesty."[38]

Reed, Lakes, Kennedy, and Reed's hired hand, Ashley, had all kept an eye on Marsh's quarries during Cope's visit, actually guarding the prime sites. "Prof Cope having gone . . . ," Lakes wrote Marsh, "probably relieves you of all anxiety here." Still, Cope's departure didn't mean that the threat was gone. If anything, his presence had made the Marsh camp all that more wary of competition. "Cope has gone to California. . . . The C. company are prospecting most of the time but we can hold most of the ground we have," Reed assured New Haven.[39]

As the summer wore on, Reed became increasingly irritated with Lakes. How much of it was Lakes's English manners and how much was the result of him spending so much time—some days not even leaving camp—drawing is difficult to say.

"I cannot possibly work here any longer," Reed informed Marsh on August 19.[40] "It is impossible to get along with certain parties here peaceably and the matter of working with men so far above me."

The next day, Reed wrote a more pointed letter to Williston. "I am gong to quit the bone business the first of Sept. and go to work at something else or collect independently for I cannot get along with lakes," Reed said.[41]

"I have put up with him as long as I can and if I was to try it another month some one would get hurt and I don't want any such thing to happen," Reed warned, "so I wil quit Prof. Marsh. . . . I don't know as lakes means any harm but his Oxford education places him far above the comon uneducaed american. . . . I have bin taught that all men are equals so you see I can not worship this high born english man and war is the consequence."

A couple of days later, Lakes wrote to Marsh saying that Reed's resignation had arisen "from some misunderstanding between us" and then added, "It remains for me to do the same as I would not in any way wish to stand in his way. . . . He is the man for the place & will carry out the work here better than I or any other man could."[42]

Faced with two resignations at Como was bad enough, but Reed also reported that Cope was coming back and another scientist, Harvard's A. S. Packard, was also expected. "So you see times are going to be quite lively at Como," Reed said.

Reed and Lakes had each performed valuable work, and in an effort to keep them both, Marsh instructed them to work separately. So Lakes went off to the west end of the bluff—near Robber's Roost—and Reed went to the east end, about five miles away. It was there that he discovered Quarry No. 13, which turned out to be the single richest dinosaur site on Como.

Reed and Ashley worked Quarry No. 13 that fall, and eventually out of this single pit would come about nine different dinosaur species, including *Camarasaurus lentus, Coelurus fragilis, Camptosaurus dispar, Stegosaurus affinis,* and a huge, beautiful *Brontosaurus.*

By September, there was also good news about the competition at Como. Cope had not come back, and Reed said, "I think Copes party wil throw up the sponge pretty soon. I hear money is very scarce with them."[43]

Winter was coming, and both Reed and the Hubbells started building dugouts, little cottages with earthen embankments. Reed had estimated that such a "shanty" would cost fifteen dollars to build, making it five dollars cheaper than a tent.

In October, Reed, with Ashley's help, began to dig out of Quarry No. 10 the remains of a *Brontosaurus excelsus*—the skeleton was almost complete.

One day it would stand grandly in the large hall of the Peabody Museum. The snows came that month, and winter settled in on Como Bluff. Reed took to his dugout, and Lakes took up residence with the railroad crew in their section house for five dollars a week.

Toward the end of the month, Marsh complained about a jawbone reaching New Haven in pieces. Reed explained that "the rocks have to be loosened in the first place with large picks and often things get broken then and if they do the pieces are hard to find, but we are using white cloths now."[44] The small bones were being shipped back east in old tin cans and cigar boxes stuffed with old newspaper. (Marsh and Williston were asked several times to send more old newspaper to Como.)

On December 18, Lakes noted in his journal, "Williston told me of the sudden death of my kind and good friend Prof. Mudge." Benjamin Mudge had died of a stroke in Manhattan, Kansas, on November 21, at the age of sixty-two. Lakes noted that "letters of sympathy from many quarters seem to have in some way mitigated the loss" for Mrs. Mudge.[45]

In January, Reed hired Fred Brown, the miner, to join him and Ashley. The weather was cold and nasty, but the three fossil hunters continued to work the quarries. Lakes remained a burr under Reed's saddle, and he complained about "haughty Oxford ways" and called Lakes an "absent-mined English gentleman." Still, Lakes worked through a bitter Wyoming winter filled with snow and subzero temperatures.

On February 28, 1880, Lakes wrote in his journal, "Fearfully cold. Thermo[meter] 30 degrees below zero and blowing a blizzard and a perfect river of blinding snow. Clocks stopped by the cold. Water buckets frozen solid. Knife handles like icicle. No heat from the red hot stove. Track men dare not go out as it would have been fatal."[46]

On March 19, Lakes left Como and returned to Golden, where he obtained a teaching appointment at the new state school of mines. While the loss of Lakes might have hurt the exploration and excavation of the bluff, at least one would have thought it would bring some peace to the Marsh camp. But that was not to be, for at about the same time Lakes left, Marsh hired the railroad man Kennedy to work at Como.

Kennedy had been a great help to Reed when he had come back to Como in early 1879, but now since he had been hired directly by Marsh, he didn't think he had to take orders from Reed. The fight between Reed and Kennedy was a sharp one, and Brown and Ashley found themselves caught in the sniping. They both quit. In a June letter, Reed laid out the problem to Marsh and again voiced the thought of quitting. But he swore, "You may rest ashured *I shall never go to work for Cope.*"[47]

Marsh again suggested that the two men work independently and far apart. He also arranged for Frank Williston to return to Como Bluff. This, however, didn't quite lead to the results Marsh had hoped for.

Meanwhile, Cope's efforts at Como had been faltering. A small crew had worked for part of the winter, but by the spring, activity had pretty well petered out. "I think the Cope party is going to break up," Reed reported in May. "His boss come to me the other day and wanted to know if I did not want to buy some packing material cheap." Reed got five dollars' worth of paper and twine for two dollars.[48] The Hubbells were finished. But just when the Marsh men thought they were rid of Cope, Carlin came back and started a sheep ranch along Rock Creek.

Reed, Kennedy, and Frank Williston began working the quarries. Two new laborers—Dixon and Kenny—were hired to replace Brown and Ashley. With five men working, and Cope mounting no serious opposition, Como Bluff was once again Marsh's. In September, Marsh inspected Como and ordered that work focus on Quarry Nos. 9 and 13—the best of the lot.

But then another fight broke out among Marsh's workers, this one starting with Frank Williston, who eventually quit the Marsh camp and bunked with Carlin at his ranch. "Having been charged by W. H. Reed of theaving and many other absurd suppisitions . . . I deem [it] unnecessary to triffle with such selfish principals," Frank Williston told Marsh in his resignation letter.[49]

Soon it became apparent that Williston had switched allegiances and was working with Carlin for Cope. Williston, Reed heard, was being paid $150 a month by Cope. Marsh immediately sent a telegram to Reed urging him to take precautions at the most valuable sites. The problem was compounded by the fact that Dixon and Kenny had just quit, leaving only Reed and Kennedy to guard Marsh's interests. Reed replied to Marsh's wire.

"Your telegram recd wil do all I can to keep all parties out of the places you mention they have shiped a Box to Cope to day so *it is a shure* thing that is what they mean if you wish I can tell you something by which you can make them trouble."[50]

The "something" was a plan to take control of the bluff under the Desert Lands Act, which would allow Marsh to buy a three-year lease hold on the land at twenty-five cents an acre. After three years, Marsh would have to pay a dollar an acre for a deed. But Reed was confident that "three years is ample time."

Marsh approved the plan, and Reed set it into motion. At the same time, the activity in the Cope camp became more pronounced. A shipment with a pick, shovel, wrapping paper, lumber, and gunnysacks arrived at the station for Carlin. And soon he was again on the bluff.

"The Cope party was up to 13 yesterday they did not come to the quarey but was all around it," Reed reported to New Haven in December. "I find their tracks all around No. 9 but they have not done any work there." Reed reassured Marsh that these important sites were being checked every day.[51]

Cope had collectors making sorties onto the bluff well into the next year. But by then, lots of other people were interested in Como Bluff. In 1881, several collecting parties turned up, including one from Harvard University, under the auspices of Prof. Alexander Agassiz. Harvard tried unsuccessfully to hire some of Reed's men. They ended up engaging the railroad section foreman, Peter McDermott, who, Reed said, "did not know a bone from a stone." So McDermott struck a deal with Frank Williston to split their take of bones.

Williston and Carlin had found another fossil area to the north of Como Bluffs, and although they did not develop it themselves, in a few years the Bone Cabin Quarry would come to rival Como.

Reed said that he had followed the wagon tracks made by McDermott and Williston and saw where the bones were loaded. "On Monday there was Boxes on the platform marked for Prof. A. and the others marked for Prof. C.—and they all came from one quarey."[52]

There would be many more collectors now, but Marsh's early and continued presence—thanks to Reed, Lakes, and Kennedy—had given him a decided edge. He might not have been able to lock Como Bluff in his attic, but he came pretty close.

Marsh would operate quarries at Como until 1889. Reed, however, would finally break camp in 1883. At first, he would try sheep ranching, but in 1897 he would receive an appointment as an assistant geologist and museum curator at the University of Wyoming.

Conflicts between Marsh's field hands never seemed to abate. After Reed left, Kennedy and Fred Brown worked the quarries. But the arguments over who was in charge continued. "Brown assaulted me at the station with two revolvers and wanted me to fight him," Kennedy reported to Marsh in December of 1883. "i Refused on account of my family."

In six years of work, Reed sent 152 boxes and eighty-four cans of fossils to New Haven and Marsh paid him and his helpers a total of more than eight thousand dollars in salaries, although not necessarily in a punctual manner. Reed was in a continual struggle to get his pay. There were repeated threats, work stoppages, and shipment delays. At one point, Reed pleaded for his check so he could buy a Christmas turkey.[53] But it was impossible to prod Marsh.

Still, when Reed married Ann E. Clark, of Milford Center, Ohio, in 1880, Marsh promptly and politely took notice. Reed had met Miss Clark through an advertisement he had placed in the *Detroit Free Press* offering to exchange fossils and Indian artifacts for books.

Marsh, in a timely fashion, sent a wedding present, and in a fine, elegant hand, the new Mrs. Reed wrote from Como Station, "Dear Professor Marsh, Please accept many, *many* thanks for your beautiful set of silver knives and forks."[54]

❖

By 1881, Cope and Marsh had named a bevy of new dinosaurs. Marsh had pieced together the *Apatosaurus excelsus, Camptosaurus dispar, Diracodon laticeps,* and *Stegosaurus ungulatus.* Cope had found the *Hypsirophus seeleyanus* (named in honor of his friend Harry Grovier Seeley) and *Camarasaurus leptodirus.*

So many bones were being shipped to Philadelphia that there wasn't enough room at 2102 Pine Street. Cope arranged to store the bulk of this material in the basement of the glass-and-iron-domed Centennial Exposition Building in Fairmount Park, a memento of the 1876 fair.[55] Even with all those bones, Cope was clearly losing the dinosaur race now.

But as happens in a race, the pace quickens and with it the chance of a misstep. As bones rapidly rolled into the Peabody Museum, the risk of confusion and error grew—despite Marsh's penchant for detail. Compounding that was the pressure created by the pesky, agile Cope.

Both men contributed to the hazard by publishing short, hastily written papers that didn't give enough information about the finds. The result, according to contemporary paleontologists David Berman and John McIntosh, was that Cope and Marsh created "confusion and misconception about the animals they described that lasted long after their deaths."[56] It was the Bridger Basin all over again.

Cope and Marsh were littering the literature with mistakes. For example, Marsh's *Morosaurus* was really a juvenile *Camarasaurus.* But once Marsh thought that *Morosaurus* was a smaller animal, it led him to make mistakes in identifying several adult *Camarasaurus* specimens. Similarly, Cope's *Hypsirhopus* was Marsh's *Stegosaurus.*

In the years to come, paleontologists would have to untangle the taxonomic jumble that Cope and Marsh had once again created. But in all fairness, although they were egregious perpetrators, the problem wasn't just limited to them. Everyone in the field—Huxley, Seeley, Owen—was struggling to understand the bones unearthed and was making mistakes.

It would turn out that for every ten dinosaur genera proposed since 1824, nine of the names were not valid. Some were names for animals already named. Some were described based on too little material to be scientifically accurate. And some simply weren't dinosaurs. Yes, there was an abundance of mistakes.[57]

The biggest mistake, however, would be Marsh's, and it was literally the biggest mistake in the history of paleontology, and like Cope's *Elasmosaurus,* it would involve putting a skull in the wrong place. In doing so, Marsh would create a dinosaur that simply had not existed. It was O. C. Marsh, not the forces of nature, who created the *Brontosaurus.*

The tale of *Brontosaurus* began in 1877 when Lakes sent from Morrison a large sacrum—the fused vertebrae that fit into the pelvis. Based on this fragment and a few loose vertebrae, for there was a race on, Marsh named a new dinosaur—*Apatosaurus ajax.* The following year, a few more pieces were found, and a more complete paper identifying the animal was written.

By this time, Lakes was in Como, where in August of 1879, Reed and Ashley found Quarry No. 10, from which they pulled two very large, nearly perfect, sauropod skeletons, which Marsh decided were species of a new genus—*Brontosaurus.*

The skeleton that came out of Quarry No. 10 was the most complete sauropod skeleton that had ever been found, and as a result, it would be described and illustrated in greater detail and used as an example more often than any other animal. But Reed could find no head in No. 10.[58]

So Marsh had a decision to make, and he guessed that a head found in one of the other quarries, about four miles away, was the right kind of head. So that's the one he used in his 1883 reconstruction of the *Brontosaurus.* What Marsh had, in fact, done was place a *Camarasaurus* head on an *Apatosaurus.*

There were other little errors in the reconstruction, based in part on the fact that Marsh had, as in the case of the *Morosaurus* and *Camarasaurus,* mistaken a young *Apatosaurus* for a *Brontosaurus.* In 1891, Marsh did a revised reconstruction of the *Brontosaurus.* This time, he used a skull from Canon City—four hundred miles away from Como Bluff. It was still the wrong skull. (After Williston left Canon City, M. P. Felch worked the quarry for five years, exhuming a host of Jurassic dinosaurs, which he sent to New Haven.)

It did not take long for some paleontologists to suspect a mistake had been made. Samuel Williston, who was working at the Peabody when the reconstruction was done, thought that *Apatosaurus* and *Brontosaurus* might be similar. In 1903, Elmer Riggs of the Field Museum in Chicago also raised the issue. William Holland, the director of the Carnegie Museum, also believed there was an error. In 1914, he wrote, "The association of this skull material with what Marsh denominates the *Brontosaurus* is wholly arbitrary, and I doubt its correctness."

Still, Marsh's vision of the *Brontosaurus* was subscribed to by many other paleontologists, and it endured for almost a century, until modern researchers would put it right. Marsh's *Brontosaurus* survived in part because it was such a complete and compelling model. But it also survived because Marsh had gained so much power. For now as he entered a new decade, he was poised to vanquish Cope.

Chapter Fifteen

 CLARENCE KING'S APPOINTMENT AS the first director of the U.S. Geological Survey was seen by his friends as a grand victory and fair recognition of the man's promise and certain greatness. But by the beginning of 1881, King had been absent from his job for more than four months. He wasn't even in the United States. No, he was mulebacking through the foothills of Mexico's Sonora Mountains looking at mining properties.

The truth was that King's coterie had always been more anxious and interested than their friend in winning the new survey's directorship. While the honor was desirable, the actual job had come with all sorts of liabilities.

First of all, the agency's annual budget was modest, just $106,000, and its mandate was blurred. The survey was, according to law, supposed to study and classify the lands in "the public domain." But what constituted the public domain? Schurz quickly ruled that meant public lands. That, of course, blocked King from assaying most mining properties, which happened to be privately held, and mining was what interested King most.

Powell might want to classify soils, forests, and water resources, but King was a mining man. Besides it wasn't even clear how rigorous a classification of its lands Congress desired, for the more detailed and scientific the survey, the more expensive and time consuming it would be. King had no appetite for wrestling with congressmen over such questions. Remember, during the thick of the battle over the survey merger, he didn't even show up to testify at a key congressional hearing, leaving it to Powell to carry the banner.

King's biggest initiative as director was to launch, in collaboration with the 1880 national census, a "statistical survey of mineral resources and production" in the country. He also commissioned a study of Nevada's silver-rich Comstock Lode. Mining simply had a hypnotic allure for King. And why not? Jay Cooke, bankrupt from his railroad venture, was able to rebound and turn three thousand dollars invested in a Utah silver mine into a million dollars. Such stories drove thousands of men in pursuit of gold and silver. So what if most would-be mining millionaires failed and ended up broke? At Como Bluff, Reed and Lakes had seen such men— destitute after failing to find gold in the Black Hills—hoboing west on freight trains in search of another strike. Still, the stories of glittering wealth drove King.

Indeed, the two greatest annoyances of his director's job was the fact that he was precluded from holding mining interests in the United States and that the job only paid six thousand dollars a year. That was more than the annual salaries of two senior Yale professors, but it wasn't nearly enough for King, who employed a valet, belonged to expensive clubs, collected art, and had a taste for champagne suppers. No, a few thousand a year wasn't nearly enough.

In September of 1880, King, then in poor health, took a leave of absence to recuperate in Arizona. But when revived, instead of returning to Washington, he headed for Mexico, where the laws did not restrict him from searching for treasure.

Near Hermosillo, he found a promising silver mine and convinced the Mexican owners that the introduction of modern mining techniques could make everyone—King included—rich. He returned to the States in February of 1881, with an authorization to develop the Prietas Mines. King now headed not for Washington, but New York City. The capital was the place to make laws, but New York was the place to raise money.

Meanwhile, there were big changes in Washington. After a single term, Rutherford B. Hayes had left office and with him Carl Schurz. James Garfield had been elected president the previous November, after fending off a bid by Grant to reclaim the White House. The congressional appropriations committee was already beginning hearings on the coming year's budget, and King's top aide at the survey, John McChesney, was sending out volleys of telegrams trying to locate his boss.

King was huddling with the money men, among them Harvard's Alexander Agassiz, already wealthy from his Michigan copper mines, and King's brother-in-law, Henry Lee Higginson, who would be best remembered as the founder of the Boston Symphony Orchestra. Both thought the Prietas Mines looked like a good investment, or at least they thought that King was a good investment. Even Henry Janin, the mining engineer who had vouched for a Wyoming diamond field that King had proved was a fraud, took a piece of the action. The Grand Central Mining Company was created, and on March 11, 1881, King sent his resignation to President Garfield.

"The chances were great," Henry Adams waxed of his friend King, "that he could, whenever he chose to quit Government service, take up the pick of the gold and silver, copper or coal, and build up his fortune as he pleased." Now King had done just that. Adams predicted he would end up the richest man in America, but in truth, King would end up closer to the Wyoming hobos than to the Nevada silver kings.

Within a week, John Wesley Powell was named to replace King. King said he recommended Powell. But Powell needed no recommendation. It was Garfield who, a decade earlier, had gotten Powell his first congressional appropriation, and he had fought alongside the one-armed major in the reform movement. Garfield said that the only man he consulted was Spencer Baird. Baird and Powell were not only friends, but colleagues at the Smithsonian. The intersecting links were firm and numerous. Powell slid into the directorship.

"King went away for good on Monday to our extreme regret," wrote Henry Adams's wife, Clover, on March 17, "having got out of office, named and seen confirmed his successor, Powell of Illinois, in whom he had great confidence. He did it so noiselessly that Professor Hayden, who would have done his best to upset it, knew nothing of it till it was done." But the truth was Hayden was beaten and weary. Cope, however, would now have to deal with yet another director to get his final studies published.

The survey under Powell would be a much different entity. Powell was still driven by his belief that government-based science was the key to the manner and method of settling the West. One of the first things he did was to reorganize the survey into divisions based on scientific disciplines— geology, topography, chemical and physical studies, and paleontology. Paleontology. Who would head the survey's division of paleontology?

At the same time Powell was pondering this question, Spencer Baird was embarking on the grand expansion of the National Museum. The new museum building—a redbrick castle between the Capitol and the Washington Monument—had just been completed, and now Baird faced the task of filling it. One natural supplier was the survey, for all collections made under it were the property of the government. Marsh had written that into the law (although, truth be told, Baird turned virtually every branch of government and every federal employee from soldiers to lighthouse keepers into a network to feed the museum).

So, when it came to naming the survey's chief paleontologist, once again the intersection of interests made it obvious that the man should be none other than O. C. Marsh. But the Yale professor was reluctant. Between 1868 and 1882, Marsh calculated that he had spent two hundred thousand dollars of his own money on expeditions and collections. The booty from those ventures was his and his alone. If he became connected with the survey, as a result of his own law, he could no longer claim new fossils. The federal government would hold the keys to the attic.

What concerned Marsh most was control of "type" specimens, the ones upon which the identification and classification of new species are made. He called such fossils "beacons to knowledge." More than anything else, Marsh wanted ownership of the type specimens.

The problem for Powell and Baird was that if Marsh didn't take the job, the next logical and most qualified candidate was Cope. From the outset of the campaign to merge the surveys, Cope had been an opponent of Powell's position, first in the National Academy and then in Congress. Cope's acerbic personality, his lone-wolf approach, also probably made him a less desirable alternative. Powell's friends inquired of Leidy's friends if the elder scientist might be interested in the post, but the answer came back a definite "no." Marsh was the man. Both Powell and Baird wanted Marsh.

They offered substantial aid in the way of publication and collections, but Marsh remained hesitant. Baird and Powell indicated perhaps a little deal, a verbal-wink-of-the-eye agreement, could be fashioned.

"The proposal made to me to aid the Government was more favorably presented by both the Director of Geological Survey and Professor Baird, and the position of Paleontologist in the Survey was accepted by me, July 1st, 1882," Marsh was to explain vaguely, when he finally agreed.[1]

Since it was a "gentlemen's agreement," there is no record of precisely what deal was made. But it is clear that Marsh was allowed to keep some specimens, type specimens, no doubt, as his own, separate and apart from the national collections.

Of course, that is the way it had always been done. Government agencies had often traded specimens for expertise in lieu of cash payments. In the 1850s, Louis Agassiz had such an understanding with the U.S. Coast and Geodetic Survey. Hayden had cut such deals with scientists working on his survey, but that was precisely the target Marsh had shot at in the merger legislation. Now Marsh was trying to get around his own law.

Marsh's decision to hitch his wagon to Powell's survey brought immediate benefits. Powell steadily increased the survey's budget from the original one hundred thousand dollars to more than five hundred thousand dollars by 1886, and he made certain that Marsh was well provided for. The appreciative director first gave the Yale professor an annual budget of fourteen thousand dollars. It would soon climb to sixteen thousand dollars, where it held steady for the rest of the decade.[2]

In his ten years as the survey's paleontologist, Marsh would receive about $150,000. Two-thirds of that money would be used to hire a staff, which at its peak numbered eighteen men at the Peabody Museum. With a band of collectors out in the field, and preparers, artists, and junior scientists working away in the Peabody basement, Marsh had, in a little more than a decade, successfully moved the nation's paleontology center from Philadelphia to New Haven.

Powell's survey also provided resources for publishing, and this again was a substantial inducement. Marsh proposed to Powell that the survey publish a series of ten major monographs on vertebrate paleontology, consisting of:

Vol. I *Odontornithes—Birds with Teeth*
Vol. II *Dinocerata—Terrible Horn*
Vol. III *Sauropoda—Lizard Feet*
Vol. IV *Stegosauria—Plated Lizards*
Vol. V *Brontotheridae—Thunder Beasts*
Vol. VI *Ornithopoda—Bird Feet*
Vol. VII *Theropoda—Beast Feet*
Vol. VIII *Pteranodontia*
Vol. IX *Mosasauria*
Vol. X *Jurassic Mammals*

The first volume, *Odontornithes,* had already been published by the King Survey. But just the plates for the next two volumes on *Dinocerata* (uintatheres) and sauropod dinosaurs came to $11,500 and $12,500, respectively.[3] Yes, there were definite benefits to being allied with Powell. But there were also serious liabilities, as Marsh would soon find out.

King and Agassiz weren't the only scientists bitten by the mining bug. By the summer of 1881, Cope was also careening around the West, from Idaho to New Mexico, in search of mining properties.

He was propelled by the disastrous turn of events in Washington. Not only had he lost the support of Hayden and Wheeler, but now Marsh, thanks to Powell and Baird, had the resources of the new survey. Cope was facing the prospect of seriously losing ground.

But even before these misfortunes, Cope was finding that his resources could not easily sustain his growing paleontology empire. He was sending out at least two collecting parties every year, subsidizing the *American Naturalist,* and trying to operate a laboratory and workshop out of 2102 Pine Street to rival the Peabody. In addition, he had a wife and daughter to care for and for whom he cared. Julia was approaching college age, and it was unthinkable that she and Annie should not summer on the New England coast or in the Berkshires with the rest of the Cope clan.

By his own estimation, Cope had spent nearly seventy-five thousand dollars on exploration and collections since 1871. In 1881, he was financing collecting parties not only at Como Bluff but also in Kansas, Texas, and New Mexico. Two of the collectors working for Cope that season—Frank Williston in Wyoming and David Baldwin in New Mexico—were turncoats from the Marsh camp.

Baldwin was particularly productive, and Cope was to write, "Baldwin's success had a very important bearing on . . . paleontology. He had obtained more than sixty species from [the Puerco] formation, nearly all of which were new to science."[4]

Also increasingly in Cope's employ was Jacob Wortman, a twenty-five-year-old physician turned scientist. Wortman, like Osborn and Scott, would become a loyal Cope ally in the war against Marsh. He had been sent by Cope to Oregon and Como Bluff and would return to Oregon to conduct for Cope the single most thorough exploration of the John Day Basin.

But to sustain this kind of activity, Cope needed more money, and what better way to get it than mining? With his superior knowledge of western geology, surely he would be in an exceptional position to assess prospects and make investments.

But the lesson of the Wyoming diamond scam ought to have warned Cope that mining in the Gilded Age was not simply about assaying ore and sinking shafts. No, it was about watering stock and salting mines. It was about skimming ore and hostile takeovers. There were great perils in both the financing and production of mining companies. Cope was a simple innocent. "With childlike confidence he accepted the statements of glowing prospectuses and interested promoters, and scattered his capital in many directions," said Cope's friend Persifor Frazer.[5] Like thousands of others, Cope couldn't help himself. The lure was so great, the myth so luscious.

From the first big California gold strike, at Sutter's Mill back in 1849, a belief grew that there was always a fortune just waiting to be discovered in the West. All one had to do was look. In 1859, it was the Comstock Lode in Nevada. Within four years, there were big strikes in Idaho's Snake River valley, Wyoming's Sweetwater region, and Montana's Last Chance Gulch. Then, of course, in 1874 came Custer's announcement that there was gold in the Dakota Black Hills.

Along the way, there were other discoveries of gold, silver, and copper in Colorado, New Mexico, and Arizona, all nurturing the belief that the West was simply riddled with valuable minerals and instant wealth. Before 1830, there had been perhaps two or three true millionaires in America. By 1860, the number had climbed to 350. In 1880, there were more than two thousand, and a fair number of these nouveaux millionaires had come out of the mines. The press's lavish celebration of their lives and strikes helped keep the believers believing.

John McKay, son of a poor immigrant Irish family, drifted into Nevada penniless after ten fruitless years in the California gold fields. But in Virginia City, he became part of the consortium of miners and stockbrokers that launched a hostile takeover of the Consolidated Virginia Mine, among the richest in the Comstock Lode. McKay became one of the celebrated "silver kings" and amassed a fortune estimated at sixty million dollars.

In his later years, McKay fought with Jay Gould over the trans-Atlantic telegraph business. The great Wall Street financier finally capitulated, saying, "There is no beating John McKay. If he needs another million or two he goes to his silver mine and digs it up." Now, that's just what Cope desired. If Jay Gould couldn't stand up to the deep pockets of a silver mine, how could Marsh?

So, in the summer of 1881, Cope headed west, but instead of fossils this time he was looking for precious metals. By August, he had found his way to Lake Valley Ranch, New Mexico. It was here, between the ranges of the Black and Caballo Mountains, that Cope would sink a large part of his fortune, and that first summer, the valley was filled with wildflowers and promise.

"My time has been devoted to examining the mines," he wrote to Annie. "I have gotten used to looking down deep shafts—and you have to get used to it—and have got so far as to go down with my foot in a loop of a rope, and holding the rope with my hands, while one man turns the windlass. After seeing what I have, I have no doubt of the great value of the four properties at this place. They are *all* good, probably the best in all New Mexico."[6]

The great, sparkling lure of Lake Valley was the "Bridal Chamber," a cavern fortuitously pierced by one of the first mining shafts. The chamber was so rich in silver chloride that the walls glittered and shimmered in lantern light. The seams were so thick that just holding a candle next to the wall would start the silver dripping.[7]

When Arizona governor Stafford saw the Bridal Chamber, he offered to pay fifty thousand dollars for all the ore he could remove with his own hands in just ten hours. James Hague, one of the Comstock silver kings, was also impressed. "I have before seen nothing like it," he wrote. But being savvier than most in the ways of the mines, he added, "I don't believe it will stay, but there is Millions in it for speculation."

How could Cope not be impressed? He became an investor in the Sierra Mining Companies, which operated the Plata, Grande, Bella, and Apache Mines. "This is a great mining region perhaps the best in the entire west, and the mines are becoming more successful very rapidly," he reported.

With his characteristic enthusiasm, he ardently recommended the investment to his cousin, Philip, and several other relatives. Of course, despite such claims, the Southwest was not a great mining region and had been at the bottom of the production of gold and silver in the western states, according to the federal mining survey ordered by King.[8]

Nevertheless, in the great game of mining roulette, the Southwest was a spot on which many easterners were ready to plunk down their money. "Nearly every property being vigorously worked is in the hands of people living east of the Mississippi River," the *Denver Republican* reported from Elizabethtown, New Mexico.[9] Among those eastern investors were to be Cope, his family, and his friends.

One of the reasons for the fresh interest in the region was that it had only recently been opened to development by the Atchison, Topeka & Santa Fe Railroad. The railroad, in fact, hadn't even reached Santa Fe until 1880. "The A.T. & S.F.," Cope wrote to his daughter, "is a fearfully and wonderfully made R.R. Every rain causes a 'washout' and the trains have to wait till the places mend. If they have no news of the condition of the road the trains lie by night." Cope was caught in a torrent that swept away tracks and telegraph poles and delayed his journey a week.[10]

Even with the railroad, many a settler and investor were scared off by the ferocious and free Apaches. At the very moment that Cope was investing in the Apache Mine, the last of the Indian wars was being waged between General Crook, who had headed the Sioux campaign, and guerrilla bands of Apaches led by Geronimo, Ulzana, and Natchez, the son of the famous Apache chief Cochise.[11]

It was a fluid battle of Indian raids and cavalry pursuits, played out along the border mountains of the Sierra Madre. Crook once even chased Geronimo all the way into Mexico. But the Apaches were fierce and fleet.

"The Apache can endure fatigue and fasting and can live without water for periods that would kill the hardiest mountain men," Crook said. "In fighting them we must of necessity be the pursuers, and unless we can surprise them by sudden and unexpected attack, the advantage is all in their favor. In Indian combat it must be remembered you rarely see an Indian; you see a puff of smoke and hear the whiz of bullets."[12]

Just a couple of years before Cope arrived, the Apaches blazed through the Lake Valley killing sixteen miners. In December of 1883, Apache bands would launch a three-day raid through the towns of Solomonville and Alma, stealing horses and massacring a dozen settlers.[13]

The Indians' ferocity and spectral nature frightened Cope. "The Apaches are making it hot. I think that sooner or later the savages will give some trouble here," Cope wrote to his wife from Lake Valley. "They have been doing much mischief all around us and in fact have been seen near the mines. . . . Daley our supt. is, however, an old Indian fighter & knows how to manage them, especially Apaches. The days of these savages is, however, short."[14]

Even though his first priority was silver and his second was to pick up any fossils he might encounter, Cope still made time to devise a carton that was tightly sealed and lined with wet paper so that he might send Julia a bouquet of Lake Valley's dazzling wildflowers.

But this was more than simply an act of fatherly love. It was also an exercise in botany, Cope noting, "I have put in 20–30 species nearly all with pretty flowers. . . . They belong to many orders, some I do not know. I give thee a few notes on what one sees."

Cope had taken to calling Julia by the pet name "Mammani," or "my sweet Mammani," and by degrees, as his daughter, now fifteen, approached maturity, she became her father's intellectual confidante and sounding board, filling a void left by Alfred Cope's death six years earlier.

In June of 1882, Cope led a small group of Philadelphia and California investors on a tour of the Lake Valley mines. "The party examined the mines yesterday and are very well pleased. The most conservative are feeling well about it," Cope told Annie.[15]

Things continued to look promising. "Stocks have been behaving queerly in our absence," he noted in the same letter. "Railroad stocks have gone down, but our mines have risen. We have two brokers along & they are sending and receiving dispatches all the time. The mill started yesterday, and works without a hitch, which was more than we expected. As a consequence Grande has gone to $8.00 & Plata to $5.00, which is a pretty good profit on what thee paid viz; $2.50 and $1.60."

The Lake Valley mines were remote—eighteen miles from the railroad—and the Apaches were still roaming the mountains, so a company of soldiers was detached to guard the camp. "I do not approve of war, but in this country, the soldiers are the only armed police and they have to be," Cope told Julia, who was then finishing her first year at Smith College's Classical School for Girls, in Northampton, Massachusetts.[16]

Cope wasn't satisfied with just his Lake Valley investments. In El Paso, which he considered "not much of a place," he "got on the track" of important silver mines in Chihuahua, Mexico. He passed on inspecting them because they were "too near the Apaches."[17] He did, however, visit the North Horn Mine in the San Francisco Mountains of New Mexico and then headed north to the mines at Rocky Bar, Idaho.

Cope spent his days traveling through a string of mining camps—hard, sad places, with rough, unpainted shanties, hemmed in by huge man-made mountains of mine tailings and debris; towns whose citizenry consisted of grim and grimy-faced miners and whose only commerce was in bars, brothels, and outrageously priced company stores.

He reveled in the adventure. Sporting his new merino-wool shirts, soft as cashmere, and a brown, low-crowned hat, he traipsed across the West. "I have shaved all my beard except moustache and goatee as an experiment," he wrote to Annie, "and I think I look like a gambler, or some other piratical craft." A gambler is truly what Cope had become.

There were lots of things that could go wrong with a mine. Even when precious metals were found, and there were plenty of dry holes or "horses," as they were called, the ratio of ore to rock in the vein could be too low to make mining it profitable. Labor problems—miners were paid about three dollars for a ten-hour day—could cripple an operation. Pilfering ore could skim off any profit. Well-planted rumors could send stock prices plummeting or soaring to abet the stratagems of speculators. Unscrupulous company officials could sell stock issue after stock issue—watering down the investment—while lining their pockets with fees and commissions. At Lake Valley, the woes began to surface as early as 1883.

One big problem was that the Bridal Chamber had created huge expectations, and everything was done with the belief that more treasure caverns would be found. A huge and expensive mill was built for one hundred thousand dollars, and a thirty-ton smelter was erected at a cost of twenty thousand dollars. In the early years, dividends were issued to clamoring investors, so little working capital was set aside. But while one other promising vein—Jackson's Baby—was discovered, there were no more Bridal Chambers.[18]

For a few months now, however, mining was to assume a minor role in Cope's life as his mammoth work on western fossils finally moved toward publication. This was the fruit of his many seasons in the field and was a remnant of the Hayden days that King and Powell had agreed to publish. Cope described it as "the big book I have been at work on for ten years."

Titled *The Vertebrata of the Tertiary Formations of the West,* it was quickly dubbed "Cope's Bible." But comparing it with the Bible seems unfair, the Bible being so much more modest a volume.

Cope's study of Eocene and lower and middle Miocene life in the West covered 1,002 pages of text, with 134 lithographic plates. It included Cope's discoveries and those of other researchers from the Puerco of New Mexico, the Bridger of Wyoming, the White River of Dakota, and the John Day of Oregon. In all, it described about 350 different species. The book was a foot thick and weighed fifteen pounds. In this volume, Cope continued his battle with Marsh, not giving him nearly enough credit for his work on horses and still quibbling over the uintathere debate.[19]

February found Cope in Washington putting the final touches on the manuscript and angling for a permanent position at the Smithsonian or on the survey. "How would my Mammani like to go to Washington to live?" he asked Julia. "They have been asking me to go; and I have a great notion to do it." This was, like his speculation about succeeding Henry at the Smithsonian, merely wishful thinking.[20]

Tertiary Formations was slated to be the first of three works summing up the paleontology of the Hayden Survey; the other two, still sitting incomplete on Cope's desk, dealt with life from the upper Miocene and the Pliocene epochs.

In his preface to *Tertiary Formations,* Powell wrote, "At the time when the work was turned over to the Director of the Geological Survey an important portion of the manuscript was yet unprepared; but through the energy of Prof. Cope, the volume has been rapidly brought to completion. . . . The yet unpublished volume will be pushed to completion at an early date." But in reality, the remaining work would become yet another bitter battleground between Cope and Powell.

Stunned by the size and the cost of Cope's Bible, Powell tried to both speed the delivery of the remaining work and limit the size of the manuscript to no more than five hundred pages. Cope was suspicious that this was part of a plot to prevent him from publishing. "Can't we scotch Powell?" he asked an old friend at the survey. The answer was "no."

By the spring, Cope's Bible was heading to the government printing office, and Cope made one more bid to get a full-time position, this one in Philadelphia as curator at the Academy of Natural Sciences.

Cope attempted to oust Charles Parker, the academy's mortally ill curator, who had been put on a leave of absence. He introduced a motion on the evening of July 10 removing Parker. Cope's allies then nominated him for the freshly vacated job, but his opponents managed to stay the action for a week on a parliamentary technicality. Word went out around town, and the following week sixty-four members showed up for the weekly meeting—about three times the average—and Cope was voted down.[21]

"We were beaten as usual last night; vote 27 against 37 . . . ," Cope reported to Annie. "Our defeat was due to Hayden who gave the other side notice by his wild talking. . . . I shall let the Academy alone for a while— perhaps always, for the university people talked to me yesterday in a practical way."[22]

So it was back to the sorry state of affairs of the Sierra Mining Companies. At the July stockholders' meeting in Philadelphia, Cope led a charge to oust the board of directors. Here he was more successful than at the academy. "They made me President!" Cope announced in the same letter. "So we are rid of disgrace and it is left to me to save the reputations of several members of the society of Friends."

One of the first actions of Cope and his new board took was to fire the mine superintendent and hire Fred Endlich, an American who had learned his geology in Germany at Stuttgarts's Polytechnic School and then served as a top aide in the Hayden Survey. He was also one of the men sitting around Powell's living room the night the Cosmos Club was founded.

A week later, Cope was trying to quell the worries of his family investors. "I would write to Mary about the Grande . . . ," Cope told Annie, who was summering in Copake, New York, along with other members of the Cope family. "She must not be scared at the proceedings of the stock robbers, who put the price down by telling falsehoods. I have good news from Endlich, and we will pay a divvy before long—say in September or October."[23]

After a few days in the country with Julia and Annie, Cope returned to a sweltering Philadelphia for some Sierra meetings, only to learn the company had now encumbered four lawsuits, which threatened to soak up any profits Endlich could generate. "I am disgusted but will have to stand it," Cope lamented. "Were it not for that, everything would be lovely for the stock robbers are out entirely."

Ever optimistic, Cope told Annie, "Give my love to Julia & Lilly. Tell Philip he had better buy Bella. We have just struck a lot of high grade ore at 54 ft on the dividing line of Littleboy and Comstock claims."[24] (In the middle of all this, Cope had to rush to Washington for a few days to search for a mislaid portion of his Bible, which was fortunately found before he was forced to rewrite it.)

By August, Endlich had gotten the monthly production up to eighty-two thousand dollars in ore. Cope himself arrived at the mines on September 21 and announced to Annie, "We will not go to the poor-house yet awhile, though I know some people who ought to go to Jail.[25]

"As I suspected the talk of exhaustion of the properties had the object to frighten the stockholders into selling out," he wrote. ". . . I take to myself the credit of having balked their game, and the same men will not try it again, if I can help it, *anywhere or anybody."* Cope's optimism also seemed intact. "I feel the trouble of the last two years is over and I shall succeed in this enterprise."

At a meeting of the Sierra board, held at Lake Valley in October, Endlich and Cope argued that too much time had been spent working easy breasts and holes, and too little sinking shafts to find more lucrative veins like the Bridal Chamber. The two men charged that management had done this to drive down the price of the stock and stampede the investors.

Despite the strong charges, the *Republican,* the newspaper from neighboring Las Cruces, said that the "contest was decidedly intellectual" and decorous. The fact that board member W. B. Jones kept the meeting in good cigars, claret, and Mumm's extra dry probably helped. "Prof. Cope," the newspaper reported, "wore a high collar shirt and tight pants, but did not in the least look like a dude."[26]

Lake Valley was, according to Cope's letters, a busy place now. "Blasts are booming night and day," he wrote. So robust were the underground charges that they shook the entire camp. The mill ran continuously with the roar of a great waterfall, and convoys of mule-drawn wagons moved in and out of town hauling ore eighteen miles to the rail line.

The streets were filled with a "good many rough looking people," and Endlich warned that while there was no trouble at the moment, they would have to keep an eye out for men ready to help themselves to a few mules or a cartload of ore.[27]

There was even a prospect that at least one or two of the mines would be able to pay small dividends soon. "I had too much on hand last winter," he wrote apologetically to Annie. "My row with the mining board cost me a good deal of energy and the ANS [Academy of Natural Sciences] didn't make it any better. The mining business was also very bad. . . . Had the management continued much longer in the hands of the robbers I should have lost ⅔ of what I was worth. The danger from that is now passed, but it will take me a little while to recover financially. . . . I hope to be more amiable to everybody and display more Christian graces at home."

Before returning to Philadelphia, Cope made a quick fossil-hunting trip and a visit to Mexico. "I am writing by a fire of dry cedar sticks which give a good light," Cope reported home from his camp in the San Francisco Canyon. "The moon lights up the wall of the canyon, and the rush of the water never slackens its voice. Besides this nothing is audible except the crickets, and the noise of the horses feet as they occasionally change position. This was once the land of the cruel Apaches. . . . They are now well out of this country, or I would not be in it. . . . I dreamed of home the other night. I will see what I can do tonight."[28]

For a brief moment, things seemed to have righted themselves. But not for long. In Monterey, Mexico, Cope learned that he had been ousted as president of the Sierra Mining Company and dropped from its executive committee. "I thought it rather rough under the circumstances," he told Annie. It was an omen that the Cope's mining troubles were not over yet.

The ledger accounts of the mines were an augury of still more turmoil to come. Between 1881 and the start of 1883, the Sierre Grande properties had sold a little more than a million dollars in silver bars and ore. But they had run up a little more than a million dollars in expenses. A dividend had been paid, but the financial balance of Lake Valley was clearly precarious.[29]

Back in Philadelphia, Edward and Annie Cope lived a life that included dinner parties among friends and family, lectures, concerts and receptions. Cope was also increasingly absorbed in managing Julia's education.

"Mama and I attended the reception of the graduates of the Woman's Medical College last evening," Cope wrote to his daughter. "The class is large 35. Some of them are very pretty ladylike girls. It is very important for women to know something more than how to get food ready & to make clothes, though these things lie at the foundation of all living. . . . Whatever women do—whether to marry or have a trade, as they like, the more they know the happier they will be. Most women marry. I suppose my Mammani will someday do like the rest. If she knows more & things better & doesn't hide it, she will attract a better style of man than if she does not."[30]

The teenage Julia clearly responded, studying chemistry, mathematics, physics, French, and German. She also gave her father a variety of "commissions," as he called them, asking him to send her a hand-held microscope for botany studies, a horned lizard from New Mexico, and various mineral samples.

Julia was even bold enough, and this was very daring, indeed, for a genteel Victorian girl, to collect snakes on her summer vacations. A clearly delighted Cope asked Annie to "Tell Mammani her little snake is a *Diavophis functatus,* one of the family of *Colubridae.*" After completing her studies in Northampton, Julia proposed going to Bryn Mawr College, just outside of Philadelphia. "Thy plan seems good," her father replied, *"provided . . .* they have a good teacher of Nat. Sci. at Bryn Mawr."

After spending the first winter months of 1884 at home, Cope left for the mines in late March. The trains heading west were filled with immigrants as the towns and cities of the West continued to swell. The railroads were now running entire "immigrant trains," which were slow, long, frequently halting, but cheap.

There was such a shortage of coaches for the immigrant trains that stock cars were impressed into service. Holes were cut in the sides for windows, rows of backless, wooden benches bolted to floor, and a rough coal stove placed in the corner. Straw-filled mattresses to sleep on were sold for two dollars a piece.[31]

Whenever possible, Cope tried to stick to the more direct express trains, but on occasion, he would find himself rumbling along with the great wave of European pilgrims, who were in plodding pursuit of their American dream.

Reaching Kansas City, Cope wrote, "The city has grown enormously and numbers many say now 96,000. When I first saw it in 1871 there were about 20,000. Parts of it are handsomely built and it is a very lovely place."[32]

But for Cope, who made sure to count how many Irishmen and blacks were in town when he had moved to Haddonfield, and who despite all his years traveling still lived in his closed circle, the hordes filling the West were extremely distasteful.

"It is astonishing what a number of Jews travel with huge families in the sleeping cars," he wrote to his wife. "I have them all the way out. They are often unmannerly people. The men go about half dressed and smoke everywhere. The babies make night vocals. Some day they may learn to be less selfish, but I doubt it."

At the mines, Cope was a perpetual-motion machine, checking the works, studying the ore, examining drilling cores, and at day's end, wandering the nearby hillsides looking for fossil shells and corals. But he simply could not will the mines to make money. "With mines it is either everything or nothing," he told Annie. "I went in hoping to increase my income. I did so for awhile then it fell to nothing." Still, he continued to hope. "I will begin to recover with proper management," he predicted, "but it is going to take time."[33]

The railroad had been extended to the mines, and money had been set aside by the company to erect a community building to be used as a church, schoolhouse, and meeting hall. "Under our management we hope this community will improve in morals," Cope told Annie. "It has improved some but the town is a bad place yet."

The months passed, and still the mines made no money. In February of 1885, Cope once again headed for Lake Valley. He spent his time on the train ride out writing freelance articles for the popular press, because he was facing "the prospect of short money for some time yet."

And the news at Lake Valley did not help. "I have not gone fully over the mines here, but I have seen enough to know that we are not making anything but expenses," Cope reported to Annie. "This means no income for me for so long."[34]

And still he was indefatigable, for in the next breath, he spoke of a new project—securing two new claims "by 'jumping'; that is taking possession on account of vacancy." Cope proposed naming the two new mines the Annie and the Little Julia. Would he never learn? No. Cope simply couldn't accept that with his superior intellect he was unable to make a fortune in mining. If an illiterate Irishman could do it, surely he could, too. He took a ten-thousand-dollar mortgage on his Pine Street property and sunk that into the mines as well.

"He was almost immediately hit with losses which alarmed and confused him," Persifor Frazer wrote. "Instead of accepting these as severe warnings that he was entering upon unknown dangers and withdrawing on the best terms available, with a diminished but still handsome fortune, he plunged deeper and deeper and lost so heavily that his whole subsequent life was harassed and even the moderate requirements of himself and his family were inadequately met."[35]

Leidy had also dabbled in mining stocks, even briefly becoming president of Colorado's Bullion King Silver Mining Company. But the mine was a swindle, and Leidy lost eight thousand dollars. Leidy, however, knew when and how to cut his losses.

Now Cope was beset with "horrible financial anxiety." He was even exploring the possibility of selling his fossil collections to a buyer such as the University of Missouri or the American Museum of Natural History in New York City.

And if that wasn't bad enough, he and Powell were now arguing over the fate of the remaining manuscripts. "Powell has not answered my letters or fulfilled his promises, although he may do so yet. The situation is bad and I am weighed down with constant anxiety. The last thing I did was offer my entire collection to the British Museum, but I would greatly dislike to see it leave the U.S.," Cope wrote in the summer of 1885.

In that same letter to his wife, he casually mentioned that, "Mr. Baur, Marsh's assistant, is coming here today. He wants to see me very much about something. He is a good man so far as I know."[36] What could this Mr. Baur possibly want with Cope?

When news that Cope was trying to market his collections made it to New Haven, Marsh immediately wrote to Spencer Baird saying, "I hear Cope is trying to sell his collections in Europe. As an important part of it belongs to the National Museum it should not be allowed to leave the country."[37]

Cope also found himself increasingly distant from his colleagues at the academy and the Philosophical Society. Another Cope attempt to reform the academy—by creating a professional cadre within the institution—had also been rebuffed by the general membership, leaving him frustrated and infuriated.

He warned Leidy that unless more emphasis was placed on professionalism, Philadelphia's place in the science community would slip. Leidy agreed but said the academy simply didn't have the money for a professional staff.

There seemed to be no hope for him in his native city. "I would rather live in Philadelphia and I would like to help develop the place," he wrote to Julia. "But it is going to take too long, & I will lose every opportunity for the future if I wait any longer. There are a great many slow people in Philadelphia."[38]

For the moment, however, there was no relief to be found anywhere else. Back in 1877, Cope had set up a comfortable and convenient base of operations in the pair of townhouses on Pine Street. One for a workshop, and one for a family home. By the fall of 1885, he could no longer afford to maintain both. He moved his family out of their home, hoping to rent it for one thousand dollars a year. "If properly packed," he wrote to Annie, "the greater part of the furniture should go into the third story room and kitchen of 2102 Pine St."[39] Cope had set out to amplify his fortune so that he could expand his paleontological dominion, but now everything seemed to be crumbling around him.

Chapter Sixteen

IF THERE WAS SUCH a thing as fate, if a man, even if he were a scientist, nurtured some small belief in divine justice, then O. C. Marsh just had to be delighted and feeling quite vindicated by the turn of events.

For every defeat and hardship Cope suffered, Marsh could count a victory and an indulgence. While Cope had frittered away his wealth and energy, gravely crippling his scientific work, Marsh could depend on the ample resources of Powell, the ever-growing science faculty at Yale, the stream of specimens flowing into the Peabody, and his own personal wealth, which was still very much intact. For Marsh, now came a time of great professional and personal consolidation.

In his early years as a professor, Marsh had lived in a three-room apartment on College Street, littered knee deep with books, papers, and fossil specimens. But soon after the Peabody Museum was completed, he embarked on his own building program. He bought a seven-acre plot on Prospect Street, just where the roadway crested the hill, and informed the executors of the Peabody trust that he wanted thirty thousand dollars to build a home.

On that hilltop, Marsh built an eighteen-room, three-story brownstone mansion. It was a very Victorian house, with a welter of gables and chimneys, and it was perched so precisely on the hill's edge that the side of the house hovered over the valley and gave the enclosed porch a spectacular view of the western hills.

It was completed in 1878, but the interior wasn't finished until 1881, at a cost of another thirty thousand dollars. It may not have had a Garrett, but it did have luxurious cashmere rugs, oil paintings, and antiques. The surrounding grounds were laid out in gardens and arbors sweeping down the hill.

The huge oak front door—big enough to enter two abreast—gave way to a large octagonal reception area Marsh called the wigwam. Along one wall was a grandfather clock and perched above it, the buffalo head Marsh had won on the Kansas plains some dozen years before. There was an antelope head over one of the massive sideboards and a deer head over another sideboard, which was filled with Chinese vases and Greek amphora. Ribbons of Indian wampum were draped here and there.

A big, round pedestal table sat in the middle of the room piled with books, maps, and knickknacks. Marsh's paintings included western scenes such as Gifford Sanford's *On the Plains* and *The Mesas at Golden, Colorado.* Beyond the wigwam, through a sweeping archway, an ample, dark-wood banister swirled around on its way to the second floor.

The house was filled with Japanese enamels, Chinese porcelains, Turkish scarves embroidered with gold, and odd bits, including a Japanese execution sword and an antique brass synagogue lamp. Later Marsh would add a greenhouse and a collection of thirteen hundred rare orchids, for which he paid thirty-six hundred dollars.

Such a grand house seemed only fitting for a man living a grand life. Since the late 1870s, Marsh had been a member of the *Beaux Espirit,* a group of prominent men that met once a month in New York City to dine at Delmonico's. In the great restaurant of deep mahogany and sparkling mirrors, they would sup on Delmonico's famous dishes—green turtle soup *au clair, aiguillettes* of bass in Mornay sauce, saddle of lamb *à la Colbert*—complimented by the finest French wines and brandies.

Marsh was also a denizen of the smoking rooms and libraries of the city's University and the Century Clubs. There among the plush rugs and leather armchairs, he won a reputation as a great raconteur of Wild West stories.

Now Marsh traveled in the world of true notables. When his monograph on toothed birds was published, he sent it not only to scientists like Richard Owen and Charles Darwin but also to the commander of the army, General William Sherman, and jurist Oliver Wendell Holmes.

"I am very much obliged to you sir for the copy of your admirable monograph," Holmes wrote to Marsh in 1882. *"When I heard that you had found birds with teeth in their jaws I was as much surprised—startled, I might almost say—as the midwife who first looked into the mouth of the baby Richard Third. The fact is of profound interest in many points of view, not the least of which is that it hints at our coming upon 'the missing link' some day. . . . I often envy you Champollions of Nature's hieroglyphics, and when I think of all that a single generation may teach I could wish to reverse the order of the figures which tell me I am myself a fossil.*

"Thanking you most cordially for your polite attention in sending me this beautiful volume with its wonderful revelations."[1]

And beautiful it truly was, for Marsh had spent his own money on a special author's edition, with gilded pages and a thick, red Morocco-leather binding.

Augusta Astor sought out the professor, hoping that he could advise the Spanish diplomat Adolfo Munoz Del Monte on where his sons should go on their western tour of the United States.[2] Marsh was also invited to the Astor's Fifth Avenue mansion one evening "for refreshments and to hear the new Phonograph," a clever invention from Thomas Alva Edison.[3]

Sometimes, traveling between New York City and New Haven, Marsh would get off in Bridgeport to visit P. T. Barnum. Barnum provided complimentary passes for Marsh to his "Greatest Show on Earth" circus and, more important, made ten donations to the Peabody Museum, including the placenta of the second elephant born in America. (In the years that followed, this curiosity was misplaced and then simply disappeared.[4])

Once his house was completed and suitably furnished, Marsh also became a great host. In January of 1883, he even had Chief Red Cloud as a houseguest. (Marsh dispatched Thomas Bostwick to meet Red Cloud in Jersey City and escort him to New Haven.) The visit was marked with a photo of Red Cloud, in frock coat and cravat, handing a peace pipe and wampum belt to the professor.

Returning to the Pine Ridge Reservation in May, where his people were plowing and seeding, Red Cloud wrote a note of thanks. "I have made so many warm friend to stand by the poor Indian and help them. . . . May you well remember me to all your friends. I close by saying good bye my friend Marsh."[5]

That fall, Marsh hosted a reception for the entire National Academy of Sciences. Marsh was once again president of the academy as the result of a death. This time it was William Rogers, the respected geologist and founder of the Massachusetts Institute of Technology, who had died while holding the academy's presidency.

A string of notables came to the house on Prospect Street. Alexander Graham Bell dined there; so did John Hay, author Edward Everett Hale, Herbert Spencer, and Alfred Russel Wallace. Surrounded by fine things and fine people, Marsh had come a long way from a barefoot farm boy in Lockport, who had considered becoming a carpenter. And yet, there was something missing.

Marsh remained a wary character, who never completely emerged from behind his emotional barricade. There was in the man "an absence of the complete exchange of confidence which normally exists between intimate friends," said Charles Beecher, one of Marsh's most trusted assistants and his successor as curator at the Peabody. "Even where perfect confidence existed, he seldom revealed more about any particular matter than seemed to him necessary."

As the years passed, and the western stories were told and retold around the club lounges, the middle-aged Marsh became known as the "Great Dismal Swamp" by the younger wags. All too often, the professor would not even go home after a day at the Peabody but would instead dine at Mosely's New Haven House, a popular Yale rendezvous, while the great stone house, at the top of the hill, stood dark and empty.

❧

It was, however, in the Peabody Museum, not in the Prospect Street house, that Marsh's steeliness created the most serious problems, as a war of intellect and nerves was waged in the museum's basement workshops.

Upstairs, the museum was really taking shape. The first floor had a lecture hall and mineralogy room. On the second floor was the osteology collection—including the dinosaur bones. The third floor was devoted to zoology and the fourth floor to anthropology.

In the western room on the second floor, a huge *Brontosaurus* leg bone lay on the floor, as did some massive vertebrae. Glass cases held the bones of stegosaurs, mosasaurs, and *Hesperornis.* The bones were displayed individually.[6] Marsh had not been a booster for the centennial *Hadrosaurus* and was not interested in trying to recreate full-scale dinosaurs for the public at the Peabody.

In the mid-1880s, perhaps to celebrate the publication of the *Dinocerata* monograph, Marsh did relent and build a full-scale model of *Dinoceras mirabile* (or Leidy's uintathere). But not with the real bones. No, they weren't for such play. The reconstruction was made of papier-mâché, using a paper made of ground-up greenback dollars, redeemed by the U.S. Treasury. Well, that was certainly one way to deal with the inflationary problems caused by paper currency.

The heart and the soul of the Peabody, however, was the basement studios, where between his own resources and those provided by Powell, Marsh was able to build arguably the finest paleontology laboratory in the world.

True, Louis Dollo had an extraordinary workshop at the Royal Museum in Brussels. There he was reconstructing thirty-nine *Iguanodon*s, all found in a coal mine in Bernissart, Belgium. So many specimens of the same species presented a unique opportunity in paleontology, and Dollo was doing groundbreaking work. Nevertheless, he could not match in breadth and volume the fossil work of Marsh's Peabody staff. No one could.

Part of Marsh's strength came from the great fossil fields of the West and the tenacity of collectors like Reed, Lakes, and Baldwin. But an equally important part came from the fact that the Peabody drew to it the next generation of ambitious young scientists. Williston, Grinnell, and others would work for Marsh because he had the bones, the money for salaries, and a great university at his doorstep. No one else in America could offer that combination.

Marsh, however, was a difficult man to work for. He was casual in his payment of salaries, tight lipped in his counsel, imperious in his manner, and he absolutely forbade any of his budding scientists from publishing their own work in vertebrate paleontology. From the mid-1870s to the late 1880s, Marsh would employ fifty-four different staff members, which was the equivalent of the entire staff turning over almost four times.

There was a constant war of nerves being waged at the Peabody. Of course, not everyone was a combatant. George Bird Grinnell, who had accompanied Marsh on his first expedition, then bought dead animals from Barnum, and went with Custer into the Black Hills, was happily employed at the Peabody while he completed a Yale Ph.D. He even worked for free. In the *Birds with Teeth* monograph, Marsh made a point of acknowledging Grinnell's "valuable assistance, especially while the volume was in press." Marsh also named a fossil in his honor, *Crocodilus grinnelli*. When he received his doctorate, in 1880, Grinnell left New Haven to become an ethnologist and explorer, and after Marsh's death, he would write a highly complimentary profile for a book titled *Leading Men of American Science*.

It seems, however, that Grinnell was the exception. Assistants like Oscar Harger, Samuel Williston, Erwin Barbour, and George Baur seethed and clashed with Marsh and his ways. These were all bright, well-schooled, and ambitious young men. But in Marsh's Peabody autocracy, all was done for the greater glory of Marsh.

Marsh's methods reinforced that feeling. He would parcel out sets of fossil bones to each assistant with instructions on what kind of analysis or comparisons he desired. Marsh would then quiz the assistant on what he had found, taking notes, but never revealing his own thoughts. Much later when a Marsh scientific paper was published, the staffer might find a phrase or an insight of his embedded in the Marsh text, or he might find that Marsh had totally disagreed with the original analysis but had not had the courtesy of a colleague to raise those objections face to face.

The longest serving of Marsh's assistants was Oscar Harger. Poor, undersized, and hobbled with a heart condition, Harger worked his way through

Yale doing mathematical calculations for insurance companies. Still, he managed to graduate with honors and trek across the West with Marsh in 1871 and 1873. Marsh hired him at a salary of thirty-five dollars month in 1872.

Perhaps because of his physical limitations, Harger was a studious and patient fellow, who read widely in all the fields of science, much more widely and deeply than his boss. As the years passed, Harger developed great expertise in paleontology, and Marsh came to depend on him as a valuable critic and editor of his manuscripts. But despite Harger's repeated pleas, Marsh absolutely refused to let him publish on his own or even coauthor papers in the field of vertebrate paleontology. Harger, Marsh said, was free to write about invertebrate biology—so long as it didn't interfere with his duties at the Peabody.

Harger lamented his situation to his fellow workers, and at least two professors tried to intercede with Marsh on his behalf. Prof. S. I. Smith, one of Harger's supporters, said the young man had a "truly philosophical grasp" of evolution and classification. But Marsh would not yield, although Harger's salary by the 1880s had risen to fifteen hundred dollars a year.

Yet shackled as he was by poor health and poverty, the Peabody was a refuge for Harger. He did manage to publish a few papers on spiders and microscopic pond animals. But his thoughts on the great beasts he worked with in the Peabody basement remained at best veiled in Marsh's own work. "Only a few who knew his attainments can appreciate how much paleontological science would have advanced had he been allowed to publish," Smith said.

When Samuel Williston arrived in New Haven in 1876, he ran into the same problems. While working on the Kansas plains, he had collected fossil fishes, animals in which he knew Marsh had no interest. But back in New Haven, Marsh refused to let him work on the Cretaceous fish, saying that it would distract him from his duties.

Like Harger, Williston switched his own studies far away from Marsh territory. He began studying flies. Reed even took time out from digging bones at Como Bluff to catch some for his friend Williston. Williston was able to extract concessions from Marsh that enabled him to attend Yale. He did this by pointing out that he could collect for Cope during the summers with "a salary sufficient during the season to pay my expenses at College the following winter."[7]

Anything was better than Williston going over to the Cope camp. So Williston received his M.D. from the Yale Medical School in 1880 and a Yale Ph.D. in zoology for his work on flies in 1885.

But where Harger was, in the words of Yale President Timothy Dwight, a "kindly and gentle spirit," Williston was hardened by western life and combative. Venting his frustration to his wife, Williston wrote, "Science is the slowest and hardest of professions to make pecuniary success. My employer is a man I cannot respect. . . . I came very near having a quarrel with the Prof. last Saturday. . . . I talked pretty severely to him about money matters and the way he was trying to prevent me from acquiring any sort of independent reputation."[8]

Marsh was paying Williston twelve hundred dollars a year, with U.S. Geological Survey funds, and at one point, Williston was so frustrated about tardy payments, he wrote a letter of complaint to Powell. Powell passed the letter on to Marsh. In 1885, with his Yale studies nearing completion, Williston broke with Marsh.

"From a review of *all* the circumstances, and after mature deliberation, I have finally and definitely resolved to sever any relations with you," Williston wrote to Marsh in February of 1885. "I beg that you will accept this without further discussion. I do not wish to have any trouble nor to leave in an unfriendly spirit. . . . I must seek out another occupation and I cannot afford to lose more years of my life."[9]

For five years, Williston practiced medicine in New Haven and served as a public health officer. In 1890, he landed a professorship in geology at the University of Kansas, and twelve years later, he moved to the University of Chicago as a professor of paleontology.

Although he tried to part on amicable terms, Williston's sense of injury showed when Harger died from a cerebral hemorrhage in 1887. Harger was just forty-four years old and had been in Marsh's employ for fifteen years. Here was, Williston thought, a brilliant life, stifled, denied, and now cut short. At least, he should get his due posthumously.

In an obituary written for the *American Naturalist,* Williston said that Harger was responsible for much of the good work Marsh claimed. "To my personal knowledge nearly or quite all the descriptive portions of Prof. Marsh's work on *Dinocerata* was written by him [Harger] and was published without change . . . ," Williston said. "The descriptive portion of the *Odontornithes* was likewise his work."[10]

That such sharp criticism should appear in Cope's journal wasn't at all surprising. Indeed, Cope was cultivating Marsh's unhappy assistants and collecting whatever dirt he could gather. He was certain that some day it would come in handy.

His co-conspirators in this effort were Scott and Osborn, now both junior professors at Princeton and staunch enemies of Marsh. "Marsh's egoism, his extreme selfishness and unscrupulous duplicity aroused very strong feelings in me," Scott was to write in his memoirs.[11] Once, under the cover of going to the Yale-Princeton football game, Scott went to New Haven to meet secretly with Marsh's assistants to try to organize a revolt. But nothing came of it.

One of the most dissatisfied and perhaps the most brilliant of all Marsh's assistants was the German-born George Baur, who had received his Ph.D. in 1882 from the University of Munich. His doctoral dissertation dealt with the similarity between birds and dinosaurs.

Baur came to Marsh with a sound background in microscopy, anatomy and embryology. But most of all, he brought to the Peabody a strong view of the "recapitulation" theory developed by the German biologist Ernest Haeckel. While Marsh might be trying to reconstruct the path of evolution by assembling millions of years' worth of bones, Haeckel argued that evolution could be seen in the development of the embryo of the higher forms of life.

"Ontogeny recapitulates phylogeny" was the mantra of these theorists. Quite simply, they believed an organism passed through its ancestral forms on its way to its mature development. The gill slit of an early human embryo, for example, represented the ancestral fish; the temporary tail, the reptilian stage. Each organism proceeds down the same evolutionary path, but more advanced forms go farther.

Recapitulation was among the most influential ideas of the century. "It dominated the work of several professions," said Stephen Jay Gould, the Harvard paleontologist and science historian, "including embryology, comparative morphology, and paleontology. All these disciples were obsessed with recreating evolutionary lineages."[12] The Neo-Lamarckians, Gould said, were particularly taken with the theory and "exalted recapitulation."

Indeed, Baur's background in biology offset a serious deficiency in Marsh, who had been trained primarily in geology and mineralogy. In fact, there has been speculation that Marsh's reliance on his staff in part came from the "major handicap" of his not having a solid grounding in biology and anatomy.[13]

So Baur brought both biology and recapitulation theory to New Haven, and in a Yale research proposal, "Paleontology as assisted by Embryology," he argued, "It would be of the highest importance if Paleontology and its sister-science, Embryology, would go hand in hand. I will give an example: Dinosaurs are now generally considered as the ancestors of Birds; if this view is correct we must find in embryos of the Birds, especially the oldest birds, the Ratitae, characters of the Dinosauria."[14] Marsh paid Baur more than his other assistants, quickly raising his salary to eighteen hundred dollars a year, and he permitted Baur to publish sixty-four short papers and eleven long ones during his six years at the Peabody.

Still, Baur was restless and felt blocked by the slow, methodical, taciturn Marsh. Baur, however, was perpetually broke and forever in debt to Marsh. Between July and December of 1884, for instance, Baur received a half-dozen salary advances, adding up to three hundred dollars. This gave Marsh a hold over Baur, and he used it.

In the spring of 1888, Harvard offered Baur a position. "We lack a man for vertebrates," Harvard President Charles Eliot explained in a note to Marsh. The salary was smaller than the one Baur received from the U.S. Geological Survey at the Peabody. Nevertheless, Baur was interested. Marsh blocked the move. "Professor Marsh does not like that I leave him, I therefore decided to stay here," Baur wrote to Alexander Agassiz.

Baur finally resigned from the Peabody in 1890—after paying off $470 in debts to Marsh—and took a job as a lecturer at Clark University in Worcester, Massachusetts. Two years later, he was appointed professor of paleontology at the new University of Chicago, a post he held until, suffering from paralysis, he returned to Germany in 1897.

Yes, there was much unhappiness in the Peabody workshops, and Cope and his allies were continually lurking around trying to pick up scraps of information. For just as Marsh had doubted the honesty of Cope's dates, now Cope questioned whether Marsh simply wasn't engaged in plagiarizing the ideas of his brilliant staff.

"The four men who have left Marsh wish to place themselves & him right before the Scientific public . . . ," Cope told Osborn in 1885. "It is clear to me that Marsh is simply a scientifico-political adventurer who has succeeded, in ways other than those proceeding from scientific merit."[15]

❖

Marsh seemed, however, to live a charmed life. Even before one gifted assistant would leave, another would be clamoring to take his place. Williston was just a few months away from handing in his resignation when a new graduate of the Sheffield Scientific School boldly walked into Marsh's office.

The Yale professor looked up to see slight, wiry young man with cool, gray-blue eyes that looked back at him unflinchingly. The young man wanted a job, and for whatever reason, Marsh decided that John Bell Hatcher would have one.

Marsh knew that Hatcher had worked in coal mines and collected Carboniferous fossils before coming to New Haven. So he dispatched the
would-be paleontologist to Long Island, Kansas, where a new bone quarry
was being worked for Yale by none other than Charles H. Sternberg.

During his twenty-one-year association with Cope, Sternberg would
spend a total of thirteen seasons in the field for the Philadelphian, and he
would always feel great loyalty and admiration for him. But Sternberg had a
family that had to be fed every year, and when Cope couldn't afford to pay,
Sternberg had to work for those who could.

In 1882, he was fossil prospecting for Harvard when he first came upon
the promising Long Island site. But it wasn't until 1884, when he was
financed by Yale, that he could properly develop it. Sternberg had begun
work that spring. Hatcher arrived on July 8, 1884.

It is difficult to say precisely what Marsh expected out of the twenty-
three-year-old Hatcher, but he would soon realize that he had hired one of
the most energetic, resourceful, and meticulous field paleontologists ever to
work the western plains. He had hired a man who would be a legend in his
own right.

Sternberg had successfully been collecting fossils for eight years, and he
saw Hatcher as "an enthusiastic student from Yale," who was making "the
first collection of his life."[16] But Hatcher was as impatient as enthusiastic and
quickly determined that he could do a better job than Sternberg.

He had been at the site just two days when he wrote to Marsh asking to
be allowed to work on his own. In a stream of five letters that month,
Hatcher argued for autonomy. Sternberg, he said, was "a hard-working
industrious man but quite careless."[17]

In August, while Sternberg was away, a dispute over access to the quarry
arose with the property's owner, James Overton. Hatcher struck a new
agreement with Overton that gave Marsh exclusive rights to the site. What
had been the Sternberg Quarry, now became the Marsh Quarry.[18]

More than ever, Hatcher pressed for his independence. When Sternberg
returned, he was furious and immediately wrote to Marsh. "I wish to write
to you on a subject which if not fully settled I will resign my position . . . &
collect either for myself or Prof. Cope.

"Now if after two years work I have discovered the only rich formation
on this deposit in the state, I am to be turned out of the locality by an assistant & all the work given to him, I have had enough of it," Sternberg
declared.[19]

Either Hatcher was to be sent to "Colorado or elsewhere," Sternberg
warned, or he himself was gone on September 1. Marsh tried to resolve the

situation, as he had done at Como Bluff, by having each man work separate sites.

While a stinging rebuff to Sternberg, the arrangement now allowed Hatcher to apply his own approach. He divided his site into a checkerboard of five-foot squares and systematically excavated, square by square. He sent Marsh a chart of the site and then a chart of each square showing the location of each bone found. Hatcher also demonstrated remarkable skill in the excavating, and out of a single square, he was able to unearth sixty-seven bones.

Hatcher's techniques offered a major advance in fieldwork, and Marsh visited Kansas in September to tour the site. By November, when work ceased for the year, 143 boxes of fossils had been prepared for shipment to New Haven.

Sternberg left Long Island brooding about the events of the summer. Marsh had paid him about $1,130 for the season—including expenses—but he had lost access to the quarry for future excavation. Years later, it would still be a sore point. In a 1904 letter written to Henry Fairfield Osborn at the American Museum of Natural History, Sternberg would say, "Thank you for sending me your memoir and a photograph of the specimen of the rhinoceros that was collected in 'my quarry' and not Marsh's, for ever the laborer is worthy of his hire."[20]

A month after closing down the Kansas quarry, Marsh sent Hatcher to northern Texas to search the Permian beds that had proved so valuable for Cope. Now Hatcher began experiencing the same money problems as Marsh's other field hands. On February 9, Hatcher trudged into Wichita Falls after his blankets and supplies had been stolen. He had "not enough money for a postal card."[21]

Hatcher reached the town—a string of timber buildings on the flat, desiccated plains, sitting alongside the half-built Fort Worth and Denver City Railway—expecting relief in the form of a check from New Haven, but it wasn't there.

The Comanche and Kiowa were no longer threats, but Texas was still a rough-and-tumble place. It was the kind of place, Hatcher said, that if two men had a gunfight, and one man was killed, the authorities would promptly arrest the dead man.

But neither western stories nor fossils from the field could move Marsh. In early March, after walking sixteen miles and wading through the ice-choked Big Wichita River to reach the Seymour post office only to find once again no mail and no check, Hatcher sent a message to New Haven. "Unless there can be a change I had rather stop work." It was a threat that Hatcher would use again and again over the next eight years.

In 1886, Hatcher was dispatched to Nebraska to collect brontotheres. Back on his first western expedition, Marsh had collected these hoofed, horned, rhinolike animals, which lived about thirty-five million years ago during the Oligocene. Cope had also collected specimens of the genera and had written about the animals. But now Marsh proposed doing with the brontotheres what he had done with the Dinocerata—collecting such a vast quantity of bones and writing such a detailed monograph (to be published by Powell's survey) that it would be the definitive work. Hatcher, true to form, collected 24,136 pounds of brontothere material. And the next year, 1887, he was back adding even more brontothere skulls.

In the next four years, Hatcher was to surpass his performance with bronotheres, in the pursuit of Ceratopsian dinosaurs. This quest had begun rather doubtfully when Hatcher tried going over the Judith River territory Cope had explored back in 1876.

"I am having very poor success . . . ," Hatcher reported back. "I am commencing to think that Sternberg *lied* about the rich fossil bed that he talked about here."[22] After gathering a few boxes worth of fossils, including some interesting horn cores, Hatcher abandoned the river valley. But on his way east, he stopped in southern Wyoming to look at some bones gathered up by ranchers. Here again, he came across a huge fossil horn.

When the material arrived in New Haven, Marsh sorted through it and compared it with some other horns, including one he originally believed belonged to a huge, ancient buffalo. He realized he was on to a new dinosaur. Hatcher was sent once more into the field to search for the remains—especially skulls—of these horned beasts.

Hatcher went back to the Wyoming ranch where he had seen one of these gigantic horns and excavated a thousand-pound skull, which proved to have had a horn on the nose and two on top of the head, Marsh called the dinosaur *Triceratops*. Over the next three years Hatcher would scour the Dakotas and send back to Marsh the remains of fifty ceratopsians, including thirty-three nearly perfect skulls, one of them weighing 6,850 pounds.

This was truly a breakthrough, an entirely new type of dinosaur. Harry Grovier Seeley, for one, was deeply impressed. "I offer you my hearty congratulations on your discovery of the skull of Triceratops," he wrote Marsh. "It is one of the most interesting beasts of the long series which you have made known; and after this anything in skull structure is possible."[23]

Marsh developed an extensive description of these horned dinosaurs, but as far as Cope was concerned, Marsh was simply following in his wake, for he had discovered the first horned dinosaur—*Monoclonius crassus*—in Montana back in 1876. "Marsh has been duplicating this work," he wrote to Sternberg in 1887, "in his newest shameless style. According to him nothing has been done on this field before! He made a good beginning by describing the horns of one of these fellows as a new species of *Bison!*"

Hatcher did this work despite recurrent bouts of rheumatism and the standard western hardships. "My horse tried to play circus the other day & fell over backwards on me injuring my legs a little, but not seriously," Hatcher reported one day from Hermosa, Dakota. "It might have easily been much worse."[24]

(Indeed, eight months earlier, it had been much worse for Fred Brown, up at Como Bluff, when his horse had run off and then pitched and fell atop of him, breaking Brown's collarbone.[25])

But as the fossils flowed into the Peabody, Hatcher became concerned that the analysis and publication of the material wasn't proceeding at an equally a quick pace, and he was growing worried about the competition. "Bone hunters are as thick as sparrows in New Haven," Hatcher warned from the Dakotas in 1888.[26]

"I think you are a long way ahead of Cope so far as material is concerned & do not see why you should let him get ahead of you on the literary part of the work, with all your assistants back there to help you," he wrote from Wyoming. "I will certainly try to keep the end out here a good, long pull ahead of any party that attempts to come in."

"But," he warned, "if Osborn or Cope or anyone else sees fit to send *collectors* in this rich field (which they have a right to do) there are bones here for the millions & it would be the utmost folly to attempt to keep them from getting some of them."[27]

There was no question that things seemed to have slowed down over the years at the Peabody. Marsh was no longer prodded by Cope—who had neither access to government publications nor ample funds of his own—and so he felt no imperative to publish.

In fact, his slow, methodical inclination coupled with his penchant for secrecy frustrated even his assistants down in the basement. And then there were his receptions up on Prospect Street, his evenings in the New York clubs, his dinners at Delmonico's, not to mention his duties for the National Academy of Science. "During most of my time in his employ," Williston charged, "I never knew him to do two consecutive honest days' work in science."

Marsh also had a habit of dawdling, of procrastinating, some might say. It was a flaw that was exacerbated by his habit of taking on too many things at one time. His most recent campaign, for example, was to raise additional funds to build the second wing of the Peabody, as called for in the original design. Marsh even tried to tap Barnum.

The showman, however, who was now in his seventies, said reports of his wealth had been greatly exaggerated. "The newspapers mark me down as worth *five times* the amount I ever was or wished to be," he told Marsh. Barnum, who would die in 1891, said his first concern was "to do justice to my 2 children and 9 grandchildren." This, he declared, might be a "drawback to further charitable contributions from your humble servant."[28] The money for the second wing of the Peabody would have to come from elsewhere.

But "the real cause of his inadequate productivity after 1882," said Marsh's biographers Charles Schuchert and Clara Mae LeVene, "was that he had become overwhelmed and confused by the very mass of his fossil riches, and by the effort required to direct his superabundant staff in the laboratory and in the field."[29]

It was true that as Hatcher, Sternberg, Baldwin, and all the other collectors unearthed more and more bones, the view of prehistoric life—particularly concerning dinosaurs—became more and more confused. Marsh was "almost literally being buried by tons of dinosaur bones," said paleontologist and historian Edwin Colbert.

It was perplexing for everyone. Germany's Hermann von Meyer even suggested doing away with "dinosaurs" altogether and instead calling these animals *Pachypoda*. Certainly "elephant foot" didn't seem as grand a name as "fearfully great lizard." Not surprisingly the dinosaurs' creator, Owen, opposed the name change. He argued that von Meyer's *Pachypoda* emphasized an affinity to mammals that simply didn't exist. Owen had only used the elephant as crude model for the dinosaur. "There is, in fact, not a single specially mammalian feature in their whole organization," he maintained. Owen was even prepared to concede that dinosaurs were closer to birds.[30]

Dinosaurs stayed dinosaurs. But Owen's own criteria for what made a dinosaur a dinosaur were breaking down. Initially, this was a group of huge animals. But species like Marsh's Canon City *Nanosaurus* were tiny, and while all the initial species had five fused vertebrae, now some specimens with just three were being called dinosaurs. Some of the animals had armor plating, and some didn't. Things really were getting confusing.

Huxley, Cope, and Marsh each took a stab at trying to organize the ever-growing menagerie of dinosaurs. It was a tricky exercise. The criteria had to be general enough to sort this large, diverse bunch of animals into mean-ingful groupings. But it couldn't be too general, because that would leave everything just as muddled as before.

As underscored by the story of Owen's Thecodontia and Cope's reworking of that broad group of Triassic reptiles into a group called Archosauria, the key was to be thoughtful and elegant.

Cope tried to sort the dinosaurs by their ankle structure and a hipbone. His dinosaur groups were:

Orthopoda (straight feet)—Armored and duck-billed dinosaurs
Goniopoda (angle feet)—Carnivorous dinosaurs
Symphopoda (grown-together feet)—Small carnivorous dinosaurs

The problem with Cope's effort was that things were still a jumble. Orthopoda contained both armored quadrapeds and armorless bipeds. Symphopoda contained both herbivores and carnivores. In an effort to clean things up, Cope added a fourth classification, Opisthocoela, for the gigantic swamp-dwelling dinosaurs, but this was a name Owen had created and was not really based on ankle structure.

Huxley rejected Cope's efforts, arguing that the ankle bones simply were not the key determinant. He tried to classify dinosaurs based on teeth, jaws, a hipbone, and a leg bone. Huxley came up with three groupings:

Megalosauridae—Carnivores, such as *Dryptosaurus* and *Megalosaurus*
Scelidosauridae—Armored species, such *Hylaeosaurus*
Iguanodontidae—Herbivores, like the *Hadrosaurus* and *Iguanodon*

The first problem with Huxley's method was that a dinosaur like the little *Compsognathus* managed to fit into all three categories. So Huxley added a fourth category, Orntithoscledia, that in turn was divided into two cate-gories—Dinosauria and Composagnatha. But by this point, Huxley's system was both complicated and messy.

Marsh also came up with four different and distinct orders of dinosaurs, proposing:

Stegosauria—Armored dinosaurs
Ornithopoda—Iguanodonts, duck-billed dinosaurs, and so on
Sauropoda—Gigantic, marsh-dwelling dinosaurs
Theropoda—Carnivorous dinosaurs

This sorting was based on a wide range of characteristics, including teeth, backbones, feet, hips, and shoulders. Marsh had come closer to the essence of the dinosaurs than either Cope or Huxley. But Marsh's system required very complicated sorting, and something was still missing.

In 1887, Cope's English friend, Harry Grovier Seeley, solved the riddle of organizing the dinosaurs. The key Seeley saw was that dinosaurs weren't one huge group with a great variety of forms. They were two large, but distinct, groups or orders.

Seeley pointed out that all these specimens had one of two types of hips, which varied by the position of one of the hipbones, the pubis. In one of these groups the hips were similar to those of a bird and in the other, to those of a reptile.

"Dinosauria has no existence as a natural group of animals, but includes two distinct types of animal . . . which show their descent from a common ancestry rather than their close affinity," Seeley wrote in "On the Classification of the Fossil Animals Commonly Named Dinosauria."

"These two orders of animals," Seeley proposed, "may be conveniently named the Ornithischia and the Sauricha"—bird-hipped dinosaurs and lizard-hipped dinosaurs.

Seeley had done more than simply sort fossil bones. He had given paleontology a vision that dinosaur evolution had proceeded along two separate lines and clearly had taken the source of the animals back to the Triassic. But even more important than that, he had intimated that dinosaurs were part of a much larger evolutionary pattern involving other reptiles and birds.

Eventually, Marsh's classifications would be absorbed into Seeley's system. The Ornithopoda and Stegosauria would be placed underneath the bird-hipped dinosaurus, and the Sauropoda and Theropoda under the lizard-hipped dinosaurs.

All this, however, would take years, and in the meantime, the bones were piling up in the basement of the Peabody, overwhelming Marsh and his staff. "At times, his assistants were left for a day or more with nothing to do except talk over their grievances," Schuchert and LeVene wrote, "while Marsh lingered in New York at the University Club or the Century Club, where he undeniably liked to 'spread himself.' "

In Marsh's defense, there were some major distractions, not the least of which was still another full-scale congressional investigation into the role of science. It was an investigation that opponents of Powell and Marsh would use as a weapon of attack, and in it, they would also find a new ally, a former Confederate solider and current Alabama congressman, named Hilary Abner Herbert.

Powell and Marsh would have to summon up all their political acumen to counter their enemies. Worst of all, one of their greatest allies, the president, James Garfield, had been killed by an assassin. A disgruntled office seeker had shot Garfield. But there were those who said it wasn't the assassin who was responsible for murdering Garfield, but rather the doctors and scientists who were supposed to be taking care of him.

Chapter Seventeen

PRESIDENT JAMES GARFIELD WALKED into the Washington railroad depot on the morning of July 2, 1881, heading for the Berkshire Hills of western Massachusetts and his alma mater, Williams College.

The first few months of Garfield's presidency had been filled with the tumult that seemed to mark Washington politics, no matter who was in office. Another fraud investigation had broken—this one involving postal officials who were cheating the government out of revenues on western mail routes. The newspapers were calling it the "Star Route Scandal." The trial had just begun.

But of even greater concern to Garfield was the terrible fracture in his Republican Party, a product of his struggle for the presidency. It was a divide that only seemed to be getting worse. The 1880 Republican nomination had been ferociously fought over by Maine senator James G. Blaine and a nostalgia-driven Ulysses Grant. But neither man could muster enough delegates. On the nominating convention's thirty-sixth ballot, Garfield was offered as a compromise candidate, and with Blaine's support, the Ohio congressman took the nomination.

The general election was another war, with Garfield beating Democratic candidate General Winfield Scott Hancock by less than ten thousand popular votes. (Garfield did have a better than two-to-one margin in the electoral college.) It was, at least, a more or less, honest race.

Garfield's inaugural ball was one of the first official functions held in Baird's new National Museum, and it was a fitting venue for celebrating a man who had served as a Smithsonian regent and fought alongside Powell and Marsh in the struggle to recast the national survey. The ball's centerpiece was a large plaster statue of the Goddess of Liberty, but instead of holding aloft a torch, she gripped one of Thomas Edison's new incandescent light bulbs.

The election, however, had left hard feelings on all sides, particularly between Blaine supporters, called Half-Breeds, and Grant men, known as Stalwarts. Garfield owed his nomination to the Half-Breeds, and they received the lion's share of administration appointments, inflaming the wounds even more.

That morning, at the Baltimore and Potomac train station, the president, accompanied by his new secretary of state, James G. Blaine, was approached by Charles J. Guiteau, a lawyer and Republican Stalwart. Guiteau had sought a political appointment, preferably as ambassador to France, and had been rejected. Now Guiteau walked up to Garfield and shot him twice in the back.

Garfield, who never lost consciousness, was rushed to the White House. One bullet had grazed Garfield's arm, the other was lodged somewhere in the president's torso. But doctors did not know where.

The accepted procedure of the day to find a slug was to use a probe to follow the bullet's path through the wound. Dr. Willard Bliss did this on his first examination of Garfield. Bliss used his unwashed finger and then a nonsterilized probe. (The "germ theory" for disease was only then being worked out in Germany and France by Robert Koch, Paul Ehrlich, and Louis Pasteur.) Bliss couldn't find the bullet.

After Bliss, a string of doctors paraded into the White House. They predicted a quick demise for the president, but Garfield lingered. He developed a fever. He was put on a diet of milk spiked with brandy. The doctors weren't sure what to do.

Newspapers across the nation ridiculed the indecision and limited ability of the president's physicians. Here they were living in the most modern of times, and still nothing could be done. People from all over the nation began deluging the White House with their home remedies, poultices, herbs, and patent medicines, as well as their own advice and theories.

A committee of scientific men—lead by Powell and Simon Newcomb—was gathered to devise a way to ease the president's discomfort in the humid oven of a Washington summer, and Alexander Graham Bell appeared on the scene with a plan to use science to find the bullet.

Employing electricity running through wire coils and a telephone apparatus to amplify the signal, Bell believed that he could detect the location of the bullet since his coil hummed when placed near a metal object.

Before going to the White House, Bell took the apparatus to the Old Soldiers Home, where Civil War veterans, with bullets still in them, allowed Bell to pass his coils over their bodies. In each case, the coils hummed, and Bell was able to locate the bullet.

But Bell had no such luck at the White House. No matter where the coils were placed on Garfield's body, they hummed. Bell was now in for taunts in the press similar to those the doctors had received. Editorials charged he was merely a self-promoter and "publicity seeker."

Back to the lab Bell went. More tests. More successes. Bell persuaded the doctors to let him have another try. But the results were the same. At the end of July, a dejected Bell left the White House and returned to Boston.

Meanwhile, with Garfield's condition deteriorating, the doctors decided to operate. They cut the president open, but still could not find the bullet. The best relief the Powell committee had been able to devise was a crude air conditioner—a contraption that blew air over a cake of ice.

In August, Garfield was finally moved to his family's summer home in Elberon, New Jersey, and there he died on September 19, 1881. The nation was dismayed by the news. The presidential record in the sixteen years since the Civil War had been grim: two presidents assassinated, one president nearly impeached, one president who stole his election, and one president presiding over the most corrupt administration of all time. What was the nation coming to?

Fifteen-year-old Julia Cope followed the Garfield story with the avid interest of a teenager just becoming aware of the world of events around her. She questioned her father about Guiteau. "I think he is crazy in a certain way," Cope replied. "He has emotional insanity, but his intellect is not much out of order."

At his trial, Guiteau's defense was that while it was true that he had shot Garfield, it was the doctors who had killed him. The jury was not agreeable to the argument, and even though it believed Guiteau was insane, he was found guilty and hanged.

It was not the finest moment for American medicine or American science. And it deprived Powell and Marsh of a valuable ally just when they were about to face still another attack. If only Bell's invention had worked.

There was, however, a good reason why it had not. Bell had been undone by another modern invention—the just patented, coil-spring mattress. The White House, in fact, was one of the few places in the country that had this marvelous advance in sleep technology. Bell didn't realize Garfield was lying on metal springs. If the president had been moved off the mattress, perhaps his life would have been saved.

No, it hadn't been a shining moment for science, and soon Congress would take another run at the questions of science in government, and government in science. The law creating the U.S. Geological Survey had cleared up the problem of the competing surveys, but little else. The Public Lands Commission, of which Powell was the leading member, had, after extensive hearings and a fact-finding trip across the West, issued recommendations that read a lot like the original *Arid Region* report and received a similar, unenthusiastic reception by Congress.

The General Land Office was still dishing out parcels, and the other scientific bureaus, like the U.S. Coast and Geodetic Survey, were still in business. But with each year, the presence of the scientist grew in Washington. Powell, in particular, was pushing and expanding the field. So, in July of 1884, Congress decided that it would again investigate the proper role of science in the federal government.

This time they created a special joint House-Senate commission charged with looking at a host of scientific agencies, with a "view to secure greater efficiency and economy of administration of the public service in said Bureaus." The commission was to report back in six months.[1] Ostensibly, the role of the commission was to consider things such as whether printing costs were reasonable, the administrative efficacy of bureaus, and the appropriate place for the U.S. Weather Bureau (then part of the Army Signal Corps). But in reality, the commission became a podium for debating the role of government in science, and science in society.

One of the first acts of the commission, which was chaired by Senator William B. Allison of Iowa, and thus known as the Allison Commission, was to seek the opinion of the National Academy of Sciences. Marsh, who was once again the academy president, formed a committee. He had wanted to put his old friend Simon Newcomb on the panel, but the navy blocked his appointment, concerned it represented a conflict of interest for the astronomer.

The academy came back with a soaring proposal that science be elevated to the position of an essential national activity—like war, treasury, and interior. "The country will demand the institution of a branch of the executive government devoted especially to the direction and control of all the purely scientific work of the Government," the academy proposal maintained.

"In this day the pursuit of science itself is, visible to all men of education, directly connected with the promotion of the general welfare . . . ," the committee continued. "The study of electricity has resulted in the telegraph, the telephone, the electric light, the electric railway." These inventions, the scientists pointed out, were worth millions of dollars in revenue and jobs.

"None who have lived with open eyes during the development of purely scientific investigations doubt that the cultivation of the sciences 'promotes the general welfare,' " the academy maintained.[2]

Perhaps, but the academy committee spoke of "educated men" and those "who have lived with their eyes open." What about Congress? The legislators were looking for less bureaucracy, not more. Besides, administration officials, like Navy Secretary William Chandler, were opposed to losing their scientific agencies to a new department. Scientific research, Chandler argued persuasively, "should be conducted within and under the direction of the Department that needs the scientific assistance."

The National Academy of Sciences, realizing that its Department of Science might "be now impractical," suggested that at the minimum the observatory (navy), the weather service (army), the geological survey (interior), and the coastal survey (treasury) all be placed in the same department. The department heads didn't care for that either.

Powell offered an alternative, which was to take the purely "informational" bureaus—such as the geological survey, the fish commission, and the naval observatory—and make them part of the Smithsonian. No support for that one either.

Although Newcomb, as the navy's senior scientist, had been prevented from participating on the academy's committee, he was able to send a letter to the Allison Commission, with his views. He believed the "evils of the scientific bureaus" came from "the want of adequate administrative supervision." There was, he said, "but one adequate remedy . . . to place all the scientific work of the government . . . under a single administrative head to be selected by the President."[3]

Newcomb's proposal didn't garner much support. But while the debate was about bureaucratic organization, the subtext was really about ways of legitimizing science and also about controlling it. Much of this had been forced by Powell and his persistent expansion of his survey.

The U.S. Geological Survey's budget had quadrupled since King's day, and Powell was making all sorts of agreements and alliances with state surveys and independent researchers. This worried many congressmen—even Abram Hewitt. They feared that Powell was building an empire within the government.

Alabama congressman Hilary Herbert, one of the members of the Allison Commission, had an entirely different idea. As far as Herbert was concerned, government's role when it came to science should be none at all. No federal dollars should be spent, no federal facilities constructed, and those that existed should be sold.

The son of a South Carolina planter, with one year of study at the University of Alabama and one year at the University of Virginia, Herbert had a low opinion of science, and after serving as a colonel in the Confederate Army, an even lower opinion of the federal government.

After the war, he had been a lawyer in Montgomery, Alabama, and was elected to Congress in 1877. Now he took up the banner of John Calhoun, who had fought against the Smithsonian, and Simon Cameron, who had "had enough of this thing called science." Herbert's goal was to use the Allison Commission to purge science from the federal government.

"I am radically democratic in my views," Herbert would explain to Marsh. "I believe in as little government as possible—that Government should keep hands off and allow the individual fair play. This is the doctrine I learned from Adam Smith & Mill & Buckle, from Jefferson, Benton and Calhoun."[4]

These were not idle words for Herbert. In 1878, he opposed a government guarantee on bond payments for the Texas and Pacific Railway, despite the strong support for the project by both his constituents and the Alabama legislature. He was prepared to be voted out of office, but saw his reelection as a vindication of his views. He was a tough opponent for anyone to have to face.[5]

The end of 1884 came, and still the Allison Commission labored on. On March 4, 1885, Grover Cleveland became the first Democrat in the White House since 1861. It was time to clean out Republican waste and find patronage posts for Democrats. It was also a time for faithful Southern Democrats, like Herbert, to call in their political markers. The Cleveland administration also took aim at the survey.

For Cope the Allison Commission was one more chance to make a run at Powell and Marsh. It was another opportunity, at least in his mind, to set things right. Unfortunately, his avatar would be Hilary Herbert.

"This winter there is to be a thorough ventiliation of the Geological Survey at Washington. Marsh will probably try to get the National Academy to boost the organization," Cope wrote to Osborn in October of 1885. "There is a good deal of Marshisms in other departments . . . as I am told. In any case such an opportunity of placing Marsh in his true position will not soon occur again."[6]

Cope's major goal was to discredit Powell and Marsh, and he began this campaign by trying to gather dirt. During the commission hearings, Endlich, apparently at Cope's urging, wrote to several of the former Hayden men still on the survey. The letter to one of them, Henry Gannett, asked:

> *I presume you are aware of the fact that the Powell Survey is going to the wall. I have been called upon for certain information which I cannot now get without calling on my friends. I want to know all about the deadheads on the survey, favoritism, misapplication of funds, waste of money &c. If you are in the position to give me information, I shall be very much obliged, and will remember it in the sweet by and by. Your name will not appear in any way, and I will ask you to keep this letter quiet.*[7]

But Gannett and the others all turned their letters over to Powell. Cope also tried to raise money to pay off Baur's debts to Marsh, so Baur would be free to testify before the commission. But cash poor himself, Cope could not find the few hundred dollars Baur needed.

Cope also tried to enlist Hayden in the campaign. But Hayden, who was in steadily failing health, declined. In a letter to Leidy, Hayden said he even tried without success to defuse Cope. Enough was enough. Cope's passion, however, knew no moderation, and soon a twenty-three-hundred-word document viciously attacking the survey was floating around Capitol Hill. Herbert picked up the ammunition.

Powell and the survey would have been targets of the inquiry under any circumstances given the agency's high level of activity. Besides, Powell's numerous political enemies in the western development camp were always looking for a way to take the major down a peg or two. But Cope made doubly sure the survey was a target, and what's more, he made certain that paleontology and the publication of major studies would also be issues.

Cope's principal aim was to ensure that Marsh was not forgotten. In fact, he had been lobbying against him even in the days before the commission convened. "I wrote Prof. Baird," Cope told his wife, "that a man who employs others to [do] his work for him, only needs money enough to fill or control all the positions in the country. The fact is Marsh cannot and will not live in Washington and does practically no work, and why they give him the preference I do not see, for they admit his selfishness and his bad qualities."[8]

It was a remarkably self-destructive performance, because Cope was still trying to get the last two volumes of his Hayden work published by Powell. But this was the unyielding, almost–rabid Cope that had proven so distasteful to the polite scientific societies in Philadelphia. This was, as Leidy had once called him "the unnecessarily offensive" Cope.

Back in Philadelphia, Cope had once again been rebuffed in an attempt to win a paying position. This time he was passed over for an appointment at the Wagner Free Institute—one of the city's scientific museums and schools. What was even more galling was the selection of Professors Heilprin and Leffmann to the posts.

"Both as you know are Jews," Cope wrote to Leidy, who was a trustee of the institute. "In the next place Leffmann has no scientific standing whatever," Cope said, while Heilprin, was he charged, "scientifically on trial."

"It is remarkable too that Americans & Philadelphians of good standing and ability could not have been found for the positions," he said. "I myself was an applicant."[9]

He complained to Hayden, who wrote to Leidy. "Can you find a place for Cope in Wagner . . . ," Hayden asked. "Will he work in double harness?"[10]

A week later, Cope was still fuming. "The association of your name with two Jews of . . . unsavory scientific antecedents is not a good thing," he told Leidy. Leidy's reply was that both men had been affiliated with the institute, had done good jobs, and were deserving of the one-year appointments. But he added, "should they not prove efficient or otherwise wanting," the trustees might consider other candidates "for the future."

Cope was hired by the Geological Survey of Canada, which sent him fossils for analysis. The work was intermittent, and the fees were modest. There was no fieldwork, although he did travel to Ottawa and Montreal and was able to report home that "Canadians all wear fur caps" and that "in Montreal the girls and women are rather better looking than in Ottawa."[11]

Cope's real focus, however, remained south of the Canadian border, where it turned out that he was not the only prominent scientist taking aim at Powell's survey and raising questions about government-funded science. Alexander Agassiz also emerged as a valuable ally in Herbert's holy war and a comfort for Cope. The Harvard professor, however, was motivated not by personality but rather by ideology.

Agassiz believed that decentralized, private science was more powerful and more appropriate than centralized, government science. The robust and powerful German scientific community was scattered among its regional states, Agassiz pointed out, while the weaker French science was controlled by the government. "It would be a great disaster if Washington should ever become the Paris of the United States," Agassiz warned.

There were some areas where government action was acceptable, he conceded, but government ought not to do whatever can be done by private interests. "I do not see why men of science should ask more than any other branches of knowledge, literature, fine arts &c," Agassiz said.[12]

This "laissez-faire" approach to science was right in the spirit of the times, and it was a powerful argument that Herbert promptly adopted. The fact that Agassiz was independently wealthy and the curator of Harvard's Museum of Comparative Zoology, one of the prime competitors of the Smithsonian, was lost on the Alabamian—but not on Powell.

Herbert, Agassiz, and Cope whipped up a good deal of mischief by the fall of 1885. "There is a daily flood of paragraphs . . . showing a systematic attempt on the part of some newspapermen to write [all the scientific bureaus] down," Newcomb wrote to Marsh that September. "So far I think our best policy is silence at least until we see a chance to kill somebody," the astronomer roguishly advised.[13]

In the same letter, Newcomb included a September newspaper article that had run in the *New York Times* and the *Boston Advertiser,* reporting on a federal audit of the U.S. Geological Survey. "It is claimed," the dispatch reported, "that large collections of fossils have been made by various branches of the geological survey, which instead of being deposited in the national museum as the law directs have been diverted to the museums of private parties notably those of Prof. Marsh of Yale College and Professor Cope of Philadelphia. The report said that the costs direct and indirect to the government for making these collections to have been fifty thousand dollars for those been held by Professor Marsh and one hundred thousand dollars for those retained by Professor Cope. These were kept in the first instance, under the plea that it was for the purpose of legitimate study preparatory to making reports but the work is now done."

In late 1885, Herbert and Agassiz had an exchange of letters that became part of the commission records. In a November letter, Herbert outlined a series of four different studies on Nevada's Comstock Lode done by surveys dating back to the first King party. He also raised the question of the value to the nation of the many paleontology studies published by surveys.

"To me," Herbert wrote, "it is very clear Major Powell is transcending the rule you lay down that the Government ought not to do scientific work which can properly be accomplished by individual effort."[14]

Agassiz obligingly replied, "Private individuals have learned nothing from the works you refer to . . . [and] are all such that they fall within the limits of individual investigation. . . ."

"As regards paleontology," Agassiz went on, "that is just one of the things which private individuals and learned societies can do just as well as Government. They will do it cheaper. There are always in different universities plenty of people who will be too thankful to do such work for the sake of doing it, and who will get the gist of their results published by scientific societies to which they belong."[15]

After getting a peek at Agassiz's letter before it was public, Newcomb wrote to Marsh, "Herbert wants to lop off everything he can, and that seems to be all he cares to do." But he held out some hope, believing that "the rest of the commission favors science."[16]

That was the hope of the science community, as the National Academy of Sciences was also campaigning for a new Naval Observatory. The scientists reported to Congress that the dome of the current building was "warped," the heating was failing, the equipment old, and the building falling apart.[17]

It is clear from the volume of return letters he received that Marsh was worried and was writing about affairs in Washington to many of his friends and allies. But the general counsel he received was to sit tight and let Powell handle things. Marsh's own words or presence would only inflame the situation.

Powell was not cowed by Herbert or Agassiz, and as the loyalty of his Hayden men showed, he had Cope well in check. Between December of 1884 and June of 1886, the major testified before the Allison Commission seven times, making him its star witness. He also submitted a long, detailed, written statement and a follow-up letter. Powell, in a word, thrived on the challenge.

Once more he would articulate a bold and sweeping vision of what science was and what it should be for the nation. Taking up the theme that the academy had sounded, Powell told the commission that science was not just an exercise in knowledge, but also an exercise in the public interest. America needed science to prosper. It was too vital to be left to just the private sector.

Herbert did draw some political blood. Yes, Powell had to concede no maps had yet been produced by the survey and that the cost per map was more than anticipated. Yes, at least one of the Comstock Lode studies probably did not need to be done. Yes, Powell had made agreements with state surveys and private researchers beyond the bounds of his survey's legal mandate—but in doing so, he had saved the federal government money. Marsh's relationship with the survey and his four-thousand-dollar annual stipend was also defended. Marsh was simply a full-time government employee, because he received no salary from Yale. (Marsh actually used that money to fund other work at the Peabody.)

Powell's records showed that he certainly spent money. But they also showed that he did not steal it. The dollars were accounted for, and while Herbert could disagree on whether the U.S. Geological Survey maps had to be so detailed, the money really was used for maps.

Powell's survey was politically impregnable, but the political process, and the Cleveland administration, needed a scapegoat. So the heat swung from the U.S. Geological Survey to the U.S. Coast and Geodetic Survey and its aging director, J. E. Hilgard. Charges were made, and Hilgard was forced to step down. "I am afraid we shall not see a scientific man in the post again," Newcomb predicted. Cleveland proved Newcomb a prophet, appointing as the survey's new director F. M. Thorn, a political crony from the president's hometown of Buffalo. Thorn had headed the investigation that ousted Hilgard.

Powell, however, was no such easy mark. In his own testimony to the Allison Commission, he went right after Agassiz and laissez-faire science. He pointed out that the Harvard professor had accumulated "a great fortune," which he was now using to "make the museum over which he presides the American center for scientific research." But Powell went on, "a hundred millionaires could not do the work in scientific research now done by the General Government." Besides, should the "scientific research and progress of American civilization wait until the contagion of [Agassiz's] example inspired a hundred millionaires to engage in like good works?"

No. Even rich scientists, like Marsh and Cope, had needed at least a little government support to elevate and speed their work. Without the surveys and the government printing office, American paleontology might still be a backwater instead of a leader.

But Powell also made it clear that government science was a public good for the use of all the people. Science paid for with federal dollars "should be given back to the people at large through the agencies of the public libraries which they have established. To turn over all this material to private societies and museums for publication would be to defraud the people of that for which the money was expended."[18]

Cope had made the collections an issue, and now Powell had no choice but to affirm that what the government paid for, the government should get. Cope had created a little beast that would bedevil both him and Marsh in the years to come.

Herbert was first to issue a bill with his proposed reforms. The aim was to sharply restrict the role of the geological survey to mapping and limit its publications to a single annual report. "The Geological Survey shall not . . . expend any money for paleontological work," the legislation stated.

In his accompanying report, Herbert said that it was clear that the survey's research and publications plan "promises to be very expensive and we think ought to be curtailed. . . . In the Act of 1879 [creating the survey], to wit, it is also true Congress did not then expect such a lavish expenditure as has followed." Herbert went so far as to actually name Marsh and use his work as an example of what the survey ought not to be doing.

This issue of printing expenditures became the last battleground of the fight. Agassiz had told Herbert that the "methods of publication adopted by the various bureaus, the size of the editions, were extravagant and wasteful." Was he thinking of Cope's Bible and Marsh's Dinocerata?

These works troubled even supporters like Hewitt. "I never contemplated the establishment of a scientific publication department for original works," Hewitt wrote Marsh. "It seems to me the attempt has been too ambitious, and like pride has o'er lept itself."[19]

With suicidal fervor, Cope jumped on the issue. "Agassiz's letter has had a very great influence with the Commission," Arnold Hague, one of Powell's top aides wrote to Marsh in May of 1886. "Cope has followed it up closely having had interviews with several members of the Commission. He states that he is ready to publish material at his own expense and at the expense of societies, thus relieving the Government of the cost. This of course is a direct blow at you."[20]

Cope's assertions were like a self-inflicted wound, for at that very moment, he was still hoping that the cost of printing his remaining Hayden Survey manuscripts would be borne by either the geological survey or an independent congressional appropriation. What was Cope thinking? Meanwhile, Marsh was fearful that the Allison inquiry had turned into a campaign to get him.

"I do not think there is any reason to be anxious," Newcomb tried to assure Marsh. "Last Monday evening Powell and I had quite a talk with Mr. Herbert. He was perfectly frank and courteous in expressing his decided opinion that the Geological Survey has gained influence by employing professors in various parts of the country and that it ought to confine itself to the function of making maps. I am sure your are mistaken in supposing there is anything personal in his opposition."[21]

A few days later, Hague sent Marsh an update saying that Powell was "pretty well pleased" with that morning's appearance before the Allison Commission.[22] Hague also included a clipping from the *Washington Capital,* which said:

> I am informed that the raid of Senator Morgan and Congressman Herbert upon the Geological Survey grows out of the feud between Prof. Marsh of Yale College, and Prof. Cope, the two eminent paleontologists. Major Powell, the director of the survey, has placed Prof. Marsh in charge of that branch of the investigation of the bureau, instead of Prof. Cope. . . . Both are able men but are not satisfied with the work of each other and have not been for years. . . . At the Cosmos Club, where the scientific men of Washington make their rendezvous, the details of the squabble are well understood and are the topic of constant discussion.
>
> There is only one voice concerning the report that Congressman Herbert has made, and only one opinion as to its authorship. They all say that no one but Cope could have written it; that it bears his imprint in every line.

Cope!
Standing on the House floor, Herbert charged that the academy had ceased to be a scholarly body and turned into "one of the active political

forces of the country." Marsh could stand it no more. In early July, he wrote to Herbert saying that while he did not believe the congressman wished to do an injustice to himself or the academy, he had "unintentionally done both."

The academy, Marsh maintained, had never become involved in an issue without the request of the government. "Individual members may have done so, but not the Academy or its officers."

Marsh went on to defend his role in the U.S. Geological Survey. His affiliation with Yale actually saved the government rent, and he himself had been devoted to his survey duties. "I have never received a single dollar as salary for twenty years' service in Yale College," Marsh said.

As to the charge of extravagance, Marsh stressed that he himself had paid for the illustrations in his *Birds with Teeth* monograph, "and cost the government nothing."[23]

When the majority report of the commission was issued—two years after it was originally ordered—it spared the U.S. Geological Survey any significant cuts or changes. It did call for a tightening of the survey's appropriation and disbursement procedures and suggested splitting off publications into a separate and more easily monitored budget.

The rest of the government bureaus also weathered the storm, but the commission saw no need for a Department of Science. Still, it was, in its way, a great victory for government science. By endorsing the status quo, the commission was favoring the slow and steady growth of federally funded science over Herbert's Luddite beliefs or Agassiz's laissez-faire approach.

Marsh had also come through without damage. His position as chief paleontologist, his budget, and his collections were all intact. Perhaps he felt that by associating himself with Powell, he had opened himself up to this attack. Perhaps Powell felt the same way about Marsh. But the relationship continued.

"You and the Geological Survey have been so completely victorious in the late fight that I hope you are now very happy over the matter," Newcomb wrote Marsh in July. But the issues raised in the battle had really not been settled, and the last had not yet been heard from Cope or the Honorable Hilary Herbert.

In that same letter, Newcomb said he wanted to enlist Marsh's help in another "little measure of reform" at the academy. He wrote, "You remember that last spring, on a motion of Professor Baird, Colonel Gilder was invited to entertain the Academy with an account of his proposed plan for reaching the North Pole. You may have seen in yesterday's papers that Gilder has been arrested in New York on charges of embezzling a $1,000 bond, the accuser being a woman supposed to be 'his girl.' Comment is superfluous. If Baird has any more suggestions to make about inviting people I shall want to know more about them."[24]

That line between science and scam was still, after all these years, still perilously thin.

Chapter Eighteen

 IN THOSE WARM, TORPID DAYS OF JULY 1886, as Washington was preparing to close down for the summer, and congressmen and senators were planning to flee to the seashore, mountains, or even their hometowns, it seemed that Cope, too, was nearing his own legislative success. His bill for an appropriation to publish the last volumes of his Hayden work had slowly and painfully worked its way toward a vote in Congress.

It had been a time-consuming and humbling exercise. First, Cope had sought the support of the new secretary of the interior, Quintus Lamar. A Mississippian and son of the South, like Hilary Herbert, Lamar was not particularly interested in science. But the South was faithfully Democratic, and the Cleveland administration paid obeisance.

Lamar suggested Cope write to Powell. How could Cope explain that Powell was his problem, that Powell and Marsh had been "squelching" his writings for more than two years? Cope dutifully wrote a letter. There was no prompt reply.

This should not have been a surprise. Cope had gone as far as writing an editorial in the *Naturalist* vilifying Powell and charging that "a verbal promise made to Dr. Hayden and Professor Cope by Maj. Powell . . . was not fulfilled."[1]

Cope went back to Lamar, or at least he tried to. "I went 5th day to the office of the Sec. of the Interior & waited 2 hours without seeing him. Next day I waited an hour and then he left the Department. . . . Seventh day (yesterday) I waited an hour, and then Gen. Warner came along & saw the Secretary himself on my acct. He made an engagement for me to go tomorrow, and tomorrow I go, with considerable hope of seeing him," Cope wrote to Annie in early June.[2]

But the next day, despite the intercession of Warner—an Ohio congressman—Cope spent five and a half hours in Lamar's outer office. "I was not idle all the time. I read some proofs & had a book to read; never the less I am a good deal disgusted." Still, Cope vowed to Annie, "I go again tomorrow and soon."

Cope was trying to muster support wherever he could find it. "I got a courageous letter from Dr. Williston for ten years in Marsh's employ. This will do great execution if it become necessary to use it. It shows M.'s modus operandi perfectly." But Hayden, now in deeply declining health, wanted no part of this fight. "I had a most cowardly letter from Hayden, who is in a pitiable state between Powell & my work, which is his work as well," Cope told Annie.

Three days later, Cope finally got in to see Secretary Lamar. "It only resulted in his dictating a letter to Prof. Baird asking for information & opinion about my work. The Sec. looked as if he was at a funeral . . . ," Cope wrote to Julia. "He doesn't want to see me at all, but I have so many recommendations that he had to."[3]

Lamar, who knew little and cared less about such esoteric matters as Pliocene fossils, simply tended to rely on those in positions of authority like Powell and Baird. "A great deal depends here on official position," Cope observed. "It regulates everything, especially society." And Cope had no position, none at all.

The day Cope met with Lamar, June 9, was also Julia's birthday. "Today thee is twenty years old. Thee is not so old but that thee can still call me Papa . . . ," Cope wrote to her. "It doesn't seem so long thee was one day old, but a good while since I was 20! . . . It has always been a great pleasure to me that thee is industrious and does thy best at whatever thee undertakes. As long as thee does thy will always have the sympathy of thy Papa, as thee does his love anyhow."

Even without the administration's support, Cope headed for Capitol Hill, where he had a difficult time in the House. The chairman of the Appropriations Committee, Representative J. S. Randall of Pennsylvania, was utterly unsympathetic.

But Fred Endlich had come east, from the Silver Lake mines, to help Cope lobby. Together, they were able to add the appropriation—Cope figured he needed about thirty-eight hundred dollars for printing and expenses—to the Sundry and Civil Appropriations Bill in the Senate. "This is the best news yet," Cope reported on June 16.

That same month, Cope was editing the final manuscript for his new work on evolution, a series of essays titled *Origin of the Fittest*. On the title page, he would be identified as "E. D. Cope, Ph.D., University of Heidelberg." It was an honorary degree conferred on Cope a few months earlier. It was his greatest academic recognition and one of which he was duly proud.

The lobbying went well, and things looked promising. "So far as words go, my appropriation is secured! But I do not allow myself to be sanguine about it or expect anything until I actually see it done. It is a great job for a whole corps of men to get an appropriation through Congress and for *one man* to succeed will be rather remarkable," Cope wrote home at the end of June.[4]

In July, Annie and Julia went to the coastal village of West Falmouth, Massachusetts. Cope's efforts were approaching their end. "The further it gets, the more likely it is to get through," Cope believed, and he hoped "Congressmen anxious to get through for the summer . . . may not feel disposed to object."[5]

Jacob Wortman was also in Washington, and one day, he and Cope spent an afternoon in the country. "We explored some great woods & got some 'sallys' [salamanders] . . . ," Cope told Julia. "I obtained three lots eggs & brought them home." At his boardinghouse, Cope fixed sets of eggs with chemicals on successive days so he could study the development of the salamander embryos, thus turning his lodgings into his laboratory.

The days passed slowly, and Cope was simultaneously impatient and listless. "I have had a grand fight with a bad tooth, which ached fiercely" he reported to Julia. "I bathed it in carbolic acid and it is now quiet. I am getting of tired of staying here, and want to get up to West Falmouth. I am so tired of it that I can scarcely do any work."[6]

On July 27, it was all over. *"My bill was thrown out* on a technicality, no doubt in the interest of Powell," Cope wrote to his wife. "This means a great deal for us. First, I will have to be here again next winter. Second, we will have to live very cheaply for a year. I will have to figure up what I will have *exactly,* so that I cannot say about going to Berkshire, or as to Julia's future at Bryn Mawr."

Cope left Washington to join his family on the New England coast, but along the way, he stopped in New Haven to spend a day with Williston and Baur. The very day he was in town, Baur's wife gave birth to a girl.

Within two weeks of his defeat, Cope was planning his new Washington campaign. "Next winter I intend to try again," he told Osborn. "It will however, require all the aid I can muster from all quarters to preserve myself from the attacks of Powell, Marsh and some of their adherents. I met all sorts of statements circulated by them among congressmen." One argument, Cope heard, was that "the Government should publish nothing from specimens that do not belong to them." Cope's demon was loose on Capitol Hill. Of course, he pointed out that, there was "not a volume of Marsh's past or to come, that is not based on his own materials."[7]

At the end of August, Cope and Marsh crossed paths—almost—at the American Association for the Advancement of Science meeting held in President Cleveland's hometown of Buffalo. They certainly saw one another from afar, but they did not speak. "Prof. Marsh rolls around, and a large representation from Washington is here," Cope sniffed in a letter to Annie, who was now with family in the Berkshire foothills of Copake, New York. He also reported that "the scientific girls are out rather strong." Miss Abbot, a botanist whom he had met collecting plants at Yellowstone, read two papers. And two other women—Miss Hitchcock and Miss Martin— each read one.[8]

In the fall, Cope was invited to be the main speaker at the University of Kansas dedication of the new Snow Natural History Museum. Cope spoke for an hour and a half and thought it went off quite well. It was the kind of honor and accolade that he longed for, but so rarely received.

It was to be one of his last pleasant moments, for as the year wound to a close, everything that had been slowly crumbling, now completely and totally collapsed.

❧

Cope returned to Washington in late November to "dance attendance on Sec. Lamar and S. J. Randall." He also inquired of Baird about filling a recent opening at the Smithsonian, but Baird quickly told him that the vacancy no longer existed.

Cope once again made the rounds and even sought the help of W. S. McGee, "Powell's right hand man." Lamar had asked Cope to get an official estimate of the printing project. "McGee is very friendly and diplomatic," he told Annie. "How much is one and how much the other I do not know."[9] But really, what could Cope possibly expect at the hands of Powell and his minion? Still, Cope drafted his bill and had it filed again.

By now the dream of wealth from silver mines had completely evaporated, and in early December, he arranged to sell all but a few shares of his stock. Cope was in Philadelphia when he made the arrangements, but waited until he was in New York City to tell Annie the bad news.

He wrote her a letter on stationery filched from the Smithsonian. "After I left thee I went to the Grande office & had a talk with one of the trustees," he wrote. "I found that certain things had occurred in connection with the company which will put them into tedious litigation for a long time which will use up any profits that will be made out of the ore. I concluded that the stock would probably become worthless or nearly for a time at least. More over I have not the money to pay the assessment."[10]

Cope recovered a pittance, enough to scrape through the winter, until his congressional appropriation or one of his other stratagems succeeded. If it was any consolation, the brilliant Clarence King had fared no better than Cope.

The Grand Central Mining Company had been incorporated with King as managing director, $5 million in stock, and an initial development budget of $750,000. That was more than seven times as much as King had been given for the U.S. Geological Survey.

But the money was quickly eaten up by technical problems and labor disputes at the Prietas, Yedras, and Sombrete mines. King went out and got more money from John Astor II, the tobacco magnate Pierre Lorillard, and Frederick Billings, former president of the Northern Pacific Railway. Additional stock was sold in Europe in a venture called the Anglo-Mexican Mining Company.

But when Agassiz went to the Anglo-Mexican shareholders meeting in London, he found the operation in total chaos. "The more I see the Yedras business," Agassiz wrote Higginson, "the less . . . I understand the total absence of common sense [in] King." In 1877, Agassiz forced King out of his directorship. It was the beginning of a long and bizarre descent for "the most brilliant man of his generation" that would end in both mental and financial collapse.

King's tale of woe probably offered no solace for Cope. He had, after all, more than enough of his own worries. The reason Cope was in New York was to seek out a new publishing house for the *Naturalist,* its former publisher having gone bankrupt—owing Cope four hundred dollars. When things turned bad, they turned horribly bad. For a while, Cope even considered abandoning the review. "He has done more foolish things than that," Hayden wrote to Leidy. "I have written him to hang on—His personal power is nothing, but as long as he [owns] such a journal he will be something of a power."[11]

The problem in finding a new publisher was that the magazine never actually made money. In the past, Cope could offer guarantees to make up the difference between costs and revenues. He was, however, no longer in a position to provide such subsidies. If he could find a sympathetic publisher willing to take on the magazine, he would have to beg his friends and allies to ante up the surety money.

So now came a time of great hardship. The Copes moved into a modest little cottage, once servants' quarters, which sat behind their grand townhouse. They had scraped together enough for another year at Bryn Mawr for Julia. But they could not see what would happen after that.

The nineteenth-century Quaker marriage vows did not ask a man and woman to take one another for "richer or poorer." Edward and Annie simply promised be "loving and faithful . . . until it shall please the Lord by death to separate us."[12] Still, how must Annie have felt? If she maintained that Quaker common sense for which Cope had married her twenty-two years before, she could not help but be dismayed. Such a very large fortune, and now it was all gone. It was probably just such a result that Alfred Cope had tried to thwart by keeping his son on the farm. But it is hard to bend the destiny of someone as strong willed, as "mule headed," to borrow Hayden's description, as Cope.

It is difficult to penetrate the inner life of a marriage, even when there is much said. In the case of Edward and Annie, all we know is that from this time on there is more business and less affection in the letters that remain. Perhaps it is a hint of how things were.

Then again, when one is living hand to mouth, business becomes a good deal more important. "Mamma says thee is bankrupt & so I write thee a brief letter with pay," Cope says to Julia in one letter. "Return to me the check for I am informed my back account is over drawn," he writes to Annie in another. "I am afraid thee is short of money and I am trying to raise some. I am trying to sell the casts [of fossils] Jacob is making but have not yet succeeded."

Once again, Cope pondered selling his fossils. The problem was that most of the material was still in crates, waiting to be cleaned and identified. Cope wasn't even certain precisely what he had to offer, although surely it was of great value. "As to selling my collection for what it will bring," he told Annie, "I cannot do that with propriety until I can show what it is, and I cannot do without the assistance of Jacob and possibly of thee and Julia to mend and label and exhibit somewhere. My entire future in a financial sense, which means thine and Julia's so long as she is single, depends on that collection so far as I can see now. If anyone will make me an offer for that collection I will consider it."[13]

By the following March, Cope had once again gotten his appropriations bill through the Senate, only to see Representative Randall kill it in the House Appropriations Committee. There would be no relief for 1887.

Cope continued to pursue his attempts to secure a position in Washington, but he concluded there was little chance. "Prof. Baird is afraid of me I suspect & will give me nothing regular yet for awhile. It did not use to be so, but now J. W. Powell is in power here & O. C. Marsh, he thinks he must keep in with them. He has little backbone in some aspects," Cope said.[14]

It had to be totally galling for Cope when later that year, Baird made Marsh the Smithsonian's chief paleontologist. At least, it was only an honorary title and came with neither salary nor resources. Cope simply could not see that his repeated attacks on Powell—a friend of Baird's—and his liaison with Hilary Herbert had turned him into something of a pariah among scientists in the capital.

Back in Philadelphia, Cope spent long hours amid the clutter of 2102 Pine Street, even sleeping there on a narrow cot many nights. This had become his last refuge. The first floor, behind the heavy wooden, arched front door, looked like nothing so much as a warehouse. The windows were shuttered, and the front parlor, the dining room behind, even the kitchen at the back of the house were piled with crates, boxes, and cases. The basement was packed with bottles and jars of alcohol holding specimens of modern animals.

A mounted caribou stood in the front parlor, and scattered through the house, one could find the femur of the giant *Camarasaurus supremus,* pulled from the Colorado Rockies, the nasty talons of the carnivorous *Dryptrosaurus* of the Kansas plains, and the skull of the Montana horned *Monoclonius.* A fine layer of dust covered everything.[15]

The stairway led to a narrow second-floor hall connecting two front and back rooms. The front room was lined with shelves of paper boxes holding the smaller and more delicate specimens of Cope's Argentinean and Texas collections.

In the back room, away from the sharp strike of iron hooves on cobblestones and the shouts of liverymen and teamsters, was Cope's study. Still, Cope was moved to complain to city officials about the noise of livestock being driven through the street. His protest was answered by Philadelphia Mayor Edwin Stuart, who explained apologetically that "city ordinances do not absolutely prohibit the driving of cattle, sheep, swine, etc. through the streets in the busiest sections of the city."[16]

A huge, square desk in the middle of the room dominated the study. It was heaped with papers, a stuffed lynx, a human skull, and assorted fossil bones. Sitting in a cane-backed, swivel desk chair, Cope wrote away, still generating a steady stream of papers on paleontology, herpetology, and ichthyology.

A visitor entering the room when Cope was hard at work might be told to take the chair opposite the desk, only to find it was "piled high" with books and periodicals.

Despite his financial and political woes, Cope wrote thirty-five scientific papers in 1886, fifteen the following year, and sixteen the year after that. They included reports on subjects as varied as dinosaur breastbones, copperhead snakes, a new sabertooth tiger fossil from the Loup Fork beds, the evolution of teeth in rodents, and a comparison of the pug dog and the Chihuahua dog.[17]

Just to the left of the desk was small table with a vivarium, a Gila monster circling its glass walls. Cope liked to feed it raw eggs and scratch its head. By the window sat "a fernery," home to tree frogs and salamanders. Every chair was heaped with books and papers. There were stacks on the floor and bookcases as well. A large tortoise crawled across this obstacle course. The desk drawers held the twine and scrap paper Cope carefully collected as an exercise in economy.

But the desk's lower right-hand drawer held something far more precious than bits of paper and string. "Here is my accumulated store of Marshiana," he one day told Osborn. Here were all the letters, the notes, the papers he had gathered on his lifelong enemy. "In these papers," he announced, "I have a full record of Marsh's errors from the very beginning, which at some future time I may be tempted to publish."

Up on the third floor, Cope's one remaining, loyal employee, Jacob Geismar, lived and worked. All in all, 2102 Pine Street was a marked contrast to Marsh's mansion on the hill.

Still, Cope was indefatigable. Scott and Osborn would drop by, and the little band would go out to dine at one of the "odd, half-Bohemian restaurants" Cope had taken to frequenting. Here for twenty-five cents, they would get a slice of roast beef, mince pie, and coffee. The conversations would be lively and peppered with amusing anecdotes as Cope entertained the young scientists, much as he had done with Sternberg at Sunday dinner in Haddonfield a decade earlier.

When the meal was done, "Cope would bring out his venerable cigar case," Osborn recalled, "from which he would extract a half-burned cigar. This was smoked following our coffee, then replaced in the cigar case for future reference."[18] While raised an abstemious Quaker, Cope now indulged in both cigars and wines—but only to aid digestion.

Somehow, the Copes struggled along. Annie and Julia went to West Falmouth in July. Just a few miles away, in Woods Hole, Spencer Baird was on his deathbed. The sixty-four-year-old Baird had been failing for some time, and his doctors had ordered complete rest, but he never rallied and died that summer on Cape Cod.

"The death of Prof. Baird has given me sorrow. The Pioneers are dropping off," Hayden wrote to Leidy in August. "Mrs. Hayden is . . . anxious that your turn may come." Leidy would endure, but before year's end, Hayden himself would be gone.[19]

On November 6, 1887, Hayden died at his home in Philadelphia. His death notice appeared in the same issue of the Naturalist as that of Oscar Harger. "His removal from the position which he had won through so many years of toil," the notice contended, "was influential in bringing on the disease to which he succumbed." But in reality, neither Powell nor Marsh could be blamed for Hayden's demise from the advanced degeneration caused by syphilis.

The National Museum and Smithsonian now passed to G. Brown Goode and James Langley, younger men for whom Cope and Marsh and their feud were mostly legendary artifacts. In the fall, Julia returned to Bryn Mawr, although something as basic as the question of her new winter coat became the subject of family correspondence.

Toward the end of the year, Cope made a short, sad journey to visit one of his closest relatives, Mary Cope. He had been so fond of Mary that years later Osborn would suspect that she had been the love interest that had prompted young Cope's European trip. (Julia would insist that wasn't so.)

"Yesterday, I went to see Cousin Mary," Cope wrote to Julia. "I found the family all in her room expecting her death. . . . Of all my relatives, except my own family, I have loved Mary Cope the best. . . . I can only say how very glad I was that I went, how sweet her talk was and how happy she is. She cannot live long, indeed her death may come at any time. . . . It would be nice if thee could see her."[20]

Increasingly Cope confided in Julia. Now, father and daughter were in discussions over Parker's *Zoology* and Haeckel's monograph on the Medusae. Sometimes Cope would write his letters in French or German— an extra exercise for Julia, an extra bond between them. "I haven't heard how thee got on with the osteological examination!" Cope mentions in a chatty letter written to "a young lady at Bryn Mawr," and offers, "If thee wants a quiz before it comes off, I can give thee one!"[21]

Cope pushed, urged, cajoled, and cheered his daughter through the most demanding of studies—analytical chemistry, physics, foreign languages— and yet despite his admiration and belief that she could master these subjects, he remained an unreconstructed male chauvinist and opponent of women's rights.

In an article in *Popular Science Monthly,* titled "The Relation of Sexes to Government," Cope argued, "Woman is not only restrained by her reproductive functions from taking the same active part in the world's life as does man; but what is more important she inherits a greater disability from the . . . countless generation's of man's animal ancestors. This nature is thoroughly ingrained, and is as permanent as any other part of her organism."

Men were more rational and could deal with more physically and mentally taxing situations. Mental strain in a woman leads to a hysterical temperament. Cope maintained these were simply facts and reasons women should not have the right to vote. Besides, there were also the political and social implications.

How would a woman vote? Either she would merely follow the lead of the dominant male in her household, making such a vote meaningless, or she would vote in opposition of her husband or father, causing "unpleasant consequences."

"No man would view with equanimity the spectacle of his wife or daughter nullifying his vote," Cope warned. The New York State Association Opposed to Woman Suffrage was so impressed by Cope's article that they republished it in pamphlet form.[22]

Studies, "scientific" studies, had already turned up evidence that women were physical and mentally inferior to men. They were less evolutionary advanced and simply lacked as highly developed faculties. For example, work pioneered by Philadelphia physician and scientist George Samuel Morton in the 1830s, and then advanced by French anatomist Paul Broca in the 1860s, clearly showed that women had smaller brains, and as everyone knew, brain size correlated with intelligence. But Harvard paleontologist and science historian Stephen Jay Gould actually re-created many of Morton's experiments, and in doing so, he revealed chronic errors and glaring omissions, which Gould attributes to social bias. (Morton, for example, never adjusted his measurements of skull cavities for size and weight, and since women are on average smaller than men, it stands to reason their skulls would be smaller.)

In reality, what was going on was finding "facts," just like Owen and Huxley did with bones, that would buttress a particular point of view, dressing up opinion and prejudice as science. "Conclusions came first and Broca's conclusions were the shared assumptions of most successful white males during his time—themselves on top by the good fortune of nature, and women, blacks and poor people below," Gould said.[23]

These attitudes and this sort of science would have equally pernicious impact on the debates over race and class and turn Cope's neo-Lamarckian evolution into a loathsome, evil exercise rather than a kinder and gentler substitute for the Darwinian struggle. It wasn't surprising that such a racist science would find a comfortable home inside Philadelphia's circle.

But Cope made no apologies and voiced his opposition even to Julia. "We have too many incapable voters now, to give suffrage to all women would be to increase the numbers very greatly," he wrote. ". . . If all women's privileges based on her sex were taken away, & she was reduced to the level of man in ordinary affairs, she would find the road a hard one to travel; too hard for her lesser powers. . . .

"As a recent English physician said, if they cannot be a Bacon or a Shakespeare themselves they have and may again produce a Bacon or a Shakespeare. Now I must close on the woman question. Write and tell me what is doing in Biology and Chemistry."[24]

⚜

Later that year, *Origin of the Fittest* reached the bookstores, adding fuel to the newest debate over evolution. By this time, there was little question—at least in the scientific community—that evolution was a fact. The likes of Louis Agassiz and Andreas Wagner were now gone—dead or simply defeated.

The new debate focused on the mechanisms and implications of evolution. Many scientists, like Cope or Germany's Haeckel, accepted the process but rejected Darwin's "natural selection" as the sole evolutionary force. They believed there was direction and progress in evolution.

In the nineteenth-century spirit of imperialism, it was an article of faith that some races were more fit and clearly superior. It was one idea that Darwin's theory did not shake. The age of the world might change, the process by which animals were created might be different, but the inherent and inherited superiority of some over others endured.

It was only logical that humans would be at the top of the evolutionary ladder, since humans drew up the ladder. And it was only logical that at the very top would be white Indo-European men, since they were the particular humans drawing up the scheme.

So convinced of their superiority were the white men of America and Europe that this attitude suffused their work, their politics, and their idle conversation. Consequently, it is not surprising that Powell would start his *Arid Region* study speaking of a "new phase of Aryan civilization" coming to pass in the American West or that Alexander Agassiz would remark to Marsh after visiting California, "I saw a lot of Japs . . . who came here as laborers, it was as good as seeing a bit of Japan."

It was a different era, with a different sense of what was politically correct. Theodore Roosevelt, one of the most progressive politicians of the time, could say he "would rather address a Methodist audience than any other. . . . The Methodists represent the great middle class. . . . The Catholic Church is in no way suited to this country."[25]

Even a crusader for women's rights like Elizabeth Cady Stanton would exhort women to seize the vote, pressing "through the constitutional door the moment it is open for Sambo."

Stanton may have felt women were ready to take an equal place along-side men, but when the men of the day turned to pondering evolution, it was clear to them who was really the fittest. That science would offer proofs seemed inevitable. In reality, they were seeking facts to simply affirm what they believed. Gould argues that this is neither surprising nor limited to the Gilded Age. Science "is a social-embedded activity," he maintains and is always a reflection of its times. So these were Cope's times—and Cope's society, his closed circle.[26]

The result was that evolution theory was adapted to explain and buttress a host of social, political, religious, and economic beliefs. The most imme-diate incarnation was "social Darwinism." At a time when disparities of wealth and power were multiplying with numbing speed, when the man-sions of robber barons were rising on New York's Fifth Avenue, while cold-water slums seethed on the city's eastside, and when local millers and butchers were being put out of business by the combination of railroads, Pillsbury's grain rollers, and Swift's refrigeration cars, social Darwinism assured the populace that this was not only the way of the world but in fact all for the best. Those who could not keep up with "progress" must be allowed to fall by the wayside.

"Fostering the good for nothing at the expense of the good is an extreme cruelty," warned Herbert Spencer, the English social theorist and foremost promoter of social Darwinism. It was Spencer, not Darwin, who first coined the phrase *survival of the fittest*.

America's most articulate proponent of the new hardheartedness was Marsh's Yale colleague William Graham Sumner, the nation's first professor of sociology. Sumner's essay, "What do the rich owe the poor?" had a sim-ple answer: "Nothing." Life was an endless struggle among unequals, according to Sumner, and "hard work and self denial" were the only tools that could advance "the welfare of man on Earth."

It is not surprising that the great capitalists of the day rushed to embrace this view. "I remember that light came in as in a flood and all was clear," Andrew Carnegie wrote of his first reading of Spencer. "Not only had I got rid of theology and the supernatural, but I had found the truth of evolution."

And John D. Rockefeller was to argue, "The American Beauty rose can be produced in its splendor and fragrance only by sacrificing the early buds which grow up around it. This is not an evil tendency in business. It is merely the working-out of a law of nature and a law of God."

But what Cope and the neo-Lamarckians brought to the debate was ultimately something meaner and more vicious, although they certainly didn't see it that way. If life was a chain of evolution, moving in a particular direction, with mammals the highest expression of animal life, and man the highest expression of mammals, then there had to be intermediate stages between man and animal. For Cope, these were represented by lesser human species, such as the Negro.

These transitional aspects could be traced in the jaws and limbs of blacks—so much more apelike than those of Aryans. "We all admit the existence of lower and higher races, the latter being those which we now find to present greater or lesser approximation to the apes," Cope wrote in an article for *Lippincott's Magazine.* "The peculiar structural characters that belong to the negro in his most typical form are the kind, however great may be the distance of his remove there from. The flattening of the nose. The prolongation of the jaws constitute such a resemblance."[27]

In *Origin of the Fittest,* Cope went even further, arguing that looking at the physiognomy of the principal human subspecies, the Negro, the Mongolian, and the Indo-European "we can readily observe that in the first two named there is a predominance of the quadrumanous [apelike] features which are retarded in man."[28] Cope goes on to argue that "some of these features have a purely physical significance, but the majority of them are . . . intimately connected with development of the mind."[29]

Cope was certain that the Negro was "a species of the genus Homo as distinct in character from the Caucasian as we are accustomed to recognize today in other departments of the animal kingdom." And between the true Caucasian and the Negro were intermediates—the Mongol; the Slav; the lower white ethnic groups, such as the Irish, Jews, Italians. They were all arranged in progressive order, culminating in the Creator's most brilliant expression—the white, Anglo-Saxon, Protestant man. Wasn't it obvious?

What was surely obvious were the implications for society. These subspecies were primitive and limited. It would be as unreasonable to expect the Negro to excel like an advanced Caucasian as it would be to expect an ape to live in the trees like a chimpanzee. It simply was not in their nature. Their biology determined and limited their capacities.

Part of this was a variation of the old German recapitulation theory. These lower races exhibited childlike aspects of the early stages of human development, a stage out of which they never outgrew. This was, to some degree, Cope's argument for women also.

Doubtless, Cope would have been shocked to be considered a bigot and a villain for his views. This was after all just science. It is true that his scientific works are devoid of any race baiting or slurs. They were simply the facts, as Cope saw them. If the message was unpalatable, the messenger was not to be blame. Of course, Cope, himself, saw nothing wrong with the message.

A few years later, however, Cope would write "Two Perils of the Indo-European" for the magazine *Open Court*. Perhaps in an effort to appeal to a broader audience, this was a much more inflammatory piece. The Negro remained "mentally undeveloped," Cope warned, and his continued presence posed a threat. White society was faced with carrying "eight million of dead material." Material that had to be kept apart. Mixing the races was a recipe for disaster.

"The highest race of man cannot afford to lose or even compromise the advantages it has acquired by hundreds of centuries of toil and hardship, by mingling its blood with the lowest," Cope wrote. ". . . We cannot cloud or extinguish the fine nervous susceptibility, and mental force, which cultivation develops in the constitution of the Indo-European, by the flesh instinct, and dark mind of the African."[30]

Just look at the imagery. The white race had risen by hardship and toil, while blacks had wallowed in their dark thoughts and carnal instincts. This was not science. Whites were not only physically superior but also morally so. The solution was clear. Blacks ought to go back to Africa or be segregated. Similarly, the immigration of lower white groups—Jews, for instance—should also be limited. It was for the good of society. Cope was doing his best to keep the circle closed.

In 1893, Herbert Spencer wrote to both Cope and Marsh trying to run down a story that he had heard for use in an essay he was calling "The Inadequacy of Natural Selection." At question were reports that after a white woman had borne the child of a Negro, subsequent offspring, even when conceived with a white man, had "traces of black blood." This, Spencer heard, had been "repeatedly" observed. "I should like to be able to give something like scientific verification," he explained. If Cope or Marsh didn't know anything perhaps one or the other knew a scientist in the South who did.[31]

The understanding of heredity and environment was all very fuzzy despite Darwin's best efforts, and the fact that twenty-eight years earlier Gregor Mendel had published his groundbreaking—but largely ignored—studies on heredity. For example, Alexander Graham Bell wrote Cope querying under what conditions profoundly deaf people could be bred to create a "a deaf variety of the human race." Surely, it had to be possible, even though the majority of the children of the deaf had the ability to hear?[32]

As odious as were the implications of neo-Lamarckian progressivism, the Germans went even further. Haeckel, along with other German naturalists and philosophers, created *Darwinismus*—a movement closer to religion than science. The core belief was another variation of recapitulation theory—the development of the individual follows and illustrates the history of the race.[33]

But by refining the species or race, Haeckel explained, it could be elevated and perfected. In a few decades, this would translate to the idea of a "master race," and the Nazis would solemnly quote Haeckel's view that "politics is applied biology."

For the Germans, the struggle for survival came not only in the competition among species, but even among political organisms such as nations. This competition, of course, was called war.

Such armed conflict, Von Bernardi would argue in *Germany and the Next War,* was "not merely a necessary element in the life of a nation, but an indispensable factor of culture, in which a truly civilized nation finds the highest expression of strength and vitality." Here was the ultimate test in the struggle of the survival of the fittest. All this from Charles Darwin pondering the finches of the Galápagos Islands.

❖

In the early months of 1888, Cope, incredible as it may seem, returned to Washington for a third try at getting an appropriation to publish his Hayden studies. Lamar was gone. Cope was now dealing with William F. Vilas, the fourth interior secretary in nine years. But Powell was still at the survey, and Randall was still running the House Appropriations Committee.

In February, the first edition of the "new" *American Naturalist* appeared, with a new publisher and fresh backing from Osborn and other Cope supporters. "It looks very well, I think, and the papers better than heretofore," he told Julia.

The story in Washington, however, was the same. In his first eight days in the city, Cope tried three times to see Vilas, without success. He made the rounds on Capitol Hill. He also paid a visit at the House Ways and Means as a representative for the AAAS, lobbying to remove the duty on imported scientific books and apparatus. But it wasn't all hard work. No, once again, even the financially beleaguered Cope was ready to flirt with the ladies.

"I room with Dr. Spencer who thee may remember," Cope told his daughter. "He is a good deal of a society man, and I have done considerable visits with him. Some of the ladies are single & some married, and they are of a good style & kind, but not oppressed with intelligence. The southern girls, which some of these are, having few aspirations in that direction. The only two that were really well informed are from Cincinnati; one of them a relation of Probasco who gave the bronze fountain that so adorns that city. She is about thy size & only 16! but she is studying and really knows something. I was pleased with her unsophisticated ways, which please far more than artificial flirtations or assumed manners of the average society woman."[34]

As the days passed, Cope became increasingly frustrated and began to "feel like giving it up." Finally, three weeks after arriving in Washington, he got his interview with Vilas, who told Cope he knew nothing about the issue and had no time to deal with it. If Powell recommended it, however, he would give it serious attention. "I concluded that my chance of finishing the work for the Hayden Survey is very slim!" he told Julia.

Still, Cope went and had lunch with Powell, who was polite, but said he simply couldn't get Vilas interested. The major, however, proposed publishing some of the work under the new survey provided Cope gave a set of fossils to the National Museum. "This will be a good beginning," Cope wrote to Julia, "& he proposes to pay a salary. I feel much relieved. This will not, however, commence until July. Between now & then I am 'short.' "[35]

It was a difficult spring. Cope didn't think he would be able to manage to send Annie and Julia to West Falmouth for the summer until he hit upon the idea of taking in a pair of boarders at six to eight dollars a week each. Julia was able to find some classmates interested in the offer.

"I feel I can hold on a while longer yet if I can get the money I asked for from the Bache Fund of the U.S. National Academy, by the time I have spent that I suspect that Whitaker Wright's new mines will begin to pay," he advised Annie in May. "I may sell one of the duplicate collection of shells."[36]

What Cope did not know was that Wolcott Gibbs, who was one of the trustees of the Bache Fund, established by the academy to promote original research, immediately informed the president of the academy—Marsh—of the application.[37]

Simon Newcomb would get a fifteen-hundred-dollar grant from the Bache Fund to study astronomy, and Powell would get one for twelve hundred dollars to drill a deep mine shaft to measure subsurface temperatures. There would, however, be no grant for Cope. Nor would Whitaker's mining stocks pay off.

The following month, the American Museum of Natural History in New York City passed on a Cope proposal that they hire him and purchase his collections. "As this is the second time they have done that, I think I can consider the place definitely out of the question," he wrote.[38]

While Annie and Julia spent the summer in West Falmouth, Cope was on Block Island running down reports of the sightings of a giant "sea serpent," which he suspected was nothing more than a large eel. Perhaps things would change in the fall, but at the moment, Cope had no prospects in New York, Philadelphia, or Washington. A sad state of affairs for one of the most prominent paleontologists in the country. "The financial position has not improved & I will have to do all possible things to get through the winter, when I hope better times arrive. I have no word from Powell yet as he is not in town," he wrote to Julia from Washington in September.[39]

Julia had a plan herself—she would get a job. Cope agreed to ask the publisher of the *Naturalist* to see if he had anything that might be "agreeable," and that fall Cope's daughter prepared to switch from student to secretary. So much for the weaker sex not being able to deal with adversity and stress.

But now into Cope's inexhaustible optimism crept a strain of bitterness. "Learned societies," he was to conclude, were "largely filled with professional failures, and the shifty disciples of personal expediency."

Even his humor took on a rancorous tone. In a parody of a scientific article, titled "Some Points in the Zoology and Geology of Glycaphutal," by Robert Ramrod, Cope wrote of a mythical Caribbean island inhabited by a race largely without backbones. These Petromogli, as he called the species, ate sugar and went around in groups of three or four slumped together so they could support each other's spineless bodies. "The result of this gelatinous state . . . ," he wrote, "is that they are continually engaged in taking care of their feelings." There were a few individuals with spines on the island, but they were outcasts. "These backboned people are disliked by the others," he wrote, "who are apparently jealous of them, and obstruct and interfere with them in almost every possible way."[40]

In the spring of 1888, the British paleontologist Richard Lydekker unwittingly inflamed old wounds an ocean away when he published his paper "Icthyosauria and Pleisauria." Somehow Lydekker had a copy of Cope's *Elasmosaurus* paper, with the head on the wrong end. Cope had tried to buy them all up, but at least one had managed to make it all the way to England.

In the August issue of the *Naturalist,* Cope once again tried to stamp out the old error, insisting Lydekker had misquoted him and that "no such plate appears in the Transactions of the Am. Phil. Soc. or in any other society." This, of course, was technically true.

The subterfuge, however, troubled Leidy, and in the fall, he wrote to Marsh asking his thoughts. "This we know to be virtually false," Leidy wrote of Cope's contentions, "or is so only in the fact that after I had pointed out the error . . . Cope managed to get possession of most of the copies of the original Transaction."

What concerned Leidy now were the few remaining copies that told the truth. Marsh had two of the originals. "I have, as you no doubt remember, one copy," Leidy said. ". . . I have a mind to present my copy to the Ecological Society of London or to the British Museum. What do you think of it? If it remains here it may come into the possession of some one who may destroy it. The librarian of the Academy tells me that the copy presented to it was stolen."[41]

❧

As 1889 opened, there seemed to be no relief yet in sight. Cope was working away on his newest project—a paleontology manual—while still hunting for some permanent position.

California's former governor, and now the state's U.S. senator, Leland Stanford Jr., was preparing to use some of the wealth he amassed in the building of the Central Pacific Railroad to fund a new university. "Stanford is looking for a president for his big university in California. I advised him to look in at 2102 Pine Street if he wants one!" he told Julia.

Cope inquired after a "scholarship" position at the brand new Clark University, in Worcester, Massachusetts. But did not hold much hope in obtaining it. "I suspect the University will require such a person to live at Worcester, but this is not settled," he said.

In the meantime, Cope was scrambling to come up with five hundred dollars to pay the mortgage interest on his two Philadelphia townhouses. "I do not know where it is to come from, but I shall have to do some begging and then only get a part of it I suppose," he wrote.

For her part, Julia had received an offer of employment from James Rhoads, the president of Bryn Mawr and a family acquaintance. It was not an offer in which she took much relish.

"I have thy letter. Mamma has explained matters to me and I have been thinking over the question," Cope told Julia in May. "The situation is one of necessity and not choice. Were it not for this I could find thee more congenial and not more confining employment, but at present $ have to be considered first.

". . . I have some reason to anticipate that next winter the finances will look up, but as this is too uncertain to rely on, there is nothing to do but accept Dr. Rhoads proposition mentally at least. And when he will wait no longer for an answer, and nothing has turned up meanwhile, tell him thee accepts."[42]

Meanwhile, Cope was being considered for a spot at the Smithsonian, but alas his history and reputation weighed against him. "I am almost brought to the reluctant decision not to offer the Curatorship of Reptilia to Professor Cope, who is beyond all other men so eminently fitted for it," Langley wrote to Goode—in a letter marked "private and confidential."

There was no question that Cope's "scientific abilities rise to genius," Langley said. The problem was his brawls and behavior. "I think that if Professor Cope were connected with the Museum in some way which would oblige him to recognize that there were certain rules laid down for him, as to what he was to do, and more particularly, as to what he was not to do . . . something might perhaps be done." But nothing ever was.[43]

That spring, Marsh ran for reelection as president of the National Academy of Sciences. There was, however, a general feeling that after six years in the chair, it was time for him to step down. Cope led the campaign against him. He was promoting the candidacy of mathematician Benjamin Gould, although some members preferred Wolcott Gibbs.[44] But Cope's attack was so vituperative that it caused a backlash, and Marsh managed to retain the gavel.

"He sought re-election as 'vindication.' Why he should think he needs 'vindication' is what I do not understand, and why sage physicists etc. should want him to have it, is stranger still," Cope wrote his daughter.[45]

"You see that the Natl. Academy disgraced itself again. The vote was 22 to 13. I know of 5 or 6 men whom remained away who would have voted against him. Such is the cowardice of certain specimens of alleged man," he complained to Osborn.[46]

In the fall, Cope went to Washington yet again seeking an appropriation to finish his Hayden work. Times were increasingly desperate. He owed the publisher of the *Naturalist* $455, but had only managed to raise $45. "Can you give me a lift with this difficulty?" he inquired of Osborn, adding, "Sorry to have to ask." In October, he faced another five-hundred-dollar mortgage payment.

In late 1889, Cope finally obtained a teaching appointment in geology at the University of Pennsylvania. The salary was modest, but dependable. Now, if he could only get his Hayden papers published, perhaps his financial nightmare would, after three hard years, be over.

Cope prepared to deal with his fifth secretary of the interior, John W. Noble. As had his predecessors, Noble referred the matter to Powell. By this time, Powell had been dealing with Cope and his publishing hassles for nine years. It must surely have seemed to him that it would never end. So the crafty Powell adopted a new tack.

In a letter to Noble, Powell outlined the history of Cope's manuscripts pointing out that based on Cope's Bible, it would "require twelve to fifteen years' time and an expenditure of not less than $60,000" to publish the remaining work—not counting the cost of engraving and printing. "The estimate of $3,800 mentioned in Professor Cope's letters will make but a small beginning," Powell warned Noble.

But Powell did not leave it there, he struck right at Cope's heart, charging that the "collections upon which Professor Cope was working were chiefly the property of the government. The extent of the collection is unknown.

"Before sending an estimate to Congress for the completion of the work the director recommends that Professor Cope be informed that the government collections now in his hands in Philadelphia should be transferred to the National Museum at Washington," Powell wrote.

On December 16, 1889, Noble sent a letter to Cope, along with a copy of Powell's letter to the secretary. Following Powell's "reasonable suggestion," Noble directed Cope to "place the collections in the National Museum at Washington, as I understand them to be the property of the United States."[47]

After the ravages of the 1880s, Cope's entire professional and financial life hinged on that collection, and Powell was trying to take it away. This was the most serious threat Cope had ever faced. He immediately wrote Noble. "Major Powell never 'understood . . . this collection was chiefly the property of the government.' He has known the contrary for many years and his assertion to this effect is an attempt to deceive Your Excellency and an attempt to rob me. In my last letter I wrote that this collection had cost me $75,000, which sum must be refunded to me by the government of the United States before it becomes its property."

Powell's aim, Cope said, was to prevent him from besting the survey's own researchers. "One of those men, Professor O. C. Marsh, of Yale College, is now engaged in duplicating that work in a way that is disgraceful to science."[48]

This was war, and if Powell and Marsh wanted war, well Cope would give them war—an all-out, no-holds-barred war.

Chapter Nineteen

COPE'S WAR WITH MARSH forever seemed to be throwing him into bad company—be it his sympathy for Columbus Delano or his collaboration with Hilary Herbert. Now it would make Cope a conspirator with William Hosea Ballou. Worse than either a crooked bureaucrat or political demagogue, Ballou was a journalist.

The world of the Gilded Age newspaper was a rough one, populated by the penny press, the Police Gazette, yellow journalism, crusading muckrakers, and imperious press lords like Pulitzer and Hearst. The goal here, above all else, was to sell newspapers. This was a world that didn't put much stock in civility or, for that matter, the truth.

"An ideal morning edition . . . ," a critic wrote of the Hearst papers, "would have been one in which the Prince of Wales had gone into vaudeville, Queen Victoria had married her cook, the Pope had issued an encyclical favoring free love . . . France had declared war on Germany, the President of the United States had secured a divorce in order to marry the Dowager Empress of China . . . and the Sultan of Turkey had been converted to Christianity—all these being 'scoops.' "

Still, Cope saw the newspaper page as his final field of battle. "When a wrong is to be righted, the press is the best and most Christian medium of doing it," he said. "It replaces the shot gun & bludgeon & is a great improvement."[1]

So it was here in the daily press that Cope sought his redress and vengeance, and it was Ballou who would be his champion. Once again, Cope could have chosen better. Ballou was a freelance journalist, a writer of popular-science articles. He was, as one biographer put it, "a mushroom collector with delusions of grandeur."[2]

Ballou had—as his own entry in *Who's Who* showed—a habit of making things up. He said that he had attended Northwestern University and the University of Pennsylvania, but neither school had any record of him. He said he had received an honorary degree from the Chicago Law School, but there's no record of that, either. He listed himself as a member an 1884 Arctic rescue expedition, but there is no indication he was there. This was the man who was to tell Cope's story.

Ballou and Cope had met some time before, and the journalist knew of the feud with Marsh. Doubtless, Ballou had offered to tell the tale, and Cope now took up that offer. He removed the Marshiana from his desk drawer and gave it to the journalist. Cope knew that Ballou was "a rough customer," but at that moment, that's just what he was looking for.

Ballou quickly cobbled together a long exposé and shopped the article around to the major New York papers in late December of 1889. The *New York Times* passed on the article, and so did the *New York Sun,* but the *New York Herald* bought it. Now Cope's descent into the journalistic nether-world was complete.

The *Herald* was one of the original penny-press newspapers, aimed at the emerging working-class readership. The newspaper thrived on equal parts of breaking news—*Herald* reporters were experts at using the new telegraph to send dispatches—and sensationalism. It was the *Herald* that sent Henry M. Stanley in search of the missing African missionary David Livingston. By the 1860s, the newspaper had become the New York's circulation leader, with a readership of nearly eighty thousand, even though upper-class New Yorkers would cast only a disparaging glance its way.

Weeks before the story went to press, the scientific community knew that it was coming. The *New York Times* had tipped everyone off when they sent a reporter to the American Geological Society's December meeting to check out the allegations in Ballou's article. Among those at the meeting were Hall, Newberry, and Arnold Hague of the U.S. Geological Survey.

The reporter was told this was "an old controversy, and a very deplorable one [that] has been thoroughly investigated by the National Academy of Sciences and has been discredited." The *Times* might not be interested, but the story was around, and Marsh quickly learned what was up. By the first week of 1890, he was hard at work trying to stop publication.

He went to William Pepper, president of the University of Pennsylvania, demanding that Cope withdraw this "libelous" article or be fired. Pepper was leading an ambitious expansion of the university, adding thirteen departments including the coeducationl School of Biology. Cope had been part of his expansion, but now Pepper found himself entangled in the Cope–Marsh web.

There was no tactic Marsh would not use to stop the story. The word was that Pepper had himself been involved in a blackmailing case, and Marsh threatened to air that scandal if the university president did not silence Cope.

"Marsh has made a dead set on Pepper . . . ," Cope wrote to Osborn on January 5, "so as [to] secure my resignation or expulsion. Pepper is terribly frightened & yields everything to him. The two are making such a fuss that they are pretty sure to get the article published. It will require considerable effort to prevent my being 'retired' from the University. . . .

"What I need is some credible person to inform Pepper as to the facts. Marsh fills him with lies & Pepper does not believe a word I say. Can you come to Philadelphia very soon—say *tomorrow.* "[3] Osborn dutifully took the train from Princeton to Philadelphia and spoke to Pepper, relieving at least some of the anxiety. The *Herald* also heard about Marsh's threats and warned Pepper that he would have "cause to regret" any attempt to interfere with Cope's freedom of speech. Poor Pepper was trapped.[4] Cope's position at Penn was safe, and Ballou's article was just days away from hitting the streets.

❖

On Sunday morning, January 12, 1890, the *New York Herald* offered its daily cornucopia of news to the city. There was a story from South Carolina, headlined "The Genesis of the Negro Exodus," explaining that blacks in the South, now abandoned by their carpetbagging white northern friends and facing increasingly hostile local whites, were contemplating a return to Africa. "The intelligent Negro realizes that he is considered an interloper here. The fact that he was unwillingly brought does not change the fact," the article stated.

There was also a fashion report—"Frocks and Gowns from Paris Town"—which told of a Russian princess who went to the theater in a dazzling outfit with a green satin skirt, a corsage of green spangles, and dark-green velvet sleeves. The ensemble giving her the allure of a mermaid.[5]

But biggest story in the paper—at least in the number of columns—was on pages 10 and 11, under a cascade of headlines that read:

SCIENTISTS WAGE BITTER WARFARE
PROF. COPE OF THE UNIVERSITY OF PENN-
SYLVANIA BRINGS SERIOUS CHARGES
AGAINST DIRECTOR POWELL AND
PROF. MARSH OF THE GEO-
LOGICAL SURVEY

CORROBORATION IN PLENTY
LEARNED MEN COME TO THE PENNSYLVANIAN'S SUPPORT WITH ALLEGATIONS OF IGNORANCE, PLAGIARISM AND INCOMPETENCE AGAINST THE ACCUSED OFFICIALS

IMPORTANT COLLATERAL ISSUE

THE NATIONAL ACADEMY OF SCIENCES, OF WHICH PROFESSOR MARSH IS PRESIDENT, IS CHARGED WITH BEING PACKED IN THE INTEREST OF THE SURVEY

RED HOT DENIALS PUT FORTH

HEAVY BLOWS DEALT IN ATTACK AND DEFENSE AND LOTS OF HARD NUTS PROVIDED FOR SCIENTIFIC DIGESTION

WILL CONGRESS INVESTIGATE?

So there it was out in the open for everyone to see—the meanspirited little fight between Cope and Marsh that had been going on since Bridger Basin days. Oh, it had laced the pages of science journals and been hinted at here and there in the daily press, but now it was all over the streets of New York—a full page in the *Herald* with portraits of Cope, Marsh, and Powell. It also had a little something extra, the hyperbole of William Hosea Ballou.

"For some time past a volcano has been slumbering under the Geological Survey, and of late there have been indications that the time for eruption was not far distant," Ballou told his readers. "Now it has arrived and the long pent-up forces have gained their freedom with a rush and a roar which, if it does not indeed carry the present management of the survey to official destruction, will certainly disturb the entire scientific world of America, and bring in its train a series of charges and counter charges, recriminations and reproaches which will ring from one end of the land to the other."

The charges, the article noted, "covered a great deal of ground." They were, in fact, a grab bag of all the accusations and complaints gathered over nearly two decades. As for Powell, it was alleged that he had turned the U.S. Geological Survey into a "gigantic politico-scientific monopoly, run on machine political methods." It was a machine so large and unwieldy that it was out of control.

The survey, according to the article, was giving Marsh a budget of sixty thousand dollars a year, plus a salary of four thousand dollars to run the paleontology division. But this simply wasn't about science. No, in return for the money, Powell received the prestige of Yale College and control of the National Academy of Sciences.

For these advantages, Powell was ignoring Marsh's behavior, which included destroying specimens out west to prevent any other researchers from obtaining them and sequestering his plunder in New Haven so no one else could see it. Marsh was basically depending on the skill and intellect of his assistants to write his scientific papers, and at the same time, he was shortchanging his employees on their federal salaries. All in all, Marsh was a villain, a cad, and a plagiarist.

"Major Powell has been sufficiently warned of Professor Marsh's doings during the past years, and that but for Marsh's usefulness he would long ago have gotten rid of him," the article stated. "He has had faith that Marsh's connection with Yale College would somehow pull things through."

All of this might have been kept from the public, the *Herald* explained, were it not for attempts to suppress the work and seize the collections of the distinguished Philadelphia researcher—Professor Edward D. Cope, the chair of paleontology and geology at the University of Pennsylvania.

Here Ballou practiced a singular bit of conceit, concocting an encounter with Cope for his readers that went like this:

I saw Professor Cope at his residence, No. 2102 Pine Street, Philadelphia, a few days ago. He was engaged in naming new species of fossil animals, but cheerfully put aside his work when the nature of my call was made known to him. He is a man of not over forty-five years of age and of distinguished appearance.

"What is the origin, Professor, of this war against the Geological Survey?" I asked.

So began Ballou's interview. How much really occurred and how much Ballou made up is difficult to say, although it is revealing that the journalist didn't even get the forty-nine-year-old Cope's age right.

In the interview, Cope explained that his attack was prompted by the secretary of the interior's order to turn over his collections. Cope maintained that he had spent eighty thousand dollars (the figure had grown by five thousand dollars since the previous month) of his own money on gathering fossils. "I have no more than a bushel of specimens belonging to the government," he insisted.

"Who is the author of the order?" Ballou asked.

"Why to be sure, who but Major Powell," Cope replied. "The object of this absurd order to place my collections in the National Museum is to gain control of them, so that my work may be postponed until it has been done by Professor Marsh."

Cope then recounted in great detail the problems of Marsh denying access to other researchers to government specimens, his reliance on his staff to write papers, and his misapplication of funds.

On the plagiarism issue, Cope charged that Marsh had lifted his ideas about the evolution of fossil horses from the Russian paleontologist Vladimir Kovalevsky; that his monograph on toothed birds was written by Williston; and that *Dinocerata* was the work of Baur. Cope also went after Powell's scientific background, contending that he wasn't much of geologist. "Major Powell must be held responsible for the blunders of his agent, Professor Marsh. He had used Marsh as a tool, and Marsh has used him as a tool. They together have used the National Academy of Sciences as a tool for their mutual purposes," Cope concluded.

As unpleasant as this public airing was for the scientific community, what was even more distressing was the number of other scientists named in the article. Cope indicated that Scott, Osborn, C. Hart Merriam, and Newton Winchell were all in a position to "offer evidence." Merriam, one of the country's foremost mammalogists, worked for the federal Department of Agriculture, and Winchell was a professor of geology at the University of Minnesota.

Marsh's former assistants—Williston, Baur, Barbour, Hatcher, Otto Meyer, and Max Schlosser—were also named, as were Cope's closest scientific supporters Endlich, Persifor Frazer, and T. Sterry Hunt. A good number of the men named in the article were aghast at being publicly linked to the Cope and Marsh vendetta.

But published right there in the *Herald* were letters written by Williston and Otto Meyer. "Prof. Marsh performs very little, I might say almost no scientific work, at least in the later years," Meyer's letter stated.

Of course, not everything was to be believed. Ballou had telephoned Scott at his Princeton home and used Cope's name to bring up the subject of Marsh. They chatted for a few minutes, and then Scott hung up. On Sunday when he picked up the *Herald,* Scott was mortified. Ballou had not identified himself as a reporter, and Scott had not agreed to speak for the record. Perhaps that didn't matter because he never said some of the things attributed to him.[6]

"If these things charged against the Geological Survey are true, ought not scientific men who had the facts speak and root out the evil doers?" Ballou is supposed to have asked.

"They ought, perhaps, but we fear that in rooting out the evil doers we may destroy the survey, and that would be a public calamity indeed," Scott is supposed to have replied. "I can testify that Professor Marsh is wholly incompetent as a paleontologist," Scott reportedly said.

Endlich and Frazer were also interviewed. Each man raising his own set of complaints. Endlich pointed out that Powell had sent researchers to look at Hawaiian volcanoes but still hadn't produced a systematic report on mineral geology inside the country. Frazer, a geologist and professor of chemistry at Philadelphia's Franklin Institute, charged that Powell had tried to ride roughshod over other geologists at an international congress set up to standardize mapmaking procedures. This was just an example of the high-handed, autocratic way that Powell operated, Frazer said.

To dampen the threat of a libel suit, as well mix up the cauldron, Ballou had sent advance copies of his article to both Powell and Marsh. Powell responded immediately, and his reply was part of the article. The methodical Marsh was preparing a voluminous rejoinder to run later that week.

In his Powell-ish way, the major started off by thanking the *Herald* for displaying "eminent fairness" in allowing him a response. Indeed, it was almost a relief to get it all out in the public. "A covert enemy may maliciously stab, and his unseen blows may injure because they cannot be parried, but an overt assailant may be met face to face," Powell said.

He explained that in examining the manuscript, it appeared to be largely the handiwork of four men led by Cope. The others being Endlich, Frazer, and T. Sterry Hunt. Powell charged that they had been engaged in a campaign to "reorganize" the survey, "or rather to change its management by putting themselves in charge of the work."

Had not both Cope and Hunt—a geologist and chemist,—repeatedly applied for survey positions? Had not Endlich been a top aide to Hayden and lost his chance to advance when Hayden was bested? "I suppose Frazer aspired to be chief geologist, though I have no written evidence of that fact," Powell wrote. He referred to the group as "Professor Cope and his coparceners in martyrdom."

Powell ran through the history of the survey and how Cope and Endlich had been thwarted in 1879 and again in 1885. Then he set out to address point by point the scattershot charges made by Cope and Company. It was easy. Powell was able to knock down one after another.

He had only put the relative of one congressman on the payroll, and he was an honor student. He had hired a journalist not to spew out propaganda but rather to serve as the editor for the numerous survey reports and publications.

Powell said it had been necessary to have a paleontologist because paleontology is crucial to being able to identify geological horizons, and Marsh was the best man for the job. "He has exhibited in his work great industry, having made vast collections in the field and produced great results in the laboratory," the major said. "For a number of years the National Academy of Sciences has kept him for its president."

Marsh was not getting sixty thousand dollars a year, but just twelve thousand to sixteen thousand dollars, including his own salary, and while it was true that his assistants helped with publications, it was merely "a method of writing adopted by most public men."

What had really been the survey's transgression? Not hiring or publishing Cope, and in so doing, Powell said, it stood guilty of "nothing less than to put under a bushel the light and glory of the genius of Professor Cope."

Cope, Powell conceded, was "fair systematist" and decent scientist. He could do good work "if his infirmities of character could be corrected by advancing age . . . if he could be made to realize that the enemy which he sees forever haunting him as a ghost is himself."

Marsh had not been idle either, having contacted everyone mentioned in the piece, demanding to know if they supported the article and what charges they were making.

He received telegrams from a half-dozen scientists, which he forwarded to the *Herald* and which were then run under a headline "They All Deny." But did they?

Obsborn wired, "Have not seen or authorized any article whatever." Baur said, "I never authorized the use of my name." Williston replied, "I have given no one authority to use my name in connection with charges against you."

Not one of them, however, said the charges were false. Indeed, soon there would be even more explicit challenges from Osborn, Baur, and others. Williston was so delighted with the exposé, he cut out every article and pasted them in a scrapbook.

✤

VOLLEY FOR VOLLEY IN THE GREAT SCIENTIFIC WAR
PROFESSOR COPE RETURNS TO THE AT-
TACK RIPPING UP MAJOR POWELL'S
ANSWERS TO THE FIRST CHARGES
AND HEAPING MORE ON
TOP OF THEM

MEN OF SCIENCE AGOG
SOME SHOCKED, ALL STIRRED UP, BY THE
SENSATIONAL DISCLOSURES IN THE HERALD,
AND MANY UNABLE TO BELIEVE
THE ACCUSATIONS
LONG SMOLDERING EMBERS OF HATRED

And so the second day's story in the *Herald* began. "The war between the scientists . . . goes bravely on and the fur is flying in great shape," Ballou announced. "It is a very pretty fight as it stands."[7]

Ballou led off with Cope's retort to Powell. He defended the size of his manuscripts, like Cope's Bible, saying, "It is not my fault if formations were found to be rich and that my report reached considerable dimensions. That is the fault of nature.

"But Major Powell would have no report exceed five hundred pages in length, and told me that if any exceeded that amount he would cut off the manuscript with a pair of scissors."

Cope got in some more jabs at Marsh, charging that he had written a paper on fossil frogs based on discovery by Otto Meyer—a discovery that Marsh initially didn't understand. "No man can, by the use of money only, palm himself off successfully as a representative of the science of America," Cope asserted.

A large part of Monday's story, however, was what is known in the newspaper business as a reaction story. Ballou and a small band of correspondents had fanned out on Sunday and buttonholed some of America's most distinguished scientists for their opinions. In general, the reaction was one of dismay.

Ballou himself interviewed Pepper at the University of Pennsylvania. Pepper made it clear that when he learned what Cope was up to he had "endeavored to get him to abandon the project." Pepper was most fearful that his university "was to be dragged into the squabble," but now hoped Cope would substantiate his serious charges.

Scott, still feeling the sting of Ballou's little subterfuge, told the *Herald*. "I have been grossly misrepresented." It was, Scott thought, "unbecoming in men of science to wash their dirty linen in public." He went on to stress he had never said anything critical of Powell. Still, even Scott could not help but say "I am glad the subject has come out."

"Though I thoroughly disapproved of Marsh," Scott would explain in his memoirs, "and would have rejoiced to see him removed from any connection with the U.S. Geological Survey, I did not at all like the sensational method of a newspaper attack."

Osborn was "foxy" when the *Herald* reporter called on him. "I am glad the matter has at last come out. It will clear the atmosphere. The truth will be sifted out from the falsehood, and a great good will be accomplished," Osborn said. "I don't think I want to say another word."

Marsh did have his supporters. Merriam told a reporter, "I place no confidence in what Professor Cope says. His whole attack is due to jealousy." Harvard geology professor Nathaniel Shaler said, "You can say for me and the Harvard men interested in geological matters that little weight should be attached to Professor Cope's statements, as they grow out of disappointment and envy."

The reaction was the same from scientists at Cornell and, of course, at Marsh's home field, Yale. But one voice not heard was that of James Dana. A reporter had gone to his home on Hillhouse Avenue and knocked on the door. But other than expressing surprise that the story was in the newspaper, Dana declined comment. "He refused to talk on the subject and said that the controversy had a tendency to make scientific matters ridiculous."

That Monday morning, the *New York Times* and the *Philadelphia Inquirer* published short stories on the dispute. The *Times* story, under the headline "An Old Grievance Aired—Why Scientists Make Light of Professor Cope's Charges," was on the last page of the paper.[8]

Based on the reporting done at the Geological Society meeting in December, it was a brief, balanced story, sketching the feud's history in a few paragraphs. It largely discounted Cope's charges, but it did note criticisms against Marsh.

"I do not say that I approve altogether of what Prof. Marsh has done," said Alexander Winchell, a geology professor at the University of Michigan. (Winchell's younger brother Newton had been mention in Ballou's Sunday story.) "But such criticism as I have to make I will make in his presence. I have told Prof. Marsh that he ought to be more liberal with the younger men who were employed by him and ought to allow them the credit and honor of their discoveries. . . . Prof. Cope is a genius in his way, and has all the erratic peculiarities of genius."

The *Philadelphia Inquirer* called the report "a sensational scandal" and sent a reporter to Leidy's home on Sunday evening for a comment. Leidy obliged, saying, "It is very unfortunate that this thing should have gotten to the newspapers. It will simply cause strife and vexation among the scientific men of the country."

Leidy went on to lay the blame on Cope's "consuming restlessness." Leidy praised the Geological Survey, and as for the charges of Marsh's plagiarism, he said, "I do not see how it can be so. . . . All his descriptions are original and all his reports are excellent."[9]

Cope was not happy. "Poor old Leidy has come out against me in the Phila. Enquirer, just as he has always done," he complained to Osborn.

On Tuesday, a third story ran in the *Herald,* but it was nothing more than a rehash of what had come before. The story had also been picked up by the *New York Sun* and the *Philadelphia Record,* but the issue was clearly losing steam.

In Tuesday's story Ballou compared Cope to Don Quixote tilting at his windmills, which might have been more accurate a comparison that he actually intended, considering that Quixote was delusional. "Although his adversaries are rich, powerful, and have influential friends in almost every department of the government, the plucky Pennsylvania professor springs on gallantly to the fray as ever any knight of old," Ballou sang.[10]

Cope was delighted. "You have seen Sunday's Herald & by this time Monday's. I have a good stock of hot shot & shell on hand as you see," he wrote to Osborn on the first day of publication. This was a great crusade. "It has to be done or American Science [will] sink into eternal disgrace. . . . There is nothing wrong with speaking the truth about Marsh. . . . Either he or I must go under."[11]

The next day, responding to concerns about the excess and license in the stories, Cope wrote, "Ballou is a rough customer but I doubt whether anybody else would have pushed the matter to the conclusion it has reached. I am not responsible for the long preface & I must specifically disavow it, as I seem to be credited with it."[12]

Cope, however, had no regrets for turning over his personal communications to Ballou. "Williston, Meyer & others, must not write such letters if they cannot stand by them," he said. But Cope had fired his pistol, and as in a duel, he now had to stand and await Marsh's return fire.

On Sunday, January 19, a week after the initial *Herald* story, Marsh's reply became the grist for one more story.

MARSH HURLS AZOIC FACTS AT COPE
YALE'S PROFESSOR PICKS UP THE GAUNT-
LET OF THE PENNSYLVANIA PALEONTOL-
OGIST AND DOES ROYAL BATTLE
IN DEFENSE OF HIS SCIEN-
TIFIC REPUTATION

HURTFUL ALLEGATIONS DENIED

Marsh, as always, was methodical, and deliberate. Like Powell, the Yale professor had little trouble dismantling Cope's scattershot assault, which was filled with unsubstantiated accusations, half-truths, and errors. Marsh organized Cope's charges into a series of allegations and then knocked them off one by one—in the sharpest, nastiest of manners.

The National Academy of Sciences was populated by the nation's most eminent men; how could Marsh manipulate such a distinguished group? Besides, all academy actions were open to scrutiny. Could Cope's hostility come from the fact that there had been a move to expel him from the group?

The national and college collections at Yale were marked and separated. "Every specimen belonging to the government is kept by itself, and no mixing with Yale Museum collections is possible," he assured.[13]

As for his assistants at Yale, the work they did was primarily "clerical" and "mechanical." When one of them did render an intellectual contribution, it was duly noted. For the most part, assistants took "dictation" from Marsh, and that is why some extensive manuscripts are in their handwriting, not his.

"Little men, with big heads, unscrupulous in warfare, are not confined to Africa, and Stanley will recognize them here when he returns to America," Marsh wrote. "Of such dwarfs we have unfortunately a few in science."

Marsh fiercely denied the charges of plagiarism and intellectual panhandling from other scientists. "My work on the genealogy of the horse was entirely my own," he insisted. He hadn't even read Kovalevsky's papers. (Considering Marsh's reputation for not keeping up with the literature, that might have been true.) Since then, the troubled Russian paleontologist had committed suicide. "Kovalevksy was at last stricken with remorse," Marsh wrote, "and ended his career by blowing out his own brains. Cope still lives unrepentant."

Marsh's final jab at Cope was at an old wound, but he simply couldn't resist. He dredged up the story of the *Elasmosaurus* one more time. Marsh's defense was followed by yet another reply from Cope, but it could hardly be called news.

It looked like Marsh had won the day. "The thoroughness and ability with which this reply was prepared indicated that it was by no means the work of a single week, but years of preparation," Osborn concluded. "Whereas Cope attacked after a truly Celtic fashion, hitting out blindly right and left with little or no precaution for guarding the rear, Marsh's reply was thoroughly of a cold-blooded Teutonic, or Nordic type, very dignified and under the cover of wounded feelings reluctantly breaking the silence of years, as if his reply had been forced upon him."[14]

There followed two more stories in the *Herald* on January 20 and January 26. But these were rehash of the rehash, an effort by Ballou's sleight of hand to keep the story going. There were, however, a few interesting admissions. Cope conceded that there might have been inaccuracies in dates on his papers. "I am not infallible, but I have not on that account turned my work over to assistants to have it done for me," he said. As for the *Elasmosaurus,* Cope said, "I answer 'peccavi' to some extent." It was a curious confession depending on the obscure word *peccavi,* an acknowledged sin. Even then Cope couldn't help modify it with "to some extent." The extenuating circumstance, he explained, was misleading information from another scientist, Cope's "predecessor in the same field." At least, he had the grace not to publicly name Leidy.

But Cope insisted there remained a serious question of scientific ethics to be settled—a position with which others, like Michigan's Winchell, agreed. "If anybody is being robbed of intellectual property in any government bureau or university laboratory it is a good time to speak out," Cope proclaimed. "There must be no class of privileged brains in this country.

"In America, where the number of men devoted to pure science is relatively small, the standard of excellence of scientific work is constantly liable to be lowered by the entrance into the field of men who are more or less incompetent and sometimes by mere seekers after notoriety," Cope argued.

Almost half a century earlier, Joseph Henry had bemoaned, "Our newspapers are filled with puffs of quackery, and every man who can burn phosphorous in oxygen and exhibits a few experiments to a class of young ladies is called a man of science." American science had come a long way since then, or had it? Surely, such a public display of scientific pettiness and mean spirits would have sent poor Henry into despair.

The end of Ballou's campaign slipped into rhyming buffoonery, which was titled "Paleozoic Poetry."

The Unfortunate Pterodactyl Wings Its Flight through Prosody

I.

Professor Cope to Professor Marsh:
Your ignorance of saurians is something very strange;
The mammals of the Laramie are far beyond your range.
You fail to see that certain birds enjoyed the use of teeth,
That pterodactyls perched on trees, nor feared the ground beneath.
You stole your evolved horse from Kowalevsky's brain,
And previous people's fossils smashed, from Mexico to Maine.
To permian reptiles you are blind—in short, I do insist
You are—*hinc illae lachrymae*—you are a plagiarist!

II.

Professor Marsh to Professor Cope:
'Tis strange that you, who always get the cart before the horse,
Should dare to state, my equine screed I filched without remorse.
'Tis strange that you, who helped to kill a moribund magazine,
Should hint that I have fossils smashed of prettiest pliocene.
Your reference to a horn cone on an ischium sends a chill.
Professor Huxley is my friend, and likewise Buffalo Bill.
Though paleontologic facts you've studied since your youth,
You shun the streptasauria as if they were the truth!

⚜

Then, at last, it was finally over. "The great sensation was not even a nine days' wonder; it fell flat. The public of those days knew nothing and cared less about such matters; vertebrate paleontologists were few, feeble folk," Scott said.[15]

Well, actually, it wasn't quite over. The March and April editions of the *American Naturalist* carried extensive articles by Baur and Erwin Barbour about the conduct of research at the Peabody Museum. Both men had served as Marsh assistants, both were now in academe—Baur at Clark University and Barbour at Iowa College—and both had tales to tell.

There is no question that the two hated Marsh. "If there is any truth left under the sun then judgment must fall on the scientist who walks the halls of the Yale Museum," Barbour intoned. He called Marsh a "scheming demagogue" and the Peabody a place of "deceit and falsehood."

But unlike Cope's careening, ill-aimed broadside assault, both Barbour and Baur had specific allegations, and Baur, a true German, could display as much Teutonic rigor in his attack as Marsh had shown in his own defense.

In the March *Naturalist,* Baur went over Marsh's statements point by point in a six-page article. He contended that while the national and college collections were kept separate, Marsh had the option of deciding which specimens went into which collection and had a tendency to keep the best for himself.

Furthermore, he had actually seen Marsh tell visiting scientists that particular specimens were boxed and inaccessible when in fact they were in the very room, lying on a large table, covered with a cloth.

Baur cited a litany of small errors over the years Marsh had preferred to bury rather than correct and noted that his approach to his staff was to give them a set of fossils and a set of questions to answer, such as "What are the principal characteristics of the skull of Sauropoda?" or "What are the relations between the different groups of dinosaurs?" Marsh would then use the answers to "dictate" his papers. So while it was his dictation, it was his assistants' answers he was relying on.

"Only a short time ago I had the opportunity to observe Prof. Marsh's passion to adorn himself with other's plumes . . . ," Baur wrote. Baur, himself, had found some trends in the evolution of the ostrich skeleton that threw "new light on the relationship between birds and dinosaurs." Baur told Marsh about it and did not publish himself.

When Baur saw the proofs on Marsh's *"Ornithomimus"* paper, there was his discovery, without any credit at all. The two argued for nearly two hours, and Marsh relented. But he put the credit not in the text, but in the caption for an illustration. It was, Baur complained, "a place where it could easily be overlooked."[16]

The following month, Barbour's piece appeared. He had two basic charges against Marsh. First, Marsh was using "government time and money in beautifying his own private collection." Second, Marsh had used plaster of Paris to dress up and improve his fossils without noting the restorations. "His assistants are asked not how nearly they can approximate truth, but instead 'How closely can you imitate the coloration and texture in the missing part?' Which translates into 'How cunningly can you deceive.' "[17] Barbour concluded, "A certain unfaithfulness runs through all his doings. . . . He cannot but be weighed in the balance by scientists and found wanting."

Then at last, it was really and truly finally over. James Hall tried to console Marsh. "The attack was so gross and uncalled for," Hall wrote from Albany, "that it has reacted against the parties who violated all pledges and decency in the course they pursued. It has done harm to no one except themselves."[18]

It did appear that Marsh and Powell had weathered Cope's gale. The public had not taken notice. Congress had not even blinked. Indeed, if there was any loser, it seemed to be Cope, for Secretary Noble informed him that the Hayden work would definitely not be published.

There was, however, one reader who had followed the battle with great interest, a reader who thought this spat proved a point he'd been trying to make for years. There was one reader who would make use of the facts and fictions that had tumbled forth. That reader was Hilary Herbert.

Chapter Twenty

 COPE'S ACCUSATIONS IN THE *Herald* might have just melted away. As Scott had said, hardly anyone really cared about something as obscure as paleontology. But for a change, timing was on Cope's side. His attacks came just at the moment that Powell's western enemies were watching one of their most cherished myths wither away.

For years, western developers had assured hopeful homesteaders that rain would follow the plow. Why, back in the 1860s, Louis Agassiz had postulated that the building of railroads might even change electrical fields, altering climate. Hayden had scientists seriously try to measure climatic changes.

But the promise was at best a dream, at worst a come-on. Wyoming might have had a lush, humid forests fifty million years ago in the Eocene, but most of it was now bone dry, and that's the way it would remain. Powell had said as much in *Arid Region,* back in 1878.

Powell's report could be dismissed and ignored, but the truth was driven home to enterprising developers and hopeful settlers in 1886 when drought descended on the West. If that lesson wasn't learned, it was repeated the next year, and the year after that, and the year after that. By 1889, there had been four relentless years of drought. Wells dried up, wheat fields shriveled, and dreams evaporated.

Something had to be done. Powell had warned that the West could not be developed in the same way as the lands east of the Mississippi. The West needed a more careful analysis of land and soil, alternatives to the quarter section, and most of all, it needed significant irrigation. Western political interests now agreed with Powell, at least when it came to irrigation.[1]

In 1888, the "irrigation clique," lead by Senator William "Big Bill" Stewart of Nevada, and Senator Henry Teller of Colorado, pushed a resolution through Congress directing the secretary of the interior to make an "examination of that portion of the United States where agriculture is carried on by means of irrigation" and determine where dams should be placed "together with the capacity of streams, and the cost of construction and capacity of reservoirs."

Secretary Vilas passed the job onto Powell, who happily embraced it.

Powell had tried to impress his vision of development on the West in 1878 with *Arid Region,* and again in the early 1880s with his management of the U.S. Geological Survey, but this was the greatest opportunity he would ever have.

What Stewart and Teller had envisioned was a quick scan of the rivers and streams, followed by the designation of some dam sites, followed by an ambitious dam-building program, followed by water getting to the fields of constituents.

Powell, of course, had other ideas. This was a chance to do complete topographical and hydrological surveys, a comprehensive categorization of land, plus basic engineering studies for public works. In short, Powell saw this as an occasion to organize and manage the West—an area that covered nearly two-fifths of the nation.

One thing was certain, whether it was done Stewart's way or Powell's way, it was going to take time—years to survey the land and build the dams. In the gap between initial surveys and the finished dams lurked the threat of land speculators and corporations gobbling up the acres most likely to benefit from government water. There were visions of the land grabbers with their checkbooks following the surveying crews. As far as many in Congress were concerned, there had been enough of that already. So Colorado Congressman George Symes added an amendment that withdrew from settlement "all lands made susceptible of irrigation" under the survey, until the work was completed. That was modified in the conference committee to enable the president to restore lands to the market as he saw fit under the Homestead Act.

In a bit of legislative expediency, the irrigation survey, like the legislation to merge the old surveys, was attached to the Sundry and Civil Appropriations Bill, which passed on October 2, 1888. Powell got one hundred thousand dollars and set to work. He had told a legislative committee that, all in all, it would take six or seven years and six or seven million dollars to do the job.

But none of this dampened the efforts by both homesteaders and speculators to file land claims. So, in late 1888, the General Land Office closed its windows and canceled all claims filed after October 2. In effect, the West was closed for business. Western political and economic interests howled. Nevertheless, the General Land Office bureaus were officially closed on August 5, 1889.

An effort was made to get the offices open again, but in early 1890, Solicitor General William Howard Taft ruled that until the president had certified the land, "entries should not be permitted . . . upon any part of the arid regions which possibly come within the operation of this act." President Cleveland concurred. Some 850 million acres were off limits. The president would certify land when the survey was completed, and it was Powell who would determine when it was done.

So, as 1890 opened, western political interests were getting ready to attack Powell and his irrigation survey with any club they could seize. Imagine with what interest Stewart and the others read the *New York Herald* in late January. Here was ammunition against Powell they hadn't even expected. Cope's complaints had nothing to do with Powell's *Arid Region* theories or his irrigation survey. Still, scandal was scandal.

It was the last thing Powell needed to worry about when he went up to Capitol Hill that spring for appropriation hearings. But it turned out what the politicians wanted to talk about most were water and money, not fossils. "Every representative of the arid region—I think there is no exception—would prefer there would be no appropriation to having it continued under Major Powell," Stewart announced.

Powell defended the plan as best he could. Wasn't it better to hold onto the land for just a little while than have helter-skelter development and failed homesteads? Congress did not agree. The lands were open once again for settlement, and Powell's request for a $720,000 appropriation for the irrigation survey was cut to $162,500. The major's vision for western settlement had been thwarted once more.

Perhaps Powell could find some solace in the U.S. Geological Survey's appropriation of $719,000 for the year. That made it one of the best-funded entities in the government and the best-financed scientific agency in the world. If Powell could find some satisfaction there, Hilary Herbert could not. Herbert had been stewing over the growth of government science since his days on the Allison Commission. The fact that Alabama state geologist Eugene Smith had his own war with the survey and was a member of the Cope camp doubtless added fuel to Herbert's fire.

Now he had Cope's allegations and that residue of ill will between Powell and the western legislators. The time was ripe to try once more to curb government science.

⚜

Powell and Marsh knew something was coming, although they weren't sure when. In April of 1892, Marsh was in Washington trying to rally support. One of the allies he was most depending on was Representative Joseph Outhwaite of Ohio, who happened to be his cousin.

"I heard various rumors in Washington about a change of Directors [at the U.S. Geological Survey], as Powell has had about enough of it," Marsh wrote Outhwaite. ". . . I also heard that Herbert was still hostile to the Survey, which surprised me, as I had been told that his animosity of five or six years ago had been removed." Marsh enclosed a letter outlining the limits of his funding from the federal government. "This letter you are free to use," Marsh told his cousin, "if the matter comes up in Congress."[2]

And come up it did. On May 18, 1892, Hilary Herbert rose on the floor of the House brandishing a copy of Marsh's monograph *Odontornithes*. A huge volume about birds with teeth! What was the government doing? Why just look at it with its red Morocco-leather binding, gilt edges, and tinted paper. And if that wasn't enough, Herbert added, two years later, "the same book, with very few changes, was published again by this same Government, and it was then called 'Birds With Teeth.' "[3]

Charles Darwin had called *Odontornithes* "magnificent . . . the best support for the theory of evolution which has appeared in the last 20 years." Sir Richard Owen told Marsh it was "the best contribution to Natural History since Cuvier." Hilary Herbert, however, wasn't much impressed. "Now when you come to examine the book you found that it was simply going back into the past ages to show that at some prehistoric period of the world there existed birds of a certain type which had teeth," Herbert explained incredulously.

Herbert put the challenge to his colleagues. "If the House is bound at all by its repeated promise to reduce expenditures, we ought to begin upon the Geological Survey," he said. "Especially, we ought to put the knife where moneys are expended that are not necessary to carry on the Government, not necessary for the preservation of order, or the protection of life, liberty or property."

It just had to stop. "We are expending today on science twenty times more than any government in the world," Herbert announced. Clearly, this was a bad thing. With Marsh's volume sitting on his desk, Herbert took special aim at paleontology.

"What is paleontology?" Herbert asked. "It is the science of ancient fossils. These fossils or rocks are picked up by parties in the field, brought here, and investigated in laboratories. . . . In this manner the scientists weave out eventually what they call the story of the rocks. . . . If there is on this earth an abstract science, it is paleontology. What practical use has the Government for Paleontology?"

Herbert had been waiting years for this moment, and he went on and on. "When the morning of resurrection shall come, some paleontologists will be searching for some previously undiscovered species of extinct beings," he proclaimed. ". . . There is no end to it." He read Agassiz's letter of 1885 again stating that paleontology was "one of the things private individuals and learned societies can do just as well as the Government." Finally, tying science to Powell and his hated irrigation survey, Herbert concluded, "Paleontology, paleobotany and even general researches into the science of geology, are of no value whatever to the surveys which are intended to aid in the irrigation of our Western country."

Herbert's amendment cutting the U.S. Geological Survey budget by thirty-seven thousand dollars and virtually wiping out paleontology passed by a vote of ninety to sixty. Where was cousin Outhwaite through all this?

"I had watched and waited two days for that part of the bill in which you are so deeply interested . . . ," Outhwaite wrote to Marsh. "Yesterday, being called out upon committee business—the Committee of the Whole being engulfed over a silver coinage proposition, I though it safe to leave for a short time. I was accidentally detained a half-hour. Upon my return the motion had been made by Mr. Herbert. Debate was closed and the vote was being taken. I then did all I could to get votes. . . . This House is extremely utilitarian and has its teeth sharpened for everything simply scientific."[4]

The letter Marsh had sent Outhwaite specifically went into the issue of *Odontornithes,* and the following day, Herbert, under questioning, conceded that Marsh also had sent him a letter back in 1886 pointing out that monograph had been published before the creation of U.S. Geological Survey, that the Yale professor had paid for all the illustrations, and that the leather-bound copies were from a private author's edition. But the damage was done, and the truth would not easily be set straight.

Marsh was seething. "As to the practical value of paleontology," he wrote to Outhwaite, "there is more money wasted every year in the United States searching for coal in places where a paleontologist would know at a glance none could be found than would pay for all the works ever published on paleontology."[5]

Powell had also been caught by surprise. "This was sprung in the Committee of the Whole, by Herbert, who made a violent speech against Paleontology and no one came to the rescue," Arnold Hague explained to Marsh. "An attempt will be made to reinsert these items when the bill is reported from the Committee of the Whole to the House."[6] But that attempt failed, too. "It shows a black eye so far as the Survey is concerned," Hague said. Still, there were hopes the damage could be repaired. "Powell tells me this morning to say to you that he thinks there will be no difficulty in having the Senate reinsert the items."[7]

The Senate, however, was the home of Big Bill Stewart, a man who brimmed with venom when it came to Powell and his survey, and if that weren't enough, there were the Cope charges and allies still lingering about.

❧

When the appropriation bill reached the upper house, Senator Allison asked Henry Osborn for his assessment of the value of paleontology to the U.S. Geological Survey. It seemed like a reasonable request, for at that moment the thirty-five-year-old Osborn, whom Ballou described as look-ing "like a college senior and athlete," was the country's emerging light in the science. Just a year earlier, Osborn had been simultaneously appointed chairman of the new biology department at Columbia University and head of the division of mammalian paleontology at the American Museum of Natural History in New York City.

In many ways, as Cope's star had set and Osborn's rose, it was the protégé rather than the master, who had become Marsh's real rival. But unlike Cope, Osborn with his links to Princeton, Columbia, and the American Museum of Natural History was well connected professionally and politically.

Osborn and Marsh had been going at one another since the late eighties. In 1890, Osborn wrote to Marsh saying he was postponing a visit to Yale in protest, after learning that Marsh had blocked Baur's Harvard appointment. In the same letter, he accused Marsh of having covered up Dinocerata bones on his last visit to the Peabody.

A few months later, Marsh was fretting over Osborn's western expedi-tions. "I learn that Osborn has been imitating Cope in trying to secure spec-imens from one of my men," Marsh wrote to Leidy. "If the facts are, as stated to me, he has acted most dishonorably. . . . You will do me a great favor, if you will let me know all you know about this. I will regard anything you say as strictly confidential. I do not want to believe that Osborn would do anything wrong intentionally, but he is so completely under the influ-ence of Cope and Baur."[8]

By this time, Marsh's ace fossil collector, John Bell Hatcher, was feeling increasingly frustrated not only by his boss's laggardly salary payments, but by the sense of being blocked from advancement. Marsh was reluctant to have him work at the Peabody and had sponsored Charles Beecher, instead of Hatcher, for a doctoral degree.

In the spring of 1891, Hatcher decided to try for a position as an assistant in paleontology at Princeton, but Osborn warned him that there was "some difficulty in carrying this through, partly because of representations as to your character."[9]

Hatcher knew what that meant and immediately demanded a response from Marsh, showing him Osborn's letter. Marsh sent a telegram at once assuring him that "statements implied in the enclosed letter are absolutely false."[10] Hatcher apparently accepted Marsh's word, but he still did not get the job. That fall Marsh increased Hatcher's salary to two thousand dollars a year.

Even as the Herbert amendment was working its way toward the Senate, Marsh was complaining about Osborn. Marsh had staked out patches of Wyoming as "government" research sites, but Osborn simply refused to let the Yale professor lock up the west. "Osborn's men . . . In spite of my protests they went directly to my localities," Marsh complained to Powell in a June letter.[11]

So, when Senator Allison asked for Osborn's opinion of the survey, what would he say? First, he defended invertebrate paleontology studies as a key for being able to determine the age of geological strata, saying it was "at the basis of all geological work."

Vertebrate paleontology was not as essential, he said, but was still important and valuable, although he did concede it was "of a less practical and of a more purely scientific character." The real problem was the error-filled, high-handed way it was conducted by the survey. "The systematic work is inaccurate and if published by the Government will subsequently require complete revision," he said.

"Secondly," Osborn continued, "the department is conducted as if it were the private bureau and the collections were private property, instead of as a public bureau with public responsibilities."

The government's expensive collections, he noted, *are retained in the private store rooms of a college museum,* instead of being transported directly to the National Museum." Compounding the problem was the fact that it was difficult for visiting scientists to see the material.

To make matters worse, the survey's paleontology division also tried to thwart other institutions from gathering collections. "Professor Marsh," Osborn charged, "used every means to prevent the [American] Museum [of Natural History] from collecting in one of the great horizons of Wyoming, upon the grounds that the Government had prior rights there."[12]

The problem wasn't vertebrate paleontology. The problem was Marsh!

Marsh learned of Osborn's charges and wrote to Allison. He pointed out that some of Osborn's friends and associates were enemies of the survey. Marsh also vowed that the government collections were "carefully labeled and preserved by themselves, and as fast as their investigation is completed or even before, they are sent to Washington."[13]

Suddenly, the collections in New Haven were becoming yet another political headache for Powell. The fate of these fossils had initially been raised by Cope during the Allison Commission hearings. Powell paid back Cope when he suggested to the interior secretary that Cope's final papers couldn't be published until the Philadelphian's own fossils were turned over to the National Museum.

That ploy had backfired and led to the *Herald* exposé. The result of that had been to swing the light of scrutiny back onto the collections at Yale. By this point, no one was asking after Cope's fossils anymore. After all, he had never gotten a single cent from the Powell-run survey. Marsh, on the other hand, had received nearly $150,000.

In the wake of the *Herald* series, Powell dispatched one of his most trusted aides, Charles Walcott, to New Haven to "consult" with Marsh about the collections. "The information desired relates to the method of recording and caring for the collections, the means used to clearly distinguish the specimens belonging to the Survey," Powell explained in a letter. They were also to discuss the transfer of those collections to Washington.[14]

Powell was trying to cover his flanks, to leave no vulnerable targets for his opponents. But Marsh and paleontology had clearly become a weak link, and if the critics had seen some of the private correspondence between the Peabody and the Smithsonian, they would have known just how chaotic things really were.

In the early summer of 1890, the Smithsonian made several inquiries about whether it might get some *Triceratops* bones, but it got no clear answer from New Haven. The fact was that a great deal of the collections was not unpacked, cleaned, or organized. Marsh's assistant Beecher tried to accommodate the Smithsonian, but finally had to give up.

"I have had another look for the [neck bones] of *Triceratops,* so little of the material is . . . worked out or unpacked that it is difficult to say just what we have," Beecher explained.[15]

One other effect of Cope's *Herald* attack was that this time other scientists and institutions would stay away from the fight. Marsh and Powell would find few vocal supporters in the science community. Everyone just wanted this embarrassing episode to end.

⚜

On July 13, a red leather copy of *Odontornithes* was once again held aloft in the halls of Congress, this time by Big Bill Stewart, who described it as "an elegant book" that had to cost between three and four thousand dollars a volume. What was the government doing promoting such a book?[16]

The next day Senator Hawley of Connecticut once more tried to set the affair straight, reading into the record a letter from Marsh. But Stewart was unrepentant. He compared the original volume to the one that had been reprinted by the U.S. Geological Survey. Stewart found them "substantially" the same. "If this is a year's contribution by Professor Marsh as an employee of the Geological Survey, it is a very meager contribution," he charged. Did Marsh, Stewart asked, do "anything else to earn his $4,000 salary?" "Professor Marsh is a gentleman and everybody knows it," Hawley shot back in his constituent's defense.

"Professor Marsh may be a most estimable gentleman," said Senator Joseph Carey of Wyoming, "He is a learned man . . . and he has made some very valuable discoveries; but I do not believe in carrying on the rolls of government college professors."

Then summing up the feelings of many of the western legislators, Carey said, "Democrats are elected to office, Republicans are elected to office, heads of bureaus change, but this bureau under Powell goes on forever."

Powell had also sent a letter to Congress emphasizing that *Odontornithes* had been done under King's survey of the fortieth parallel, and that these fossils were "of great importance." The fact that the toothed birds were found in Kansas hundreds of miles away from King's survey was not mentioned.

The only defender for science was Senator Call of Florida. "In regard to the question of whether scientific investigation is of any value . . . the world is too full of all the practical triumphs of applied science to deny it," he said. "We see it every day in the new motors, in the applications of electricity to a thousand uses."

Call went on to quote Sir Francis Bacon—the sixteenth-century English philosopher who pioneered the idea of scientific method. But even "Lord Bacon" could not save the day. Stewart called for the "yeas and nays," and when the counting was done, not only was paleontology gone from the survey, so was more than two hundred thousand dollars—a 40 percent cut in Powell's budget request. Just as bad, the appropriation specified the staff positions and salaries to be paid.

Powell launched a frantic lobbying effort and was able to restore some of the money—the final appropriation coming in at $430,000. But two paleontology posts and fourteen other positions were lost. Coupled with the cut in the irrigation survey funding, Powell's plans had been smashed.

Damn those birds with teeth. Powell had spent precious time and political resources defending them, and really the senators didn't care. They were just convenient clubs with which to hit Powell. "There is nothing important connected with these two paleontologists," Colorado senator Edward Wollcott had confessed, "but here is a chance to cut the survey appropriations."

As soon as the vote was final, Powell fired a telegram—brief and bitter—to Marsh in New Haven: "Appropriation cut-off. Please send your resignation at once.

"Powell, director"[17]

The same day, Hague posted a letter to New Haven. "My dear Marsh . . . The game has been played and we are badly out. Much to the surprise of everybody, the House concurred with the Senate amendments. . . . Not only is paleontology badly damaged, but geology is equally badly hurt. . . . Order has not yet come out of chaos, and we do not know exactly where we stand. I think all geological fieldwork will be stopped at once. . . . I see no way out of it."[18]

Defeated, Powell cleared out of Washington for the summer, leaving it to his aides to pick up the pieces and write his annual report. After tidying up affairs, he would hand in his resignation in 1894 and return to the Smithsonian's Bureau of Ethnology. If only he hadn't taken up with Marsh and his tar baby Cope, things might have gone differently. Of course, Marsh undoubtedly felt that he had been put through a political wringer because of Powell's irrigation survey.

Well, Cope might have had it right when he told Ballou that Powell and Marsh had used each other as tools. Now they had each paid a price. Cope had to feel vindicated.

⚜

There was a time when the loss of the four-thousand-dollar salary from the U.S. Geological Survey wouldn't have meant all that much to Marsh. For many years, he had received ample sums from two funds created by George Peabody for his relatives—the Boston Trust and the Peabody Trust. In its peak years, 1872 and 1877, Marsh had received as much as fifty thousand dollars. But the Peabody Trust had issued a distribution payment of $37,598 in 1888 and since then had yielded hardly anything. Now as the markets went soft, and were about to get even weaker, the Boston Trust also went down.[19]

Marsh's remaining income, several thousand dollars for the year, was still larger than Cope's. But then he lived a larger life. Marsh mortgaged his house to Yale for thirty thousand dollars, and for the first time in his twenty-four years at the university, he was forced to ask for a salary.

Hatcher was still out searching for Ceratopsian dinosaurs, but Marsh could no longer afford to ship huge quantities of bones back to New Haven. He ordered his collector to study the distribution of the dinosaur beds instead.

The situation would grow worse as the year moved to a close. In addition, to attacking Powell and his survey, Congress had been busy passing laws that were seriously destabilizing the nation's economy.

Since 1890, the country had been laboring under the stiff tariffs shepherded through Congress by Ohio congressman William McKinley. The tariff movement had gotten a boost when Germany and France closed off their markets to American meat. But in the tit-for-tat trade war, high tariffs on manufactured goods just added to inflation, so the economic squeeze would be felt in the city as well as the country. It also hurt the federal budget, as import duties—an important source of federal revenues in the days before federal income taxes—plummeted.

A further strain on federal resources had come from the Sherman Silver Purchase Act, which required the federal government to buy four and one-half million ounces of silver each month and enabled the government to pay its debts in either gold or silver.

Western political interests pushed through the act to bail out the troubled mining industry. But it created anxiety among European investors, who held a large chunk of American debt, and they began calling their loans in gold. The finances of the times were precarious, and on February 25, 1893, they received a jolt that sent the entire economy in a downward spiral.

The Reading Railroad, which had already passed through several receiverships, declared bankruptcy. With a few weeks, the National Cordage Company—the "Rope trust"—also collapsed. Like withered autumn leaves, other railroads and corporations started to tumble, and the crash of 1893 was on. And this crash was far worse than Jay Gould's Black Friday in 1869 or Jay Cooke's fall in 1873.

By the end of the year, 642 banks would be closed; dozens of railroads, covering a quarter of a million miles of track, would be in receivership; and a quarter of heavy industry would be idle. Grain and cotton prices also plunged, and suddenly hundreds of thousands of men were jobless.

No one escaped the crash. "The convulsion of 1893 left its victims in dead-water," Henry Adams wrote. ". . . While the country braced itself up to an effort no one thought within its power, the individual crawled as best he could through the wreck. . . . And among the earliest wreckages had been the fortune of Clarence King."[20]

After being bounced out of the Anglo-Mexican Mining Company by Agassiz, King had returned to New York City and pursued a variety of business ventures. Under an assumed name, he married a Negro woman, Ada Todd, in a secret wedding held in a tenement. King set up Todd and the five children he had with her in an apartment in Brooklyn.

His friends were only a little surprised, for they knew of his "appetite" for dark skin. "He loved the Spaniard, as he loved the Negro, and the Indian and all the primitives," Adams said of his friend in a memorial speech at the Century Club.[21]

Meanwhile the real wealth King sought always eluded him, and the crash of 1893 wiped him out completely. His friend John Hay advanced a loan against King's art collection, and, depressed and exhausted, the brightest man of his generation was admitted to the Bloomingdale's Asylum.

There were other victims. Fred Endlich, sitting in a Tucson hotel room, put a pistol to his head and pulled the trigger, and in August of 1893, after limping along year after year, the mines at Lake Valley closed for good. In eleven years, the Sierra Grande Mining Company produced between five and seven million ounces of silver but consistently lost money.[22]

The crash truly marked the end of an era. "Much that had made life pleasant between 1870 and 1890 perished in the ruins," Adams lamented.

Ten days after the Reading Railroad collapsed, Grover Cleveland was inaugurated for a second term. He moved to repeal the Sherman Silver Purchase Act and put America on a single gold standard. But by 1894, the federal government was desperate for a new bond issue to sustain its treasury.

Cleveland was forced to go to J. P. Morgan and August Belmont to float the loan, and the two financiers, along with the help of the Rothschilds' banking interests in Europe, took over the bonds—at very advantageous terms. The spectacle of rich financiers making a profit off America's misery led to bad feelings among the suffering populace. But business was business.

Although Morgan had foregone that appointment as a mathematics professor years ago, he had himself now been bitten by the paleontologist's dinosaur bug. In the 1890s, he helped finance the American Museum of Natural History's expeditions—even sending a special train to Wyoming to bring back ninety tons of fossil bones from a site near Como Bluff.

The crash had left Marsh in tight, if not dire, financial straits. By 1893, he could no longer afford to keep Hatcher in the field and finally let him go. Hatcher was hired as curator of vertebrate paleontology at Princeton,

where he put together an expedition to Patagonia, and with some more of
J. P. Morgan's money, set off for South America.

The days of collecting were over for Marsh. There would be no more
teams scouring the West. But there was plenty of material to sort through
at the Peabody. In truth, a century later, there would be matrix still waiting
to be chipped away from fossils. But life, for Marsh had palpably changed.
"Much . . . ," as Adams had said, "perished in the ruins."

Chapter Twenty-One

 ON THE DAY CONGRESS HANDED Powell and Marsh their bitterest defeat, Cope was more than a thousand miles from Washington, watching an immense thunderstorm sweep across the Dakota plains, its luminescent fingers snaking down from heaven to prairie. It was, Cope told Julia, a "black storm . . . brilliant with lightning."[1]

It had been ten years since Cope had been in the field, but now he was back thanks to a grant from the Texas Geological Survey. He had dragged his old trunk from the closet under the stairway, and dug out his gear—saddlebags, gum blanket, canteen—and headed west. True, the money was to do work in Texas, but Cope being Cope managed to end up in the Dakota badlands.

It wasn't that he had ignored his assignment. He had happily obliged the Texas survey, spending May and June of 1892 searching the Pliocene, Triassic, and Permian formations in the Texas panhandle. Riding a white stallion named Billy and carrying most of his kit in his saddlebags, Cope rode the Staked Plains. He was accompanied by W. F. Cummings, a geologist and Cope collector from the old days, and following behind, in a mule-drawn wagon, were Yancey, the cook, and "Black Bill," the teamster. Cummings's son and a friend tagged along, as well.

Cope had also salvaged from the closet trunk an old broad-brimmed straw hat, which he now tied down with a handkerchief under the chin, giving it the look, he said, of "a sun bonnet." Still, even with that and a daub of Vaseline on his nose, he managed to get a good sunburn.

Once again, he reveled in the country. "The yuccas are in bloom and they make quite a show," he told Annie. North of the Brazos River, mesquite covered the land, offering "the general appearance at a distance of an interminable peach orchard."

He watched white swallows build their nests, and listened to the ever-present song of the mockingbirds. On the parched prairie, animals would search for water wherever they could. "Two beautiful moths came to my mouth for a drink last evening," he told Julia.[2]

While the world was now coming undone for Marsh, Cope, after all the bad years, all the rejection, frustration, and penny-pinching, had finally obtained a measure of peace and security. The previous year, Joseph Leidy had died at the age of sixty-eight, and Cope was clearly his successor at the university.

In a career spanning more than four decades, Leidy had explored not only paleontology and geology but also zoology, parasitology, botany, mineralogy, and helminthology—the study of worms. He had been one of the last great naturalists, not merely a specialist in vertebrate fossils, protozoa, or vascular plants but an explorer of all things that lived. Marsh was one of his pallbearers.

The loss of one more of the elder lights left open the presidency at the Academy of Natural Sciences, and the chair of zoology and comparative anatomy at the University of Pennsylvania. By the 1890s, Cope had become almost a persona non grata at the academy, but he was quickly appointed to Leidy's zoology chair. It was a promotion of sorts, if only because of the distinction Leidy had given the post. It was also an affirmation of Cope's security at the university.

Cope was also in the midst of one of his most fertile periods of writing. He had always been a facile and prolific writer, perhaps too much so for his own good. Surely, he could be brilliant. "Often with only a small amount of fossil evidence before him, Cope could see through to the true interpretation, where a man with full documentation would fumble," Alfred Romer, Harvard's great paleontologist, would write decades later.[3]

But Cope was also forever peppering his work with errors and odd ideas, which more thought and editing might have caught. Cope's most productive years, fueled by the great dinosaur finds, were 1884, when he wrote seventy-nine papers, monographs, and articles, and 1885, when he published sixty-two.[4]

But in the nineties, with life a bit more settled, he would churn out an average of forty-three publications a year. A good chunk of this would be popular pieces and reviews on topics as disparate as "the effeminization of men" and Kedzie's *Gravitation, Solar Heat & Sun Spots*. Still, this would also be a time of a great scientific summing up.

He and Marsh had battled over fossil life, most notably over dinosaurs and fossil mammals, and this had consumed the greatest portion of his personal, financial, and intellectual life. He had, however, never given up his boyhood fascination for fish, amphibians, and reptiles. They had really been his first curiosity and his first success.

"A good while ago I caught a large water snake or water wampum as they are called here—one of the Colubers—in the Brandywine and I brought it home," a fourteen-year-old Edward had written to his father in 1855. ". . . Everybody almost about here thinks water wampums are poisonous, & indeed the way it struck at me scared me a little, but I soon convinced myself it was not by examining its mouth which wanted fangs & as all non venomous have, it had 4 rows if small teeth in its upper & 2 in its lower jaws."[5]

Four years later, Cope delivered his first scientific paper at a weekly meeting of the Academy of Natural Sciences. It was titled "On the Primary Divisions of the Salamandridae."[6]

Over the years, whether it was examining rain puddles on the Colorado plains or experimenting with salamander eggs in his Washington boardinghouse, Cope continued to study fish, amphibians, and reptiles. He would write fifty articles on living fish species and, using to good advantage all those specimens Williston left behind on the Kansas prairies, seventy-four pieces on fossil fishes.

He also wrote a total of eighty-four articles on living and fossil amphibians, and more than three hundred on living and fossil reptiles. About a third of the those reptile articles dealt with dinosaurs, pterodactyls, plesiosaurs, and other forms of prehistoric life. But Cope also wrote about the iguanas of the Greater Antilles, crocodiles from West Africa, and a Central American boa found wrapped around the stem of bunch of bananas imported to Chicago.[7]

All the time Cope was chasing those congressional appropriation bills, he was also working away on another major volume, which he finally published in 1889—*Batrachian of North America*. It was the most detailed analysis and organization of the continent's amphibians and frogs ever done.

While it was an extensive listing of species, covering 515 pages with eighty-six plates, mostly Cope's own illustrations, the work also began to attempt placing this class of animals in an evolutionary context. "The Batrachians are thus intermediate in characters, and therefore in a position between fish-like forms and the reptiles," Cope wrote.[8]

He even sketched the relationship between the species and environment, explaining that "in the history of vertebrates . . . [they were] the first members of that kingdom which occupied the land as the advent of the conditions suitable for air-breathing types." Even hobbled by his neo-Lamarckian beliefs, Cope was still so very close to seeing the process of evolution in both the fossil record and nature.

Now, he was at work on an equally ambitious project, *The Crocodilians, Lizards and Snakes of North America*. This book would run 1,115 pages, with thirty-six plates. Cope had spent his life trying to identify and sort the stream of life, and in this last of his major works, he would give voice to his vision of that exercise.

"Taxonomy is science only so far as it is exact," he wrote. "If it is alleged that gradual evolution of characteristics must preclude the possibility of exact definition, I answer that will only become practical truth when all the intermediate forms have been discovered."[9] There was a world of work still to be done.

These two extensive works, plus his mass of shorter papers, would make Cope one of the pillars in the study of fish and reptiles, so much so that the foremost American scientific journal specializing in herpetology and ichthyology would be named in his honor—*Copeia*.

In all, Cope would write a total of more than twelve hundred scientific papers—still a record among scientists—and hundreds more general interest articles and *American Naturalist* editorials. He would generate reams of studies on a theory of evolution that was really more prayer than science and fashioned an anthropology that was marred by racism. Still, he produced so much, and so much that was valuable.

When it came to mistakes, friend and colleague Theodore Gill conceded, "Unquestionably he did make many. But error seems inseparable from investigation, and if he made more than other great masters he covered more ground and did more work."[10]

Cope, however, had not lost his taste for dinosaurs, and that is why he headed for the Dakotas after his Texas sojourn. "This is a region from which Dr. Hayden brought some good things years ago, and no one has found it since. I suspect that I am on the track of it," he wrote to Julia in early July.[11]

How times had changed. Cope and his guide, a fellow named Oscar Hotchkiss, the son of a Philadelphia doctor who married "a squaw," now traveled the prairies completely alone and depended upon Sioux hospitality. "At Basil's, I was thoroughly in the hands of the Sioux. . . . Five pure bloods were there, three of whom belonged to the police and wore belts and pistols . . . ," he wrote. "We had a civilized supper at a table, the women waiting. We had tea, jerked beef fried, boiled bacon, fried eggs, boiled potatoes, and boiled jack rabbit."[12]

The land wasn't completely safe, as bad blood and resentment still simmered beneath the surface. "The trip involved some risk," Cope conceded to Annie. "The Sioux have been angered lately by trespassers on their reservation who have stolen their horses and cattle, and they are very suspicious of white people who want to go on their land. They have a way of killing stray people whom they don't know."

It had been only nineteen months since several hundred Lakota Sioux were massacred on the banks of Wounded Knee Creek—just 180 miles to the south. The army had raked a Sioux camp with small cannons, called

Hotchkiss guns, emphatically and cruelly ending the campaign against tribes of the plains.

While there might be danger, there was also beauty on the plains. The prairies were covered by a verdant carpet "spangled with many beautiful flowers . . . and birds abound and sing," Cope reported. "All would be perfect except for the mosquitoes."

Cope stopped at the Little Eagle settlement, where he enjoyed the hospitality of a missionary, Miss Collins, who ran a prayer meeting and YMCA for the tribes. Her house had "mosquito bars," or screens, which Cope said "made life endurable." Cope found Miss Collins and her assistant Miss Pratt both "good New England types," and it was from them that he learned the Sioux legend of the big bones.

Once, evil, giant monsters roamed the land. Then the Great Spirit sent powerful shafts of lightning to destroy the beasts. Their bones were left scattered across the prairies and badlands. The Sioux would not touch the bones for fear that a similar fate would befall them. But a boy at the settlement knew just where a great many of these big bones were to be found, and the next day, he led Cope across the prairie to the spot.

Sure enough, the boy brought Cope to a rich boneyard. It was, Cope wrote, "covered with fragments of dinosaurs, small and large . . . all around on banks and flats, bones everywhere. This was our destination." The greatest prize was a nearly complete skull of a dinosaur similar to a *Hadrosaurus.*

They had reached this boneyard as evening and its summer thunderstorms approached. So, after making camp and supper, Cope said he lay down to "dream of Dinosaurs except when the thunder and mosquitoes woke me." He crawled out of his nest of canvass and crates to see storms sweeping the plains on three sides, with "lightning . . . in forked streams" playing across the sky or descending to Earth in "blinding bolts." Black skies, low pale cliffs, alkali pools, and the bone mound looking like a grave in the flickering light. It was, Cope thought, an eerie scene. He could almost believe the Sioux legend.

The storms never reached Cope's camp, and at the first hint of dawn—about 4:30 A.M.—he was up and working to clean and free his great skull, which turned out to belong to a *Trachodon mirabilis.* Leidy had first identified the dinosaur species in 1856 based on teeth collected by Hayden. But Cope would excavate a head and skeleton of the duck-billed dinosaur, which would one day stand in the American Museum of Natural History. In three days, Cope collected twenty-one fossil species, primarily dinosaurs and other reptiles.

By July 31, he was back in Philadelphia, having shipped twenty boxes of fossils from Texas and a similar number from the Dakotas. It was like old times.

✤

The following season, Cope was out collecting once more. In July of 1893, he was at Fort Yates, in North Dakota, searching the Laramie formation and finding dinosaurs of the Hadosaurus, Cerotopsian, and Carnosaurus orders.

Cope moved south, stopping once more to visit with Miss Collins at Little Eagle. This year mosquitoes were not a problem, so he was able to swim in the Grand River and sit on the porch sipping lemonade and chatting with the missionary. At Little Eagle, Cope also met Miss Pingree, the young lady doctor from Maine who was in charge of the mission hospital. "She is about the best of her kind that I have seen," he wrote to Annie, "and is certainly actuated by a missionary spirit."[13]

Again, Cope searched the bluffs, riverbanks, and badlands around Little Eagle, amassing fossils, but not finding the large, complete skulls that he coveted the most. By the middle of August, Cope had fifteen hundred pounds of material ready to send back east. It represented, he estimated, about fifteen reptilian species. Among the dinosaur fossils were bones of an *Edmontosaurus,* a *Triceratops,* and a *Thescelosaurus.* Cope wrapped the bones in pages of the *Fargo Forum* and the *Sioux County Herald* for shipment to Philadelphia.[14]

Cope took a steamer down the Missouri and then continued across Kansas and Oklahoma by train until he reached Dickens County, Texas, once more. This year Cope would spend barely two weeks exploring the Triassic red beds, which Cummings had named after the nearby town of Dockum. But even in such a brief visit, Cope was to make another key discovery. The Dockum formation was "a major source" of Triassic amphibians and reptile fossils. Cope, himself, would never get back to the beds, but over the next century, paleontologists from the University of Michigan, the University of Texas, and Texas Tech would work Cope's Dockum beds with great success.[15]

On his way home, Cope stopped in Wellington, Kansas. In a few days, Oklahoma's Cherokee Strip was going to be opened for settlement. Wellington, like all the towns bordering the strip, was packed with homesteaders hoping to stake a claim in the bar of land 226 miles long and 58 miles wide.

The federal government was preparing to open the entire tract on Oklahoma's northern border—an area bigger than Rhode Island, Connecticut, and Delaware combined—for settlement at noon on September 16. Settlers were to race across the strip, stake their claims, and get to one of the land offices set up by the federal government to pay a filing fee of $1.00 to $2.50 an acre.

The Department of Interior had already designated four county seats in the strip with land offices. But it also set up makeshift offices in tents, just for the day. More than one hundred thousand homesteaders had gathered along the borders of the strip in hopes of claiming one of the estimated forty-two thousand quarter sections. The army patrolled the perimeter keeping out "sooners" before the pistol shot at noon.

"Everybody in this country is intensely excited about the opening of the Cherokee Strip," Cope wrote to Annie. "It is one of the few parts of the U.S. where a man can get a homestead. . . . Thousands of poor people, with wagons and camp outfits, are waiting on the border for the opening day, and there will be a great scramble when the time comes. The fastest riders will get the land. They are practicing horses . . . preparatory to making a run for a home."[16]

On September 16, the pistols fired at noon, and the race was on. By sunset, tent cities dotted the strip, seemingly endless lines wrapped around the federal land offices, and it could be said that the West had been settled.

By then, Cope was in Chicago visiting the Columbian Exposition, a grander, more fanciful world's fair than the one in Philadelphia seventeen years earlier. With its domes, colonnades, and sparkling lagoons dotted with gondolas, the exposition certainly had a dreamy air about it.

Buffalo Bill was appearing at the exposition, and the exotic dancer, Little Egypt, had titillated the town with her *Danse du Ventre*. What everyone wanted to see, however, was the massive, bigger than a building, rotating iron wheel that had been designed to eclipse Paris's Eiffel Tower. There was no question that George W. Ferris's wheel was the hit of the fair.

Munching on chocolates and strolling the fairgrounds, Cope indulged in the sorts of luxury that a few years earlier he simply would have been forced to forgo. But life had grown a little easier. That summer, in fact, while Cope was camping on the prairies, Annie and Julia had even gone to the exposition—by themselves. This left Cope in a tizzy.

"I haven't much opinion of women traveling alone for long distances, especially to such an attractive center for rascals of the World as Chicago," Cope wrote to Annie from the Dakotas. "When all goes well no bad results follow, but accidents often happen and then women have a poor chance. I shall not rest easy until you are safely back."[17]

The entire Cope family made it home to Philadelphia without incident.

❧

Now came a time of great changes in the personal and financial life of the Copes. For years one of the subjects Cope and Julia discussed in their letters was love and marriage. "The proper man to marry all other things being equal is the man one loves," Cope once told his daughter. But he advised, "let love be based on a knowledge of real character and not appearances, manners or accomplishments."[18]

Nevertheless, through the hardest years, which also happened to be Julia's most eligible, there were no nuptials. But on May 22, 1894, Julia Cope married William H. Collins, an astronomy professor at Haverford College. The bride was just a few weeks shy of her twenty-eighth birthday, and the groom was thirty-five. Both were past the conventional ages for proper marriage in Victorian society. Did that signal that this was a relationship of convenience, resignation, or perhaps one of genuine respect and love?

Mr. and Mrs. Collins spent their honeymoon in Europe and returned to Haverford in the fall. Soon, Annie Cope followed her daughter to Haverford. Cope did not. In theory, he was commuting the twelve miles between city and town, and, according to Osborn, "spending whatever nights involved late lectures or engagements at the Pine Street house."[19] That was the official line.

But in private correspondence Osborn conceded that after thirty years of marriage, Edward and Annie had separated. "There are plenty of scandalous stories attached to Cope you know," Osborn wrote to a book editor years later. "His wife left him, but largely for financial reasons I judge, and of course that made talk in the nineties. . . . There is also a story that Mrs. Cope left him because she found one snake too many in her shoe. They continued on amicable terms however."

Osborn couldn't help but suspect that Annie simply wasn't up to coping with Cope, and this gave him the "idea that a lot of the trouble was convention vs. unconvention, orthodoxy vs. unorthodoxy, physical and mental disparity, and the usual difficulties of keeping house with a genius."[20]

Of course, it is distinctly possible that after being put through the marital wringer by her brash, willful, self-absorbed, cavorting husband, Annie had simply had had enough. Besides, Cope's ideas about marriage, like everything else, were increasingly peculiar.

He had shaped his singular thoughts into a long article, turned pamphlet, titled "The Marriage Problem." The problem, as Cope saw it was this: "Marriage is an agreement between men and women for the satisfaction of passion." But sometimes that passion flags or disappears. What then?[21]

Then marriage—or at least the tradition-bound Victorian marriage—becomes an impediment to an honorable and virtuous life. The result of "compulsory marriage" and limited divorce, Cope argued, was prostitution and vice. "So long as each sex has maintained its natural relations to each other, life has been worth living," he contended.

Society's aim, he said, should be "securing a practicable and protected monogamy," but one that was more flexible than currently existed. To that end, he proposed a series of "renewal marriage contracts." The first contract would be for less than five years. If after that time both parties wanted to continue, a second contract would be drawn for ten to fifteen years. After that, a third contract would make the relationship permanent.

As the length of the marriage increased, so did the obligations of the man to the woman, even if the contract was not renewed. Cope felt that a woman past her prime would have trouble attracting another mate. "Such a system," he explained, "would offer a safe opportunity for the correction of matrimonial error."[22]

"Laws," Cope believed, "should not separate a man and a woman nor unnecessarily keep them together."

If Annie still placed her fidelity in the simple Quaker marriage vow to be "loving and faithful . . . until it shall please the Lord by death to separate us," the Copes had a much more fundamental dispute than simply dealing with the follies and foibles of life with a madcap genius.

In any case, Annie moved to Haverford, and Edward, for the most part, took up residence on Pine Street. They might have been separated, but they did not appear to be estranged. Cope did visit Haverford and requested Annie to visit him in Philadelphia. Cope, Annie, and Julia made a trip together to the American Museum of Natural History in New York City. Certainly, these new arrangements were made financially easier by the sale, at long last, of significant parts of Cope's fossil collection.

After a year of negotiations, the American Museum of Natural History finally agreed in 1895 to purchase Cope's fossil mammals for thirty-two thousand dollars. This represented about 40 percent of his material and consisted of about ten thousand specimens representing 463 species. Cope's asking price had been fifty thousand dollars, but the museum's president, Morris K. Jessup, held firm as to what he would pay. To finance the purchase, the museum took up a subscription from some of the biggest names in New York society—Morgan, Vanderbilt, and Dodge. There was, after all, only so much the blue bloods would pay for old bones.

In a letter to Cope, Obsorn, showing himself a friend but no sentimen-talist, explained that since collection techniques had improved so much in the last two decades, it would be foolish to pay too much for the material. The money could better be invested in expeditions that would soon surpass the collections of both Cope and Marsh.

President Pepper also urged the University of Pennsylvania Museum of Archaeology and Anthropology to purchase some of Cope's ethnological artifacts, which it did for about fifty-five hundred dollars.[23] Absent from the bidding on Cope's treasures was Philadelphia's foremost museum, the Academy of Natural Sciences. The enmity between Cope and the academy's leading members was enough to keep them from even inquiring. As a result, Cope's major finds would eventually leave the city that had once been the nation's paleontology capital.

Cope had warned Leidy that if Philadelphia didn't move away from the sociable science of the gentlemen's society, the city would be lose its place as a center for science. Cope had been brash and caustic in his attempts to make Philadelphia science more professional, and he had been rebuffed. But his prediction was holding true, and his collection leaving Philadelphia for New York was one symbol of the change in fortunes and position.

In August of 1895, Cope also gained a measure of the public honor, so long sought after. He was elected, yes elected, president of the American Association for the Advancement of Science. Scott and Osborn, both better connected to their scientific brethren than Cope, had worked hard in their mentor's behalf. "The seeds you sowed . . . brought forth fruit. Although I spoke to nobody I was elected on the 1st ballot," a grateful Cope told Osborn.[24]

Although life had become more mellow, Cope himself remained the same cantankerous soul who had irritated and incited so many over the years. At one meeting of the American Philosophical Society in March of 1892, Cope repeatedly interrupted a fellow member, William Bonwill, who was trying to deliver a paper. Bonwill protested to the secretary about Cope's behavior and declared, "I shall read it if it takes all Summer."

At the end of 1895, Cope was once again battling with the academy to defeat a front-runner in the election of officers. Urging Osborn to send in his proxy vote, Cope called the offending candidate "the compound of knave & ignoramus."

A few months later, Cope delivered a paper on paleontology and evolution as part of an American Philosophical Society symposium. But when the society went to publish the symposium papers, Cope objected, saying there wasn't anything new in his piece. When the society officers said they were going to publish it anyway, Cope "exploded and informed the society he was consulting a lawyer." The symposium proceedings were eventually published with a note stating that Cope had been "unwilling to furnish the Society with the text of his remarks."[25]

❖

One of the other benefits of Cope's new infusion of cash was that, after a hiatus of more than a decade, he was able to hire his old fossil collector, Charles Sternberg. Cope sent Sternberg to Texas to continue the hunt in the Permian formations. Sternberg explored the Wichita Brakes, a section of north Texas that 250 million years ago had been an almost tropical bayou filled with reptiles and amphibians. Sternberg was able to send back forty-five complete or near complete skulls of Permian lizards and batrachians—ranging in size from less than half an inch to two feet. It really was like old times once more.[26]

Sternberg went out again for Cope in early 1896. But without the same success, in part because his employer directed him to search a region that was devoid of fossils. To make matters worse, the weather was cold and wet. A despondent Sternberg asked Cope for permission to end the expedition.

Cope wrote back expressing concern over his collector's "very blue letter" and tried to buck him up. Science, he said, was a hard, difficult road. "Few men pursue a more useful life than yourself, and when the final account comes to be recorded you shall have no occasion to be ashamed of your record," Cope told Sternberg. "I personally have the highest respect to your devotion to science."[27]

The letter displayed a sensitivity and largess that Marsh's collectors would never have received. It was, Sternberg thought, an example of "the very best side of Cope's character," and it spurred him on. "Although I was just ready to give up from exhaustion and homesickness, I decided to remain another month in those barren fields," Sternberg said.

As 1896 came to a close, Cope was discussing the sale of another portion of his collection to the American Museum of Natural History. On the block this time were the Pampean fossils he had bought in Paris in 1878, his collection of fossil fishes, and some Miocene fossils from Europe. Once again Cope thought that they were worth about fifty thousand dollars. The museum, on the other hand, thought they were worth about half that figure.

Osborn also had the idea for a new project—a complete bibliography of Cope's works "to stand beside those of Marsh and Leidy." Osborn told Cope he was certain the National Museum would publish it. "Please do not fail to let me know about this soon," he wrote in a letter on February 20, 1897.

But the letter arrived to find Cope ill with a severe gastrointestinal ailment he called cystitis. Cope had suffered a bout of the same ailment the previous spring, and he was now laid low once more. "I must remain quiet now until certain troubles I have are well," he wrote to Annie on February 26. Cope asked Annie to come to town to see him, but she was ailing herself.[28]

Five days later, he was still sick and pretty much confined to his room. "I am not doing much work," he wrote to Osborn, "but feel like going at it soon." Osborn wrote that he would try to come for a visit.

A few days later, Cope got out of bed to give his course lecture at the university and ended up "the worse for it." The next day, he skipped one of his two lectures and felt a little better. He told Annie, "I go backward easily and must keep as still as possible."

Annie and Julia's husband, William, were both suffering from the grippe, and Cope said, "Julia must have her hands full with Wm & thee." It was, he thought, "too bad that we should both be sick at the same time."

Cope had to rely for his care upon his part-time secretary, Miss Anna Brown, and his doctor. Between fits of pain, he tried to work, but he seemed to be making no progress toward recovering. Osborn pressed him to think about surgery.

"My trouble will probably finish me in the course of time if it goes on," Cope told his wife, "but it can be eradicated by a surgical operation, that I will probably have to under go sooner or later."[29]

But going under the knife was still seen as a highly risky exercise, even though there had been tremendous advances since the days of the Garfield shooting. Cope delayed. Besides, his condition seemed to be improving. He started getting around town a bit. He delivered his lectures. Julia came for a visit. Charles Knight, the artist of prehistoric life, came and spent a few days, working with Cope on sketches of some of his prized discoveries—*Laelaps, Elasmosaurus, Camarasaurus,* and *Nanosaurus.*

But the health problems lingered. "I do not seem to get well, but remain stationary," he told Annie. Still, he had bounced back last spring; maybe it would happen again. "My Dr. says my general health is good, I should overcome this difficulty."[30]

Osborn, however, continued to urge Cope to have surgery. He went as far as speaking to a prominent surgeon in New York City about the case and making hospital arrangements. Still, Cope hesitated.

"Many thanks for your kind attention to the hospital question & the details," Cope wrote to Osborn at the end of March. "I will probably undertake the operation, but the time is as yet uncertain & will depend on my physician's advice." Cope had endured another acute attack, he explained, and was much weakened. "I must recover my strength before going into any surgery, I suspect."

Always a great believer in patent medicines, Cope self-administered morphia, belladonna, and formalin (a formaldehyde and methanol solution) in an effort to ease his pain. The drugs, which Cope described as a "combination that makes even the strongest constitutions stagger," left him deeply depressed, so that that "nothing in life is in any degree enjoyable, except an occasional draught of water."

Osborn wanted Cope to come to New York immediately and check himself into the hospital, where he could "try to build himself up for a week with good food and care." He realized that his old friend's will and courage were failing. If only he could get him to the hospital.

Cope, however, was now fading, and a tone of resignation was creeping into his words. On March 27, he wrote his last-known letter to his wife.

> *Dear A—*
>
> *I had a good night last night, & am feeling pretty well excepting that I am weak. I am recovering a little my appetite, but my head is somewhat swimmy. The crushed strawberry cushion is doing nicely and gets crushed a good deal.*
>
> *The sky looks beautiful out of the window, and I dare say that in a few days the country will be charming, I am anxious to get out, but cannot yet awhile.*
>
> With love to all
Thy husband
Edward [31]

On the last day of March, Cope managed a three-page letter to his Aunt Jane for her birthday. He had been more or less bedridden for five weeks at that time and had been worn down by bad nights and strong drugs. "To be well now seems to me to be something extraordinarily fortunate," he wrote.

"I know that many suffer more than I do, & so I am thankful," he said. "I do not expect to leave the world yet a while, but I shall do so when the time comes with a full belief that it will be a change greatly for the better. The relation of the Supreme to man is that of Father to children, and if we keep the relation true. He will not fail."[32]

In early April, Osborn was still hoping to get Cope into a New York hospital, but Cope seemed more resigned to his fate that his young friend.

"Cope was old and weary at fifty-six," Osborn said. "He had borne the heat of battle and wanted to rest." He had also been hit by another severe attack, and the chances of moving him to New York had vanished.

On Sunday April 5, Osborn made his last visit. Cope was lying on his cot in the second-floor front room surrounded by towers of paper boxes holding Permian vertebrates. The skull of a giant amphibian sat on the floor. Osborn asked after Cope's pain, but all the elder scientist wanted to talk about was Osborn's views on the origin of mammals.

As word of Cope's condition spread, visits were made by friends and colleagues. Persifor Frazer came a few days after Osborn to find Cope delirious. Frazer listened while, in that flushed and wild condition, Cope delivered a lecture on Felidae, cats, that was charming and complete.

On April 12, Cope died. The exact cause is not known. Osborn told Scott that Cope was suffering from uremic poisoning and an enlarged prostate. Whatever the cause, the career of Edward Drinker Cope ended sixteen weeks short of his fifty-seventh birthday.

That spring, Sternberg was once again working for Cope in the Permian beds of Texas. He was sleeping in his tent at his camp on Indian Creek when a liveryman rode up and roused him. The man, who had been searching for him since the day before, handed Sternberg a message. It was a note from Annie saying that Cope had died three days earlier. "I had lost friends before, and had known what it was to bury my own dead, even my firstborn son, but I had never sorrowed more deeply than I did over the news," Sternberg wrote in his memoirs.

The same day that Sternberg was mourning for Cope on the Texas plains, Osborn walked up the steps of 2102 Pine Street for the last time. He entered the hallway, went past the parlor still stocked with dinosaur bones, and climbed the stairs to Cope's study. There sitting on two study tables was Cope's coffin, draped with a dark cloth, a spray of magnolia blossoms and green leaves on top.

Chairs for six mourners were arranged around the coffin. Osborn, Scott, Frazer, Harrison Allen, Horatio Wood, and Cope's son-in-law, William Collins, each took a chair. "We all sat in perfect Quaker silence for what seemed to be an interminable length of time," Osborn said. The only sound was the scraping on the floor of Cope's tortoise as it moved around the room. Osborn's gaze wandered to the Gila monster endlessly circling in its glass bowl, and he could not help but think of how Cope had a habit of scratching the lizard's head.

As was the way of the Quakers, no one would say anything until "moved by the spirit." Osborn anticipating that, and the fact the silence might be intolerable, had brought along a Bible. He rose and read a long excerpt from the Book of Job, which began:

> Where wast thou when I laid the foundations of the earth? declare if thou hast understanding.

And ended:

> Behold now behemoth which I made with thee; he eateth grass as an ox.
>
> Lo now, his strength is in his loins, and his force is in the navel of his belly.
>
> He moveth his tail like a cedar; the sinews of his stone are wrapped together.
>
> His bones are strong as pieces of brass; his bones are like bars of iron.
>
> Then Job answered the Lord, and said,
>
> I know that thou canst do everything, and that no thought can be withholden from thee.
>
> Who is thee that hideth counsel without knowledge? therefore have I uttered that I understood not; things too wonderful for me, which I knew not.

Then Osborn said, "These are the problems to which our friend devoted his life."

The coffin was loaded on a hearse, and the men followed in carriages as Cope was carried on a final trip to his father's home, Fairfield, where a large gathering of family and friends waited.

The "spirit" was also slow in arriving at Fairfield, and for a long time, the large assembly was silent. Then a single person rose and said a few words of tribute. "By this time," Osborn said, "I was thoroughly exhausted with suppressed emotion."

At the close of the long, silent service, the coffin was removed. Cope's friends and family mingled and talked. Frazer was struck by how differently each side remembered the man. "Few men," he concluded, "succeeded so well in concealing from anyone, friend or relative, however, close, all the sides of his multiform character. . . . His scientific friends were amazed at the profound religious feelings, which he had always exhibited to nearest relatives, and these at the broad views of social problems which he imbued his intercourse with the world."[33]

Frazer was certain it wasn't duplicity by Cope. "The dominant motive of

Cope's character," he said, "was reverence for pure religion and pure science. . . . In his view these occupied totally different fields."

Osborn was getting ready to follow the coffin to the grave, but William Collins touched him on the shoulder and said softly, "Friend, in the next room thee will learn something of interest." Osborn followed him into the room, where a small gathering was getting ready to read Cope's will.

Osborn and Cope's brother-in-law, John Garrett, were named by Cope to be his executors. Cope gave family members the first selection of his books, with the remainder to go to the University of Pennsylvania or to be sold.

Once debts were taken care of, Cope left small bequests to Jacob Geismar (twenty-five hundred dollars) and Anna Brown (five thousand dollars). Julia also received five thousand dollars. The remainder of Cope's estate went to Annie. In July 1897, a notary put the total value of the estate at $75,326.95. That was considerably less than the quarter of a million dollars Cope had inherited from his father, but considerably more than the family's hand-to-mouth days in the 1880s.

Soon that figure was to be enlarged with two more fossil sales. The Pampean and European collections were purchased by the American Museum of Natural History in 1902 for $28,550, and in a third sale, the museum bought Cope's North American fish, amphibian, and reptile fossils for $18,550. Altogether, Cope's collections were sold for a total of $84,600, pretty much justifying his estimates of their worth.

As the will continued to be read, Osborn learned that there would be no graveside service and no burial, for the final codicil stated, "I direct that after my funeral my body shall be presented to the Anthropometric Society and that an autopsy shall be performed on it. My brain shall be preserved in their collection of brains, and my skeleton shall be prepared and preserved in their collection in a locked case or drawer, and shall not be placed on exhibition, but shall be open to the inspection of students of anthropology."

In the tradition started by Morton and Broca of measuring skulls and brains in an effort to glean some insight to intelligence, eminent men of the time were urged to donate their brains for study. The belief still haunted science that by weighing brains, and counting convolutions, something could be proved about intelligence.

The Mutal Autopsy Society in Paris and the Anthropometric Society in Philadelphia were leaders in this research. Although a newcomer to the field, the Cornell Brain Association had gathered seventy brains of "educated, orderly persons."

The poet Walt Whitman donated his brain, as did John Wesley Powell, the brilliant mathematician K. F. Gauss, and the German electrical engineer and industrialist Werner Seimans. Joseph Leidy and William Pepper had donated their brains as well.

In 1906, Edward Sptizka, a professor of anatomy at the Jefferson Medical College, read a paper before the Philosophical Society on his study of the brains of six eminent scientists and scholars—including Leidy and Cope.[34]

Cope's brain had weighed 1,545 grams, making it larger than the brains of John Wesley Powell (1,488 grams) and the American statesman Daniel Webster (1,518 grams). That probably would not have come as any surprise to Cope.

But Sptizka announced, "Joseph Leidy's brain is even larger than that of Cope." Leidy had beaten Cope in the brain derby by five grams. One brain Cope wasn't matched against was that of Walt Whitman. A clumsy laboratory assistant had dropped the poet's brain, and it had splattered on the floor.

As for the rest of Cope, the codicil in his will concluded, "The remainder of my body, I direct, shall be burned and my ashes be preserved in the same place as shall contain the ashes of my esteemed friends, Dr. Jos. Leidy and Dr. Jno Ryder." (Ryder and Leidy's ashes were kept in a bronze urn at the Wistar Institute, a research organization affiliated with the university.)

And so, to the very end, Cope was a man of science, although one has to suspect that Leidy might have viewed the idea of being in Cope's company for eternity with some dismay, even if he had the bigger brain.

Chapter Twenty-Two

WOLCOTT GIBBS, HARVARD'S EMERITUS Rumford Professor of Chemistry and a Marsh confidant, was now old, sick, and unable by his own hand to write to his friend in New Haven. So he dictated a letter to his niece.

"I have just heard from Chandler in Cambridge of the death of Cope, that makes the sixth prominent member whom the Academy has lost within the year," Gibbs said. At seventy-five, Gibbs had already seen so many men pass—Bache, the elder Agassiz, the elder Silliman, the younger Silliman, Henry, Leidy, Baird, Hayden. So many.

"It will be my duty to appoint someone to write his obituary notice can you suggest the proper person?" Gibbs asked. "Whatever you and I may think of his personal character Cope was I suppose a distinguished man in his own science. I am sure that you will act impartially in the matter."[1]

As one might have expected, the *America Naturalist* made much of Cope's passing. It ran four photographs, a two-page memoriam by Frazer in which he called his friend "a great master of science," and a six-page obituary by J. S. Kingsley, the journal's editor. Cope, Kingsley said, was "a man of quick decision and strong conviction. There were with him only two conclusions: a thing was either right or wrong."[2]

The National Academy of Sciences' official memoir, submitted years later, was written by Osborn. In it, Osborn could not help but compare Cope with Leidy and Marsh. "In Leidy we had a man of the exact observer type, Cope was a man who loved speculation . . . ," Osborn said. But he noted both men were true naturalists, casting a broad net over biological inquiry. "Marsh, with less breadth and less ability, nevertheless was a paleontologist of a very high order," Osborn granted.[3]

In its May 1897 issue, the *American Journal of Science* ran a bare-bones obituary for Cope, comprising six paragraphs. It described him as "former medical student" at the University of Pennsylvania. It also got his age wrong, saying was forty-six at his death.[4]

That was the end of it. There was no more posturing, no more backbiting to be done. Marsh's long war with Edward Drinker Cope was over. That first week of May also brought Marsh another letter from the past. "Dear friend," Chief Red Cloud began, "I presume you will be surprised to hear that I visit Washington once more. As you may know that I have not been for sometime able to come to this city on account of my eyes, and I believe even now it was unwise for me to travel such a distance." Yes, they were all getting old. Marsh himself, now gray and portly, had been having circulatory problems that sometimes made walking difficult.

"I shall never forget my troubles during the earlier days of reservation life. Your kind assistance rendered at that time I shall never forget," Red Cloud said. "The events associated with those days came back to me when I arrived here and wished to write to you a few lines."[5]

The note was, however, more than just a bit of sentiment. Red Cloud had come to Washington for his "last appeal to the government to fulfill all the promises of the treaties that were made." Perhaps, the old chief suggested, Marsh might be able to help once more.

But the Dakotas were now so very far away, and Marsh had so little time or money to finish his work. He could no longer rely on the U.S. Geological Survey or afford to pay for his longer, and tardier, papers to run as appendices in Silliman's journal, and Dana refused to assume the cost. "I am sorry that you think that the *Journal of Science* should pay for your papers when they are inserted . . . ," he curtly told Marsh. "I would be impossible to keep the journal afloat if we did so."[6]

Dana never did like Marsh very much and declined his dinner invitations—even when there was an English earl at the table. He could not, however, help but be enthused when Marsh sent him, in the dead of winter, a luscious orchid from his hothouse for his eightieth birthday. "Your beautiful orchid has outlived all other birthday flowers," he wrote in thanks.[7]

In 1895, Marsh had finally stepped down from the presidency of the National Academy after twelve years in the chair. The following May, the Yale Corporation voted to give him a thirty-five-hundred-dollar annual salary. Marsh still taught no classes and devoted himself to the Peabody.

Although not teaching, Marsh had begun to invite small groups of undergraduates—fresh-faced boys—to Sunday luncheons at the mansion, where he would expound upon science, but mainly retell his western adventures.

After lunch, the group would gather in the wigwam, where Red Cloud's peace pipe and Brigham Young's Bible sat on the big pedestal table. Marsh would drift from reverie to reverie. "Here a scalp or a pair of buckskin leggings, or a frontiersman's pistol would recall some incident of the west and the Yale seniors became small boys again, listening to tales of Indian savagery or of hairbreadth escapes from stampeding buffalo," one student recalled.[8]

To this new generation of Yalies, Marsh was not the brilliant scientist, the wily political operative, or the steely autocrat. To them, he was just a "pompous, but kindly old gentleman, who hunted buffalo in the dim past."

But Marsh's allusions to his western explorations in his papers left both Hatcher and Williston bemused and a little irritated. "Prof. Marsh has stated or left it to be inferred that his personal exploration in this as in other fields were extensive and that the larger part of the fossils described by him were the result of these explorations," Williston wrote in 1897.

"The actual fact is that since 1875, when my personal relations with Professor Marsh began, he himself did no fieldwork, his knowledge of the frontiers being derived from a few transient & hasty visits. . . . His references to the personal dangers encountered by hostile Indians is amusing in the extreme to all those who know the facts. I think that Prof. Marsh never ran any greater danger from Indians than when he entertained Red Cloud in New Haven."[9]

That was harsh, perhaps too harsh. Williston hadn't been there when the prairies were set ablaze or when Sitting Bull's armed braves blocked the way into the Dakota badlands. But Marsh remembered. He had those memories and his old bones.

There was little new material coming into the museum now. The last great flurry of acquisition was the purchase of fossil impressions of the ancient palmlike plants called cycads. Marsh wasn't so much interested in the plants themselves but in a geological dispute over whether the strata in which they were found were Jurassic or Cretaceous. It was another part of the puzzle work of trying to piece together that long, deep picture of Earth's history. Marsh spent fifteen hundred dollars in 1897 on cycad specimens from the Black Hills of South Dakota.

For a brief time, the Peabody had been the center of America's paleontology community, but no more. In New York City, the American Museum of Natural History under Osborn was vigorously pushing exploration, as well as purchasing large quantities of specimens from Cope's collection. Osborn had also hired Jacob Wortman, one of Cope's most valued field men, and sent him out west.

In Chicago, Marshall Field, the wealthiest man in town, was backing a new natural history museum. The Field Museum would also launch expeditions that led to major discoveries. Soon, Williston would arrive at the University of Chicago as a professor of paleontology, and he would recommend that Osborn hire one of his prize students, a fellow named Barnum Brown.

Brown did go to work for the American Museum of Natural History, and he would become one of the most famous dinosaur hunters of the new century. It was Brown who returned to the Hell Creek formation in Montana, twenty-six years after Cope had first identified it as a promising stratum, and discovered the dinosaur of dinosaurs, the *Tyrannosaurus rex.*

And just as J. P. Morgan had caught dinosaur fever in New York, and Marshall Field had gotten it in Chicago, so too had Andrew Carnegie in Pittsburgh. He was lavishly financing his new Carnegie Museum. "I have $50,000 a year to spend *forever,*" Carnegie told Marsh in a letter, "which in a few hundreds of years or so must give Pittsburgh something noble." The Carnegie Museum, officially founded in 1895, was now in the midst of receiving a ten-million-dollar infusion of money from its namesake.

Carnegie knew what he wanted straight away. "I astonished the committee with the *Brontosaurus excelsus,* knocked them flat—every one. Told them the first thing that went into the museum was that," he wrote Marsh.[10]

But efforts to buy a *Brontosaurus,* or at least part of one, were unsuccessful. The museum was going to have to find its own dinosaurs. Carnegie's new curator, J. B. Hatcher, immediately launched a series of western expeditions. One Carnegie expedition uncovered a fantastic dinosaur boneyard in Utah, just south of the Bridger Basin. Perhaps those Indians tales Marsh had heard back in 1870 had been true after all.

One thing was clear, however, the attic had been unlocked and thrown wide open. Marsh could no longer control the flow of bones. The world of dinosaurs was growing bigger every day.

Marsh's own scientific work now was focused more on the past than on new discoveries. He, too, was trying to sum things up. Of the ten monographs he had proposed to Powell back in 1882, only two, the infamous *Odontornithes* and *Dinocerata,* were completed.

The others on sauropods, brontotheres, and such were in various states of progress. He could never finish everything, so Marsh turned his back on all but his dinosaurs. What was really known about the great beasts? In 1892, he had written a survey paper on the certopsians titled "The gigantic Certopsidae, or horned dinosaurians of North America," with ten plates.

Four years later, he had a sixteen-page paper in the *American Journal of Science,* "On the Affinities and Classification of the Dinosaurian Reptiles," with plates showing the restoration of "the twelve best known Dinosaurs" in the world. The eight American dinosaurs included *Anchisaurus, Brontosaurus, Camptosaurus, Laosaurus, Stegosaurus, Triceratops, Certosaurus,* and

Claosaurus. They were all Marsh dinosaurs. Apparently, not a single Cope dinosaur was famous. Well, perhaps the feud wasn't completely dead. (The four European dinosaurs included the celebrated, little, birdlike *Compsognathus,* Mantell's *Iguanodon,* Huxley's *Hypsilophodon,* and Owen's *Scelidosaurus.* A politic, if not comprehensive list.)

"Many new discoveries have been made, and some very strange forms have been brought to light in America," Marsh said. This required a reassessment and reclassification of the ancient animals.[11]

Marsh tried to do just that in his 1896 *Dinosaurs of North America* and *Vertebrate Fossils* [Denver Basin]. In these two thick quartos, Marsh summed up nearly fifty-five papers already written and named seventy-six new species and thirty-five new genera of fossil animals. *Dinosaurs of North America* also had eighty-five plates and numerous text figures.

In this last monograph published by the U.S. Geological Survey, Marsh noted that by this time dinosaurs had been found on all the inhabited continents of the world and that their "placement in the animal kingdom [was] a matter of much discussion."[12]

Marsh observed that "some of the large earlier forms are apparently related to the crocodiles, while some of the later small, specialized ones have points of resemblence to birds. These diversified characteristics have made it difficult to classify dinosaurs among themselves."[13]

Marsh still had not accepted Seeley's designation for bird-hipped and lizard-hipped dinosaurs, which would have clarified some of his confusion. Over time, future generations of paleontologists would reorder, simplify, and elucidate Marsh's work, and some of the species and genera named in *Dinosaurs of North America* would disappear. But Marsh's volume would be the foundation upon which American paleontology was built. It would be the first, best reference. It would also be the last major scientific work in Marsh's lifetime.

While his papers continued to be studded with excellent plates and detailed dinosaur restorations, Marsh remained as reluctant to mount a dinosaur skeleton for display as he had been back in 1876 when the Smithsonian wanted to build a *Hadrosaurus* for the Centennial Exhibition. The bones were for scientists, not to be ogled and gawked at by the public. But the other museums were doing just that, and there was a push among some at the Peabody to do the same. Marsh, however, was immovable.

"The Dinosaurs seem . . . to have suffered much from both their enemies and their friends," Marsh once remarked. "Many of them were destroyed and dismembered long ago by their natural enemies, but more recently, their friends have done them further injustice in putting together their scattered remains, and restoring them to supposed lifelike forms. . . . So far as I can judge there is nothing like unto them in the heavens, or on the earth, or in the waters under the Earth."

But the desire for a dinosaur in New Haven was great, and the *Yale Alumni Weekly* would run a poem years later:

> Methinks I hear a chorus,
> The Ajax Apatosaurus
> Each Triceratop, each Saurian, each Spoon-bill Dinosaur,
> Crying out in desperation:
> 'Oh respect our age Cretacian
> Give us room to live our lives out! Can't you set us up once more?

Of course, at the moment, there wasn't even a room big enough at the Peabody to hold the biggest of the animals, and Marsh fixed himself once again on raising the money for the never-built second wing, the wing that had been on the architects original plans some twenty-five years ago.

Marsh earnestly campaigned for the new wing. Speaking before a Yale alumni dinner in New York City, he explained to the old boys that the reason "Yale gets so little money is mainly theological. She is not quite good enough to secure the saints, nor wicked enough to catch the sinners. Princeton gets the first and Harvard the second, while Yale's left between upper and nether mill stones."[14]

But it did not have to be that way. "I hope," Marsh concluded, "the friends of Yale will now come forward and complete the museum building in time for our bicentennial celebration in 1901."

All that was left of Marsh's scientific career was fifteen short papers over three years, no more than a couple of months' production for Cope. Marsh's total output would be 270 publications, or a fifth of Cope's bibliography. Nevertheless, they included three comprehensive monographs and provided vital material to the understanding of both paleontology and evolution.

Besides, Marsh would win the dinosaur race, naming eighty-six species to Cope's fifty-six.[15] Even in the months before his death, Marsh named two more dinosaurs—a bipedal, *Hadrosaurus*-like *Prosaurolophus breviceps* and a massive sauropod, *Barosaurus affinis*. (These names, however, would, like so many, disappear as paleontologists continued matching, merging, and reclassifying species.)

In the ten years he was associated with the U.S. Geological Survey, Marsh wrote only forty papers, and eventually his remaining unfinished work—

two hundred lithographic plates, dozens of drawings and engravings, but no manuscripts—would be turned over to the survey's new vertebrate paleontologist, Osborn. Osborn would parcel this material among several researchers in the hopes of completing the monographs. Two decades later, the work was still going on.

❧

After stepping down as president of the National Academy of Sciences, Marsh spent more time traveling. He went to Europe in 1895 to attend the International Congress of Zoology at Leyden. In 1897, he went again to Moscow for the International Geological Congress. It was a grand gathering. Haeckel was there from Germany, Albert Gaudry from France, Archibald Geikie from England. Among the Americans was James Hall, now eighty-six, but as animated as ever. Marsh reported that Hall "took in the Ural excursion, and everything else, Banquets, Ball, etc., without injury."[16] Marsh, even though he was twenty years younger than Hall, was nowhere near as spry, with his poor circulation and aching leg.

At the end of 1897, Marsh received the Cuvier Prize from the French Academy. Awarded every three years for the "most remarkable work either on the Animal Kingdom or on Geology," Marsh was just the third American—preceded by Louis Agassiz and Joseph Leidy—to receive this honor.

Marsh had already received the Biggsby Medal from the Geological Society of London and honorary degrees from Harvard and the University of Heidelberg. But the Cuvier Prize, if only for the company it put him in, was special.

As 1898 began, Marsh truly started settling up his accounts. He deeded to Yale, as a gift, all his collections. These included not only bones of dinosaurs and other extinct animals, but also the skeletons of a gorilla and several other rare modern animals. There were also mineral samples, some going back to his student days in Nova Scotia, and archaeological artifacts from Central America and Mexico, including those he spirited away from P. T. Barnum.

Yale president Timothy Dwight accepted Marsh's gift with "grateful acknowledgment of his generosity." Dwight went on to praise Marsh for the "unselfish devotion of his time, his talents and his energies" to science and to Yale.

Still, Dwight found Marsh a puzzling fellow, one with whom he could never strike an easy attitude. Every time Marsh would come to his office, even on the most mundane of errands, Dwight said, "It was as if we had been two ministers of state having little acquaintance with each other, who had met for the settlement of some great public question." Marsh imposed such formality that "one could not talk after the ordinary manner."[17]

Down in Washington, the announcement of Marsh's gift caused some consternation and worry at the U.S. Geological Survey. The government collections were still at Yale, but the time had clearly come to get them out of the Peabody and to the nation's capital.

Nine days after the announcement of the bequest to Yale, Charles Walcott, Powell's successor as chief of the survey, wrote to Marsh congratulating him on his donation and suggesting that the professor clarify "how, in the event of your death, government collections could be readily distinguished and taken charge by some one connected with the Survey."

Walcott and Marsh met in New York City to discuss the issue. Walcott wanted a memorandum outlining the collections. Marsh returned to New Haven and wrote a detailed history of his involvement with the survey in pamphlet form. The gist of this history was that it was really at the behest of Spencer Baird that Marsh got involved in collecting for the government in the first place. He also intimated that Baird and Powell had made concessions to him.

When Walcott saw the pamphlet, he immediately wired Marsh telling him not to distribute it or have it printed in the *American Journal of Science.* All Walcott wanted was a simple list, no history. That spring, Marsh sent a shipment of twelve Ceratopsian skulls to Washington, as a peace offering. (It represented Marsh's fourth shipment to Washington since 1886. But the bulk of the government collection remained in New Haven.)

It would not be until after Marsh's death that the survey would send a F. A. Lucas from the National Museum to sort and pack the government collection. It would take Lucas, with the help of two preparers, six months to organize and crate the fossils, which weighed eighty tons and filled five railroad freight cars.

Riding the train from New Haven to Washington were the remains of twenty-one dinosaurs, including the *Allosaurus, Triceratops, Stegosaurus, Hadrosaurus,* and *Camarasaurus.* Lucas estimated the shipment's value as upward of $150,000. The four earlier shipments were thought to be worth about $43,000. So Hilary Herbert would have been happy to know that the government got better than dollar for dollar on its $150,000 investment in Marsh, although, doubtless, he would have remained distressed that all they had gotten for the money were old bones.

In the summer of 1898, Marsh again went to Europe, as a leading member of the American delegation to the International Congress of Zoology, meeting in Cambridge, England. He then attended the annual meeting of the British Association for the Advancement of Science in Norwich.

While in England, Marsh was invited to visit young Walter Rothschild's zoological museum and park in Tring, just outside London. Marsh and his friend Sir Walter Smith Woodward were met by Rothschild, who gave them a tour of the collections.

Then they were then invited by Lord and Lady Rothschild to join a luncheon party at the family estate, Tring Park. Marsh and Smith Woodward found themselves among English aristocrats and society where the talk was mainly of country sports and politics. None of them had ever heard of Marsh or his great dinosaurs. "We were treated merely as the erratic friends of the erratic son," Smith Woodward said. Marsh left for the return trip, visibly disappointed by the aristocrats' lack of interest in him, but he couldn't help but remark to his friend how spectacular the Rothschilds' solid-gold dessert service was.[18]

To those who knew him, it was clear that Marsh was in decline. The truth was he had been in poor health since his Russian trip. When Richard Lydekker, whose 1888 paper on the *Elasmosaurus* had set both Cope and Leidy stewing, encountered Marsh in Norwich, he couldn't help but notice how much trouble the older man was having getting around.

Back in the States, Walcott was continuing to press Marsh to finish up his survey monographs and send the government collections to the Smithsonian. In late February of 1899, Marsh was summoned to Washington by Walcott to discuss the issue one more time.[19]

On the way back to New Haven, Marsh stopped in New York City for a dinner honoring Carl Schurz, the former interior secretary, the man who helped engineer the merging of the surveys into one and made Clarence King the first director. Marsh's hotel room was chilly, and he awoke the next morning with a bad cold, so bad he just stayed in bed that day.

He returned to New Haven on Sunday, the train making its way through a heavy storm. For some reason—perhaps there were no cabs at the station—Marsh walked through the rain to the New Haven House. He arrived at the hotel soaked and chilled. His closest aide, Bostwick, fetched him from there and brought him home.

For the next week, Marsh, although nursing a bad cold, insisted on going to the Peabody each morning, driving around to the back door in a cab and having staffers take him up to his office in the freight elevator.

Saturday afternoon, Bostwick went into Marsh's office and found him slouched over in his chair. He hurried down to the basement workshop and announced, "The Professor's sick." Hugh Gibb, a preparer at the museum for seventeen years and one of Marsh's stalwarts, dashed up to the office.

"I'm sick, Gibb," Marsh said, stretching a hand toward him. But at the same moment, he touched a finger to his lips, as if to say the "secret's

between us." Gibb and Bostwick took the professor down the freight elevator and got him into a cab. Marsh lay back on the seat. Gibb got in after
him, but Marsh wanted no one to take him home. Gibb pleaded. Marsh was
absolutely firm. He shook the man's hand and said, "Good-bye, Gibb."

That night, the doctor feared it was pneumonia. The following morning,
there was no doubt. Bostwick spent most of the next week at the mansion.
Marsh seemed to rally on Monday, but by Wednesday he had slipped into a
semiconscious delirium. Bostwick said Marsh was "more or less flighty
although he did have some sane moments."

Thursday, the doctor ordered an oxygen tent to ease Marsh's breathing.
But there was little else to do. Near dawn on Saturday, Timothy Dwight
came and spent some time at Marsh's bedside, but Marsh did not recognize
him. There were only a few hours left.

At five minutes to ten on the morning of March 19, 1899, Othniel
Charles Marsh, in Bostwick's words, "simply stopped breathing." He was
surrounded at the last by two nurses, two maids, the doctor, and Bostwick—all staff. Bostwick reached over and gently touched Marsh on the
lids, closing the dead man's eyes.

The *American Journal of Science* ran a sixteen-page obituary by Beecher,
which praised Marsh's science and tried to explain his icy persona. "In
making an estimate of his character," Beecher wrote, "it must not be forgotten that he developed wholly without the influence of family and home
ties."[20]

But even his critics and enemies had to concede that Marsh made a great
contribution to his science. Osborn said that he had "a genius for what
might be called the important things in science. He always knew where to
explore, where to seek transitional stages."

Marsh, Williston allowed, was "a man of extraordinary detail, with profound visualization powers. . . . He made many important discoveries in
science, but he never formulated a single broad generalization. He was just
the opposite of Prof. Cope."[21]

The most telling epitaph for Marsh, however, came from a man far from
the battles and science of paleontology. "He lived apart from those about
him," reflected Timothy Dwight. "I doubt whether even his most intimate
friends penetrated the recesses, or really in any measure understood him in
that central region of the soul where it turns toward unseen things. I question, indeed, whether he had intimate friends in the fullness of intimacy
which is known by men whose inner life opens itself with greater readiness.

". . . There was a solitariness of this character in Professor Marsh's life,
notwithstanding the abundance of outward activities and its intercourse
with other men, which as I observed or thought of him, was very suggestive

to me . . . ," Dwight continued. "For himself, I think, this characteristic of his nature lessened to some degree the happiness of his life, and gave him sometimes the feeling that he was a lonely man."[22]

When Marsh died, he had just $186 in his bank account. But under the terms of George Peabody's will, Marsh was able to give through family trusts $30,000 to the Peabody Museum, to be used in publishing the results of his western explorations, and $10,000 to the National Academy of Sciences to promote research in the natural sciences.

His house and its contents he gave to Yale. The university, which already held a mortgage on the property, had the rugs, paintings, and art objects carted off for auction in New York City. The contents of Marsh's mansion filled a thick catalog and took three days to sell off. The auction made $18,694.

Although he was survived by a half brother (who was in California at the time and did not attend the funeral) and a half sister, Marsh made no bequests to his family. A nephew tried to break the will, arguing that Yale had deluded the elderly Marsh into believing that there was no hereafter and that immortality could be obtained by human agencies, such as gifts to institutions. Though novel, the courts found the argument unpersuasive.

The mansion would become the home of the Yale School of Forestry. In 1926, when the Peabody trust investments improved and debts and mortgages were finally paid off, Yale cleared another $10,000 from the Marsh estate.

Marsh's memorial service was held in the Yale's Battelle Memorial Chapel, and he was buried in the college plot in the Grove Street Cemetery. His death notice listed three survivors: a half brother, James P. Marsh of Chicago; a half sister, Mrs. Edward Walker of Batavia, New York; and his private secretary, Thomas Atwater Bostwick.

His gravestone read: "Eminent as an explorer, collector, and investigator in science. To Yale he gave his collections, his services, and his estate."

Now, at long last the feud, begun three decades before in the workshop of the old Philadelphia Academy of Natural Sciences, where the bones of the *Elasmosaurus* had been laid out not quite the correctly, was finally over.

Or was it?

❖

By first decade of the new century, big dinosaurs were going up in American museums almost as fast as skyscrapers were rising in New York or Model Ts were being turned out in Detroit.

Even at Yale, dinosaurs were now being built. Beecher, who succeeded his mentor at the Peabody, immediately set about mounting a specimen of Marsh's *Claosaurus.* A member of the Hadrosaurids, Beecher mounted the animal in 1901, in an upright and running pose.

Although Andrew Carnegie had not been able to buy a *Brontosaurus* for his museum, once the Carnegie Museum got its own crews into the field, it found a beast that surpassed Marsh's biggest dinosaur. On July 4, 1899, the Carnegie team discovered a gigantic *Diplodocus* at Sheep Creek, Wyoming.[23]

J. B. Hatcher immediately began a paper restoration of the dinosaur, which showed that it was a most enormous beast—eighty-seven feet long. It was distinctive enough to be its own species and was named *Diplodocus carnegii*.

But Carnegie wanted more than just a drawing. He wanted a solid, standing dinosaur. So Hatcher began putting together the millionaire's namesake. When Marsh reconstructed his *Brontosaurus,* he had tucked the legs under the torso, giving it an erect stance and vertical stride, like an elephant. Similarly, that it is how Cope imagined his giraffelike *Camarasaurus,* as it ambled grazing on treetops. That was the way the masters had divined these animals, and that is how Hatcher began with his beast as well.

Hatcher never got the chance to complete the *Diplodocus carnegii,* his life cut short in 1904 after a bout of typhoid fever, at age forty-three. The directorship for the museum and the job of completing the dinosaur fell to William J. Holland.

When Holland had finished it, *Diplodocus carnegii* was more than eighty-seven feet long. It stood twelve feet high at the shoulder, and its head was perched twenty feet in the air. This was far and away the largest land animal ever known to walk the planet.

England's King Edward VII was absolutely awed when he saw *Diplodocus,* and expressed the hope to Carnegie that perhaps one day the British Museum might be home to such a magnificent dinosaur. That's all Carnegie had to hear. He asked Holland if a skeleton could be provided for the king. It had taken two quarries and several years' excavation to provide enough bones for the great dinosaur standing in Pittsburgh. The chances of doing that again, at least on demand, were slim. But Holland suggested that they could manufacture a dinosaur. It seemed an appropriate exercise for an industrial town like Pittsburgh.

In early 1905, a complete set of plaster replicas of the *Diplodocus* bones arrived in London. A Carnegie Museum preparer soon followed to oversee the assembly, and in May, there was a formal ceremony for the presentation of the dinosaur. Lord Avebury officially accepted the dinosaur from Carnegie. Great scientists and peers of the realm filled the British

Museum's Gallery of Reptiles. (*Diplodocus* was too big to fit into the Hall of Paleontology.)

So delighted was Carnegie with the pomp and prestige that he made presents of *Diplodocus* to Kaiser Wilhem and French Premier Georges Clemenceau. Soon everyone was clamoring for a copy, and in short order, the *Diplodocus* arrived in St. Petersburg, Vienna, Bologna, Mexico City, and La Plata, Argentina.

This created an unprecedented phenomenon, for the first time paleontologists all over the world could look at the same bones, the same mounting. They looked, and, of course, they immediately disagreed. Some paleontologists thought that Hatcher and Holland—like Cope and Marsh before them—had made a mistake in putting together the bones.

The most strident and vocal of these critics were in Germany. A generation earlier Marsh, as other young Americans aspiring to careers in science, had made the pilgrimage to study at the great German universities. It was necessary to do so, if one wanted to be a legitimate scientist. So one might have thought that the German criticism would strike a serious blow to American confidence.

Berlin's Gustav Tornier argued that since dinosaurs were reptiles, their pose was doubtlessly more reptilian. The limbs of the *Diplodocus,* Tornier contended, stuck out from the sides, like those of an alligator. The model Carnegie gave to Frankfurt was even dismantled and reconstructed with the legs sprawling out from the sides. Other German paleontologists followed Tornier's lead and belittled their American colleagues.

Affairs, however, had changed, just as Werner von Seiman's had predicted. America had become increasingly confident in its institutions and science. The United States now had several large, well-financed museums and dozens of universities awarding doctoral degrees. In 1899, Johns Hopkins alone had 514 Ph.D. candidates and had 184 doctoral graduates teaching in colleges and universities around the country.[24] Yale, which had only four members on its science faculty when Marsh was a student, now had nearly seventy. No, the Americans were not cowed by the German critics.

Besides this spat wasn't simply about Holland's Pittsburgh *Diplodocus.* In Chicago, Elmer Riggs was mounting for the Field Museum a *Brachiosaurus* he discovered at Grand Junction, Colorado. In New York, the American Museum of Natural History had just mounted its first *Brontosaurus.* All these sauropod dinosaurs, like elephants, had their legs beneath their bodies. That is the way the Americans saw dinosaurs.

Tornier had sketched the *Diplodocus* in a crocodile pose. It looked ludicrous to the Americans. The Germans were working on theory, but

Hatcher, Holland, Osborn, Williston, and the other young American paleontologists had handled many dinosaur bones. They had a tactile, perhaps
almost visceral sense about these animals.

"Hatcher had handled scores of fossil joints," wrote Robert Bakker, one
of America's most provocative modern-day paleontologists. "He knew that
Diplodocus's thigh had a cylindrical surface at the joint that faced predomi-
nantly upward and forward. *Diplodocus*'s hipbone contained a deep socket at
the joint, whose surface correspondingly faced mostly downward and backward. Put the thighbone into the hip socket, and only one correct fit was
possible: the hind leg stood vertically, with the knee facing forward."

The Americans attacked the Germans as being "closet-naturalists" and
Holland ridiculed Tornier's crocodile sketch as at best "a contribution to the
literature of caricature." As a piece of paleontology, he snapped, it was a
"skeletal monstrosity."

In 1910, the Germans finally got their own great dinosaur graveyard in
East Africa at Tendaguru. It was filled with *Brachiosaurus* bones, and soon
paleontologists back in Berlin could see, touch, and feel what the Americans
had already known.

But just in case there were any remaining doubters, or if any scent of dis-
sent still lingered, the case was firmly settled in 1930 by Roland T. Bird,
another paleontologist at the American Museum of Natural History. Bird
had been working near the town of Glen Rose, Texas, when he found a
remarkable set of dinosaur tracks. There in the bed of the Paluxy River, in
what had once been Cretaceous mud, was the complete trail of a sixty-foot
Brontosaurus.

The beast's stride was twelve feet long, but the width of the trail was just
six feet. If the animal had had sprawled legs, the trail would have had to have
been much wider. Once again, the American West had offered up the fossil to prove the point. There was no doubt now that the Americans had been
correct.

The great dinosaurs walked Earth just as Cope and Marsh had pictured
them. It was an outcome to one more scientific battle that both Cope and
Marsh probably would have delighted in, even if they disagreed about
everything else.

Afterword

EXACTLY THIRTY MINUTES—and one hundred years—after Thomas Bostwick leaned over O. C. Marsh's deathbed and closed the old man's eyes, six-year-old Katie Lisk walked into the Peabody Museum with her kindergarten class from the Holy Family School in Fairfield, Connecticut.

This March day was not cold and rainy, but full of the coming spring, and Katie was wearing her gray Holy Family sweatshirt and blue Holy Family sweatpants—the school's kindergarten garb—and with each step her little white running shoes sparked with red lights.

The class entered the museum's great hall. Here was the *Triceratops* head that J. B. Hatcher had won in Wyoming, and a *Chasmosaurus* skull unearthed by Charles Sternberg. There was also a *Mosasaurus* from the Kansas days. But dominating the room was the huge skeleton made from the bones of Como Bluff, the fruit of Bill Reed's hard work.

The nameplate for the huge beast read *"Brontosaurus excelsus."* But Katie Lisk turned her little blond head upward and regarded the beast with her pale blue eyes. "It's an *Apatosaurus,*" she announced.

"Very good," the tour guide said. "Does anyone know what the *Apatosaurus* ate?"

"Plants," piped up Katie's classmate Hayden Collins, a bold little boy with a neo–Buster Brown haircut.

"That's right," the guide said.

The children moved from fossil to fossil mesmerized by the massive skulls with their spooky, vacant eye sockets and menacing sharp teeth.

"How did they put all the pieces together?"

"Is that blood on those teeth?"

They came to Marsh's *Stegosaurus ungulatus.* "Does anyone know what those spikes on its back were for?" the guide asked.

Katie Lisk's hand shot up. "For cooling," she said.

When asked why the dinosaurs disappeared, Katie and her classmates were less certain. "Buried in an avalanche," Katie offered. "Maybe they couldn't find enough to eat," Hayden proposed. The kindergartners' befuddlement was only slightly greater than the most distinguished paleontologists, for while science has been able to rule out avalanches, no one really knows what happened to the dinosaurs. That mystery remains part of their allure.

The next room was filled with mammal fossils, including Marsh's papier-mâché uintathere, a titantothere, and an ancient Irish elk skeleton. There were also the bones of an oreodont and the little Eocene horse *Hyracotherium vaseicciene.* But the children walked past these hard-won treasures quickly. After all, they were not dinosaurs.

The next room, however, held a small, provocative specimen—the *Sinosauropteryx*—and the children crowded around. Discovered by Chinese paleontologists in a quarry in Liaoning Province, the Cretaceous rock slab had preserved not only bone but some of the surrounding soft tissue as well. Those tissues clearly show what looks like quill points. *Sinosauropteryx* was covered with a dense coat of "protofeathers." It was a feathered dinosaur. The children buzzed at the idea. "Did dinosaurs fly?"

⚜

The idea of feathered dinosaurs has also sent a hum through the science community, and while the children imagined their flying dinosaurs, John Ostrom, one of the prime proponents of the feathered dinosaur theory, and emeritus Yale professor and Peabody curator of paleontology, was puttering around in his upstairs office.

Ostrom had come to Yale in 1961, as a thirty-three-year-old junior professor. "I was nervous. I was stepping into a great tradition and a great opportunity. I wondered if I could do it," he remembers.

Did Marsh's ghost and legacy haunt the Peabody? (Actually this was a new Peabody. Marsh's building and been torn down and replaced in 1924.) "I did not sense the presence of Marsh," Ostrom said, "but I knew he had been here. Let's face it, the guy was an SOB."

By the 1960s, it was thought, once again, that dinosaurs had been mainly reptilian, mainly cold-blooded, and mainly slow moving. Then in 1969, Ostrom found a relatively small bipedal dinosaur in the Cretaceous Cloverly sandstone of Montana. He named it *Deinonychus,* or "terrible claw." *Deinonychus,* Ostrom explained, "was just built for action." Like Cope imagining his *Laelaps,* Ostrom could see his *Deinonychus* as a leaping, agile predator, and it became the model for the dangerous and clever dinosaur that stalked the humans in Michael Crichton's *Jurassic Park.*

Deinonychus led Ostrom to revive the idea, casually posited by Sir Richard Owen more than a century earlier, that dinosaurs were, like mammals, warm blooded. It was a controversial proposal and one that Robert Bakker—just a Yale undergraduate at the time—would pursue relentlessly and artfully.

One of the main arguments against warm-bloodedness for dinosaurs was that, unlike mammals or birds, the ancient beasts didn't have coverings of fur or feathers to insulate and hold in body heat. Or did they? This is what sent Ostrom on a twenty-year search for the feathered dinosaur. It was a search that ended for the elderly Yale professor in 1998 at a quarry six hundred miles northeast of Beijing.

Along the way, Ostrom resuscitated another old idea—Huxley's link between theropod dinosaurs and birds. By examining every *Archaeopteryx* specimen in the world and comparing them to dromaesurid dinosaurs (like *Deinonychus),* Ostrom was able to detail a large number of shared similarities, similarities that birds do not share with thecodonts or crocodiles, the two other reptile families from which birds might have come.

Ostrom has gained his share of critics over the idea and one veritable nemesis in Alan Feduccia of the University of North Carolina. Rather than seeing the fossils as reptiles on their way to becoming birds, Feduccia believes they are the remains of ancient birds that had lost the power of flight and had come to resemble theropods. "In my opinion," Feduccia has predicted, "the theropod origin of birds will be the greatest embarrassment of paleontology in the 20th Century." Shades of Cope and Marsh.

Well, how does Marsh hold up in the eyes of his modern-day successor? "I think Marsh was a lot smarter than most people give him credit for," Ostrom said. "He knew paleontology was going to be big and he asked the right questions. . . . Marsh acted as if science were a big business."

Marsh's names for dinosaur groups—sauropods, theropods, and ornithopods—are still used today, Ostrom pointed out. Marsh remains the preeminent namer of dinosaurs, with nineteen genera to his credit. That's five better than anyone else.

Even more important, Ostrom said, Marsh was one of the most eloquent and important defenders of Darwinian evolution. It is, he said, an idea that still needs defending. "You know this university hasn't taken a position on evolution since the Scopes trial in the 1920s," Ostrom said. "I think it's about time it did. Science is being cowed by the Creationists today."

One hundred seventy miles to the south of New Haven, at the University of Pennsylvania, Peter Dodson could be found working in a smaller, but equally cluttered, office. Although he is a Yale man and a protégé of Ostrom, as Penn's premier dinosaur paleontologist, it could be said that he is the inheritor of Cope's mantle.

"When it came to dinosaurs, Cope was always a day late and a dollar short," Dodson said. A dollar short, indeed. Marsh's ability to collect vast amounts of material ultimately ensured his chances of being more accurate. Of the twenty-six dinosaur genera that Cope named only three survive today: *Camarasaurus, Monoclonious,* and *Coelophysis.*

Coelophysis had a featured role in *The Lost World,* the movie sequel to *Jurassic Park.* It was the friendly little dinosaur that was repeatedly hit with an electric cattle prod to amusement of one of the bad guys. But when that very bad guy lost his way he was attacked and killed by a whole pack of *Coelophysis.*

Hard times, however, still seem to dog Cope, and he may not even be able to hang on to this name. "There is a move to rename *Coelophysis,"* Dodson said. Why? The same old story. Cope made his claim and named his name based on scant material, and now paleontologists are debating whether it might not be better to rename the animal *Rioarribasaurus.*

Even with the erasing and retooling of dinosaur names, the number of dinosaur genera has grown from roughly one hundred in the days of Cope and Marsh to more than 336. Dodson calculates that there are potentially another one thousand genera waiting to be discovered.

By far and away the largest number of dinosaur discoveries—sixty-four—have been made in America. "The United States is a large country and we have geological formations that span the entire Mesozoic," Dodson explained. "It's really the only place you find that and it still makes the U.S. prime dinosaur hunting country."

The single most fertile geological vein in America has been the Judith River formation, which Cope first explored—at the risk of meeting Sitting Bull and his braves—back in 1876. Thirty different dinosaurs have been pulled from the Judith.

"Cope was really quite a good scientist and clearly a high order intellect," Dodson said. "His 1,400 published scientific papers is still a record number." And while Marsh may have found and named more dinosaurs, Dodson said, "there are no *ideas* associated with Marsh."

On the other hand Cope's concept of archosaurs and his "law" that over time species tend to become bigger are still used by and debated among scientists. For decades, Cope's law has been one of the organizing precepts of paleontology. Dodson has said, "While we now know that it isn't absolute, it is used and regularly discussed in the literature.

"Each man in his own right has left a legacy," Dodson said, "and each was a distinguished researcher. But really it seems impossible to say one name without the other. Cope and Marsh. Bonnie and Clyde. Adam and Eve. It's like that."

❖

Katie Lisk's class had just about finished its visit to the museum. The children were crowded into the gift shop to buy dinosaur postcards, dinosaur models, and dinosaur key rings. What would Marsh have thought? Probably nothing very nice. But Cope likely would have been delighted. He certainly would have found Katie Lisk adorable and perhaps would have taught her "Je suis un prince," the song he sang to his Julia when she was a little girl.

But how was it that Katie knew so much about dinosaurs? Katie, as little girls sometimes are, was shy with strangers, and could only manage to look away and say, ever so softly, "Our teachers taught us." But her classmate Hayden promptly and loudly exclaimed, "I watch a lot of dinosaur stuff."

As the Holy Family kindergartners were preparing to leave the Peabody, a small band of museum staffers also left and made its way to the Prospect Street Cemetery. The group ambled to the back corner plot where O. C. Marsh's tombstone—a squat, red-granite stone on a black base—stood in the shade of a yew tree. But on this near spring day, the group was more in the mood for festivity than a somber marking of the hundredth anniversary of Marsh's passing. So they picnicked at the graveside and laid a small bouquet of flowers on the stone. Then they scattered a few kernels of popcorn for any dinosaurs that might also stop by to pay their respects.

Notes

Chapter One

1. Hall's letter is reproduced on p. 21 of the 1869 pamphlet "The American Goliath," which was printed in Syracuse and sold at the Cardiff Giant's pavilion. A copy of the pamphlet is among Marsh's papers.

2. Henry James, *Washington Square* (New York: Penguin Books, 1986), 27; originally published in 1880.

3. Wallace Stegner, *Beyond the Hundredth Meridian* (New York: Penguin Books, 1992), 9–21.

4. David Hull, *Darwin and His Critics* (Chicago: University of Chicago Press, 1983), 37.

5. John M. Clarke, *James Hall of Albany—Geologist & Paleontologist* (Albany: 1921), 412.

6. Marsh correspondence, reel 1, frame 185, Nov. 30, 1869.

7. "The Cardiff Giant," *New York Sun,* 9 April 1899. A copy of the article is among Marsh's papers.

8. "Exposed by Prof. Marsh, Yale Man Tells Story of Cardiff Giant Episode," *New Haven Register,* 26 December 1897.

9. Marsh correspondence, reel 6, frame 1012, 5 May 1871.

10. Ibid., reel 7, frames 1, 10, 25, 13 Feb. 1873, 19 March 1873, 23 Apr. 1873.

11. Charles Schuchert and Clara Mae LeVene, *O. C. Marsh, Pioneer in Paleontology* (New York: Arno Press, 1978), 349; originally published in 1940 by Yale University Press.

Chapter Two

1. Dorothy Gordon Beers, "The Centennial City 1865–1876," in *Philadelphia, A 300-Year History,* ed. Russell K. Weigly (New York: W. W. Norton, 1983), 427.

2. E. D. Cope, "Remarks on Laelaps aquilunguis," *Proceedings of the Academy of Natural Sciences of Philadelphia* 18 (1866): 275–79.

3. *Proceedings of the ANSP* 10 (1868): 304.

4. Cope correspondence, letter 52, 4 January 1863. American Museum of Natural History Archives, New York City

5. Marsh correspondence, reel 3, frames 837–50, 28 Feb.; 1870. E. D. Cope Papers collection, Quaker Collection, Haverford College, collection 956, Haverford, Pa.

6. O. C. Marsh, "Notice of Some New Mosauroid Reptiles from the Green Sands of New Jersey," *American Journal of Science and Arts* 48 (November 1869).

7. Leidy correspondence, *ANSP,* 4 March 1868.

8. *Proceedings of the ANSP* 20 (1868): 92.

9. Cope correspondence, letter 96, 2 April 1868.

10. Adrian J. Desmond, *The Hot Blooded Dinosaurs—A Revolution in Paleontology* (London: Blond & Briggs, 1975), 10.

11. Charles Lyell, *Principles of Geology, Being an Attempt to Explain the Former Changes of the Earth's Surface,* vol. 3 (London: John Murray, 1833), 389–93.

12. James Dwight Dana, *Manual of Geology* (New York: Ivison, Blakeman & Co., 1880), 833, 391.

13. Hugh Torrens, "Politics and Paleontology: Richard Owen and the Invention of Dinosaurs," in *The Complete Dinosaur,* ed. James O. Farlow et al. (Bloomington: Indiana University Press, 1997), 175–90.

14. Marsh correspondence, reel 25, frame 427, 1864.

15. *Proceedings of the ANSP* 22 (1870): 9.

16. Ibid., 9–11.

17. Marsh correspondence, reel 1, frame 822, 20 March 1870.

18. Ibid., reel 3, frame 866, 28 February 1870.

Chapter Three

1. Marsh correspondence, reel 2, frame 194, 30 April 1870.

2. Ibid., reel 9, frame 584, 23 September 1864, and reel 9, frame 610, 22 May 1870.

3. George Bird Grinnell, *Leading American Men of Science—O. C. Marsh* (New York: Henry Holt & Co., 1910), 286.

4. Marsh correspondence, reel 21, frame 684, 15 October 1861.

5. Schuchert and LeVene, *O. C. Marsh,* 75.

6. March correspondence, reel 22, frame 471, 12 July 1868.

7. Ibid., reel 15, frame 48, 3 June 1873.

8. Ibid., reel 26, frames 547–51, chapter from Marsh's unpublished autobiography, "Fossil Hunting in the Rocky Mountains." Three draft chapters of Marsh's autobiography are among his correspondence and papers.

9. Stegner, *Hundredth Meridian,* 119.

10. Marsh correspondence, reel 26, frames 311–14, chapter from Marsh's unpublished autobiography, "My First Visit to the Rocky Mountains."

11. Ibid., reel 3, frame 851, 4 June 1870.

12. Schuchert and LeVene, *O. C. Marsh,* 37–38.

13. Don Russell, *The Lives and Legends of Buffalo Bill* (Norman: University of Oklahoma Press, 1960), 167.

14. Robert M. Utley, *Frontier Regulars—The United States Army and the Indians, 1866–1890* (New York: Macmillan, 1973), 157.

15. William F. Cody, "The Great West That Was, Buffalo Bill's Life Story," *Hearst's Magazine* (April 1917).

16. Charles Wyllys Betts, "The Yale College Expedition of 1870," *Harper's New Monthly Magazine* 43, no. 257 (October 1871): 664.

17. Ibid., 665.

18. Ibid., 666.

19. George Bird Grinnell, "An Old-Time Bone Hunt," *Natural History* 23, no. 4 (July–August 1923): 334.

20. Marsh correspondence, reel 3, frame 151, 30 July 1870.

21. "Professor Marsh's Rocky Mountain Expedition," *American Journal of Sciences & Arts* 50, no. 149 (September 1870): 292.

22. Ibid., 335.

23. Harry Zeigler, "The Rocky Mountains—Results of the Yale College Expedition to the Far West," *New York Weekly Herald,* 24 December 1870, p. 422.

24. Betts, "The Yale College Expedition," 671.

25. Clarke, *James Hall,* 346.

26. Mike Foster, *Strange Genius—The Life of Ferdinand Vandeveer Hayden* (Niwot, Colo.: Roberts Rinehart Publishers, 1994) 158–59.

27. Joseph Leidy correspondence, 11 September 1870.

28. Ferdinand Hayden correspondence, *ANSP,* 8 September 1870.

29. Ferdinand Hayden correspondence, Fryxell Collection 1638, box 44, American Heritage Center, University of Wyoming, Laramie, Wy., 16 November 1870.

30. Joseph Leidy correspondence, *ANSP,* 12 November 1870.

31. *At Home in Ellis County Kansas, 1867–1992,* vol. 1 (Hays, Kans: Ellis County Historical Society).

32. "From Kansas to Denver," *Ottawa (Kans.) Journal,* 29 September 1870.

33. P. T. Barnum, *Struggles and Triumphs* (1869; reprint, New York: Viking Penguin, 1981), 393.

34. Blaine Burket, *Wild Bill Hickok—The Law in Hays City* (Hays, Kans.: Ellis County Historical Society, 1996), 9.

35. Marsh correspondence, reel 26, frames 253–60, chapter from Marsh's unpublished autobiography, "My First Buffalo Hunt."

36. *Fossil Collecting in Cretaceous Niobrara Chalk.* Kansas Geological Survey, Open-File Report 97–62 (1997).

37. Zeigler, "Rocky Mountains," 422.

38. Marsh correspondence, reel 26, frames 260–68, chapter from Marsh unpublished autobiography, "A Thanksgiving Dinner on the Plains."

39. Ibid., frames 269–75, chapter from Marsh's unpublished autobiography, "My First Pterodactyl."

Chapter Four

1. Cope correspondence, letter 30, 1 January 1856.

2. Ibid., letter 45, 16 September 1860.

3. Ibid., letter 49, 1 February 1861.

4. Schuchert and LeVene, *O. C. Marsh,* 47.

5. Marsh correspondence, reel 21, frame 672, 4 May 1862.

6. Cope correspondence, letter 53, 10 January 1863.

7. Pamela M. Henson, "Spencer Baird's Vision for a National Museum—The Megatherium Club," *Smithsonian Research Reports* (winter 1996); http://www.150.si.edu/chp3/club.htm.

8. Cope correspondence, letter 54, 12 March 1863.

9. W. H. Ballou, "Marsh Hurls Azoic Facts," *New York Herald,* 19 January 1890, whole no. 19058, edition 11.

10. Cope correspondence, letter 70, 11 February 1864.

11. Charles Yarnall Papers collection, Quaker Collection, collection 910, Haverford College, Haverford, Pa., 13 July 1864.

12. Cope correspondence, letter 71, 23 December 1864.

13. E. R. Dunn, "Edward Drinker Cope," *Haverfordian* 59, no. 2 (May 1940): 16.

14. Presifor Frazer, "The Life and Letters of Edward Drinker Cope," *American Geologist* 26, no. 2 (August 1900): 126.

15. Edward C. Carter II, *One Grand Pursuit: A Brief History of the American Philosophical Society's First 250 Years, 1743–1993* (Philadelphia: American Philosophical Society, 1993), 34–35.

16. Henry Fairfield Osborn, "Biographical Memoir of Edward Drinker Cope," *National Academy of Sciences Biographical Memoirs* 13 (1929): 170.

17. Thomas Holmes, "The Haddonfield Home of Edward Drinker Cope." Monograph of the Historical Society of Haddonfield, N.J., 1992.

18. Cope correspondence, letter 93, 22 March 1868.

19. Ibid., letter 91, 17 March 1868.

20. William B. Gallagher, *When Dinosaurs Roamed New Jersey* (New Brunswick, N.J.: Rutgers University Press, 1997), 35.

21. Cope correspondence, letter 102, 2 February 1869.

22. Ibid., letter 103, 7 April 1869.

23. Marsh, "First Pterodactyl."

24. Marsh correspondence, reel 2, frame 270, 27 May 1871.

25. O. C. Marsh, "Notice of Some Fossil Reptiles from the Cretaceous and Tertiary Formations with a Note on a New and Gigantic Species of Pterodactyl," *American Journal of Science and Arts* 1 (June 1871): 472.

26. Marsh correspondence, reel 21, frames 781, 823, 867. There are fifty-six letters from Elizabeth Dixon covering the years 1858 to 1867.

27. Ibid., reel 21, frame 792, 29 June 1859.

28. Ibid., reel 21, frame 801, 20 July 1859.

29. Ibid., reel 21, frame 810, 27 September 1859.

30. Ibid., reel 21, frame 842, 10 January 1861.

31. Ibid., reel 21, frames 781, 821, 29 June 1859 and June 1860.

32. Ibid., reel 22, frame 175, 25 August 1861; and reel 22, frame 185, 9 January 1862.

33. Ibid., reel 21, frames 894, 904, 9 January 1863 and 16 December 1864.

34. Ibid., reel 22, frame 579, 12 December 1866.

35. Ibid., reel 26, frame 353, address by George Bird Grinnell.

36. Ibid., reel 5, frame 319, 18 April 1879.

37. Ibid., reel 2, frame 939, 31 March 1871.

38. "The Yale Expedition of 1871," *College Courant* 10, no. 5 (3 February 1872), 49.

Chapter Five

1. Cope correspondence, letter 115, 6 September 1871.

2. Ibid., letter 116, 7 September 1871.

3. E. D. Cope, "The Vertebrata of the Cretaceous Formations of the West," *Report of the United States Geological and Geographical Survey of the Territories,* vol. 2 (1875), 42–50.

4. Ibid., 42.

5. Ibid., 46–48.

6. Cope correspondence, letter 119, 19 October 1871.

7. E. D. Cope, "On Two New Ornithosaurians," *Proceedings of the American Philosophical Society* (1 March 1872): 420.

8. Richard Zakrzewski, *A Brief History of Vertebrate Paleontology in Western Kansas* (Hays, Kans.: Department of Earth Sciences, Hays State University and the Sternberg Memorial Museum), 124.

9. Cope correspondence, letter 116, 7 September 1871.

10. Ibid., letter 117, 13 September 1871.

11. W. E. Webb, *Buffalo Land: An Authentic Narrative of the Adventures and Misadventures of a Late Scientific and Sporting Party upon the Great Plains* (Cincinnati & Chicago: E. Hannaford & Co., 1872). Webb's account is problematic. There is a period of about twenty-five days from early November to early December when Cope might have made the trip with Webb. The train ride from Philadelphia to Leavenworth, Kansas, took just twenty-seven hours. But there are no letters from Kansas in Cope's correspondence during this time period. Furthermore, it is clear that some points in Webb's narrative are fictionalized. For example, the party meets Wild Bill Hickok in Hays. But Hickok had left town by the fall of 1871. They also meet Buffalo Bill, which is historically possible, but not likely. On the other hand, Cope credits Webb in several reports with helping him, and Webb's Professor Paleozoic sounds a lot like Cope. It is difficult to imagine that Webb could construct such monologues on his own. At best, *Buffalo Land* is a true narrative dressed up with a few historical characters. At worst, it is an impressionistic pastiche, but is still valuable for the way Webb describes his friend Professor Paleozoic, a.k.a. E. D. Cope.

12. Ibid., 36.

13. "Hays by Moonlight," *Manhattan (Kans.) Standard,* 8 May 1869, files of Ellis County Historical Society.

14. Burket, *Wild Bill,* 18–19.

15. Webb, Buffalo Land, 142.

16. Ibid., 108.

17. Ibid., 208.

18. Ibid., 244–45.

19. R. S. Ellison, *Fort Bridger—A Brief History* (Cheyenne: Wyoming State Archives, Museum and History Department, 1931).

20. William A. Carter Collection 3535, box 2, legal documents, American Heritage Center, University of Wyoming.

21. "Yale Expedition," *College Courant,* 50.

22. "The Yale Party—Return of the Expedition to Salt Lake," *New York Times,* 17 October 1871, vol. 21, no. 6236, edition 2.

23. Mary Faith Pusey, "The Yale Scientific Expedition of 1871," *Manuscripts* (spring 1876): 97–105. This article is based largely upon the diaries of one of the Yale students, George G. Lobdell Jr.

24. Robert M. West, "Vertebrate Paleontology of the Green River, Wyoming 1840–1910," *Earth Sciences History* 9, no. 1 (1990): 46.

25. Leidy correspondence, *ANSP,* 2 November 1870.

26. Marsh correspondence, reel 3, frame 781, 20 April 1872, and frame 783, 8 November 1890.

Chapter Six

1. Cope correspondence, letter 117, 22 June 1872.

2. Marsh correspondence, reel 3, frame 166, 6 July 1872.

3. Ibid., reel 3, frame 163, 2 June 1872.

4. Ibid., reel 4, frame 219, 11 July 1872.

5. Cope correspondence, letter 119, 27 July 1872.

6. Ferdinand Hayden correspondence, Fryxell Collection 1638, box 51, American Heritage Center, University of Wyoming, Laramie, Wy., 14 July 1872.

7. Cope correspondence, letter #118, 17 July 1872.

8. Marsh correspondence, reel 4, frame 169, 23 July 1872.

9. Cope correspondence, letter 101, 30 December 1868.

10. Osborn, Cope Master Naturalist Correspondence, American Museum of Natural History Archives, New York, N.Y., 1935 correspondence file. This file includes copies of two letters about H's review, provided by Leidy's family. One letter is from Newberry to Leidy, 20 January 1869; the other is from Leidy to Joseph Henry, 14 February 1869.

11. E. D. Cope, "The Geological Age of the Wyoming Coal," *American Naturalist* 6, no. 11 (November 1872): 670.

12. *Agthaumas* is no longer used to identify the animal. It is what paleontologists call a *nomina dubia,* based on fragmentary material. The animal is now thought to be a kind of *Triceratops.* See Brent H. Briethaupt, "Lance Formation," in *Encyclopedia of Dinosaurs,* ed. Philip Currie and Kevin Padian (New York: Academic Press, 1997), 394.

13. E. D. Cope, "On the Existence of Dinosauria in the Transition Beds of Wyoming," *Transactions of the American Philosophical Society* 12 (19 September 1872): 483.

14. Marsh correspondence, reel 3, frame 384, 16 July 1872.

15. Ibid., reel 3, frame 169, 23 July 1872.

16. Ibid., reel 3, frame 294, 25 July 1872.

17. Ibid., reel 15, frame 393, 21 July 1872.

18. E. D. Cope, "Descriptions of Some New Vertebrae from the Bridger Group of the Eocene," *Transactions of the American Philosophical Society* 12 (29 July 1872): 460–65.

19. E. D. Cope, "Second Account of the New Vertebrae from the Bridger Group," *Transactions of the American Philosophical Society* 12 (3 August 1872): 466–68.

20. Marsh correspondence, reel 26, frames 276–84, chapter from Marsh's unpublished autobiography, "A Ride for Life in a Herd of Buffalo."

21. Adrian Desmond, *Archetypes and Ancestors* (Chicago: University of Chicago Press, 1982), 124–31, 144–45, offers an excellent discussion of the issue.

22. Marsh correspondence, reel 15, frame 397, 28 August 1872.

23. William Berryman Scott, *Memories of a Paleontologist* (Princeton, N.J.: Princeton University Press, 1939), 231.

24. Cope correspondence, letter 120, 8 September 1872.

25. James Manley correspondence, vertical file Fort Bridger State Historic Site Museum, Fort Bridger, Wy., 23 September 1872.

26. Cope correspondence, unnumbered, 21 September 1872. This is the only letter by Anne Cope in the entire collection.

27. Ferdinand Hayden correspondence, Fryxell Collection 1638, box 51, American Heritage Center, University of Wyoming, Laramie, Wy., 21 July 1872.

28. Ibid., 20 September 1872.

29. Ibid., 10 October 1872.

30. Cope correspondence, letter 122, 12 October 1872.

31. Ibid., letter 123, 13 October 1872.

32. E. D. Cope, "On a New Vertebrate Genus from the Northern Part of the Tertiary Basin of the Green River," *Transactions of the American Philosophical Society* 12 (12 October 1872): 554–55.

33. Cope correspondence, letter 124, 19 October 1872.

34. T. A. Larson, *History of Wyoming* (Lincoln: University of Nebraska Press, 1978), 115.

35. Thurman Wilkins, *Clarence King, a Biography* (New York: Macmillan, 1958), 183.

36. Hayden correspondence, Fryxell Collection 1638, box 51, American Heritage Center, University of Wyoming, 30 October 1872.

37. Leidy correspondence, ANSP, 29 November 1872.

Chapter Seven

1. Laurence H. Skelton, "Kansas Skirmishes in the Cope-Marsh War," *Earth Science History—Journal of the History of Earth Science Society* 3, no. 2 (1984): 119.

2. O. C. Marsh, "On a New Class of Fossil Birds," *American Journal of Science and Arts* 5, no. 2 (February 1873): 3.

3. Sankar Chatterjee, *The Rise of Birds* (Baltimore: The Johns Hopkins University Press, 1997), 9–10, 109–12, 229–30.

4. Marsh correspondence, reel 2, frame 235, 22 August 1872.

5. Ibid., reel 2, frame 236, 30 August 1872.

6. Cope correspondence, letter 125, 1 January 1873.

7. Marsh correspondence, reel 3, frame 885, 20 January 1873.

8. Ibid., reel 3, frame 886, 27 January 1873.

9. Ibid., reel 2, frame 888, 30 January 1873.

10. Ibid., reel 3, frame 891, 3 February 1873.

11. Cope correspondence, letter 120, 5 February 1873.

12. O. C. Marsh, "The Fossil Mammals of the Order Dinocerata," *American Naturalist* 7, no. 3 (March 1873): 151.

13. Ibid., 153.

14. E. D. Cope, "The Gigantic Mammals of the Genus Eobasileus," *American Naturalist* 7, no. 3 (March 1873): 157.

15. Ferdinand Hayden correspondence, Fryxell Collection 1638, box 51, American Heritage Center, University of Wyoming, Laramie, Wy., 18 February 1873.

16. O. C. Marsh, "Supplementary Note on the Dinocerata," *American Journal of Science and Arts* 5 (April 1873): 1.

17. Cope correspondence, letter 131, 12 May 1873.

18. Ibid., letter 129, 6 April 1873.

19. Hayden correspondence, Fryxell collection 1638, box 51, 5 April 1873.

20. Ibid., Fryxell Collection, 1638 letter 207, box 44, 26 April 1873.

21. O. C. Marsh, "On the Genus Tinoceras and Its Allies," *American Naturalist* 7, no. 4 (April 1873): 216.

22. Marsh correspondence, reel 1, frame 78, 2 February 1873.

23. Ibid., reel 1, frame 85, 7 June 1873.

24. E. D. Cope, "On Some of Prof. Marsh's Criticism," *American Naturalist* 7, no. 5 (May 1873): 294.

25. O. C. Marsh, "On Tinoceras and Its Allies," *American Naturalist* 7, no. 5 (May 1873): 306.

26. Marsh correspondence, reel 7, frame 751, 23 June 1873.

27. Cope correspondence, E. D. Cope Papers collection, Quaker Collection, Haverford College, collection 956, file folder 17, Haverford, Pa., 3 June 1873.

28. Editorial, *American Naturalist* 7, no. 6 (June 1873): 384.

29. O. C. Marsh, "Reply to Professor Cope's Explanation," *American Naturalist* 7, no. 6 (June 1873): appendix, page v.

30. E. D. Cope, "On Professor Marsh's Criticisms," *American Naturalist* 7, no. 7 (July 1873): appendix.

31. Hayden correspondence, Fryxell Collection 1638, box 44, American Heritage Center, University of Wyoming, 8 September 1872.

32. Leidy correspondence, *ANSP,* 13 April 1873.

33. Leidy correspondence, *ANSP,* 16 April 1873.

34. Leidy correspondence, *ANSP,* 18 April 1873.

35. Henry Fairfield Osborn, "Joseph Leidy," *National Academy Biographical Memoirs* vol. 7 (1913): 365.

36. Walter H. Wheeler, "The Uintatheres and the Cope-Marsh War," *Science* 131 (22 April 1960): 1171–76.

37. O. C. Marsh, *Dinocerata, A Monograph of an Extinct Order of Gigantic Mammals,* vol. 10. (Washington, D.C.: U.S. Geological Survey, 1884), 189–90.

38. Cope correspondence, letter 132, 26 May 1873.

39. Hayden correspondence, Fryxell Collection, box 51, American Heritage Center Archives, University of Wyoming, 21 December 1873.

40. Cope correspondence, letter 134, 6 July 1873.

41. E. D. Cope, "On the Zoology of a Temporary Pool on the Plains of Colorado," *Proceedings of the American Philosophical Society* 14 (June 1874): 139–40.

42. Cope correspondence, letter 135, 18 July 1873.

43. "The Yale Expedition," *New York Tribune,* 7 November 1873, vol. 33, no. 10, 178, p. 3.

44. Cope correspondence, letter 137, 3 October 1873.

45. Marsh correspondence, reel 3, frame 179, 13 August 1873.

46. Ibid., reel 3, frames 184–85, 5 November 1873.

47. Hayden correspondence, Fryxell Collection 1638, box 44, American Heritage Center, University of Wyoming, 27 September 1873.

48. Ellis Paxon Oberholtzer, *Jay Cooke—Financier of the Civil War,* vol. 3. (Philadelphia: George W. Jacobs & Co., 1907), 447.

49. Marsh correspondence, reel 4, frame 224, 19 September 1873.

50. Marsh correspondence, reel 2, frame 619, 26 November 1873.

51. Hayden correspondence, Fryxell Collection 1638, box 54, American Heritage Center, University of Wyoming, Laramie, Wy., 3 December 1873.

52. Marsh correspondence, reel 9, frame 34, 8 December 1873.

53. Hayden correspondence, Fryxell Collection 1638, box 40, American Heritage Center, University of Wyoming, 29 October 1873.

54. Ibid., 12 November 1873.

55. Marsh correspondence, reel 4, frame 663, 12 December 1873.

56. Ibid., reel 4, frame 668, 15 December 1873.

Chapter Eight

1. Robert K. Bruce, *The Launching of Modern American Science* (New York: Alfred A. Knopf, 1987), 220.

2. Letters from Joseph Leidy to Ferdinand Hayden, 28 April 1863 and 7 June 1863. The letters appear in Nathan Reingold's *Science in Nineteenth Century America: A Documentary History* (New York: Hill & Wang, 1964), 209.

3. A. Hunter Dupree, *Science in the Federal Government* (Cambridge: Harvard University Press, 1957), 204–05.

4. Marsh correspondence, reel 9, frame 37, 20 April 1874.

5. Testimony of Dr. H. C. Yarrow. H.R. Rep. No. 612. 62, 43rd Cong., 1st sess.

6. Marsh correspondence, reel 9, frame 38, no date.

7. Ferdinand Hayden correspondence, Fryxell Collection 1638, box 44, letter 221, American Heritage Collection, University of Wyoming, 15 May 1874.

8. Ibid., Fryxell Collection 1638, box 44, letter 223, 30 May 1874.

9. Cope correspondence, letter 145, 22 July 1874.

10. Marsh correspondence, reel 26, frame 744, 9 June 1873.

11. Ibid., reel 12, frame 300, 6 April 1874, and frame 337, 2 October 1874.

12. Marsh correspondence, reel 13, frame 20, 6 November 1874.

13. "A Perilous Fossil Hunt—Professor Marsh's Last Trip to the Bad Lands," *New York Tribune,* March 1875, no. 27, Tribune Extras, Lecture and Letter Series, p. 48.

14. Sitting Bull's testimony before Indian Commission, Marsh correspondence, reel 26, frames 6–7.

15. George E. Hyde, *Red Cloud's Folk, A History of the Ogalala Sioux* (Norman: University of Oklahoma Press, 1937), 224–28.

16. James McLaird and Lester V. Turchen, "Exploring the Black Hills, 1855–1875: Reports of the Government Expeditions," *South Dakota History* 4, no. 3 (summer 1974): 303–17; and C. C. O'Hara, "Custer's Black Hills Expedition of 1874," *The Black Hills Engineer* 18, no. 4 (November 1929), p. 46.

17. U.S. Senate, letter from the secretary of war, transmitting a "Report of the Exploration of the Black Hills Under the Command of Bvt. Maj. General George A. Custer," Senate Executive Document 32, 43rd Cong., 2d sess. (1875): 6–8.

18. John D. Bergamini, *The Hundredth Year—The United States in 1876* (New York: G. P. Putnam's Sons, 1976), 47.

19. George Phillips, "The Indian Ring in the Dakota Territory, 1870–1890," *South Dakota History* 2, no. 4 (fall 1972): 349–96.

20. Evidence Before a Committee of the House of Representatives Charged with the Investigation of Misconduct in the Indian Office (1871): 67.

21. Report of the Commissioners Appointed by the Secretary of the Interior to Examine the Red Cloud and Whetstone Indian Agencies. (Washington, D.C. U.S. Government Printing Office, April 23, 1874), 16.

22. J. J. Saville, "First Annual Report—Red Cloud Agency," *Report and Historical Collections—South Dakota Department of History,* vol. 29, 1958 (31 August 1874): 396–97.

23. Cleophas C. O'Hara, *The White River Badlands.* South Dakota School of Mines Bulletin no. 13 (November 1920): 36–48.

24. Richard A. Bartlett, *Great Surveys of the American West* (Norman: University of Oklahoma Press, 1962), 333.

25. Cope correspondence, letter 149, 6 August 1874.

26. Ibid., letter 150, 15 August 1874.

27. Ibid., letter 151, 17 August 1874.

28. Ibid., letter 156, 14 September 1874.

29. E. D. Cope, "Part II—Report upon Extinct Vertebrata Obtained in New Mex-

ico by the Expedition of 1874," *Report upon the United States Geographical Survey West of the One Hundredth Meridian,* vol. 4, *Paleontology* (Washington, D.C., U.S. Government Printing Office, 1877), 72.

30. Cope correspondence, letter 149, 6 August 1874.

31. Ibid., letter 150, 17 August 1874.

32. Ibid., letter 148, 6 August 1874.

33. Utley, *Frontier Regulars,* 219–21.

Chapter Nine

1. Mark Twain and Charles Dudley Warner, *The Gilded Age* (1873; reprint, New York: Meridian-Penguin USA, 1994), 178.

2. Allan Nevins, *Hamilton Fish: The Inner History of the Grant Administration* (New York: Dodd, Mead, 1936),

3. Constance McLaughlin Greer, *Washington: A History of the Capitol* (Princeton, N.J.: Princeton University Press, 1962), 375.

4. Robert Bruce, *Modern American Science,* 317.

5. William S. McFeely, *Grant—A Biography* (New York: W. W. Norton, 1981), 305–18.

6. "The Indian Bureau—The Complaints of Chief Red Cloud," *New York Tribune,* 26 April 1875, vol. 35, no. 10,629, p. 1.

7. Harry J. Brown and Frederick Williams, eds., *The Diary of James A. Garfield,* vol. 3 (East Lansing, Mich.: Michigan State University Press, 1967–73), 243–44.

8. Henry Adams, *The Education of Henry Adams* (1907; reprint New York: Penguin USA, 1995), 266.

9. "A Statement of Affairs at the Red Cloud Agency Made to the President of the United States" by Prof. O. C. Marsh.

10. Marsh correspondence, reel 12, frame 362, 15 March 1875.

11. Ibid., reel 12, frame 380, 4 July 1875. The total bill for the expedition is on reel 12, frame 415.

12. Ibid., reel 12, frame 413, 5 October 1875.

13. Cope correspondence, letter 164, 29 August 1875.

14. Marsh correspondence, reel 27, frame 413, 9 September 1875. Marsh's statement covers frames 394–415.

15. Ibid., reel 27, frames 419–21, 10 September 1875. This is Marsh's pencil account of the exchange with Delano.

16. Marsh correspondence, reel 3, frame 58, 4 October 1874.

17. Frazer, "E. D. Cope," 125.

Chapter Ten

1. Marsh correspondence, reel 12, frame 455, 1 June 1876.

2. Ibid., reel 12, frame 444, 14 May 1876.

3. Ibid., reel 1, frame 362, 7 July 1876.

4. David L. Hull, *Darwin and His Critics* (Chicago: University of Chicago Press, 1973), 6.

5. Marsh correspondence, reel 13, frame 63, 19 March 1875.

6. Francis Darwin, ed., *The Life and Letters of Charles Darwin* (New York: Boyle Books, 1959), 2:64–65, Charles Darwin to J. Murray, 1860, quoted in Hull, *Darwin and His Critics,* 248.

7. Cynthia E. Russett, *Darwin in America: The Intellectual Response, 1865–1912* (San Francisco: W. H. Freeman, 1976), 4.

8. E. D. Cope, *Primary Factors of Organic Evolution* (Chicago: Open Court Press, 1896), 474.

9. Ibid., 1.

10. Ibid., 175.

11. For an excellent discussion of the British reaction to Darwin and the emerging fossil record see Adrian Desmond's *Archetypes and Ancestors, Paleontology in Victorian England, 1850–1875* (Chicago: University of Chicago Press, 1982).

12. Marsh correspondence, reel 1, frame 269, 8 June 1877.

13. Edward Danford Eddy Jr., *Colleges for Our Land and Time: The Land Grant Idea in American Education* (New York: Harper & Brothers, 1956), 8.

14. Beers, *Centennial City,* 448.

15. Charles Frederick Holder, "Spencer Fullerton Baird," in *Leading Men of American Science,* ed. David Starr Jordan (Henry Holt, 1910), 278.

16. Spencer Baird correspondence, record unit 7002, box 18, file 5, Smithsonian Institution Archives, Washington, D.C., 1 September 1875.

17. Marsh correspondence, reel 2, frame 261, 22 November 1876.

18. Baird correspondence, record unit 7002, box 18, file 5, 23 November 1875.

Chapter Eleven

1. Charles H. Sternberg, *The Life of a Fossil Hunter* (1909; reprint, Bloomington: Indiana University Press, 1990), 33.

2. Oscar Osburn Winther, *The Transportation Frontier* (New York: Holt Rinehart & Winston, 1964), 122–23.

3. Cope correspondence, letter 165, 14 August 1876.

4. Dan Cushman, "Monsters of the Judith—Dinosaur Diggings of the West Provided Competitive Arena for Fossil Discoveries," *Montana—The Magazine of Western History* 7, no. 4 (autumn 1962): 18–36.

5. "Geological Expedition," *Helena (Mont.) Daily Herald,* 15 August 1876, vol. 19, no. 12, edition 1.

6. "Montana & The Indians," *Daily Independent,* 23 July 1876, vol. 5, no. 98.

7. "The Custer Massacre," *Helena Daily Herald,* 5 July 1876, vol. 18, no. 122, edition 1.

8. Rex C. Myers, ed., *Lizzie—The Letters of Elizabeth Chester Fiske* (Missoula, Mont.: Mountain Press Publishing Co., 1989), 101.

9. Merrill G. Burlingame, *The Montana Frontier* (Helena, Mont.: State Publishing

Co. 1942); and Michael P. Malone and Richard Roeder, *Montana as It Was: 1876, A Centennial View* (Bozeman, Mt.: Montana State University, 1975). These both provide an excellent overview of the life and times of the territory.

10. Joel Overholser, *World's Inner Most Port* (Fort Benton, Mont.: River Press, 1980), 11. Overholser's personal communications, vertical files Montana Historical Society, also hold a good deal of information about Fort Benton.

11. *History of Montana 1739–1885, A History of Its Discovery and Settlement* (Chicago: Warner, Beers & Co., 1885), 730.

12. "The Northern Indians, What a Fort Benton Correspondent Thinks of the Situation," *Helena Daily Herald,* 29 July 1876, vol. 18, no. 141 edition 3.

13. *Fort Benton Record,* 14 July 1876, vol. 2, no. 12, 1.

14. "Billy Jackson's Recollection of the Battle of the Little Big Horn," as told to Jack Burton Monroe (unpublished manuscript, Montana Historical Society, Helena, Mont.).

15. The tale of Madame Moustache can be found in Duncan Aikman, *Calamity Jane and the Lady Wildcats* (Lincoln: University of Nebraska Press, 1987), and Dee Brown, *The Gentle Tamers: Women of the Wild Old West* (Lincoln: University of Nebraska Press, 1981).

16. Cope correspondence, letter 166, 20 August, 1876.

17. Cope correspondence, letter 167, 27 August 1876.

18. Cope correspondence, letter 168, 2 September 1876. It seems that Cope had a dental bridge rather than a full set of false teeth, since there are repeated references in his letters to toothaches and dentist visits. For example, he writes of a "neuralgic tooth ache" in 1884 (letter 250) and waxes about the "delightful sense of intoxication" from the dentist's nitrous oxide in 1889 (letter 362).

19. Cushman, "Monsters of the Judith," 30.

20. Cope correspondence, letter 169, 10 September 1876.

21. Ibid., letter #171, 3 October 1876.

22. Ibid., letter 170, 17 September 1876.

23. Ibid., letter #172, 8 October 1876.

Chapter Twelve

1. Michael F. Kohl and John McIntosh, eds., *Discovering Dinosaurs in the Old West— The Field Journals of Arthur Lakes* (Washington, D.C.: Smithsonian Institution Press, 1997), 12.

2. Marsh correspondence, reel 10, frames 357–60, 2 April 1877.

3. Ibid., reel 10, frames 348–56, 15 June 1877. Note: This letter is actually dated June 15, 1876, but based on its content, it seems clear that Lakes miswrote the date.

4. Marsh correspondence, reel 10, frame 403, 20 June 1877.

5. Ibid., reel 10, frames 419–24, 27 June 1877.

6. "The Bones of Monsters, Wonderful Discoveries in the Sandstone Rocks of Colorado," *New York Sun,* 27 May 1877, reprinted from the *Colorado Springs Gazette.*

7. Kohl and McIntosh, *Discovering Dinosaurs,* 24.

8. Marsh correspondence, reel 12, frame 517, 27 June 1877.

9. Ibid., reel 2, frame 78, 8 August 1877.

10. Ibid., reel 12, frame 520, 30 June 1877.

11. O. C. Marsh, "Notice of a New and Gigantic Dinosaur," *American Journal of Science* 14, no. 7 (1 July 1877): 87–88.

12. Marsh correspondence, reel 12, frame 522, 8 July 1877.

13. Kohl and McIntosh, *Discovering Dinosaurs,* 29.

14. Marsh correspondence, reel 12, frames 542–43, 4 August 1877.

15. Ibid., reel 21, frame 550, 9 August 1877.

16. E. D. Cope, "On a Gigantic Saurian from the Dakota Epoch of Colorado," *Paleontological Bulletin,* no. 26 (26 August 1877): 5–10; also *Proceedings of the American Philosophical Society* 15 (1877): 82–84.

17. Marsh correspondence, reel 12, frame 554, 12 August 1877.

18. Ibid., reel 1, frame 460, 29 June 1878.

19. W. A. Helm, "The Gate of the Mountains" (manuscript no. 438, Colorado Historical Society); and Anson S. Rudd, "Early Affairs in Canon City" (manuscript no. 409, Colorado Historical Society, Denver, 6.) Denver, Co.

20. Marsh correspondence, reel 12, frame 560, 15 August 1877.

21. Ibid., reel 12, frame 568, 21 August 1877.

22. Ibid., reel 12, frame 574, 24 August 1877.

23. Ibid., reel 12, frames 569–71, 21 August 1877.

24. Ibid., reel 12, frame 575, 26 August 1877.

25. Charles Sternberg, *Fossil Hunter,* 99.

26. Marsh correspondence, reel 18, frame 533, 22 April 1877.

27. Ibid., reel 18, frame 570, 26 July 1877.

28. Cope correspondence, letter 180, 17 September 1877.

29. Marsh correspondence, reel 18, frame 598, 21 September 1877.

30. Ibid., reel 12, frame 610, 8 October 1877.

31. Kohl and McIntosh, *Discovering Dinosaurs,* 65.

32. Marsh correspondence, reel 3, frame 273, 27 June 1877.

33. Ibid., reel 3, frame 271, 16 June 1877.

34. Edwin Barbour, the Peabody assistant given the order by Marsh to cover the fossils, became a distinguished paleontologist at the University of Nebraska. He told this story to his student, Edwin Colbert, who also became a noted paleontologist. Colbert included the story in his book, *A Fossil Hunter's Notebook* (New York: E. P. Dutton, 1980), 49.

35. Marsh correspondence, reel 10, frame 515, 11 November 1878.

36. George Olshevsky, "Dinosaur Genera," in *Encyclopedia of Dinosaurs,* ed. Philip J. Currie and Kevin Padian, (San Diego: Academic Press, 1997) 797–804; and in *The Dinosauria,* ed. David Weishampel, Peter Dodson, and Halszka Osmolska (Berkeley: University of California Press, 1990).

37. E. D. Cope, "On the Vertebrata of the Dakota Epoch of Colorado," *Proceedings of the American Philosophical Society* 17 (21 December, 1877): 219–47.

38. Leidy correspondence, *ANSP,* 14 December 1877.

39. O. C. Marsh, "Principal Characters of American Jurassic Dinosaurs," *American Journal of Science* 16 (November 1878): 411–12; and O. C. Marsh, "Principal Characters of American Jurassic Dinosaurs—Part II," *American Journal of Science* 17 (January 1879): 514–22.

Chapter Thirteen

1. "Joseph Henry," *Nation,* no. 672 (16 May 1878): 3–4.

2. Marsh correspondence, reel 3, frame 615, 14 May 1878.

3. Cope correspondence, letter 190, 14 May 1878.

4. Marsh correspondence, reel 11, frame 187, 9 January 1878.

5. Cope correspondence, letter 191, 21 May 1878.

6. Henry Fairfield Osborn, *Cope: Master Naturalist* (Princeton: Princeton University Press, 1931), 29.

7. Ibid., 12.

8. Dupree, *Science in the Federal Government,* 94–95.

9. Stegner, *Hundredth Meridian,* 221.

10. Lt. George Wheeler, "Report upon Third Geographical Congress and Exhibit at Venice," House Executive Document 270, 48th Cong., 2d sess. (1881): 84.

11. Foster, *Strange Genius,* 262.

12. Wilkins, *Clarence King,* 233.

13. Grinnell, *O. C. Marsh,* 286–87.

14. Marsh correspondence, reel 3, frame 617, 9 August 1878.

15. Powell Survey letters received, vol. 8, nos. 268–71.

16. Cope correspondence, letter 193, 18 August 1878.

17. Ibid., letter 194, 25 August 1878.

18. Ibid., letter 196, 8 September 1878.

19. Ibid., letter 198, 14 September 1878.

20. Ibid., letter 199, 29 September 1878.

21. Dinobase, University of Bristol, Bristol, U.K.; paleo.gly.bris.ac.uk/dinobase

22. Cope correspondence, letter 200, 12 October 1878.

23. *Annual Report of the National Academy of Sciences* (1878–79): appendix D, 19–22.

24. *Congressional Record,* 45th Cong., 3d sess., pt. 3 (1877, p. 2361).

25. E. D. Cope, "Letter from O. C. Marsh, etc.," *American Naturalist* 13, no. 1 (1879): 36.

26. Marsh correspondence, reel 6, frame 517, 16 December 1878.

27. *Congressional Record,* 45th Cong., 3d sess., pt. 3 (1877): The debate is on pp. 1558–69.

28. Adams, *Henry Adams,* 311.

29. *A Report on the Surveys of the Territories,* House Miscellaneous Document 5 (ser. 1861) 45th Cong., 3d sess. 1878.

30. Wilkins, *Clarence King,* 207.

31. Marsh correspondence, reel 10, frame 211, 2 January 1879.

32. Ibid., reel 13, frame 474, 20 February 1879.

33. Ibid., reel 12, frame 787, 14 March 1879.

Chapter Fourteen

1. Marsh correspondence, reel 18, frame 620, 7 November 1877.

2. Ibid., reel 18, frame 623, 14 November 1877.

3. Ibid., reel 18, frame 625, 16 November 1877.

4. Ibid., reel 18, frame 645, 24 November 1877.

5. Brent H. Breithaupt, "Como Bluff, Wyoming Territory, 1868–1877: An Initial Glimpse of One of the World's Premier Dinosaur Sites," *Dinofest International Proceedings,* (1997): 19–29.

6. Marsh correspondence, reel 2, frame 55, 17 November 1877.

7. Ibid., reel 2, frame 57, 24 December 1877.

8. Ibid., reel 2, frame 59, 26 December 1877.

9. Ibid., reel 13, frame 206, 22 December 1877.

10. Ibid., reel 18, frame 638, 30 November 1877.

11. John H. Ostrom and John S. McIntosh, *Marsh's Dinosaurs: The Collection from Como Bluff* (New Haven, Conn: Yale University Press, 1966), 56. The book contains a complete index of all the specimens found at Como Bluff by quarry number.

12. Marsh correspondence, reel 13, frame 736, 1 March 1878.

13. Ibid., reel 13, frame 740, 4 April 1878.

14. Ibid., reel 2, frame 68, 23 March 1878.

15. Ibid., reel 2, frame 74, 1 April 1878.

16. Ibid., reel 18, frame 692, 19 April 1878.

17. Ibid., reel 18, frame 695, 19 April 1878.

18. Ostrom and McIntosh, *Marsh's Dinosaurs,* 19. The authors offer this analysis.

19. Marsh correspondence, reel 2, frame 79, 19 September 1878.

20. Ibid., reel 13, frame 763, 29 November 1878.

21. E. D. Cope, "Synopsis of Extinct Batrachia, Reptilia and Aves from North America," *Transactions of the American Philosophical Society* 13 (1869): 30. Cope delivered this paper in two parts on 18 September 1868 and 12 April 1869. The entire paper is 251 pages.

22. Marsh correspondence, reel 13, frame 772, 12 February 1879.

23. Ibid., reel 13, frame 776, 24 February 1879.

24. Ibid., reel 13, frame 782, 3 March 1879.

25. Elizabeth Noble Shor, *Fossils and Flies: The Life of a Compleat Scientist, Samuel Wendell Williston* (Norman: University of Oklahoma Press, 1971), 118.

26. Marsh correspondence, reel 13, frame 784, 11 March 1879.

27. Ibid., reel 13, frames 794–97, 16 April 1879.

28. Kohl and McIntosh, *Discovering Dinosaurs,* 84.

29. Ibid., 107.

30. Marsh correspondence, reel 13, frame 816, 30 June 1879.

31. Ibid., reel 10, frame 574, 23, June 1879.

32. Ibid., reel 8, frame 359, 5 September 1878. This is a letter from S. F. Hubbell, Carlin's father-in-law and an attorney who is trying to get Marsh to pay his son-in-law.

33. Kohl and McIntosh, *Discovery Dinosaurs,* 99.

34. Marsh correspondence, reel 13, frame 817, 6 July 1879.

35. Cope correspondence, letter 202, 28 July 1879.

36. E. D. Cope, 1879 field journal. American Museum of Natural History Archives, New York.

37. Cope correspondence, letter 203, 8 August 1879.

38. Marsh correspondence, reel 10, frame 611, 11 August 1879.

39. Ibid., reel 13, frame 837, 9 August 1878.

40. Ibid., reel 13, frame 843, 19 August 1879.

41. Ibid., reel 13, frame 846, 20 August 1879.

42. Ibid., reel 10, frame 629, 22 August 1879.

43. Ibid., reel 13, frame 864, 6 September 1879.

44. Ibid., reel 13, frame 891, 29 October 1879.

45. Ibid., reel 10, frame 744, 12 December 1879.

46. Kohl and McIntosh, *Discovering Dinosaurs,* 148.

47. Marsh correspondence, reel 14, frame 27, 5 June 1880.

48. Ibid., reel 14, frame 24, 30 May 1880.

49. Ibid., reel 18, frame 421, 15 September 1880.

50. Ibid., reel 14, frame 118, 25 November 1880.

51. Ibid., reel 14, frame 125, 11 December 1880.

52. Ibid., reel 14, frame 224, "Historical Notes," 1 November 1881.

53. Ibid., reel 14, frame 238, 30 November 1881.

54. Ibid., reel 13, frame 678, 21 October 1880.

55. Osborn, *Cope, Master Naturalist,* 258.

56. David S. Berman and John S. McIntosh, *The Recapitation of Apatosaurs,* 83.

57. Peter Dodson and Susan D. Dawson, "Making the Fossil Record of Dinosaurs," *Modern Geology* 16 (1991): 3–15.

58. David S. Berman and John S. McIntosh, "Skull and Relationships of the Upper Jurassic Sauropod Apatosaurus," *Bulletin of Carnegie Museum of Natural History,* no. 8 (1978): 7.

Chapter Fifteen

1. Schuchert and LeVene, *O. C. Marsh,* 281.

2. Marsh correspondence, reel 13, frames 495, 512, 519, 528. These are all letters from Powell to Marsh concerning funding levels, between 5 June 1883 and 16 August 1886.

3. Ibid., reel 3, frame 1009, 17 April 1885, and frame 1010, 13 July 1885.

4. E. D. Cope, "The Vertebrata of the Tertiary Formations of the West," *Report of the United States Geological Survey of the Territories* 3 (1884): xxviii.

5. Frazer, "E. D. Cope," 127.

6. Cope correspondence, letter 213a, 11 August 1881.

7. Robert W. Eveleth, "Lake Valley's Famed Bridal Chamber—A Beautifully Large and Solid Looking Streak," *New Mexico Geological Society Guidebook* (Socorro, N. Mexico: New Mexico Geological Society, 1980): 293–96.

8. Paul Rodman, *Mining Frontiers of the Far West—1848–1880* (New York: Holt, Rinehardt, Winston, 1993), 112.

9. Olney Newell, "Good Things at Red River, Eastern Mining Companies Are Aplenty There," *Denver Republican,* 11 July 1897.

10. Cope correspondence, unnumbered, 15 August 1881.

11. Angie Debo, *A History of the Indians of the United States* (Norman,: University of Oklahoma Press, 1970).

12. James Haley, *Apaches, a History and Cultural Portrait* (New York: Doubleday, 1981), 396.

13. Ibid., 366.

14. Cope correspondence, letter 213, 13 August 1881.

15. Ibid., letter 225, 6 June 1882.

16. Ibid., letter 226, 10 June 1882.

17. Ibid., letter 227, 14 June 1882.

18. "The Lake Valley Mines," *The (Las Cruces, N. Mex.) Republican,* vol. 3, no. 6, 30 June 1883.

19. E. D. Cope, "The Vertebrata of the Tertiary Formations of the West," *Report of the United States Geological Survey of the Territories* 3, bk. 1 (1884): 561–62.

20. Cope correspondence, letter 236, 11 February 1883.

21. "Minutes for July 17th, 1883," *Minutes of the Academy of Natural Sciences of Philadelphia* 13 (December 1876 to December 1885): 659. Also see *Rough Minutes,* the extemporaneous notes of the meeting, 10 July 1883 and 17 July 1883, 548–50.

22. Cope correspondence, letter 238, 18 July 1883.

23. Ibid., letter 240, 25 July 1883.

24. Ibid., letter 241, 5 August 1883.

25. Ibid., letter 249, 24 September 1883.

26. "Lake Valley Mine," *The (Las Cruces, N. Mex.) Republican,* vol. 3, no. 20, edition 16 October 1883.

27. Cope correspondence, letter 250, 1 October 1883.

28. Ibid., letter 252, 10 October 1883.

29. "The Sierra Grande Mining Company, Lake Valley, New Mexico," *Engineering & Mining Journal* 35 (14 April 1883): 205.

30. Cope correspondence, letter 236, 16 March 1883.

31. W. L. Park, "Tales from Old Timers—No. 3," *The Union Pacific Magazine* (May 1923): 13.

32. Cope correspondence, letter 258, 29 March 1884.

33. Ibid., 260, 10 April 1884.

34. Ibid., 281, 24 February 1885.

35. Frazer, "E. D. Cope," 127.

36. Cope correspondence, letter 289, 1 August 1885.

37. Spencer Baird correspondence, record unit 7002, box 29, file 23, Smithsonian Institution Archives, Washington, D.C., 18 July 1884.

38. Cope correspondence, letter 256, 24 January 1884.

39. Ibid., letter 293, 18 September 1885.

Chapter Sixteen

1. Marsh correspondence, reel 9, frame 279, 19 July 1882.

2. Ibid., reel 1, frame 160, 31 October 1882.

3. Ibid., reel 1, frame 169, 18 March 18, no year noted.

4. A. H. Saxon, "Barnum, Nineteenth Century Science and Some 'Unnatural' History," *Discovery—The Magazine of the Yale Peabody Museum* 21, no. 1 (1 November 1988): 30; also, Marsh correspondence, reel 1, frame 682, 3 May 1880.

5. Marsh correspondence, reel 13, frame 669, 21 May 1883.

6. James Dwight Dana, *On the Four Rocks of the New Haven Region* (New Haven, Conn.: Tuttle, Morehouse & Taylor, 1891).

7. Shor, *Fossils and Flies,* 102.

8. Ibid., 105.

9. Marsh correspondence, reel 18, frame 754, 17 February 1885.

10. Samuel Wendell Williston, "Oscar Harger," *The American Naturalist* 21, no. 12 (December 1887): 1133–34.

11. Scott, *Memories,* 58.

12. Stephen Jay Gould, *The Mismeasure of Man* (New York: W. W. Norton, 1981), 114.

13. Alfred S. Romer, "Teaching Vertebrate Paleontology," *American Paleontological Convention,* pt. A (September 1969): 43–44.

14. Marsh correspondence, reel 1, frame 735, 13 December 1884.

15. Osborn, *Cope, Master Naturalist,* 380

16. Charles H. Sternberg, "The Loup Fork Miocene of Western Kansas," *Kansas Academy of Science Transactions* 20, pt. 1 (1905): 72.

17. Marsh correspondence, reel 7, frames 933–86. This correspondence includes twelve letters from Hatcher in Long Island, Kansas, to Marsh, starting 10 July and ending 25 October 1884.

18. Ibid., reel 7, frame 945, 11 August 1884.

19. Ibid., reel 15, frame 943, 12 August 1884.

20. Martin O. Riser, *The Sternberg Family of Fossil-Hunters* (Lewiston/Queenstown: Edwin Mellen Press, 1995), 176.

21. Marsh correspondence, reel 7, frame 1003, 9 February 1885.

22. Ibid., reel 8, frame 256, 25 June 1888.

23. Ibid., reel 14, frame 984, 16 December 1889.

24. Ibid., reel 8, frame 151, 27 June 1887.

25. Department of Vertebrate Paleontology correspondence, record unit 248, file 2, Smithsonian Institution Archives, Washington, D.C., 16 November 1886. Letter from Brown to Marsh.

26. Marsh correspondence, reel 8, frame 281, 22 October 1888.

27. Ibid., reel 8, frame 690, 20 June 1891.

28. Ibid., reel 1, frame 638, 3 February 1886.

29. Schuchert and LeVene, *O. C. Marsh,* 310.

30. For a discussion of the history of classifying dinosaurs, see Edwin H. Colbert, *Men and Dinosaurs—The Search in the Field and Laboratory* (New York: E. P. Dutton, 1968), 91–111; and W. E. Swinton, *The Dinosaurs* (New York: John Wiley & Sons Inc., 1970) 107–17.

Chapter Seventeen

1. The work of the Allison Commission is well described in Hunter Dupree's *Science in the Federal Government,* chap. 11, (pp. 215–31), and in Wallace Stegner's *Beyond the Hundredth Meridian,* "Spies and Whispers" (pp. 283–93).

2. Senate Miscellaneous Document 82, 49th Cong., 1st sess., vol. 4, 2345 (1886): 8.

3. Ibid., 999.

4. Marsh correspondence, reel 9, frame 116, 13 July 1886.

5. Thomas G. Manning, *Government in Science—The U.S. Geological Survey,* *1867–1894* (Lexington: University of Kentucky Press, 1967), 133.

6. Osborn, *Cope, Master Naturalist,* 380, letter dated 27 October 1885.

7. Reproduced in the *New York Herald,* 20 January 1890.

8. Cope correspondence, letter 258, 29 March 1884.

9. Leidy correspondence, *ANSP,* 15 August 1885.

10. Ferdinand Hayden correspondence, Fryxell Collection 1638, box 40, letter 301, American Heritage Center, University of Wyoming, Laramie, Wy., 26 August 1885.

11. Cope correspondence, letter 277, 26 January 1885.

12. Senate Miscellaneous Document 82, 1014.

13. Marsh correspondence, reel 12, frame 879, 18 September 1885.

14. Senate Miscellaneous Document 82, 1013.

15. Ibid., 1014.

16. Marsh correspondence, reel 12, frame 895, 8 February 1886.

17. "Report from the National Academy for 1885," Senate Miscellaneous Document 153, 44th Cong., 1st sess. (1885): 65.

18. Senate Miscellaneous Document 82; Testimony of J. W. Powell (26 February 1886): 1078.

19. Marsh correspondence, reel 9, frame 144, 3 May 1886.

20. Ibid., reel 7, frame 307, 5 May 1886.

21. Ibid., Marsh correspondence, reel 12, frame 911, 10 May 1886.

22. Ibid., reel 7, frame 309, 13 May 1886.

23. Ibid., reel 9, frame 113, 5 July 1886.

24. Ibid., reel 12, frame 922, 15 July 1866.

Chapter Eighteen

1. "Editor's Table," *American Naturalist* 21, no. 2 (February 1887): 164.

2. Cope correspondence, letter 304, 5 June 1886.

3. Ibid., letter 305, 9 June 1886.

4. Ibid., letter 309, 26 June 1886.

5. Ibid., letter 311, 10 July 1886.

6. Ibid., letter 312, 18 July 1886.

7. Osborn, *Cope, Master Naturalist,* 384, 6 August 1886.

8. Cope correspondence, letter 316, 23 August 1886.

9. Ibid., letter 321, 24 November 1886.

10. Ibid., letter 322, 11 December 1886.

11. Ferdinand Hayden correspondence, Fryxell Collection 1638, box 40, American Heritage Center, University of Wyoming, Laramie, Wy., 26 August 1885.

12. *Christian Doctrine, Practice and Discipline* (Dublin: Depository of the Society of Friends, 1864), 262.

13. Cope correspondence, letter 326, 14 February 1887.

14. Ibid., letter 324, 2 February 1887.

15. Descriptions of 2102 Pine can be found in Osborn, *Cope, Master Naturalist,* 371; Scott, *Memories,* 232; Sylvia M. Czerkas and Donald Glut, *Dinosaurs, Mammoths and Cavemen: The Art of Charles Knight* (New York: E. P. Dutton, 1982), 13–14; and in Henry Fowler, "Cope in Retrospect," *Copeia,* no. 1 (1963): p. 12.

16. Cope correspondence, E. D. Cope Papers collection, Quaker Collection, Haverford College, collection 956, file folder 3, Haverford, Pa., 26 April 1894.

17. "Edward Drinker Cope," *Catalogue of Scientific Papers—Fourth Series,* vol. 14, comp. Royal Scientific Society of London (Cambridge: Cambridge University Press, 1915), 342–46.

18. Osborn, *Cope, Master Naturalist,* 585.

19. Hayden correspondence, Fryxell Collection 1638, box 40, letter 504, American Heritage Center, University of Wyoming, 23 August 1887.

20. Cope correspondence, letter 338, 19 December 1887.

21. Ibid., letter 339, 22 January 1888.

22. E. D. Cope, *The Relation of the Sexes to Government* (New York: New York State Association Opposed to Woman Suffrage, 1888; originally published in *Popular Science Monthly,* October 1888.

23. Gould, *Mismeasure,* 85.

24. Cope correspondence, letter 325, 5 February 1887.

25. Charles Beard, 400.

26. Gould, *Mismeasure,* 22.

27. E. D. Cope, "On the Hypothesis of Evolution, Physical & Metaphysical," *Lippincott's Magazine* (July 1870): 40.

28. E. D. Cope, *Origin of the Fittest* (New York: D. Appleton, 1887), 287.

29. Ibid., 293.

30. E. D. Cope, "Two Perils of the Indo-European," *Open Court* 3 (23 January 1890): 2054.

31. Cope correspondence, Quaker Collection, Haverford College, collection 956, file folder 18, 8 March 1893; Marsh correspondence, reel 15, frame 733, 8 March 1893.

32. Cope correspondence, Quaker Collection, Haverford College, collection 956, file folder 5, 5 May 1888.

33. William Cecil Dampier, *A History of Science and Its Relations with Philosophy and Religion* (Cambridge: Cambridge University Press, 1966), 280–81.

34. Cope correspondence, letter 341, 26 February 1888.

35. Ibid., letter 344, 20 March 1888.

36. Ibid., letter 353, 4 June 1888.

37. Marsh correspondence, reel 6, frame 614, 3 June 1888.

38. Cope correspondence, letter 353, 4 June 1888.

39. Ibid., letter 358, 19 September 1888.

40. Frazer, "E. D. Cope," 70–71. Frazer quotes from Cope's parody.

41. Leidy correspondence, *ANSP,* 7 October 1888.

42. Cope correspondence, letter 368, 13 May 1889.

43. George Brown Goode correspondence, record unit 54, box 2, file 1, Smithsonian Institution Archives, Washington, D.C., 7 February 1889.

44. Cope correspondence, Quaker Collection, Haverford College, collection 956, file folder 3, "confidential" letter from Ira Remson to Cope, 28 March 1889.

45. Cope correspondence, letter 366, 29 April 1889.

46. Osborn, *Cope, Master Naturalist,* 391.

47. Reproduced in *New York Herald,* 12 January 1890, letter dated 24 October 1889.

48. Ibid., 19 December 1889.

Chapter Nineteen

1. Osborn, *Cope, Master Naturalist,* 14 January 1890, 411.

2. Elizabeth Noble Shor, *The Fossil Feud* (Hicksville, N.Y.: Exposition Press, 1970), 55.

3. Osborn, *Cope, Master Naturalist,* 5 January 1890, 409–10.

4. Scott, *Memories,* 219.

5. "Frocks & Gowns from Paris Town," *New York Herald,* 12 January 1890, whole no. 19,501 edition, p. 24; "Genesis of the Negro Exodus," p. 8.

6. Scott, *Memories,* 219.

7. William Hosea Ballou, "Volley for Volley in the Great Scientific War," *New York Herald,* 13 January 1890, whole no. 19,502 edition, p. 3.

8. "An Old Grievance Aired, Why Scientists Make Light of Professor Cope's Charges," *New York Times,* 13 January 1890, vol. 24, no. 11,674, p. 8.

9. "Scientists at War, Cope Charges Mismanagement in the Geological Survey," *Philadelphia Inquirer,* 13 January 1890, vol. 122, no. 13, p. 2.

10. William Hosea Ballou, "Widening That Geological Chasm," *New York Herald,* p. 14 January 1890, whole no. 19,503 edition, p. 4.

11. Osborn, *Cope, Master Naturalist,* 12 January 1890, 410.

12. Ibid., 13 January 1890, 410–11.

13. William Hosea Ballou, "Marsh Hurls Azoic Facts," *New York Herald,* 19 January 1890, whole no. 19508, p. 11.

14. Osborn, *Cope, Master Naturalist,* 405.

15. Scott, *Memories,* 219–20.

16. George Baur, "A Review of the Charges Against the Paleontological Department of the U.S. Geological Survey, and the Defense Made by Prof. O. C. Marsh," *American Naturalist* 24, no. 279 (March 1890): 303.

17. Edwin H. Barbour, "Notes on the Paleontological Laboratory of the United States under Prof. Marsh," *American Naturalist* 24, no. 280 (April 1890): 389.

18. Marsh correspondence, reel 7, frame 755, 5 April 1890.

Chapter Twenty

1. The story of Powell's irrigation survey is covered in Stegner, *Hundredth Meridian,* 295–344, and in Dupree, *Science in the Federal Government,* 232–36.

2. Marsh correspondence, reel 13, frame 51, 30 April 1892.

3. *Congressional Record* (1892), vol. 23, pt. 5, 4389–96.

4. Marsh correspondence, reel 13, frame 55, 19 May 1892.

5. Ibid., reel 13, frame 56, 21 May 1892.

6. Ibid., reel 7, frame 317, 19 May 1892.

7. Ibid., reel 7, frame 321, 28 May 1892.

8. Leidy correspondence, *ANSP,* 24 January 1891.

9. Marsh correspondence, reel 8, frame 661, 27 April 1891.

10. Ibid., reel 8, frame 663, 16 May 1891.

11. Ibid., reel 13, frame 559, 27 June 1892.

12. Ibid., reel 16, frame 685, 13 June 1892.

13. Ibid., reel 1, frame 110, 6 June 1892.

14. Ibid., reel 13, frame 546, 3 March 1891.

15. Department of Vertebrate Paleontology, record unit 248, box 1, file 2, Smithsonian Institution Archives, 13 July 1890.

16. *Congressional Record* (1892), vol. 23, pt. 6, 65151–6160.

17. Marsh correspondence, reel 12, frame 596, 20 July 1892.

18. Ibid., reel 7, frame 329, 20 July 1892.

19. Schuchert and LeVene, *O. C. Marsh,* 323.

20. Adams, *Henry Adams,* 330.

21. Henry Adams et al., *The Helmet of Mabrino—Clarence King Memoirs* (New York City: Putnam's & Sons, King Memorial Committee of the Century Association, 1904), 167.

22. Eveleth, "Bridal Chamber," 296.

Chapter Twenty-One

1. Cope correspondence, letter 392, 23 July 1892.

2. The description of life on the Texas plains comes from Cope correspondence, letters 378, 14 May 1892; 379, 22 May; 380, 29 May; 382, 7 June; 383, 10 June; and 384, 21 June.

3. Alfred S. Romer, "Cope versus Marsh," *Systematics Zoology* 8, no. 4 (30 December 1964): 202.

4. Presifor Frazer, "Bibliography of E. D. Cope's articles."

5. Cope correspondence, letter 23, 7 July 1855.

6. E. D. Cope, "On the Primary Division of the Salamandridae," *Proceedings of the Academy of Natural Sciences of Philadelphia* 11 (1859): 122.

7. E. D. Cope, "Snakes in Bananas Bunches," *American Naturalist* 24, no. 284 (August 1890): 781.

8. E. D. Cope, "The Batrachia of North America," *Bulletin of the United States Museum No. 34.* The Smithsonian Institution, United States Museum serial no. 45 (1889): 13.

9. E. D. Cope, "The Crocodilians, Lizards, and Snakes of North America," *Report of the U.S. National Museum for 1989,* 156.

10. Theodore Gill, "Address of Theodore Gill, retiring president before the AAAS," *Proceedings of the American Association for the Advancement of Science* 46 (1897): 18.

11. Cope correspondence, letter 386, 5 July 1892.

12. Ibid., letter 388, 17 July 1892.

13. Ibid., letter 391, 15 July 1893.

14. Edward Daeschler and Anthony Fiorillo, "Rediscovery of Fossil Material at the Academy of Natural Sciences of Philadelphia from Edward Drinker Cope's 1893 Expedition to the Dakotas," *The Mosasaur,* no. 4 (1989): 143; and Fiorillo and Daeschler, "E. D. Cope's 1893 Expedition to the Dakotas Revisited," *Earth Sciences History* 9, no. 1 (1990): 57–61.

15. Chatterjee, *Birds,* 31–33.

16. Cope correspondence, letter 398, 1 September 1893.

17. Ibid., letter 392, 23 July 1893.

18. Ibid., letter 345, 27 March 1888.

19. Osborn, *Cope, Master Naturalist,* 463.

20. Henry Fairfield Osborn, Cope Master Naturalist Correspondence, American Museum of Natural History, January–March 1930 file, 19 February 1930.

21. E. D. Cope, *The Marriage Problem* (Philadelphia: A. E. Foote, 1888), 11. This

essay originally appeared in two installments in *Open Court* magazine on 13 November and 22 November 1888.

22. Ibid., 25.

23. Cope correspondence, E. D. Cope Papers collection, Quaker Collection, Haverford College, collection 956, Haverford, Pa. Pepper first proposed the purchase in a letter dated 29 September 1889.

24. Osborn, *Cope, Master Naturalist,* 457.

25. Edward C. Carter II, *One Grand Pursuit: A Brief History of the American Philosophical Society's First 250 Years* (Philadelphia: American Philosophical Society, 1993), 34.

26. Sternberg, *Fossil Hunter,* 233.

27. Ibid., 238. The Cope letter is dated 16 February 1896.

28. Cope correspondence, letter 406, 26 February 1897.

29. Ibid., letter 407, 10 March 1897.

30. Ibid., letter 409, 18 March 1897.

31. Ibid., letter 410, 27 March 1897.

32. Ibid., letter 413, 31 March 1897.

33. Frazer, "E. D. Cope," 68.

34. Edward Anthony Spitzka, "A Study of the Brains of Six Eminent Scientists and Scholars Belonging to the American Anthropometric Society, Together with a Description of the Skull of Prof. E.D. Cope," *Transactions of the American Philosophical Society* 21 (1908): 175–308.

Chapter Twenty-Two

1. Marsh correspondence, reel 6, frame 666, 14 April 1897.

2. J. S. Kingsley, "Edward Drinker Cope," *American Naturalist* 31, no. 365 (May 1897): 418.

3. Henry Fairfield Osborn, "Biographical Memoir of Edward Drinker Cope," *National Academy of Sciences Biographical Memoirs,* vol. 13 (1929): 169–70.

4. "Edward Drinker Cope," *American Journal of Science,* 4th ser., vol. 3, no. 17 (May 1897): 427.

5. Marsh correspondence, reel 13, frame 672, 1 May 1897.

6. Ibid., reel 4, frame 262, 22 December 1892.

7. Ibid., reel 4, letter 264, 19 February 1893 (Dana's birthday), and letter 284, 10 October 1893 (Dana declines dinner with the earl of Sheridan).

8. Schuchert and LeVene, *O. C. Marsh,* 348.

9. S. W. Willistown, "The Kansas Niobrara Cretaceous," *Geological Survey of Kansas* 2 (1897): 243–47.

10. Marsh correspondence, reel 3, frame 81, 12 May 1890.

11. O. C. Marsh, "On the Affinities and Classification of the Dinosaurian Reptiles," *American Journal of Science* 50, no. 12 (December 1895): 483–99.

12. O. C. Marsh, "The Dinosaurs of North American," *Sixteenth Annual Report of the U. S. Geological Survey* (1896): 144.

13. Ibid., 143.

14. O. C. Marsh, "Prof. Marsh's Address to Alumni Dinner," *Yale Alumni Weekly* 2, no. 17 (24 February 1898): 7.

15. Colbert, *Men and Dinosaurs,* 93.

16. Schuchert and LeVene, *O. C. Marsh,* 325.

17. Timothy Dwight, *Memories of Yale Life & Men* (New York: Dodd, Mead & Co., 1903), 411.

18. Schuchert and LeVene, *O. C. Marsh,* 342.

19. The account of Marsh's final days is based upon Schuchert and LeVene, *O. C. Marsh,* pp. 330–31, and a letter from Thomas Bostwick to Marsh's half sister. Marsh correspondence, reel 2, frame 158, 20 March 1899.

20. Charles Beecher, "Othniel Charles Marsh," *American Journal of Science,* 4th ser., vol. 7, no. 42 (June 1899): 403–19.

21. Shor, *Fossils and Flies,* 72.

22. Dwight, *Yale Life,* 410–13.

23. The story of *Diplodocus carnegii* is told in Robert T. Bakker, *The Dinosaur Heresies* (New York: William Morrow, 1988), 201–5, and Desmond *The Hot-Blooded Dinosaurs,* 113–21.

24. *The President's Report, 1899* (Baltimore: Johns Hopkins University, 1899), 392.

Bibliography

Archival Material

O. C. Marsh Papers and Correspondence. Twenty-six boxes of microfilm available at Yale University's Sterling Archives and the American Philosophical Society in Philadelphia.

Edward Drinker Cope Correspondence and Field Journals. American Museum of Natural History, New York City.

The Quaker Collection, Haverford College, Haverford, Pa. Edward Drinker Cope Papers, Collection 956. Charles Yarnall Papers, Collection 910.

American Heritage Center Archives, University of Wyoming, Laramie, Wyo. Ferdinand Vandeveer Hayden Correspondence, Fryxell Collection #1638. William A. Carter Collection #3535.

Smithsonian Institution Archives, Washington D.C. Department of Vertebrate Paleontology Correspondence, Record Unit 684. Spencer Baird Personal Correspondence, Record Unit 7002.

Academy of Natural Sciences of Philadelphia Archives.

Joseph Leidy Correspondence.

Ferdinand Vandeveer Hayden Correspondence.

Edward Drinker Cope Correspondence.

O. C. Marsh Correspondence.

The American West

History of Montana 1739–1885. A history of its discovery and settlement. Chicago: Warner, Beers & Co., 1885.

Bartlett, Richard. *Great Surveys of the American West.* Norman, Okla.: University of Oklahoma Press, 1962.

Burket, Blaine. *Wild Bill Hickok—The Law in Hays City.* Hays, Kans.: Ellis County Historical Society, 1996.

Burlingame, Merrill G. *The Montana Frontier.* Helene, Mont.: State Publishing Co., 1942.

Darrah, William Culp. *Powell of the Colorado.* Princeton, N.J.: Princeton University Press, 1957.

Debo, Angie. *A History of the Indians of the United States.* Norman: University of Oklahoma Press, 1970.

Haley, James. *Apaches, A History and Cultural Portrait.* New York: Doubleday, 1981.

Larson, T. A. *History of Wyoming.* Lincoln: University of Nebraska Press, 1978.

Hyde, George E. *Red Cloud's Folk, A History of the Ogalala Sioux.* Norman: University of Oklahoma Press, 1937.

Malone, Michael P., and Richard Roeder. *Montana as It Was: 1876, A Centennial View.* Bozeman: Montana State University, 1975.

Rodman, Paul. *Mining Frontiers of the Far West—1848–1880.* New York: Holt, Rinehart, Winston, 1993.

Stegner, Wallace. *Beyond the Hundredth Meridian.* New York: Penguin Books, 1992.

Terrell, John Upton. *The Man Who Rediscovered America—A Biography of John Wesley Powell.* New York: Weybright and Talley, 1969.

Utley, Robert M. *Frontier Regulars—The United States Army and the Indians, 1866–1890.* New York: Macmillan Publishing Co., 1973.

Webb, W. E. *Buffalo Land: An Authentic Narrative of the Adventures and Misadventures of a Late Scientific and Sporting Party upon the Great Plains.* Cincinnati and Chicago: E. Hannaford & Co., 1872.

Winther, Oscar Osburn. *The Transportation Frontier.* New York: Holt, Rinehart and Winston, 1964.

The History of American Science and Paleontology

Bakker, Robert T. *The Dinosaur Heresies.* New York: William Morrow and Co.

Bruce, Robert K. *The Launching of Modern American Science.* New York: Alfred A. Knopf, 1987.

Carter, Edward C. *One Grand Pursuit: A Brief History of the American Philosophical Society's First 250 Years, 1743–1993.* Philadelphia: American Philosophical Society, 1993.

Colbert, Edwin H. *A Fossil Hunter's Notebook.* New York: E. P. Dutton, 1980.

———. *Men and Dinosaurs—The Search in the Field and Laboratory.* New York: E. P. Dutton, 1968.

Currie, Philip J., and Kevin Padian. *The Encyclopedia of Dinosaurs.* New York: Academic Press, 1998.

Dana, James Dwight. *Manual of Geology.* New York: Ivison, Blakeman & Co., 1880.

Desmond, Adrian. *The Hot Blooded Dinosaurs—A Revolution in Paleontology.* London: Blond & Briggs, 1975.

———. *Archetypes and Ancestors.* Chicago: University of Chicago Press, 1982.

———. *Huxley, From Devil's Disciple to Evolution's High Priest.* Reading, Mass.: Addison-Wesley, 1997.

Dupree, A. Hunter. *Science in the Federal Government.* Cambridge: Harvard University Press, 1957.

Farlow, James O., and M. K. Brett-Surman, eds. *The Complete Dinosaur.* Bloomington: Indiana University Press, 1998.

Kohl, Michael F., and John McIntosh, eds. *Discovering Dinosaurs in the Old West—The Field Journals of Arthur Lakes.* Washington, D.C.: Smithsonian Institution Press, 1997.

Gallagher, William B. *When Dinosaurs Roamed New Jersey.* New Brunswick, N.J.: Rutgers University Press, 1997.

Gould, Stephen Jay. *The Mismeasure of Man.* New York: W. W. Norton & Co., 1981.

———. *Otogeny and Phylogeny.* Cambridge: Harvard University Press, 1979.

Hull, David. *Darwin and His Critics.* Chicago: University of Chicago Press, 1983.

Huxley, Thomas H. *The Life and Letters of Thomas H. Huxley,* edited by Leonard Huxley. New York: Appleton, 1901.

———. *American Addresses.* New York: D. Appleton and Co., 1877.

———. *Collected Essays, Vol. VIII.* New York: Greenwood Press, 1968.

Lyell, Charles. *Principles of Geology, Being an Attempt to Explain the Former Changes of the Earth's Surface, Vol. III.* London: John Murray, 1833.

Manning, Thomas G. *Government in Science—The U. S. Geological Survey 1867–1894.* Lexington: University of Kentucky Press, 1967.

Ostrum, John H., and John S. McIntosh. *Marsh's Dinosaurs: The Collection from Como Bluff.* New Haven: Yale University Press, 1966.

Reingold, Nathan. *Science in Nineteenth Century America, A Documentary History.* New York: Hill and Wang, 1964.

Rudewick, Martin. *The Meaning of Fossils, Episodes in the History of Paleontology.* London: MacDonald & Co., 1972.

Russett, Cynthia E. *Darwin in America, The Intellectual Response 1865–1912.* San Francisco: W. H. Freeman & Co., 1976.

Scott, William Berryman. *Memories of a Paleontologist.* Princeton, N.J.: Princeton University Press, 1939.

Sternberg, Charles H. *The Life of a Fossil Hunter.* Bloomington: Indiana University Press, 1990 (originally published 1909).

Swinton, W. E. *The Dinosaurs.* New York: John Wiley and Sons, 1970.

Weishampel, David B., Peter Dotson, and Halszka Osmólska, eds. *The Dinosauria.* Berkeley, Calif.: University of California Press, 1990.

West, Robert H. *The Dawnseekers.* New York: Harcourt, Brace and Jovanovich, 1975.

Zakrzewksi, Richard. *A Brief History of Vertebrate Paleontology in Western Kansas.* Hays, Kans.: Department of Earth Sciences, Hays State University, and the Sternberg Memorial Museum.

Biographies of Cope, Marsh, and Others

Davidson, Jane Pierce. *The Bone Sharp—The Life of Edward Drinker Cope.* Philadelphia: The Academy of Natural Sciences, 1997.

Dwight, Timothy. *Memories of Yale Life & Men.* New York: Dodd, Mead & Co., 1903.

Foster, Mike. *Strange Genius—The Life of Ferdinand Vandeveer Hayden.* Niwot, Colo.: Roberts Rinchart Publishers, 1994.

Frazer, Presifor. "The Life and Letters of Edward Drinker Cope." *American Geologist* 26, no. 2 (August 1900).

Jordan, David Starr, ed. *Leading Men of American Science.* New York: Henry Holt & Co., 1910.

Laham, Url. *The Bone Hunters—The Heroic Age of Paleontology in the American West.* New York: Dover Publications, 1973.

Osborn, Henry Fairfield. *Cope; Master Naturalist.* New York: Arno Press, 1978.

———. "Biographical Memoir of Edward Drinker Cope," *National Academy of Sciences Biographical Memoirs* 13 (1929).

———. "Biographical Memoir of Joseph Leidy," *National Academy Biographical Memoirs* 7 (1913).

Plate, Robert. *The Dinosaur Hunters: Othniel C. Marsh and Edward D. Cope.* New York: McKay, 1964.

Shor, Elizabeth Noble. *Fossils and Flies, The Life of a Compleat Scientist, Samuel Wendell Williston.* Norman: University of Oklahoma Press, 1971.

———. *The Fossil Feud.* Hicksville, N.Y.: Exposition Press, 1970.

Schuchert, Charles. "Biographical Memoir of Othniel Charles Marsh 1831–1899." *Biographical Memoirs of the National Academy of Sciences* 20 (1937): 1–78.

Schuchert, Charles, and Clare Mae LeVene. *O. C. Marsh, Pioneer in Paleontology.* New York: Arno Press, 1978.

Warren, Leonard. *Joseph Leidy, The Last Man Who Knew Everything.* New Haven: Yale University Press, 1998.

White, Charles A. "Biographical Memoir of Ferdinand Vandeveer Hayden." *Biographical Memoirs of the National Academy of Sciences* 3 (1894): 395–413.

The Gilded Age

Adams, Henry. *The Education of Henry Adams,* New York: Penguin USA, 1995 (originally published 1907).

———. *Democracy, An American Novel.* New York: Penguin Books USA, 1994.

Bergamini, John D. *The Hundredth Year—The United States in 1876.* New York: G. P. Putnam's Sons, 1976.

Commager, Henry Steel. *The American Mind.* New Haven: Yale University Press, 1950.

Henry, James. *The American Scene.* New York: Harper & Brothers Publishers, 1907.

Jordan, David M. *Roscoe Conkling of New York.* Ithaca, N.Y.: Cornell University Press, 1971.

Kunhardt, Phillip Jr., et al. *P. T. Barnum, America's Greatest Showman.* New York: Alfred A. Knopf, 1995.

McFeely, William S. *Grant—A Biography.* New York: W. W. Norton & Co., 1981.

Morgan, H. Wayne, ed. *The Gilded Age, A Reappraisal.* Syracuse. N.Y.: Syracuse University Press, 1963.

Nevins, Allan. *Hamilton Fish: The Inner History of the Grant Administration.* New York: Dodd, Mead, 1936.

Peskin, Allan. *Garfield.* Kent, Ohio: Kent State University Press, 1978.

Rugoff, Milton. *America's Gilded Age.* New York: Henry Holt & Co., 1981.

Schlereth, Thomas J. *Victorian America, Transformation in Everyday Life, 1876–1915.* New York: HarperCollins Publishers, 1992.

Shannon, Fred A. *The Centennial Years, A Political and Economic History of America from the Late 1870s to the Early 1890s.* Garden City, N.Y.: Doubleday & Co., 1967.

Twain, Mark, and Charles Dudley Warner. *The Gilded Age.* New York: Penguin USA, 1994 (originally published 1873).

Weigley, Russel K., ed. *Philadelphia, A 300 Year History.* New York: W. W. Norton, 1983.

Wilkins, Thurman. *Clarence King, A Biography.* New York: Macmillan Co., 1958.

INDEX

Academy of Natural Sciences, 2, 10, 12, 19, 27-28, 36, 37, 46, 49, 50, 51, 122, 151, 160, 203, 261-62, 267, 349, 350, 357; Marsh's charges against Cope before, 93, 166

acquired characteristics theory, 149, 152-53, 312

Adams, Charles Francis, Jr., 116-17

Adams, Henry, 117, 129, 219, 222-23, 226, 252-53, 345-46, 347

Agassiz, Alexander, 158, 201, 215, 247, 252, 255, 276, 292-95, 297, 303, 309, 339, 346

Agassiz, Louis, 2, 7, 10, 14, 15, 17, 95-96, 108, 109, 149, 151-52, 153, 158, 254, 335, 365, 371

Agathaumas sylvestris, 75, 188, 190

Ainsworth, P. R., 125

Allen, Harrison, 361

Allison, William B., 288, 340, 341

Allison Commission, 288-98, 342

Allosaurus, 200, 232, 235, 236, 239, 372

American Association for the Advancement of Science, 108-9, 158, 164, 203-4, 301-2, 357

American Journal of Science, 7, 33, 44, 53, 72, 87, 366, 372; Cope's competitor journal, 201; Cope's obituary, 365; Marsh-Cope feud and, 90, 91, 93, 106; Marsh dinosaur articles, 190, 368; Marsh obituary, 374

American Museum, 5

American Museum of Natural History, 199, 278, 314, 340, 341, 346, 352, 367-68; Cope fossil sales to, 356-57, 358, 363, 367; dinosaur mountings, 377, 378

American Naturalist, 299, 306-7; Cope and, 201, 219, 237, 255, 303, 313, 315, 351; Cope-

Marsh feud and, 91-98, 333-34; Cope's memorium and obituary, 365; Williston obituary for Harger, 274

American Philosophical Society, 10, 14, 49, 50, 62, 76, 267, 364; Cope and, 76, 77, 82, 84, 90, 91, 191, 357-58; Marsh's charges against Cope before, 93-94

amphibian fossils, 7, 12, 15, 350, 353, 358

Amphicoelias, 192-93, 200-201

Anglo-Mexican Mining Company, 303, 346

Antelope Station, Nebraska, 26, 33, 117, 156

Anthropometric Society, 363

Apaches, 258-59, 260, 264

Apatosaurus, 190, 200, 248, 249, 379

Appleton, Frank, 120

Archaeopteryx, 80, 87, 88, 154, 155, 381

Archosauria, 235-36, 282

Army Corps of Engineers, 110, 205, 208, 215, 218-19

Arnold, Philip, 85

Astor, Augusta, 270

Astor, John II, 303

Atchison, Topeka & Santa Fe Railroad, 34, 258

Atkins, Representative, 220, 221, 224, 225

Atlantosaurus, 192, 198

Babcock, Orville, 132, 134, 135

Bache, Alexander Dallas, 108, 109, 130, 203, 365

Bache Fund, 314

Bacon, Sir Francis, 343

Baird, Spencer, 154, 297; and Cope, 300, 302; and Cope-Marsh feud, 88-89, 106, 202, 254, 291, 304; death of, 306; 365; *Hadrosaurus* exhibit, 160,

161; and Marsh, 24-25, 27, 53, 372; Powell friendship, 253; and scientific elitism, 96, 109, 130; and Smithsonian, 1, 5, 7, 10, 21, 36, 202-4, 221, 232, 266-67

Baker, I. G., 172, 176

Bakker, Robert, 378, 381

Baldwin, David, 145, 193, 256, 272, 281

Ballou, William Hosea, 319-29, 340, 344

Barbour, Erwin, 272, 324, 333-34

Barnard, George, 8

Barnum, P. T., 1, 2, 5, 6, 7, 8, 21, 34, 38, 56, 127, 159, 270, 272, 281, 371

Barosaurus affinis, 370

Barret, Laurence, 118

Bates, "Dutch Charlie," 239-40

Baur, George, 272, 275-76, 291, 301, 324, 326, 340

Beadle, H. H., 19

Beagle expedition, 146

Beckwith, Henry, 185

Beecher, Charles, 270, 340, 342, 374, 375-76

Belknap, Robert, 142, 156

Bell, Alexander Graham, 224, 270, 312, 2887

Belmont, August, 346

Berger, Frederick, 200

Betts, Charles Wyllys, 30, 31-32, 33, 35, 44

Billings, Frederick, 303

Bird, Roland T., 378

bird fossils, 80-81, 87-88, 91, 154, 158, 188, 194, 275, 283, 343, 381

Bitter Creek, 76, 82, 103

Black Buttes, Wyoming, 75, 76, 78, 82, 190

Black Hills, 112-19, 123, 135-44, 256, 272, 367

Blackmere, William, 37

Blaine, James G., 285, 286

415